50% OFF Online Praxis Elementary Education: Multiple Subjects (5001) Prep Course!

Dear Customer,

We consider it an honor and a privilege that you chose our Praxis Elementary Education: Multiple Subjects (5001) Study Guide. As a way of showing our appreciation and to help us better serve you, we have partnered with Mometrix Test Preparation to offer **50% off their online Praxis 5001 Prep Course**. Many Praxis courses cost hundreds of dollars. As a valued customer, **you will only pay half price.**

Mometrix has structured their online course to perfectly complement your printed study guide. The Praxis Elementary Education 5001 Prep course contains **in-depth lessons** that cover all the most important topics, **300+** video reviews that explain difficult concepts, **over 800 practice questions** to ensure you feel prepared, and **over 1,000 digital flashcards**, so you can study while you're on the go.

Online Praxis Elementary Education: Multiple Subjects (5001) Prep Course

Topics Include:	*Course Features:*

• Reading and Language Arts
  o Literary analysis, grammar, and more
• Mathematics
  o Algebra, trigonometry, and more
• Social Studies
  o World history, government, and more
• Science
  o Biology, chemistry, and more
	• Praxis Elementary Education Study Guide
	  o Get content that complements our best-selling study guide.
	• Full-Length Practice Tests and Flashcards
	  o With over 800 practice questions and 1,000+ digital flashcards so you can test yourself again and again.
	• Mobile Friendly
	  o If you need to study on the go, the course is easily accessible from your mobile device.

To receive this discount, visit their website: mometrix.com/university/praxis5001 and add the course to your cart. At the checkout page, enter the discount code: APEXPR5001

If you have any questions or concerns, please don't hesitate to contact them at universityhelp@mometrix.com.

Sincerely,

Free Study Tips DVD

In addition to the tips and content in this guide, we have created a FREE DVD with helpful study tips to further assist your exam preparation. **This FREE Study Tips DVD provides you with top-notch tips to conquer your exam and reach your goals.**

Our simple request in exchange for the strategy-packed DVD packed is that you email us your feedback about our study guide. We would love to hear what you thought about the guide, and we welcome any and all feedback—positive, negative, or neutral. It is our #1 goal to provide you with top quality products and customer service.

To receive your **FREE Study Tips DVD**, email freedvd@apexprep.com. Please put "FREE DVD" in the subject line and put the following in the email:

    a. The name of the study guide you purchased.

    b. Your rating of the study guide on a scale of 1-5, with 5 being the highest score.

    c. Any thoughts or feedback about your study guide.

    d. Your first and last name and your mailing address, so we know where to send your free DVD!

Thank you!

Praxis 2 Elementary Education Multiple Subjects 5001 Exam Prep

Praxis 5001 Study Guide and Practice Test Questions [2nd Edition]

Matthew Lanni

Written and edited by APEX Publishing.

ISBN 13: 9781628458428
ISBN 10: 1628458429

APEX Publishing is not connected with or endorsed by any official testing organization. APEX Publishing creates and publishes unofficial educational products. All test and organization names are trademarks of their respective owners.

The material in this publication is included for utilitarian purposes only and does not constitute an endorsement by APEX Publishing of any particular point of view.

For additional information or for bulk orders, contact info@apexprep.com.

Table of Contents

Test Taking Strategies

1. Reading the Whole Question

A popular assumption in Western culture is the idea that we don't have enough time for anything. We speed while driving to work, we want to read an assignment for class as quickly as possible, or we want the line in the supermarket to dwindle faster. However, speeding through such events robs us from being able to thoroughly appreciate and understand what's happening around us. While taking a timed test, the feeling one might have while reading a question is to find the correct answer as quickly as possible. Although pace is important, don't let it deter you from reading the whole question. Test writers know how to subtly change a test question toward the end in various ways, such as adding a negative or changing focus. If the question has a passage, carefully read the whole passage as well before moving on to the questions. This will help you process the information in the passage rather than worrying about the questions you've just read and where to find them. A thorough understanding of the passage or question is an important way for test takers to be able to succeed on an exam.

2. Examining Every Answer Choice

Let's say we're at the market buying apples. The first apple we see on top of the heap may *look* like the best apple, but if we turn it over we can see bruising on the skin. We must examine several apples before deciding which apple is the best. Finding the correct answer choice is like finding the best apple. Although it's tempting to choose an answer that seems correct at first without reading the others, it's important to read each answer choice thoroughly before making a final decision on the answer. The aim of a test writer might be to get as close as possible to the correct answer, so watch out for subtle words that may indicate an answer is incorrect. Once the correct answer choice is selected, read the question again and the answer in response to make sure all your bases are covered.

3. Eliminating Wrong Answer Choices

Sometimes we become paralyzed when we are confronted with too many choices. Which frozen yogurt flavor is the tastiest? Which pair of shoes look the best with this outfit? What type of car will fill my needs as a consumer? If you are unsure of which answer would be the best to choose, it may help to use process of elimination. We use "filtering" all the time on sites such as eBay® or Craigslist® to eliminate the ads that are not right for us. We can do the same thing on an exam. Process of elimination is crossing out the answer choices we know for sure are wrong and leaving the ones that might be correct. It may help to cover up the incorrect answer choice. Covering incorrect choices is a psychological act that alleviates stress due to the brain being exposed to a smaller amount of information. Choosing between two answer choices is much easier than choosing between all of them, and you have a better chance of selecting the correct answer if you have less to focus on.

4. Sticking to the World of the Question

When we are attempting to answer questions, our minds will often wander away from the question and what it is asking. We begin to see answer choices that are true in the real world instead of true in the world of the question. It may be helpful to think of each test question as its own little world. This world may be different from ours. This world may know as a truth that the chicken came before the egg or may assert that two plus two equals five. Remember that, no matter what hypothetical nonsense may be in the question, assume it to be true. If the question states that the chicken came before the egg, then choose your answer based on that truth. Sticking to the world of the question means placing all of our biases and assumptions aside and relying on the question to guide us to the correct answer. If we are simply looking for answers that are correct based on our own judgment, then we may choose incorrectly. Remember an answer that is true does not necessarily answer the question.

5. Key Words

If you come across a complex test question that you have to read over and over again, try pulling out some key words from the question in order to understand what exactly it is asking. Key words may be words that surround the question, such as *main idea, analogous, parallel, resembles, structured,* or *defines.* The question may be asking for the main idea, or it may be asking you to define something. Deconstructing the sentence may also be helpful in making the question simpler before trying to answer it. This means taking the sentence apart and obtaining meaning in pieces, or separating the question from the foundation of the question. For example, let's look at this question:

> Given the author's description of the content of paleontology in the first paragraph, which of the following is most parallel to what it taught?

The question asks which one of the answers most *parallels* the following information: The *description* of paleontology in the first paragraph. The first step would be to see *how* paleontology is described in the first paragraph. Then, we would find an answer choice that parallels that description. The question seems complex at first, but after we deconstruct it, the answer becomes much more attainable.

6. Subtle Negatives

Negative words in question stems will be words such as *not, but, neither,* or *except.* Test writers often use these words in order to trick unsuspecting test takers into selecting the wrong answer—or, at least, to test their reading comprehension of the question. Many exams will feature the negative words in all caps (*which of the following is NOT an example*), but some questions will add the negative word seamlessly into the sentence. The following is an example of a subtle negative used in a question stem:

> According to the passage, which of the following is *not* considered to be an example of paleontology?

If we rush through the exam, we might skip that tiny word, *not,* inside the question, and choose an answer that is opposite of the correct choice. Again, it's important to read the question fully, and double check for any words that may negate the statement in any way.

7. Spotting the Hedges

The word "hedging" refers to language that remains vague or avoids absolute terminology. Absolute terminology consists of words like *always, never, all, every, just, only, none,* and *must.* Hedging refers to words like *seem, tend, might, most, some, sometimes, perhaps, possibly, probability,* and *often.* In some cases, we want to choose answer choices that use hedging and avoid answer choices that use absolute terminology. It's important to pay attention to what subject you are on and adjust your response accordingly.

8. Restating to Understand

Every now and then we come across questions that we don't understand. The language may be too complex, or the question is structured in a way that is meant to confuse the test taker. When you come across a question like this, it may be worth your time to rewrite or restate the question in your own words in order to understand it better. For example, let's look at the following complicated question:

> Which of the following words, if substituted for the word *parochial* in the first paragraph, would LEAST change the meaning of the sentence?

Let's restate the question in order to understand it better. We know that they want the word *parochial* replaced. We also know that this new word would "least" or "not" change the meaning of the sentence. Now let's try the sentence again:

> Which word could we replace with *parochial,* and it would not change the meaning?

Restating it this way, we see that the question is asking for a synonym. Now, let's restate the question so we can answer it better:

> Which word is a synonym for the word *parochial*?

Before we even look at the answer choices, we have a simpler, restated version of a complicated question.

9. Predicting the Answer

After you read the question, try predicting the answer *before* reading the answer choices. By formulating an answer in your mind, you will be less likely to be distracted by any wrong answer choices. Using predictions will also help you feel more confident in the answer choice you select. Once you've chosen your answer, go back and reread the question and answer choices to make sure you have the best fit. If you have no idea what the answer may be for a particular question, forego using this strategy.

10. Avoiding Patterns

One popular myth in grade school relating to standardized testing is that test writers will often put multiple-choice answers in patterns. A runoff example of this kind of thinking is that the most common answer choice is "C," with "B" following close behind. Or, some will advocate certain made-up word patterns that simply do not exist. Test writers do not arrange their correct answer choices in any kind of pattern; their choices are randomized. There may even be times where the correct answer choice will be the same letter for two or three questions in a row, but we have no way of knowing when or if this might happen. Instead of trying to figure out what choice the test writer probably set as being correct, focus on what the *best answer choice* would be out of the answers you are presented with. Use the tips above, general knowledge, and reading comprehension skills in order to best answer the question, rather than looking for patterns that do not exist.

FREE DVD OFFER

Achieving a high score on your exam depends not only on understanding the content, but also on understanding how to apply your knowledge and your command of test taking strategies. **Because your success is our primary goal, we offer a FREE Study Tips DVD, which provides top-notch test taking strategies to help you optimize your testing experience.**

Our simple request in exchange for the strategy-packed DVD packed is that you email us your feedback about our study guide.

To receive your **FREE Study Tips DVD**, email freedvd@apexprep.com. Please put "FREE DVD" in the subject line and put the following in the email:

   a. The name of the study guide you purchased.

   b. Your rating of the study guide on a scale of 1-5, with 5 being the highest score.

   c. Any thoughts or feedback about your study guide.

   d. Your first and last name and your mailing address, so we know where to send your free DVD!

Introduction

Function of the Test

The Praxis Elementary Education: Multiple Subjects (Praxis EEMS) is an exam given to test one's knowledge and skills in preparedness for teacher credentialing. Most state education agencies use the Praxis exams for the licensing process. The Praxis EEMS is specifically designed to test teachers on the content they are expected to have mastered in order to teach elementary education. Most individuals taking this exam will possess a bachelor's or master's degree in Elementary Education and are on track to obtaining a license in order to teach these subject areas. The subject areas included in this exam are reading and language arts, mathematics, social studies, and science.

Test Administration

Beginning on September 1, 2018, the Elementary Education: Multiple Subjects exam will be offered continuously throughout the year in the United States. Praxis testing outside the U.S. is available only at Prometric centers for licensing within the United States. For those testing within the United States, the Praxis ETS website has the option for test takers to enter their zip code and country in order to find a test date and center that is accommodating to them.

For retesting, Praxis exams can be taken once every 21 days. The Praxis EEMS also limits those looking to retake subtests to 21 days. Retesting rules apply even if scores are cancelled. Praxis EEMS falls under the ETS commitment for accommodating those with disabilities. Accommodations should be requested on the ETS website well before the test date.

Test Format

The Praxis EEMS is a computer-based exam. An on-screen scientific calculator will be available for test-takers to use, so there is no need to bring a calculator. Food and drink are not allowed in the testing center, and some testing centers may require test takers to leave all belongings in a storage area outside the computer room. Handbags, water bottles, and scrap paper are not allowed in the testing center. Make sure to bring a Photo ID into the testing center, which may be a driver's license, passport, state or Military ID.

The Praxis EEMS contains four subtests: reading and language arts, mathematics, social studies, and science. Each exam is separately-timed. Check out the table below for specifics over the content of this exam.

Subject	Number of Questions	Time
Reading and Language Arts • Reading • Writing, Speaking and Listening	80 questions	90 minutes
Mathematics • Numbers and Operations • Algebraic Thinking • Geometry and Measurement, Data, Statistics, and Probability	50 questions	65 minutes
Social Studies • United States History, Government and Citizenship • Geography, Anthropology, and Sociology • World History and Economics	60 questions	60 minutes
Science • Earth Science • Life Science • Physical Science	55 questions	60 minutes
Total	**245 questions**	**4.25 hours**

Scoring

Many states require credentialing teachers to take and pass the Praxis EEMS exam, but each passing score per state will vary. The ETS website contains the most recent passing score requirement for each state. Some states have an automatic score report at the end of the exam. The score report will show an average performance range, where your test score falls on that range, and whether you passed or failed the exam. Scores are based on the number of questions answered correctly with no penalty for wrong answers. Thus, it is better to try and answer every question on the exam.

Reading and Language Arts

Foundational Skills

Phonological Awareness as a Foundational Skill for Literacy Development

Phonological awareness refers to the ability to understand different sounds and the way they build upon, integrate, or distinguish from other sounds when comprising speech. This ability is linked to reading ability and comprehension in the same language. On a larger scale, this ability is a part of complex, conscious neurological processes that govern one's ability to communicate. The individual must be able to think about the sounds they are hearing, the word structures in which they are found, how sounds are linked to create words, and how these words are used in speaking and listening communication with others who understand the same language. Because so much of this skill is based on distinguishing and applying value to certain types of sounds, building phonological awareness places a high emphasis on developing active, mindful listening skills that focus on sound recognition and patterns within words.

Infants develop the ability to notice speech and sound inflections unconsciously; new parents are often advised to speak (or read) to their infants as much as possible while using correct word pronunciation and grammar structure. The ability to notice speech and sound inflection is a building block to developing phonological awareness. Neurodevelopmental children can expect to show vastly increased levels of phonological awareness between the ages of three and five, although not all children exhibit the same skills at the same time. Children who exhibit speech disorders or delays by age three can benefit from tailored early intervention that focuses on phonological awareness. This is critical, as phonological awareness at ages five and six (or at the time when a child begins elementary school) is strongly correlated with reading ability, spelling skills, vocabulary development, and language development as a child progresses through the school years. Motor skills, including the abilities of the tongue and vocal cords, also play a role in phonological awareness.

Phonemes, Syllables, Onsets, and Rimes

A **phoneme** is the smallest unit of sound that can be used to distinguish one sound in a word from another. Distinguishing phonemes is one component of overall phonological awareness. Typically, a single letter or a pair of letters creates a single phoneme within a word. Therefore, skill development can be enhanced through practice of alliteration, matching sounds, games that isolate phonemes in words, sounding letters individually before blending them to make a complete word, and practicing single or dual phonemes both forward and backward.

Syllables define how a word is organized in terms of sound and pronunciation. The concept mainly focuses on the presence and placement of vowels in the word; the total number of syllables in a word is based on the number of vowel sounds that can distinctly be heard. Syllable exercises may focus on breaking up words into individual vowel-centered phonemes to distinguish each syllable. Words can be **monosyllabic** (comprising one syllable), **disyllabic** (comprising two syllables), **trisyllabic** (comprising three syllables), or **polysyllabic** (an umbrella term for any word with more than one syllable).

Onsets refer to the sounds present at the beginning of a syllable, usually consisting of one or more consonants. Monosyllabic words that start with a vowel may not have a clear onset. Onset structure varies significantly depending on the language in use. On the other hand, a **rime** refers to the vowel sound of a syllable and the sounds present after it. A rime may consist of a single consonant or a cluster of consonants, or it may also include silent vowels.

Blending, Segmenting, Substituting, and Deleting

intermediate phonics skills

Manipulating phonemes, syllables, onsets, and rimes further builds an individual's phonological awareness. **Segmenting** is a practice of breaking down a word. Segmenting a word into phonemes results in breaking the word down into each distinct sound (often in a way that enunciates each letter), while segmenting a word into syllables results in breaking the word down into consonant and vowel groupings. To segment a word by onsets or rimes, one should focus on either the initial sound before a syllable (onset) or the sound immediately after a syllable (rime). As a person's ability to segment becomes more developed, it will be easier for him or her to recognize segments in order to blend them together. In linguistics, **blending** is the practice of taking segments of a word (whether they are individual phonemes, syllables, onsets, or rimes) and increasing the rate of diction as each segment is pronounced in the sequence they are listed. **Substituting** is the practice of replacing one or more phonemes, syllables, onsets, or rimes with another that still maintains some portion of the original word yet changes the meaning (e.g., replacing the second syllable in the word *conjoin* to make the word *confine*). **Deleting** is the practice of removing some portion of the structure of the word to create a new word while still maintaining some portion of the original word (e.g., removing the third syllable in *compounding* to make the word *compound*). The manipulation of phonemes, syllables, onsets, and rimes assists learners in later understanding the concepts of root words, prefixes, suffixes, and their meanings. It also allows learners to better understand the patterns and relationships in words and their meanings as well as develop skills such as rhyming or creating effective prose.

Phonics and Word Analysis in Literacy Development

Phonics refers to the relationships that occur between letters and sounds (e.g., the letter *b* makes a different sound than the letter *d*). Teaching each letter with the sound it makes has been shown to be the most effective method of teaching phonics. Learners typically gravitate toward learning and understanding the letters and sounds in their names first. A basic understanding of phonics is the initial stepping-stone to literacy, as rote memorization of "sight words" will not teach effective reading skills in the long term. Understanding how each letter (or groups of letters, such as *sh*) makes a unique sound encourages learners to critically think when faced with words they have never seen before. Generally, knowing letters and the sounds they make allows learners to sound out most new words they might come across. However, it is also important to note that not all words follow the same linguistic rules, especially in the English language.

Word analysis supports learners in understanding small units of information to perceive the meaning of a word as well as apply it in contextual situations in which the meaning can change. For example, a learner who discovers that the word *cardi-* means "relating to the heart" may also understand the meaning of longer, more complex words that are not related, such as *cardiovascular* (describing the heart and circulatory system) and *tachycardia* (describing excessively fast heart rate). While these two words are not directly related to one another, word analysis would allow someone to realize both words have to do with the heart. A structured approach to word analysis includes developing foundational skills such as blending sounds, correct spelling of words, mentally extracting different word parts such as onsets and rimes to determine a root word, and placing meaning onto a root word, suffixes, prefixes, and words as a whole.

Common Letter-Sound Correspondences and Spelling Conventions

Letter-sound correspondence refers to the relationship a visual letter has with the auditory sound it represents. This understanding is critical for literacy. When teaching letter-sound correspondence, it is important to gauge the learner's background, hearing ability, and interests. Using materials that engage the reader (e.g., if a learner loves dogs, printed material about dogs might be an appropriate teaching tool) is more likely to make the process enjoyable, make the learner want to continue practicing, and facilitate the learning experience. Additionally, letter-sound correspondence is best taught moving through one letter at a time until it is mastered before moving on to or adding new letters. Letters that look or sound similar should be separated in the lesson. Vowels may require an additional focus, as some vowels will have a "long" sound where the letter is held for a longer period, a "short" sound where the vowel sound is more abrupt, or they may be completely silent. This is best illustrated by showing how vowel sounds change based on their location in the word (e.g., vowels at the end of a word typically indicate a long sound or are silent). Finally, once single letter-sound correspondences are mastered, double letter-sound groups (such as the *gh* pair which, when placed at the end of a syllable, often results in the /f/ sound) may be introduced.

Words that have atypical spelling conventions that do not necessarily match to letter-sound correspondences (such as the word *laugh*) may need to be taught as sight words. These types of words can be used as examples in which patterns of letters (such as *gh, oa, ei,* and *ief*) are seen within a word and typically create the same sound.

Distinguishing High-Frequency Sight Words from Decodable Words

Sight words refer to words that are typically recognized by the learner quickly. Commonly spoken and printed words are often taught as sight words so that learners are able to utilize them in their communication and reading. Words that cannot be immediately recognized are referred to as **decodable words.** Decodable words may be able to be understood by sounding out individual letters; however, many require the learner to use intermediate phonological skills such as blending sounds. Words that are not decodable are those that cannot be formed by simply sounding letters or blending them; they often are words that have atypical spelling conventions. To ensure that learners can recognize high-frequency sight words, it is important to expose those words to them regularly in a visual manner. This can be achieved through books, word art in the classroom setting, flash cards, or some other method that clearly shows the word. Additionally, regularly speaking the word out loud and encouraging the learner to say the word as he or she looks at it can assist in making the word an easily recognizable one. Finally, some students may learn best through kinesthetic avenues, such as tracing words for younger students or playing word games on a board for older students. Often, a blend of these modalities works best in a classroom setting and ensures all types of learners' needs and instructional preferences are addressed.

Decoding Unfamiliar Words Using Roots and Affixes

A **root** refers to a word or group of letters that serves as the main base for a word. The root conveys the primary meaning for the word. While a root can sometimes be a complete word on its own, it usually is not. **Affixes** provide supporting meaning around the root and, in conjunction with a root, typically create a full word. Types of affixes include **prefixes**, which are groups of letters that go before the root, and **suffixes**, which are groups of letters that go after the root. Many prefixes and suffixes are used often but in different combinations to create new words. Therefore, studying commonly used prefixes and affixes and their meanings can make decoding new words easier. For example, a student who knows the prefix *non-* means "not" could potentially understand the meaning of a number of different words that begin with this prefix. Suffixes can be a bit more difficult for learners to understand at first. A single letter has the ability to change the entire context of a word (e.g., when the letter *s* is added to make a singular item plural). Additionally, suffixes tend to change the part of speech of a word (e.g., adding -*er* often makes an adjective into an adverb).

Learning common roots and affixes is often a memorization task. Creating flash cards or matching games around pairing roots and affixes is one way to remember meaning. Adding context around affix and root groups that are relevant to, appeal to, and engage the learner can also help with memorization. Noting what the learner's personal interests are and utilizing them in reading and language lessons can help immensely with teaching topics that could otherwise become rote or tedious.

Stages of Language Acquisition

A person's first language develops in stages, although aspects within each stage may not always occur in a linear fashion. Starting during infancy, these stages are the babbling stage, one-word stage, two-word stage, and telegraphic stage. The **babbling stage** occurs beginning from birth until just under the first year of life. In this period, children acknowledge and produce sounds; they may even recognize familiar sounds. Infants tend to produce sounds that attract the attention of their parents or primary attachment figures. Studies show significant benefit from parents and caregivers speaking to or reading directly to even very young infants, including a positive correlation with language and speech development as infants age. The next stage, the **one-word stage**, occurs around one year of age or slightly later. In this stage, babies tend to gravitate toward single words made of a single, sometimes repetitive sound that cause positive reaction in their parents or caregivers. Even these simple words might have meaning, but they may be overly simplistic. For example, a baby may point to all toys and call them a "ball" but will not use the term "ball" for any non-toy item. At this stage, babies may understand a wide variety of sounds and words but cannot speak all of them.

In the **two-word stage**, which occurs around one and a half years and continues to the ages of two and a half to three years old, toddlers may begin saying two words together that may or may not make sense. Often, a toddler's vocabulary expands vastly during this stage. They may begin to understand sentence structure, though they may not use it well. For example, toddlers often say phrases such as "me up" when asked to be carried or "me go" to indicate they are leaving. In this stage, it is recommended that parents and caregivers continue to speak often with the child, speak as clearly as possible, and utilize correct pronunciation and grammar, as toddlers use these conversations to model their own language. The **telegraphic stage** is the last stage that occurs before a child begins to speak fluently and easily in their native language. It can occur any time after the age of two and a half years. After the two-word stage, children's speaking ability tends to explode into full (although sometimes improperly structured) sentences. Their vocabulary may expand at a rate of fifteen or more words per day. The period of life from birth to the telegraphic stage serves as the foundation for language acquisition.

Older students who learn a second language have slightly different stages of language acquisition. These students may simply listen at first or directly repeat after the instructor. The next stage will include forming and understanding simple questions that can be answered with a yes or no. After this, more complex sentence structures may be introduced; these skills are best practiced by having simple, routine conversations with a native speaker, studying flash cards, reading short stories, and listening and reading to mixed media in the language. Intermediate fluency may take a couple of years, while true fluency can take up to ten years to develop.

The **World-Class Instructional Design and Assessment** (WIDA) standards are utilized in many (though not all) states to guide English proficiency. This independent organization provides standards pertaining to listening, speaking, reading, and writing in English. These operate on a proficiency scale of 1 to 6, are tailored for each grade from pre-K to twelfth grade and offer additional guidance for different subjects. A framework based on these standards will be released in 2019; however, recommendations are available on the WIDA website at www.wida.us.

Common Phonics and Word-Recognition Approaches for ELLs

When teaching English, phonics and word-recognition approaches are considered in a linear manner. The first step is typically to encourage phonemic awareness in which learners distinguish between the forty-one phonemes that comprise the English language (one phoneme for each letter of the alphabet as well as single phonemes made up of letter pairs). Songs with repetition and rhyming can be especially helpful for older students for whom English is not a native language. The second step is to conceptualize phonics by encouraging focus on patterns between letters and the sounds they produce. This stage can take time for older learners whose native language is one with vastly different conventions from English (e.g., Asian languages, Russian, Hindi). There often may not be parallels between the two languages from which the teacher can draw. Emphasis should be placed on learning individual letters and their associated sounds, the way one would teach a pre-K or kindergarten student.

Once the learner has a comfortable master of phonics, lessons can progress to expanding the learner's vocabulary. The more vocabulary a person has, the better they are able to communicate, comprehend printed material, and understand more complex verbal language lessons. Vocabulary is best expanded through conversation with others, especially native speakers, and through reading material printed in the native language. It can be beneficial to discuss reading material in short sections to ensure reading comprehension is occurring accurately as well as to easily identify gaps if the learner is truly not comprehending the reading material. As reading comprehension becomes accurate and comfortable for the learner, he or she can work on improving their fluency through repeated reading and verbal practice with more complex materials.

Syllabication Patterns

Syllabication patterns refer to how syllable structures create the sound and pronunciation themes that take place across most words. Typically, the learner must have a comprehensive understanding of affixes, roots, and vowel sounds before they can grasp the concept of syllabication. Syllables can consist of a single long vowel sound or any vowel sound paired with consonants. There are six primary syllabication patterns. **Open syllables** refer to words that end with single, long vowel sound. **Closed syllables** refer to words in which each syllable in the word contains only one vowel sound. All monosyllabic words consist of closed syllables. Closed syllables are made up of different vowel and consonant patterns, usually indicated by "V" to show vowel placement and "C" to show consonant placement. For example, the word *cat* follows a "CVC" pattern. Words that end in a silent *e* will indicate as such in their syllabication notation. For example, the word *kite* would be notated as "CVCe." Often, the small "e" indicates the preceding vowel makes a long sound. However, for words in which the second-to-last letter is *v* (such as *live*) or in words where the final *e* is used to blend other letters into an unconventional sound (such as *fudge*), the preceding vowel makes a short sound. To begin differentiating these patterns, learners should begin with word analysis to distinguish affixes and roots. From there, the learner should label the first vowel that appears and the consonants around it to determine the syllable and any patterns.

Fluency and Related Terms   accuracy vs. fluency

Reading fluency in a particular language refers to a person's ability to quickly, reliably, and accurately read and comprehend text. Correct verbal pronunciation is often an additional component of reading fluency. **Reading accuracy** refers to how well the reader can correctly address sight words and correctly

rate vs. prosody

sound out foreign words; high accuracy often includes the ability to automatically comprehend words that are not typical sight words. **Reading rate** refers to the speed at which a person reads. **Prosody** refers to the inflections, pitches, and timing that are used when reading. Typically, accurate prosody indicates a higher level of fluency in a language, as emotive reading can only be done when the reader understands the meaning of what is being communicated. Prosody also varies by language; people with a native language that utilizes vastly different prosodic rules from a language they are trying to learn may struggle with appropriate inflection. Increasing fluency skills often is a systematic process that begins from the foundation of language; ensuring the learner's phonological skills are solid is the first step. Practicing reading out loud, listening to native speakers read (either in person, on audio, or on television), and focusing on foundational skills can greatly improve one's reading fluency. If strong reading fluency is not established by third or fourth grade, it can result in a cascade of learning hindrances and psychological barriers to learning that may persist into adulthood.

Fluency and Comprehension

Before a person can easily comprehend what he or she is reading, reading fluently must be an accessible skill. Fluency allows readers to gauge patterns in the text, understand themes and messages conveyed in the text, and apply the information in an appropriate manner. Additionally, once fluency is achieved, the reader is able to spend far less mental energy on tasks such as sounding out letters, blending letters, word analysis, and syllabication. Instead, the reader can focus on meaning, adding expression to reading out loud, and taking something away from the text (e.g., new information that has been learned or a story that was enjoyed). These are important components of comprehension, where the reader understands why the author of the text wrote it and how the information is applicable to the real world. Rather than rate of reading or correct pronunciation, accurate comprehension is the true goal of reading. If it appears that a reader is struggling to comprehend a text, it is important to backtrack and gain an understanding of their fluency in the language, as well as their abilities in basic phonological awareness, to determine the root cause of his or her reading comprehension obstacles.

Literature and Informational Texts

Theme and Topic *theme: conceptual   topic: concrete*

The theme of a piece of text is the central idea the author communicates. Whereas the topic of a passage of text may be concrete in nature, by contrast the theme is always conceptual. For example, while the topic of Mark Twain's novel *The Adventures of Huckleberry Finn* might be described as something like the coming-of-age experiences of a poor, illiterate, functionally orphaned boy around and on the Mississippi River in 19th-century Missouri, one theme of the book might be that human beings are corrupted by society. Another might be that slavery and "civilized" society itself are hypocritical. Whereas the main idea in a text is the most important single point that the author wants to make, the theme is the concept or view around which the author centers the text.

Key Details and Main Idea of Informational Text

The *topic* of a text is the general subject matter. Text topics can usually be expressed in one word, or a few words at most. Additionally, readers should ask themselves what point the author is trying to make. This point is the *main* idea of the text, the one thing the author wants readers to know concerning the topic. Once the author has established the main idea, they will support the main idea by supporting details. Supporting details are evidence that support the main idea and include personal testimonies, examples, or statistics.

One analogy for these components and their relationships is that a text is like a well-designed house. The topic is the roof, covering all rooms. The main idea is the frame. The supporting details are the various rooms. To identify the topic of a text, readers can ask themselves what or who the author is writing about in the paragraph. To locate the main idea, readers can ask themselves what one idea the author wants readers to know about the topic. To identify supporting details, readers can put the main idea into question form and ask "what does the author use to prove or explain their main idea?"

Let's look at an example. An author is writing an essay about the Amazon rainforest and trying to convince the audience that more funding should go into protecting the area from deforestation. The author makes the argument stronger by including evidence of the benefits of the rainforest: it provides habitats to a variety of species, it provides much of the earth's oxygen which in turn cleans the atmosphere, and it is the home to medicinal plants that may be the answer to some of the world's deadliest diseases. Here is an outline of the essay looking at topic, main idea, and supporting details:

- Topic: Amazon rainforest
- Main Idea: The Amazon rainforest should receive more funding in order to protect it from deforestation.
- Supporting Details:
  o It provides habitats to a variety of species
  o It provides much of the earth's oxygen which in turn cleans the atmosphere
  o It is home to medicinal plants that may be the answer to some of the world's deadliest diseases.

Notice that the topic of the essay is listed in a few key words: "Amazon rainforest." The main idea tells us what about the topic is important: that the topic should be funded in order to prevent deforestation. Finally, the supporting details are what author relies on to convince the audience to act or to believe in the truth of the main idea.

Making Inferences

One technique authors often use to make their fictional stories more interesting is not giving away too much information by providing hints and description. It is then up to the reader to draw a conclusion about the author's meaning by connecting textual clues with the reader's own pre-existing experiences and knowledge. Drawing conclusions is important as a reading strategy for understanding what is occurring in a text. Rather than directly stating who, what, where, when, or why, authors often describe story elements. Then, readers must draw conclusions to understand significant story components. As they go through a text, readers can think about the setting, characters, plot, problem, and solution; whether the author provided any clues for consideration; and combine any story clues with their existing knowledge and experiences to draw conclusions about what occurs in the text.

Making Predictions
Before and during reading, readers can apply the reading strategy of making predictions about what they think may happen next. For example, what plot and character developments will occur in fiction? What points will the author discuss in nonfiction? Making predictions about portions of text they have not yet read prepares readers mentally for reading, and also gives them a purpose for reading. To inform and make predictions about text, the reader can do the following:

- Consider the title of the text and what it implies
- Look at the cover of the book
- Look at any illustrations or diagrams for additional visual information

- Analyze the structure of the text
- Apply outside experience and knowledge to the text

Readers may adjust their predictions as they read. Reader predictions may or may not come true in text.

Making Inferences

Authors describe settings, characters, character emotions, and events. Readers must infer to understand text fully. Inferring enables readers to figure out meanings of unfamiliar words, make predictions about upcoming text, draw conclusions, and reflect on reading. Readers can infer about text before, during, and after reading. In everyday life, we use sensory information to infer. Readers can do the same with text. When authors do not answer all reader questions, readers must infer by saying "I think....This could be....This is because....Maybe....This means....I guess..." etc. Looking at illustrations, considering characters' behaviors, and asking questions during reading facilitate inference. Taking clues from text and connecting text to prior knowledge help to draw conclusions. Readers can infer word meanings, settings, reasons for occurrences, character emotions, pronoun referents, author messages, and answers to questions unstated in text. To practice inference, students can read sentences written/selected by the instructor, discuss the setting and character, draw conclusions, and make predictions.

Making inferences and drawing conclusions involve skills that are quite similar: both require readers to fill in information the author has omitted. Authors may omit information as a technique for inducing readers to discover the outcomes themselves; or they may consider certain information unimportant; or they may assume their reading audience already knows certain information. To make an inference or draw a conclusion about text, readers should observe all facts and arguments the author has presented and consider what they already know from their own personal experiences. Reading students taking multiple-choice tests that refer to text passages can determine correct and incorrect choices based on the information in the passage. For example, from a text passage describing an individual's signs of anxiety while unloading groceries and nervously clutching their wallet at a grocery store checkout, readers can infer or conclude that the individual may not have enough money to pay for everything.

Summarizing Information from a Text

An important skill is the ability to read a complex text and then reduce its length and complexity by focusing on the key events and details. A summary is a shortened version of the original text, written by the reader in their own words. The summary should be shorter than the original text, and it must be thoughtfully formed to include critical points from the original text.

In order to effectively summarize a complex text, it's necessary to understand the original source and identify the major points covered. It may be helpful to outline the original text to get the big picture and avoid getting bogged down in the minor details. For example, a summary wouldn't include a statistic from the original source unless it was the major focus of the text. It's also important for readers to use their own words yet retain the original meaning of the passage. The key to a good summary is emphasizing the main idea without changing the focus of the original information.

The more complex a text, the more difficult it can be to summarize. Readers must evaluate all points from the original source and then filter out what they feel are the less necessary details. Only the essential ideas should remain. The summary often mirrors the original text's organizational structure. For example, in a problem-solution text structure, the author typically presents readers with a problem and then develops solutions through the course of the text. An effective summary would likely retain this general structure, rephrasing the problem and then reporting the most useful or plausible solutions.

Paraphrasing is somewhat similar to summarizing. It calls for the reader to take a small part of the passage and list or describe its main points. Paraphrasing is more than rewording the original passage, though. As with summary, a paraphrase should be written in the reader's own words, while still retaining the meaning of the original source. The main difference between summarizing and paraphrasing is that a summary would be appropriate for a much larger text, while paraphrase might focus on just a few lines of text. Effective paraphrasing will indicate an understanding of the original source, yet still help the reader expand on their interpretation. A paraphrase should neither add new information nor remove essential facts that change the meaning of the source.

Characters, Setting, and Plot

The characters, setting, and plot of a literary text are all elements of literature. These elements, in conjunction with themes, perspectives, and points of view, are often used as analytical tools to help readers understand why the author developed the text as he or she did, what the meaning of the text is, and how readers can use lessons depicted in the text in their own lives.

Characters are the main players of the story. They are the people or groups who act out the plot. Characters can be analyzed as individuals or by the relationships they have with other characters. Typically, literature will include protagonist forces (the primary character) and antagonist forces (characters that act against the protagonist). These two roles are often at the center of character analyses, but other supporting character forces may also be analyzed for their purpose. When analyzing characters, emphasis is typically placed on who the character is (what they look like physically, who they are in relationship to others), what values the character holds, what are the perceptions of the character by others in the story, how complicated or deep the character's personality is, and the character's evolution, if any, throughout the story.

The **setting** of the story refers to the environment in which the story takes place. This can include descriptors such as historical period, geographical setting, the societal and cultural norms of the characters in the story, and the evolution of time from the beginning of the story to the end. These variables relating to the setting often influence how characters in the story act and play a role in character analysis. For example, a character in a story that is set during the American Civil War will likely hold vastly different motivational forces, have personal values, and work from different social norms than a character in a story that is set in present day.

A **plot analysis** typically includes four main variables that are often illustrated through a tool called **Freytag's Pyramid**. At the bottom of the pyramid is the "exposition," where elements of the literature are first introduced (or "exposed"). As the plot moves up the period, various events take place that can be analyzed both independently and holistically. These events typically give clues relating to the setting and characters within the story; they may also hint at what is coming next in the plot. Finally, the main event of the story, called the **climax**, occurs and is depicted at the peak of the pyramid. As the story comes to a close, Freytag's Pyramid shows a drop in activity. This drop is referred to as the **denouement** and may offer additional insight to the themes, lessons, or purpose of the previous activities illustrated in the pyramid.

Relationships Among Individuals, Events, Ideas, and Concepts

In order to better comprehend more complex texts, readers strive to draw connections between ideas or events. Authors often have a main idea or argument that is supported by ideas, facts, or expert opinion. These relationships that are built into writing can take on several different forms.

Depending on the main argument of an informational text, authors may choose to employ a variety of relationship techniques. But before relationships can be developed in writing, the author needs to get organized. What is the main idea or argument? How does the author plan to support that idea? Once the author has a clear picture of what they would like to focus on, they need to build transitions from one idea to the next. Learning the importance of transitioning from one sentence to another, from one paragraph to another, and from one idea to another will not only strengthen the validity of the writing but will also enhance the reader's comprehension.

When transitioning from one sentence to another, authors employ specific connecting words that emphasize the relationships between sentences. Taking the time to consider these transitional words can make the difference between a choppy or confusing paragraph and a well-written one. Consider the following:

> When I was growing up, the neighborhood had kids at every turn. I lived in a townhouse then. In my adult years, I live in a quiet suburb with hardly any children.

> When I was growing up, I lived in a neighborhood where there were kids at every turn. In contrast to my younger years, my adult years are unfolding in a quiet suburb with hardly any children.

Notice how the first example, although written coherently, employs sentences that are somehow disjointed. The transition between the statements is far from smooth. However, in the second example, the simple addition of the phrase "in contrast" connects the two parts of the writer's life and allows the reader to fully comprehend the text.

Learning to transition from sentence to sentence, from paragraph to paragraph, and throughout any piece of writing is an essential skill that helps authors to demonstrate similarities, differences, and relationships, and it helps readers to strengthen comprehension.

Structural Elements of Literature

Genres of literature (fiction, nonfiction, poetry, drama, comedy, prose, satire, etc.) are categorized by their structural elements. Different genres are usually critiqued according to different parameters; however, all genres comprise basic structural elements. For example, all genres have characters. Nonfiction genres include characters that have, at some point, existed in real life, while fiction genres include characters that have been invented by the author. In some forms of poetry, the author may be the primary character from whom the perspective of the poem is given. All genres have **tone**, or the voice (e.g., comedic, serious, dramatic), in which the literature is written. Tone is dictated by the structure of paragraphs, sentences, vocabulary, and persona of the characters. For example, a story with a comedic tone may have characters involved in nonsensical plots that are entertaining, whereas a story with a serious tone may use more complex vocabulary and have characters in intense or stressful situations. Structure in poetry is dictated by **meter**, a unit of rhythm that establishes structural patterns in the writing. **Drama**, which is literature that is often written to be acted out by live characters, usually includes stage directions that set the structure, tone, and environment of the literature. These directions normally tell characters how to act, what emotions to express, and how to shape their relationships with one another to convey particular meanings to the audience.

Text Features

Table of Contents and Index

When examining a book, a journal article, a monograph, or other publication, the table of contents is in the front. In books, it is typically found following the title page, publication information (often on the facing side of the title page), and dedication page, when one is included. In shorter publications, the table of contents may follow the title page, or the title on the same page. The table of contents in a book lists the number and title of each chapter and its beginning page number. An index, which is most common in books but may also be included in shorter works, is at the back of the publication. Books, especially academic texts, frequently have two: a subject index and an author index. Readers can look alphabetically for specific subjects in the subject index. Likewise, they can look specific authors cited, quoted, discussed, or mentioned in the author index.

The index in a book offers particular advantages to students. For example, college course instructors typically assign certain textbooks, but do not expect students to read the entire book from cover to cover immediately. They usually assign specific chapters to read in preparation for specific lectures and/or discussions in certain upcoming classes. Reading portions at a time, some students may find references they either do not fully understand or want to know more about. They can look these topics up in the book's subject index to find them in later chapters. When a text author refers to another author, students can also look up the name in the book's author index to find all page numbers of all other references to that author. College students also typically are assigned research papers to write. A book's subject and author indexes can guide students to pages that may help inform them of other books to use for researching paper topics.

Headings

Headings and subheadings concisely inform readers what each section of a paper contains, as well as showing how its information is organized both visually and verbally. Headings are typically up to about five words long. They are not meant to give in-depth analytical information about the topic of their section, but rather an idea of its subject matter. Text authors should maintain consistent style across all headings. Readers should not expect headings if there is not material for more than one heading at each level, just as a list is unnecessary for a single item. Subheadings may be a bit longer than headings because they expand upon them. Readers should skim the subheadings in a paper to use them as a map of how content is arranged. Subheadings are in smaller fonts than headings to mirror relative importance. Subheadings are not necessary for every paragraph. They should enhance content, not substitute for topic sentences.

When a heading is brief, simple, and written in the form of a question, it can have the effect of further drawing readers into the text. An effective author will also answer the question in the heading soon in the following text. Question headings and their text answers are particularly helpful for engaging readers with average reading skills. Both headings and subheadings are most effective with more readers when they are obvious, simple, and get to their points immediately. Simple headings attract readers; simple subheadings allow readers a break, during which they also inform reader decisions whether to continue reading or not. Headings stand out from other text through boldface, but also italicizing and underlining them would be excessive. Uppercase-lowercase headings are easier for readers to comprehend than all capitals. More legible fonts are better. Some experts prefer serif fonts in text, but sans-serif fonts in headings. Brief subheadings that preview upcoming chunks of information reach more readers.

Text Features

Textbooks that are designed well employ varied text features for organizing their main ideas, illustrating central concepts, spotlighting significant details, and signaling evidence that supports the ideas and points conveyed. When a textbook uses these features in recurrent patterns that are predictable, it makes it easier for readers to locate information and come up with connections. When readers comprehend how to make use of text features, they will take less time and effort deciphering how the text is organized, leaving them more time and energy for focusing on the actual content in the text. Instructional activities can include not only previewing text through observing main text features, but moreover through examining and deconstructing the text and ascertaining how the text features can aid them in locating and applying text information for learning.

Included among various text features are a table of contents, headings, subheadings, an index, a glossary, a foreword, a preface, paragraphing spaces, bullet lists, footnotes, sidebars, diagrams, graphs, charts, pictures, illustrations, captions, italics, boldface, colors, and symbols. A glossary is a list of key vocabulary words and/or technical terminology and definitions. This helps readers recognize or learn specialized terms used in the text before reading it. A foreword is typically written by someone other than the text author and appears at the beginning to introduce, inform, recommend, and/or praise the work. A preface is often written by the author and also appears at the beginning, to introduce or explain something about the text, like new additions. A sidebar is a box with text and sometimes graphics at the left or right side of a page, typically focusing on a more specific issue, example, or aspect of the subject. Footnotes are additional comments/notes at the bottom of the page, signaled by superscript numbers in the text.

Text Features on Websites

On the Internet or in computer software programs, text features include URLs, home pages, pop-up menus, drop-down menus, bookmarks, buttons, links, navigation bars, text boxes, arrows, symbols, colors, graphics, logos, and abbreviations. URLs (Universal Resource Locators) indicate the internet "address" or location of a website or web page. They often start with www. (world wide web) or http:// (hypertext transfer protocol) or https:// (the "s" indicates a secure site) and appear in the Internet browser's top address bar. Clickable buttons are often links to specific pages on a website or other external sites. Users can click on some buttons to open pop-up or drop-down menus, which offer a list of actions or departments from which to select. Bookmarks are the electronic versions of physical bookmarks. When users bookmark a website/page, a link is established to the site URL and saved, enabling returning to the site in the future without having to remember its name or URL by clicking the bookmark.

Readers can more easily navigate websites and read their information by observing and utilizing their various text features. For example, most fully developed websites include search bars, where users can type in topics, questions, titles, or names to locate specific information within the large amounts stored on many sites. Navigation bars (software developers frequently use the abbreviation term "navbar") are graphical user interfaces (GUIs) that facilitate visiting different sections, departments, or pages within a website, which can be difficult or impossible to find without these. Typically, they appear as a series of links running horizontally across the top of each page. Navigation bars displayed vertically along the left side of the page are also called sidebars. Links, i.e. hyperlinks, enable hyperspeed browsing by allowing readers to jump to new pages/sites. They may be URLs, words, phrases, images, buttons, etc. They are often but not always underlined and/or blue, or other colors.

Organizational Structures of Informational Text

Text structure is the way in which the author organizes and presents textual information so readers can follow and comprehend it. One kind of text structure is sequence. This means the author arranges the text in a logical order from beginning to middle to end. There are three types of sequences:

- Chronological: ordering events in time from earliest to latest

- Spatial: describing objects, people, or spaces according to their relationships to one another in space

- Order of Importance: addressing topics, characters, or ideas according to how important they are, from either least important to most important

Chronological sequence is the most common sequential text structure. Readers can identify sequential structure by looking for words that signal it, like *first, earlier, meanwhile, next, then, later, finally;* and specific times and dates the author includes as chronological references.

Problem-Solution Text Structure

The problem-solution text structure organizes textual information by presenting readers with a problem and then developing its solution throughout the course of the text. The author may present a variety of alternatives as possible solutions, eliminating each as they are found unsuccessful, or gradually leading up to the ultimate solution. For example, in fiction, an author might write a murder mystery novel and have the character(s) solve it through investigating various clues or character alibis until the killer is identified. In nonfiction, an author writing an essay or book on a real-world problem might discuss various alternatives and explain their disadvantages or why they would not work before identifying the best solution. For scientific research, an author reporting and discussing scientific experiment results would explain why various alternatives failed or succeeded.

Comparison-Contrast Text Structure

Comparison identifies similarities between two or more things. **Contrast** identifies differences between two or more things. Authors typically employ both to illustrate relationships between things by highlighting their commonalities and deviations. For example, a writer might compare Windows and Linux as operating systems, and contrast Linux as free and open-source vs. Windows as proprietary. When writing an essay, sometimes it is useful to create an image of the two objects or events you are comparing or contrasting. Venn diagrams are useful because they show the differences as well as the similarities between two things. Once you've seen the similarities and differences on paper, it might be helpful to create an outline of the essay with both comparison and contrast. Every outline will look different, because every two or more things will have a different number of comparisons and contrasts. Say you are trying to compare and contrast carrots with sweet potatoes. Here is an example of a compare/contrast outline using those topics:

- Introduction: Talk about why you are comparing and contrasting carrots and sweet potatoes. Give the thesis statement.
- Body paragraph 1: Sweet potatoes and carrots are both root vegetables (similarity)
- Body paragraph 2: Sweet potatoes and carrots are both orange (similarity)
- Body paragraph 3: Sweet potatoes and carrots have different nutritional components (difference)
- Conclusion: Restate the purpose of your comparison/contrast essay.

Of course, if there is only one similarity between your topics and two differences, you will want to rearrange your outline. Always tailor your essay to what works best with your topic.

Descriptive Text Structure

Description can be both a type of text structure and a type of text. Some texts are descriptive throughout entire books. For example, a book may describe the geography of a certain country, state, or region, or tell readers all about dolphins by describing many of their characteristics. Many other texts are not descriptive throughout but use descriptive passages within the overall text. The following are a few examples of descriptive text:

- When the author describes a character in a novel
- When the author sets the scene for an event by describing the setting
- When a biographer describes the personality and behaviors of a real-life individual
- When a historian describes the details of a particular battle within a book about a specific war
- When a travel writer describes the climate, people, foods, and/or customs of a certain place

A hallmark of description is using sensory details, painting a vivid picture so readers can imagine it almost as if they were experiencing it personally.

Cause and Effect Text Structure

When using cause and effect to extrapolate meaning from text, readers must determine the cause when the author only communicates effects. For example, if a description of a child eating an ice cream cone includes details like beads of sweat forming on the child's face and the ice cream dripping down her hand faster than she can lick it off, the reader can infer or conclude it must be hot outside. A useful technique for making such decisions is wording them in "If...then" form, e.g. "If the child is perspiring and the ice cream melting, then it may be a hot day." Cause and effect text structures explain why certain events or actions resulted in particular outcomes. For example, an author might describe America's historical large flocks of dodo birds, the fact that gunshots did not startle/frighten dodos, and that because dodos did not flee, settlers killed whole flocks in one hunting session, explaining how the dodo was hunted into extinction.

Recognizing Events in a Sequence

Sequence structure is the order of events in which a story or information is presented to the audience. Sometimes the text will be presented in chronological order, or sometimes it will be presented by displaying the most recent information first, then moving backwards in time. The sequence structure depends on the author, the context, and the audience. The structure of a text also depends on the genre in which the text is written. Is it literary fiction? Is it a magazine article? Is it instructions for how to complete a certain task? Different genres will have different purposes for switching up the sequence of their writing.

Sequence Structure in Informational Texts

The structure in informational texts depends again on the genre. For example, a newspaper article may start by stating an exciting event that happened, and then move on to talk about that event in chronological order, known as *sequence* or *order structure*. Many informational texts also use *cause and effect structure*, which describes an event and then identifies reasons for why that event occurred. Some essays may write about their subjects by way of *comparison and contrast*, which is a structure that compares two things or contrasts them to highlight their differences. Other documents, such as proposals, will have a *problem to solution structure*, where the document highlights some kind of problem and then offers a solution toward the end. Finally, some informational texts are written with lush details and description in order to captivate the audience, allowing them to visualize the information presented to them. This type of structure is known as *descriptive*.

Structural Elements Related to a Literary Text as a Whole

Narrative Structure
The structure presented in literary fiction is also known as *narrative structure*. Narrative structure is the foundation on which the text moves. The basic ways for moving the text along are in the plot and the setting. The plot is the sequence of events in the narrative that moves the text forward through cause and effect. The setting of a story is the place or time period in which the story takes place. Narrative structure has two main categories: linear and nonlinear.

Linear Narrative
Linear narrative is a narrative told in chronological order. Traditional linear narratives will follow the plot diagram below depicting the narrative arc. The narrative arc consists of the exposition, conflict, rising action, climax, falling action, and resolution.

- Exposition: The exposition is in the beginning of a narrative and introduces the characters, setting, and background information of the story. The importance of the exposition lies in its framing of the upcoming narrative. Exposition literally means "a showing forth" in Latin.

- Conflict: The conflict, in a traditional narrative, is presented toward the beginning of the story after the audience becomes familiar with the characters and setting. The conflict is a single instance between characters, nature, or the self, in which the central character is forced to make a decision or move forward with some kind of action. The conflict presents something for the main character, or protagonist, to overcome.

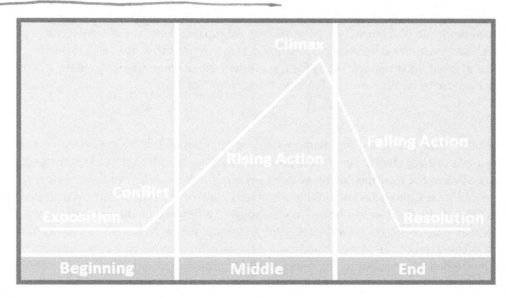

- Rising Action: The rising action is the part of the story that leads into the climax. The rising action will feature the development of characters and plot, and creates the tension and suspense that eventually lead to the climax.

- Climax: The climax is the part of the story where the tension produced in the rising action comes to a culmination. The climax is the peak of the story. In a traditional structure, everything before

21

the climax builds up to it, and everything after the climax falls from it. It is the height of the narrative and is usually either the most exciting part of the story or is marked by some turning point in the character's journey.

- Falling Action: The falling action happens as a result of the climax. Characters continue to develop, although there is a wrapping up of loose ends here. The falling action leads to the resolution.

- Resolution: The resolution is where the story comes to an end and usually leaves the reader with the satisfaction of knowing what happened within the story and why. However, stories do not always end in this fashion. Sometimes readers can be confused or frustrated at the end from lack of information or the absence of a happy ending.

Nonlinear Narrative

A nonlinear narrative deviates from the traditional narrative in that it does not always follow the traditional plot structure of the narrative arc. Nonlinear narratives may include structures that are disjointed, circular, or disruptive, in the sense that they do not follow chronological order, but rather a nontraditional order of structure. *In medias res* is an example of a structure that predates the linear narrative. *In medias res* is Latin for "in the middle of things," which is how many ancient texts, especially epic poems, began their story, such as Homer's *Iliad*. Instead of having a clear exposition with a full development of characters, they would begin right in the middle of the action.

Modernist texts in the late nineteenth and early twentieth century are known for their experimentation with disjointed narratives, moving away from traditional linear narrative. Disjointed narratives are depicted in novels like *Catch 22*, where the author, Joseph Heller, structures the narrative based on free association of ideas rather than chronology. Another nonlinear narrative can be seen in the novel *Wuthering Heights*, written by Emily Bronte, which disrupts the chronological order by being told retrospectively after the first chapter. There seem to be two narratives in *Wuthering Heights* working at the same time: a present narrative as well as a past narrative. Authors employ disrupting narratives for various reasons; some use it for the purpose of creating situational irony for the readers, while some use it to create a certain effect in the reader, such as excitement, or even a feeling of discomfort or fear.

Point of View

When a writer tells a story using the first person, readers can identify this by the use of first-person pronouns, like *I, me, we, us,* etc. However, first-person narratives can be told by different people or from different points of view. For example, some authors write in the first person to tell the story from the main character's viewpoint, as Charles Dickens did in his novels *David Copperfield* and *Great Expectations*. Some authors write in the first person from the viewpoint of a fictional character in the story, but not necessarily the main character. For example, F. Scott Fitzgerald wrote *The Great Gatsby* as narrated by Nick Carraway, a character in the story, about the main characters, Jay Gatsby and Daisy Buchanan. Other authors write in the first person, but as the omniscient narrator—an often-unnamed person who knows all of the characters' inner thoughts and feelings. Writing in first person as oneself is more common in nonfiction.

Third Person

The third-person narrative is probably the most prevalent voice used in fictional literature. While some authors tell stories from the point of view and in the voice of a fictional character using the first person, it is a more common practice to describe the actions, thoughts, and feelings of fictional characters in the third person using *he, him, she, her, they, them,* etc.

Although plot and character development are both necessary and possible when writing narrative from a first-person point of view, they are also more difficult, particularly for new writers and those who find it unnatural or uncomfortable to write from that perspective. Therefore, writing experts advise beginning writers to start out writing in the third person. A big advantage of third-person narration is that the writer can describe the thoughts, feelings, and motivations of every character in a story, which is not possible for the first-person narrator. Third-person narrative can impart information to readers that the characters do not know. On the other hand, beginning writers often regard using the third-person point of view as more difficult because they must write about the feelings and thoughts of every character, rather than only about those of the protagonist.

Second Person

Narrative written in the second person addresses someone else as "you." In novels and other fictional works, the second person is the narrative voice most seldom used. The primary reason for this is that it often reads in an awkward manner, which prevents readers from being drawn into the fictional world of the novel. The second person is more often used in informational text, especially in how-to manuals, guides, and other instructions.

First Person

First person uses pronouns such as *I, me, we, my, us,* and *our*. Some writers naturally find it easier to tell stories from their own points of view, so writing in the first person offers advantages for them. The first-person voice is better for interpreting the world from a single viewpoint, and for enabling reader immersion in one protagonist's experiences. However, others find it difficult to use the first-person narrative voice. Its disadvantages can include overlooking the emotions of characters, forgetting to include description, producing stilted writing, using too many sentence structures involving "I did....", and not devoting enough attention to the story's "here-and-now" immediacy.

Perspective of Multiple Accounts

Gauging point of view and perspective is an important part of literary analysis. Literature can be written from first-person, second-person, or third-person point of view. **First-person point of view** refers to literature in which the main character is telling the story from his or her perspective, using the pronouns *I, we, us,* and *our*. **Second-person point of view** refers to literature in which the story is told to the reader, telling the reader what to experience. The pronoun *you* is primarily used. **Third-person point of view** in literature refers to writing in which a narrator, or someone who is external to the plot or reader of the plot, is telling the story. The narrator can have a limited, objective perspective or have an omniscient, objective perspective when telling the story. Pronouns used include *she, he,* and *they*.

The point of view from which a story is told shapes how the reader perceives the story. When comparing multiple accounts of the same topic, it is important to note the point of view from which the story is told (e.g., from the view of a main character in the plot, a spectator to the plot, a supporting character in the plot, or an outsider). First-person points of view are limited to the character from whose perspective it is told, while third-person point of view can range from extremely objective to holding the narrator's biases. When comparing multiple accounts of the same story, readers should pinpoint differences between the accounts and try to determine as well as understand what influences are driving those differences.

Point of View and Overall Structure of a Text

"Point of view" refers to the type of narration the author employs in a given story. "Perspective" refers to how characters perceive what is happening within the story. The characters' perspectives reveal their attitudes and help to shape their unique personalities.

Consider the following scenario:

> The family grabbed their snacks and blankets, loaded up the van, and headed out to the neighborhood park, even though Suki would have preferred to stay home. Once they settled in at their spot on the grass, the celebration was about to start. Within minutes, the fireworks began—crack, bang, pop! Hendrix jumped up and down with glee, Suki angrily put down her phone, and the dog yelped and buried its head under the blankets.

Each character was experiencing the same event—fireworks—and yet each character had a different reaction. Hendrix seems excited, Suki, angry, and the dog, frightened. No *one* perspective is the "right" perspective, just as no particular perspective is wrong; they are simply perspectives. What makes characters unique within a story are their unique perspectives. When authors develop characters with unique personalities and differing perspectives, stories are not only more believable, but they are more alive, more colorful, and more interesting. If all characters had the same one-dimensional perspective, the story would likely be quite dull. There would never be a protagonist or antagonist, and there would be no reason to examine why each character acts and reacts to situations in such unique ways. Differentiating between various perspectives in a story can also lead to a much deeper understanding. For instance, it seems relatively easy to consider the perspective of the protagonist in any story since most readers connect with good and reject evil. But readers might wish to explore the story through the eyes of the antagonist. They might want to discover how the antagonist ended up so villainous, what events led to their corruption, and what, if anything, might lead them back to truth and justice.

Perspectives are how individuals see the world in which they live, and they are often formed from the individual's unique life experiences, their morals, and their values. Differentiating between various perspectives in literature helps readers to develop a greater appreciation for the story and for each character that helps to shape that story.

Written, Visual, and Oral Information from Texts and Multimedia Sources

Most people learn language and literacy best through written, visual, or auditory means; typically, an integration of the three methods allows for the most comprehensive learning (especially when teaching to a classroom setting in which students might encompass multiple learning preferences). Some research suggests creating mental imagery from written and oral information is not an automatic process for all people or it can be further enhanced through integration skill building. Skill building tasks may include taking single words, written passages, or oral information and asking what, if any, mental imagery is invoked from the media. Comparatively, some learners may learn better by looking at pictures or videos and then writing or speaking descriptions to give them meaning. Signs a learner may need to practice integration skill building include poor reading comprehension, the need to reread often, and written communication or oral presentation that lacks clear organization, structure, or purpose. These learners may also struggle to accurately interpret and apply appropriate meaning to media sources.

Visual and Oral Elements

Learners, especially younger ones, can benefit from the addition of visual and oral elements to a literary text. Many young students enjoy and are easily engaged through activities that engage the senses. For learners that are building connections between information and mental imagery, pictures and sounds can confirm the mental imagery they are creating is appropriate for the words they are reading. It can confirm whether the intended meaning of written text is being received correctly. New readers may benefit from pictures in stories that confirm they are reading the text correctly and understanding the plot of the story.

Additionally, visual and oral elements can add a new layer of information to interpret and provide deeper meaning to a plot. For example, a visual depiction of a written story, such as a movie based on a book, may add visual elements that provide additional meaning about the historical period in which the story is set, show subtle body language dynamics between characters that add meaning, or provide context about how characters develop throughout the story. The addition of oral elements in this same situation can also add meaning and enhance the effects of the literary text. For example, hearing the accents associated with a character's speech can share additional details about the character that cannot always be fully experienced through text. Furthermore, a movie's soundtrack often provides foreshadowing effects (such as loud, dramatic music to hint a scary event may be coming).

Comparing Literary Text with Oral, Staged, or Film Version

A number of written texts are converted to oral readings, staged productions, or films. Comparing the written text to its auditory or visual counterpart includes noticing what is different between the two formats, what is similar, and what qualities are presented in one format that either enhance or detract from the purpose. Students may want to develop a matrix organizer in which they can break down all sections of the written version first by performing an analysis on each character, the setting, the plot, and themes that present. From there, a comparison can be made across each section for other types of media. Often, oral performances are similar to written texts but with more emotive passages for characters; the performer may infuse his or her own interpretation of meaning and emotion into the sections that are being read. Staged performances typically combine written text, oral reading, and interpretation on behalf of the performers and directors. Performers will likely bring their own interpretation into individual character and relationship roles, while directors may incorporate their interpretation into the stage setting and props that are used.

The audience plays a large factor in stage performances, and these types of performances can become an interactive experience. For example, if the audience begins laughing at a scene that was not initially intended to be funny, it can shift the mood of the performance or affect how the performers choose to progress forward in the story line. This can be a positive or negative experience for those involved in the stage production. Comparatively, films may use a number of special effects to enhance both the visual and auditory experiences of a story; however, readers of the written text who had created mental imagery based on their experience while reading may find this either disruptive or an enhancement to the story line. Films do not take the audience reaction into account, so real-time changes to the production are not made.

Comparing Literary Texts that Address the Same Theme

Throughout time, humans have told stories with similar themes. Some themes are universal across time, space, and culture. These include themes of the individual as a hero, conflicts of the individual against nature, the individual against society, change vs. tradition, the circle of life, coming-of-age, and the complexities of love. Themes involving war and peace have featured prominently in diverse works, like Homer's *Iliad*, Tolstoy's *War and Peace* (1869), Stephen Crane's *The Red Badge of Courage* (1895), Hemingway's *A Farewell to Arms* (1929), and Margaret Mitchell's *Gone with the Wind* (1936). Another universal literary theme is that of the quest. These appear in folklore from countries and cultures worldwide, including the Gilgamesh Epic, Arthurian legend's Holy Grail quest, Virgil's *Aeneid*, Homer's *Odyssey*, and the *Argonautica*. Cervantes' *Don Quixote* is a parody of chivalric quests. J.R.R. Tolkien's *The Lord of the Rings* trilogy (1954) also features a quest.

One instance of similar themes across cultures is when those cultures are in countries that are geographically close to each other. For example, a folklore story of a rabbit in the moon using a mortar and pestle is shared among China, Japan, Korea, and Thailand—making medicine in China, making rice cakes in Japan and Korea, and hulling rice in Thailand. Another instance is when cultures are more distant geographically, but their languages are related. For example, East Turkestan's Uighurs and people in Turkey share tales of folk hero Effendi Nasreddin Hodja. Another instance, which may either be called cultural diffusion or simply reflect commonalities in the human imagination, involves shared themes among geographically and linguistically different cultures: both Cameroon's and Greece's folklore tell of centaurs; Cameroon, India, Malaysia, Thailand, and Japan, of mermaids; Brazil, Peru, China, Japan, Malaysia, Indonesia, and Cameroon, of underwater civilizations; and China, Japan, Thailand, Vietnam, Malaysia, Brazil, and Peru, of shape-shifters.

Two prevalent literary themes are love and friendship, which can end happily, sadly, or both. William Shakespeare's *Romeo and Juliet*, Emily Brontë's *Wuthering Heights*, Leo Tolstoy's *Anna Karenina*, and both *Pride and Prejudice* and *Sense and Sensibility* by Jane Austen are famous examples. Another theme recurring in popular literature is of revenge, an old theme in dramatic literature, e.g. Elizabethans Thomas Kyd's *The Spanish Tragedy* and Thomas Middleton's *The Revenger's Tragedy*. Some more well-known instances include Shakespeare's tragedies *Hamlet* and *Macbeth*, Alexandre Dumas' *The Count of Monte Cristo*, John Grisham's *A Time to Kill*, and Stieg Larsson's *The Girl Who Kicked the Hornet's Nest*.

Themes are underlying meanings in literature. For example, if a story's main idea is a character succeeding against all odds, the theme is overcoming obstacles. If a story's main idea is one character wanting what another character has, the theme is jealousy. If a story's main idea is a character doing something they were afraid to do, the theme is courage. Themes differ from topics in that a topic is a subject matter; a theme is the author's opinion about it. For example, a work could have a topic of war and a theme that war is a curse. Authors present themes through characters' feelings, thoughts, experiences, dialogue, plot actions, and events. Themes function as "glue" holding other essential story elements together. They offer readers insights into characters' experiences, the author's philosophy, and how the world works.

Comparing Informational Texts that Address the Same Topic

Informational texts about the same topic can include vastly different pieces of information, perceptions, or opinions. When comparing two or more informational texts that address the same topic, the first comparison to make is to determine and understand the source of each text. Based on the source, the authors may hold rather different intentions for writing the text. For example, an author of an academic textbook is likely to present information that is evidence based, instructional, and/or reviewed by peers with expert-level credentialing. A journalist who writes about the same topic may present similar information yet include a personal editorial opinion, such as the application of the information in the real world. These two authors are writing on the same topic but presenting to largely different readerships; therefore, their method of information sharing is likely to be different. Understanding the audience for whom the author is writing, the purpose of writing their text, and the author's own credentials can be useful components of a comparison analysis.

Additionally, the point of view from which an informational text is written can also be useful in understanding the different values between two pieces of text that address the same topic. For example, the first-person account of a historical event from someone who experienced it directly will likely present different information, a different perspective, and evoke different emotions from the reader than the recount of the same event by an objective researcher who is simply sharing facts about the event. In addition to focusing on where the two accounts differ, readers should note similarities between the two passages (such as factual information or similar feelings that are expressed by both authors).

Visual and Multimedia Elements in Informational Texts

Line Graphs

Line graphs are useful for visually representing data that vary continuously over time, like an individual student's test scores. The horizontal or x-axis shows dates/times; the vertical or y-axis shows point values. A dot is plotted on the point where each horizontal date line intersects each vertical number line, and then these dots are connected, forming a line. Line graphs show whether changes in values over time exhibit trends like ascending, descending, flat, or more variable, like going up and down at different times. For example, suppose a student's scores on the same type of reading test were 75% in October, 80% in November, 78% in December, 82% in January, 85% in February, 88% in March, and 90% in April. A line graph of these scores would look like this.

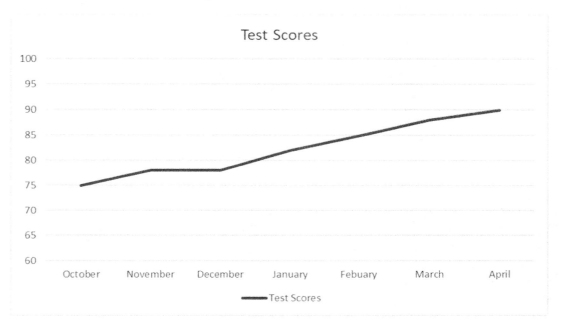

Bar Graphs

Bar graphs feature equally spaced, horizontal or vertical rectangular bars representing numerical values. They can show change over time as line graphs do, but unlike line graphs, bar graphs can also show differences and similarities among values at a single point in time. Bar graphs are also helpful for visually representing data from different categories, especially when the horizontal axis displays some value that is not numerical, like various countries with inches of annual rainfall.

The following is a bar graph that compares different classes and how many books they read:

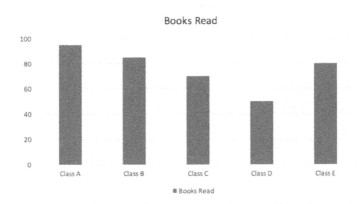

Pie Charts

Pie charts, also called circle graphs, are good for representing percentages or proportions of a whole quantity because they represent the whole as a circle or "pie," with the various proportion values shown as "slices" or wedges of the pie. This gives viewers a clear idea of how much of a total each item occupies. To calculate central angles to make each portion the correct size, multiply each percentage by 3.6 (= 360/100). For example, biologists may have information that 60% of Americans have brown eyes, 20% have hazel eyes, 15% have blue eyes, and 5% have green eyes. A pie chart of these distributions would look like this:

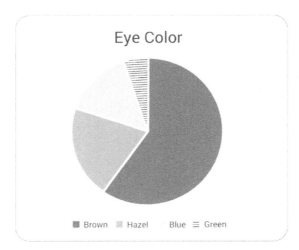

Line Plots

Rather than showing trends or changes over time like line graphs, line plots show the frequency with which a value occurs in a group. Line plots are used for visually representing data sets that total 50 or fewer values. They make visible features like gaps between some data points, clusters of certain numbers/number ranges, and outliers (data points with significantly smaller or larger values than others). For example, the age ranges in a class of nursing students might appear like this in a line plot:

```
XXXXXXXXX    XXXXX    XX        X        XXX        XX    X


_____

   18          23      28       33        38        43    48
```

Pictograms

Magazines, newspapers, and other similar publications designed for consumption by the general public often use pictograms to represent data. Pictograms feature icons or symbols that look like whatever category of data is being counted, like little silhouettes shaped like human beings commonly used to represent people. If the data involve large numbers, like populations, one person symbol might represent one million people, or one thousand, etc. For smaller values, such as how many individuals out of ten fit a given description, one symbol might equal one person. Male and female silhouettes are used to differentiate gender, and child shapes for children. Little clock symbols are used to represent amounts of time, such as a given number of hours; calendar pages might depict months; suns and moons could show days and nights; hourglasses might represent minutes. While pictogram symbols are easily recognizable and appealing to general viewers, one disadvantage is that it is difficult to display partial symbols for in-between quantities.

Key Claims and Their Evidence

When authors want to strengthen the support for an argument, evidence-based data in the form of statistics or concrete examples can be used. Statistics and examples are often accompanied by detailed explanations to help increase the audience's understanding and shape their ideas. Expert opinions are another way to strengthen an argument. But all this effort toward supporting a given argument does not necessarily make the argument absolute. After all, the word "argument" implies that there is more than one way to think about the subject. Arguments are meant to be challenged, questioned, and analyzed.

Authors will generally use one of two argument models: deductive or inductive. Deductive arguments require two general statements to support the argument. Inductive arguments employ specific data, examples, or facts to support the argument.

Deductive	Inductive
All fruits contain seeds. Tomatoes contain seeds. Therefore, tomatoes are fruits.	9 out of 10 dentists prefer soft-bristled toothbrushes. Therefore, soft-bristled toothbrushes are the best type of toothbrush for optimal dental health.

No matter what evidence is presented, readers should still challenge the argument. In any text, readers are encouraged to ask specific questions to evaluate the overall validity of the argument.

Some important points to consider include:

- Has the author employed logic in the argument?
- Is the argument clearly explained?
- Is the argument sufficiently supported?

- Who conducted the research, and for what purpose?
- Is the supporting data qualitative, quantitative, or a mixture of both?
- Is the presented data representative of the typical cross-section of society or of the phenomenon being discussed?
- Does the author present any bias?
- Has the author overlooked any related areas that should be explored in order to form a well-rounded argument?

Although informational writing should be written objectively, such writing still constitutes the author's particular point of view or belief about a given subject. The author's main idea will likely be backed up with reasons, evidence, and supporting details, but it is important for the audience to question the main idea and evaluate the presented evidence. Although the author's ideas and shared details drive the overall argument, readers should feel compelled to explore the topic further, assess the evidence, and determine whether they agree with the overall message. Authors present the argument in order to convince their readers, but readers must strive to evaluate and assess the information to arrive at an informed opinion of the subject matter.

Three Factors that Measure Text Complexity

Text complexity indicates how easy or challenging a particular passage is for a reader. Generally, learners begin with simple texts and move toward more complex texts as their fluency and comprehension increase. Additionally, choosing to read texts with higher levels of text complexity can also strengthen and encourage higher fluency and comprehension levels. These skills work in tandem with one another. Learners who are comfortable with higher levels of text complexity at a younger age have a higher positive correlation with college attendance.

Quantitative text complexity refers to concrete phonological features related to text, such as the number of letters or syllables in a word. **Qualitative text complexity** refers to more abstract features related to text, such as the vocabulary used, how formal or informal the author's tone is, the ideas and connections that are presented in the text, how information is organized, and whether the text is presenting a topic superficially or with a number of meanings. Qualitative text complexity can also refer to the language being used, as some languages are more difficult to pick up based on one's native language. For example, a native English speaker will likely find an Eastern language such as Hindi to have higher text complexity, due to the differences in letter writing, letter placement, and sentence structures, than another Romance language, such as Spanish, which has roots and sentence structures that are similar to English. Additionally, qualitative text complexity may include factors such as the level of background knowledge the reader should have in order to understand the information presented.

Reader and task factors of text complexity focus primarily on characteristics of the reader, how the reader manages passages with different levels of quantitative and qualitative complexity, and whether presented tasks are appropriate for the reader's abilities. This aspect of text complexity encompasses the reader's individual strengths and interests; for example, readers who are interested in the topic of the text presented may be more likely to push themselves to read and try to comprehend more complex passages, while readers who are not interested may give up sooner. Additionally, the tasks the instructor ties with a reading should match the level of text complexity presented in the passage. Instructors should ensure activities paired with reading passages are relevant to the information provided and students are able to approach the task that is asked of them. For example, if students read a passage about the history of transportation in the United States, they may or may not be able to answer a question (or task) that compares older American transportation methods with those of ancient Rome. This level of comprehension would require background knowledge of a different time period and location that is not available in the text at hand, therefore making the task more complex than average.

Text-Leveling Systems

Text-leveling systems integrate certain complexity indicators to holistically determine a text's level of reading difficulty. These indicators can include qualitative measures such as the purpose of the passage, sentence structures, language and vocabulary usage, visuals and graphics, passage organization, and expected background knowledge or deductive ability of the reader. Text-leveling systems also focus on quantitative indicators such as sentence length, the number of letters and syllables in each word, total word count, number of sight words, and number of decodable words. Combining these features together, text-leveling systems will typically distinguish passages by grade level. Common text-leveling systems include the Lexile Framework for Reading, which focuses on vocabulary and sentence length to assign a numerical difficulty level to a piece of literature; the Developmental Reading Assessment, which focuses on reading accuracy, fluency, and comprehension to assign difficulty by grade level up to eighth grade; the Fountas and Pinnell Guided Reading system, which categorizes texts by complexity from level A (simplest quantitative, qualitative, and reader/task measures) to Z (most difficult quantitative, qualitative, and reader/task measures); and Common Core, a standardized text-leveling and testing system used in public schools in most states.

Writing

Common Types of Writing

Narrative Writing
Narrative writing tells a story. The most prominent examples of narrative writing are fictional novels. Here are some examples:

- Mark Twain's *The Adventures of Tom Sawyer* and *The Adventures of Huckleberry Finn*
- Victor Hugo's *Les Misérables*
- Charles Dickens' *Great Expectations*, *David Copperfield*, and *A Tale of Two Cities*
- Jane Austen's *Northanger Abbey*, *Mansfield Park*, *Pride and Prejudice*, *Sense and Sensibility*, and *Emma*
- Toni Morrison's *Beloved*, *The Bluest Eye*, and *Song of Solomon*
- Gabriel García Márquez's *One Hundred Years of Solitude* and *Love in the Time of Cholera*

Some nonfiction works are also written in narrative form. For example, some authors choose a narrative style to convey factual information about a topic, such as a specific animal, country, geographic region, and scientific or natural phenomenon.

Since narrative is the type of writing that tells a story, it must be told by someone, who is the narrator. The narrator may be a fictional character telling the story from their own viewpoint. This narrator uses the first person (*I, me, my, mine* and *we, us, our,* and *ours*). The narrator may simply be the author; for example, when Louisa May Alcott writes "Dear reader" in *Little Women*, she (the author) addresses us as readers. In this case, the novel is typically told in third person, referring to the characters as he, she, they, or them. Another more common technique is the omniscient narrator; i.e. the story is told by an unidentified individual who sees and knows everything about the events and characters—not only their externalized actions, but also their internalized feelings and thoughts. Second person, i.e. writing the story by addressing readers as "you" throughout, is less frequently used.

Expository Writing

Expository writing is also known as informational writing. Its purpose is not to tell a story as in narrative writing, to paint a picture as in descriptive writing, or to persuade readers to agree with something as in argumentative writing. Rather, its point is to communicate information to the reader. As such, the point of view of the author will necessarily be more objective. Whereas other types of writing appeal to the reader's emotions, appeal to the reader's reason by using logic, or use subjective descriptions to sway the reader's opinion or thinking, expository writing seeks to do none of these but simply to provide facts, evidence, observations, and objective descriptions of the subject matter. Some examples of expository writing include research reports, journal articles, articles and books about historical events or periods, academic subject textbooks, news articles and other factual journalistic reports, essays, how-to articles, and user instruction manuals.

Technical Writing

Technical writing is similar to expository writing in that it is factual, objective, and intended to provide information to the reader. Indeed, it may even be considered a subcategory of expository writing. However, technical writing differs from expository writing in that (1) it is specific to a particular field, discipline, or subject; and (2) it uses the specific technical terminology that belongs only to that area. Writing that uses technical terms is intended only for an audience familiar with those terms. A primary example of technical writing today is writing related to computer programming and use.

Persuasive Writing

Persuasive writing is intended to persuade the reader to agree with the author's position. It is also known as argumentative writing. Some writers may be responding to other writers' arguments, in which case they make reference to those authors or text and then disagree with them. However, another common technique is for the author to anticipate opposing viewpoints in general, both from other authors and from the author's own readers. The author brings up these opposing viewpoints, and then refutes them before they can even be raised, strengthening the author's argument. Writers persuade readers by appealing to their reason, which Aristotle called *logos;* appealing to emotion, which Aristotle called *pathos;* or appealing to readers based on the author's character and credibility, which Aristotle called *ethos.*

Effectiveness of Writing Samples

While all effective writing should have a clear message; utilize correct spelling, grammar, and punctuation; and be generally easy to follow in terms of idea organization, some types of writing require that different variables are met in order to serve their purpose. When evaluating narrative writing, the work should include a clear plot and setting; have a defined beginning, middle, and end; have a developed set of characters; and show an evolution of events and characters. When evaluating descriptive writing samples, the work should have sensory details that create a visual, describe sounds, produce smells, share tangible experiences, and describe tastes where applicable. Authors should provide as much descriptive language as possible to create imagery for someone (the reader) who is not present in the experience alongside them.

When evaluating expository writing, the work should showcase objectivity, leverage evidence-based facts, and refrain from directly including or hinting at the author's personal opinions or biases. The writing should also focus on organization; since much of expository writing explains a process, ensuring the steps of the process are presented sequentially is an important evaluation component. Finally, when evaluating persuasive writing, the work should focus on a main stance and provide evidence, reason, or opinion to support the stance. Persuasive writing should not focus on the positive and negative aspects of two competing stances. Additionally, this type of writing should encourage the reader to take a specific action (such as donate to a cause, buy a product, or engage in some other outcome that is relevant to the main body of the writing).

Evaluating the Appropriateness of a Text

Authors may have many purposes for writing a specific text. Their purposes may be to try and convince readers to agree with their position on a subject, to impart information, or to entertain. Other writers are motivated to write from a desire to express their own feelings. Authors' purposes are their reasons for writing something. A single author may have one overriding purpose for writing or multiple reasons. An author may explicitly state their intention in the text, or the reader may need to infer that intention. Those who read reflectively benefit from identifying the purpose because it enables them to analyze information in the text. By knowing why the author wrote the text, readers can glean ideas for how to approach it.

The following is a list of questions readers can ask in order to discern an author's purpose for writing a text:

- From the title of the text, why do you think the author wrote it?
- Was the purpose of the text to give information to readers?
- Did the author want to describe an event, issue, or individual?
- Was it written to express emotions and thoughts?
- Did the author want to convince readers to consider a particular issue?
- Was the author primarily motivated to write the text to entertain?
- Why do you think the author wrote this text from a certain point of view?
- What is your response to the text as a reader?
- Did the author state their purpose for writing it?

Students should read to interpret information rather than simply content themselves with roles as text consumers. Being able to identify an author's purpose efficiently improves reading comprehension, develops critical thinking, and makes students more likely to consider issues in depth before accepting writer viewpoints. Authors of fiction frequently write to entertain readers. Another purpose for writing fiction is making a political statement; for example, Jonathan Swift wrote "A Modest Proposal" (1729) as a political satire. Another purpose for writing fiction as well as nonfiction is to persuade readers to take some action or further a particular cause. Fiction authors and poets both frequently write to evoke certain moods; for example, Edgar Allan Poe wrote novels, short stories, and poems that evoke moods of gloom, guilt, terror, and dread. Another purpose of poets is evoking certain emotions: love is popular, as in Shakespeare's sonnets and numerous others. In "The Waste Land" (1922), T.S. Eliot evokes society's alienation, disaffection, sterility, and fragmentation.

Authors seldom directly state their purposes in texts. Some students may be confronted with nonfiction texts such as biographies, histories, magazine and newspaper articles, and instruction manuals, among others. To identify the purpose in nonfiction texts, students can ask the following questions:

- Is the author trying to teach something?
- Is the author trying to persuade the reader?
- Is the author imparting factual information only?
- Is this a reliable source?
- Does the author have some kind of hidden agenda?

To apply author purpose in nonfictional passages, students can also analyze sentence structure, word choice, and transitions to answer the aforementioned questions and to make inferences. For example, authors wanting to convince readers to view a topic negatively often choose words with negative connotations.

Evaluating the Development, Organization, or Style of a Text

Development, organization, and stylistic elements of a piece of writing are typically first contingent on the ability of the writer (e.g., a first-grade student's writing would be evaluated differently than a ninth-grade student's writing) and/or the genre of the writing (e.g., an evidence-based academic research paper would be evaluated differently than a personal memoir). Beyond this first step, assessing the writing's development, organization, or style usually focuses on qualitative complexity factors such as sentence structure, vocabulary usage, individual paragraph development, and how paragraphs transition from one to the next.

Additionally, instructors will need to look for a few other factors when evaluating the development, organization, or style of a piece of writing. For assignments that have multiple drafts in which feedback is provided, it may be useful to see how students incorporated feedback and evolved their writing over the course of several versions. In the final version, evaluators may want to ensure a writing sample has a clear theme that is supported by all of the sentences (or paragraphs, for longer samples) in the sample. It is also important to note whether or not related ideas are grouped together and presented in a logical or sequential (where applicable) manner.

This indicates clear and well-thought-out organization. Stylistically, evaluators may want to look for variance (rather than repetition) in sentence structure. Based on the purpose of the writing sample, descriptive language may play a factor in writing style. Evaluations may be partially analytical and/or objective when examining the organization and development of a writing sample but may also be partially subjective when examining a sample's style. For example, some evaluators may enjoy certain types of humor that are presented in a writing sample, while others may subconsciously reject ideas that do not align with their personal beliefs. Therefore, when evaluating creative, persuasive, or narrative pieces, a number of institutions ask multiple evaluators to review and score a piece of writing independently. Ratings are then averaged to produce a final score for the writer.

Identifying Revisions to Strengthen a Piece of Writing

Revising offers an opportunity for writers to polish things up. Putting one's self in the reader's shoes and focusing on what the essay actually says helps writers identify problems—it's a movement from the mindset of writer to the mindset of editor. The goal is to have a clean, clear copy of the essay.

The main goal of the revision phase is to improve the essay's flow, cohesiveness, readability, and focus. For example, an essay will make a less persuasive argument if the various pieces of evidence are scattered and presented illogically or clouded with unnecessary thought. Therefore, writers should consider their essay's structure and organization, ensuring that there are smooth transitions between sentences and paragraphs. There should be a discernable introduction and conclusion as well, as these crucial components of an essay provide readers with a blueprint to follow.

Additionally, if the writer includes copious details that do little to enhance the argument, they may actually distract readers from focusing on the main ideas and detract from the strength of their work. The ultimate goal is to retain the purpose or focus of the essay and provide a reader-friendly experience. Because of this, writers often need to delete parts of their essay to improve its flow and focus. Removing sentences, entire paragraphs, or large chunks of writing can be one of the toughest parts of the writing process because it is difficult to part with work one has done. However, ultimately, these types of cuts can significantly improve one's essay.

Lastly, writers should consider their voice and word choice. The voice should be consistent throughout and maintain a balance between an authoritative and warm style, to both inform and engage readers. One way to alter voice is through word choice. Writers should consider changing weak verbs to stronger ones and selecting more precise language in areas where wording is vague. In some cases, it is useful to modify sentence beginnings or to combine or split up sentences to provide a more varied sentence structure.

Writing Clearly and Coherently

Regardless of how brilliant their ideas may be, writers who do not present them in organized ways will fail to engage readers—and fail to accomplish their writing goals. A fundamental rule for paragraphing is to confine each paragraph to a single idea. When writers find themselves transitioning to a new idea, they should start a new paragraph. However, a paragraph can include several pieces of evidence supporting its single idea; and it can include several points if they are all related to the overall paragraph topic. When writers find each point becoming lengthy, they may choose instead to devote a separate paragraph to every point and elaborate upon each more fully.

An effective paragraph should have these elements:

- Unity: One major discussion point or focus should occupy the whole paragraph from beginning to end.

- Coherence: For readers to understand a paragraph, it must be coherent. Two components of coherence are logical and verbal bridges. In logical bridges, the writer may write consecutive sentences with parallel structure or carry an idea over across sentences. In verbal bridges, writers may repeat key words across sentences.

- A topic sentence: The paragraph should have a sentence that generally identifies the paragraph's thesis or main idea.

- Sufficient development: To develop a paragraph, writers can use the following techniques after stating their topic sentence:

  o Define terms
  o Cite data
  o Use illustrations, anecdotes, and examples
  o Evaluate causes and effects
  o Analyze the topic
  o Explain the topic using chronological order

A topic sentence identifies the main idea of the paragraph. Some are explicit, some implicit. The topic sentence can appear anywhere in the paragraph. However, many experts advise beginning writers to place each paragraph topic sentence at or near the beginning of its paragraph to ensure that their readers understand what the topic of each paragraph is. Even without having written an explicit topic sentence, the writer should still be able to summarize readily what subject matter each paragraph addresses. The writer must then fully develop the topic that is introduced or identified in the topic sentence. Depending on what the writer's purpose is, they may use different methods for developing each paragraph.

Two main steps in the process of organizing paragraphs and essays should both be completed after determining the writing's main point, while the writer is planning or outlining the work. The initial step is to give an order to the topics addressed in each paragraph. Writers must have logical reasons for putting one paragraph first, another second, etc. The second step is to sequence the sentences in each paragraph. As with the first step, writers must have logical reasons for the order of sentences. Sometimes the work's main point obviously indicates a specific order.

Planning, Revising, and Editing in the Process of Writing

- *Pre-Writing/Planning*
One of the most important steps in writing is pre-writing. Before drafting an essay or other assignment, it's helpful to think about the topic for a moment or two, in order to gain a more solid understanding of what the task is. Then, spend about five minutes jotting down the immediate ideas that could work for the essay. Brainstorming is a way to get some words on the page and offer a reference for ideas when drafting. Scratch paper is provided for writers to use any pre-writing techniques such as webbing, freewriting, or listing. Some writers prefer using graphic organizers during this phase. The goal is to get ideas out of the mind and onto the page.

- *Editing*
Rather than focusing on content (as is the aim in the revising stage), the editing phase is all about the mechanics of the essay: the syntax, word choice, and grammar. This can be considered the proofreading stage. Successful editing is what sets apart a messy essay from a polished document.

The following areas should be considered when proofreading:

- Sentence fragments
- Awkward sentence structure
- Run-on sentences
- Incorrect word choice
- Grammatical agreement errors
- Spelling errors
- Punctuation errors
- Capitalization errors

One of the most effective ways of identifying grammatical errors, awkward phrases, or unclear sentences is to read the essay out loud. Listening to one's own work can help move the writer from simply the author to the reader.

During the editing phase, it's also important to ensure the essay follows the correct formatting and citation rules as dictated by the assignment.

Developmental Stages of Writing

As a young child begins to learn how to write, his or her "words" go through many stages before they begin to look familiar to experienced readers. Scribbling is typically the beginning stage of learning how to write. In this stage, children make random marks on paper that may look like wiggly lines, haphazard circles, or other shapes. This process is important because children learn and refine fine motor skills that aid them in controlling writing instruments; these fine motor skills will eventually help them in creating recognizable letters. Additionally, children often place meaning on their scribbles. Encouraging a child to share what his or her scribbles mean can hone communication skills and interpersonal skills and support critical-thinking processes. These are important aspects of assigning meaning to a visual representation and using both to communicate information to others.

After scribbling, children typically work toward forming recognizable letters. Often, the first recognizable letters they are able to create are ones in their own name. They may not space accurately between letters or may make mistakes such as creating the letters backward. Eventually, children will move toward writing recognizable letters they attempt to place together; however, spaces between letters may remain very large, or alternatively, children may write letters practically on top of one another.

Next, children move toward spacing letters appropriately but may struggle with spacing words accurately. For example, they may write multiple words together as one single word (e.g., "Thedog runs" rather than "The dog runs"). Eventually, as children begin to learn all consonant sounds and better recognize syllabic patterns, their ability to space words appropriately will get better. They may also learn proper punctuation rules at this time and have generally comprehensible writing with clear sentences and a simple meaning. However, they may struggle to spell all words correctly. Often in this stage, students may form letters and words well but spell most words the way they sound.

Finally, students learn various letter-sound patterns (e.g., *ief* is always pronounced "eef") to achieve standard spelling, a stage in which their writing becomes primarily error-free. Words are used and spelled correctly, and sentences may become more complex. Full writing samples may have a deeper meaning and message than previous samples.

Grade-Appropriate Continuum of Student Writing

As students enter kindergarten and advance through grade school, their writing abilities tend to fall and progress through a continuum. Early writers on the continuum tend to use present tense when writing and share information that describes a picture, makes a factual statement, or describes something common in their lives. Pictures and their descriptions make up a large part of the early stages of the continuum, which include the **Readiness** stage and the **Preconventional** stage. These typically occur in the pre-K and kindergarten years and include skills such as making stories from pictures, describing what is occurring in pictures, scribbling, making basic shapes, and attempting simple sentences. Many students in these stages will read aloud their scribbles and create story lines within them.

In the next stages, **Early Emergent** and **Emergent**, students begin to write more legibly and produce work others can read without assistance from the student. They may also write story lines based on their own ideas and observations rather than simply describing a picture. They may also benefit from teacher-led checklists to check their writing samples for organization, development, and stylistic features. These stages take place between kindergarten and second grade.

Through the third and fourth grades, students enter the **Developing** stage and the **Bridging** stage and typically begin to write more complex stories. They are able to better describe their own feelings and emotions, which they may incorporate into their work. Many students enjoy journaling or beginning a diary at this age. They may also begin to recognize different genres and write within those parameters. Students may benefit from receiving feedback and enjoy using feedback to revise their own work. Computer skills may develop in these stages as well.

Toward the end of fourth grade and through fifth grade, students become familiar with language and literacy tools, such as spellcheck and dictionaries, and utilize these to refine their work. They may experience writing across all four styles (narrative, expository, persuasive, and descriptive) and be easily able to distinguish between them. This final stage is referred to as **Expanding**. As students progress through middle school and high school, these skills are compounded as they begin to read more complex and meaningful literature and analyze them. This type of exposure supports refinement of one's own writing capabilities.

Digital Tools for Producing and Publishing Writing

Technology provides a number of new avenues for today's students to produce and publish writing material. In addition to traditional writing tools such as journals, notebooks, and writing software, students can also utilize a variety of publishing software, digital applications, and internet platforms on which to publish their writing. Many of these tools also integrate visual and audio components with written content.

For example, students can develop personal online blogs on platforms such as WordPress, Blogger, or SquareSpace through which their content can reach wide audiences. Collaborative tools such as online group writing applications (e.g., Google Docs, Basecamp) allow students to write together and save their work in real time; additionally, these types of tools allow students to begin work at school and continue it in their free time as long as they have a computer and internet connection. Social media is a way for students to create shorter pieces of writing, often with the incorporation of graphics.

Finally, a number of digital tools provide learning aids. For example, e-books often have built-in dictionaries to allow readers to immediately find the meaning of an unfamiliar word. Some e-readers allow students to hover over different words and learn more complex synonyms. Students who have been diagnosed with literacy-related learning disabilities such as dyslexia have found digital tools to equalize their struggles with traditional paper books; they are now able to learn the same content through a visual medium or an audiobook.

It is important to note that, while technology has greatly expanded the types of learning, writing, and publishing accessible to students, teaching internet safety and security rules should be a component of lessons that heavily rely on technology. For example, students should familiarize themselves with the permanence and wide reach of online posts, the positive and negative sides of their work "going viral," and how to handle cyberbullies or online trolls. Additionally, students should continue to learn critical-thinking and problem-solving skills. For example, even though many digital writing tools come with automatic spellcheckers, students may want to practice writing without these aids in order to ensure they are actually learning and not relying extensively on a digital tool. These are aspects of technology that must be addressed or filtered in order to ensure students' digital experiences are enriching rather than harmful.

Digital Tools for Interacting with Others

Today's young children will likely grow up understanding how to use digital tools to interact with others from a very early age. Far beyond television and computers, children are now exposed to smartphones, tablets, e-readers, electronic toys, internet applications, virtual reality, video gaming systems, and other interactive digital devices. It is important to leverage these with a meaningful, valuable, and educational purpose in mind rather than allowing students to mindlessly, excessively, or harmfully utilize them. There remains mixed research about how to best utilize technology with young children. Some research indicates technology is harmful for children, leading to addictive technology behaviors, less human and personal connection, sedentary lifestyles, decreased language development, consumption of pointless information, poor sleep habits, and cyberbullying. However, utilizing technology deliberately, with purpose, and alongside students so human interaction remains may support educational initiatives. Therefore, it is important that instructors understand technology and how to best implement it in instructional settings. For example, utilizing an application that provides information in an accessible way for a student with a learning disability is a beneficial use of technology, while playing a video to a classroom for an hour without any related discussion may be a less valuable teaching choice. These decisions may be subjective based on the types of students in the classroom at any given point.

In general, research indicates that children under age two do not benefit from using digital tools; in fact, some research indicates that repeated interaction with screens may disrupt neural pathways relating to attention, focus, and problem-solving skills. After age two, children may benefit somewhat from digital tools if their purpose is to foster interpersonal communication, quality time with an adult caregiver, and/or developmentally appropriate educational activities. For example, a preschooler who video calls a parent who is on a business trip and has a meaningful conversation is likely benefiting from using a digital tool (e.g., interaction with a loved one, practicing vocabulary and speaking skills) than if that same preschooler played with an electronic toy alone for the same period of time. Relatedly, if a kindergarten student plays an educational online game that reinforces material that was learned that day at school, this game may be a benefit for this student. If this student's younger sibling plays the same game and simply stares at the computer screen without understanding what is going on, it may be a less beneficial tool even though both siblings interacted with the same game.

As children get older, into the middle and high school years, it may be imperative for them to have an understanding of digital tools to keep up with their peers. As high school students consider future careers, they need to have a stronger grasp of technology in order to set career goals, as the economy is rapidly changing to encompass a high proportion of technology-oriented jobs. These students may need to focus more on technology and digital tools to remain competent for part-time jobs, college applications, and future careers. Older students may also begin to utilize social media and the internet for interacting with others that have similar interests or finding resources to support their schooling (such as researching topics, finding informational videos, or engaging in online tutoring). Again, it is important to note that online safety and security is an important lesson to teach as students become more engaged with digital tools.

The Research Process

Any type of research to be conducted should clearly identify the justification for the research as well as outline how the research is to be conducted. Once students have had the opportunity to carry out the research and interpret the results, they must consider the implications. For example, the results might affect the way students will conduct further experiments or research. Data implications could change the way certain industries conduct business, how teachers approach education, or how individuals manage their diet or their health and wellness regime.

The implications of scientific studies may lead medical researchers toward breakthroughs in treatment or guide them that much closer to finding a cure for a disease. In the world of education, data results are the basis for teaching methodologies, and the more data that is collected, analyzed, and interpreted, the more informed the teaching profession is about the optimal ways to prepare for instruction, teaching, and evaluation.

Research on any given topic is multi-faceted. It starts with knowing just enough about a subject to develop a detailed inquiry, which then leads to experimentation or data collection. The data must then be analyzed and interpreted. The final stage is considering what immediate or future implications this discovery may have. Implications of any research study lead to innovative practices across all sectors, provide insights, lead to new discoveries, inspire new research, and create new questions to explore.

Steps in the Research Process

A hypothesis is a well-defined research statement. An experiment then follows, usually using quantitative research. Quantitative research is research based on empirical data.

The results are then analyzed to determine whether the hypothesis was proven or disproven. Examining a hypothesis is also called hypothesis testing. Examining a hypothesis happens most often in science, and it isn't really appropriate for social sciences such as social studies and history. However, qualitative hypotheses can be made in these disciplines to further examine a social or historical event. A hypothesis, in this light, should clearly state the argument that the writer wishes to examine, and the reason or reasons why the author feels it is relevant. This type of hypothesis statement generally requires the "what" and the "why." Consider the following qualitative hypothesis:

> "The Métis in Canada were less discriminated against than were Canada's First Nations since they were partly descendants of European fur traders."

The first half of the hypothesis—"The Métis in Canada were less discriminated against than were Canada's First Nations"—reveals the "what," and the second part—"since they were partly descendants of European fur traders"—is the "why."

In science, hypotheses are generally written as "if, then" statements that require the collection of unbiased, empirical, and quantitative data to either prove or disprove the hypothesis. Consider the following:

> "**If** a hibiscus flower is placed in direct sunlight and watered twice a day, **then** it will thrive."

The basic steps that lead to the formation of a hypothesis and ultimately, a conclusion, include:

Step ONE	Making an observation
Step TWO	Forming a question based on the observation
Step THREE	Forming a hypothesis (a possible answer to the question)
Step FOUR	Conducting a study (social studies and history) or an experiment (science)
Step FIVE	Analyzing the data
Step SIX	Drawing a conclusion

In order for conclusions to be accepted as valid and credible, it is extremely important that the data collected isn't biased. The researchers must consider all possible angles of the study or experiment, and they must refrain from collecting the data in such a way as to purposely prove the hypothesis. Conducting studies and experiments of this nature helps to advance the different disciplines, challenge widely accepted beliefs, and broaden a global understanding of the fields of social studies, history, and the sciences.

Primary and Secondary Sources

A primary source is a piece of original work. This can include books, musical compositions, recordings, movies, works of visual art (paintings, drawings, photographs), jewelry, pottery, clothing, furniture, and other artifacts. Within books, primary sources may be of any genre. Whether nonfiction based on actual events or a fictional creation, the primary source relates the author's firsthand view of some specific event, phenomenon, character, place, process, ideas, field of study or discipline, or other subject matter. Whereas primary sources are original treatments of their subjects, secondary sources are a step removed from the original subjects; they analyze and interpret primary sources. These include journal articles, newspaper or magazine articles, works of literary criticism, political commentaries, and academic textbooks.

In the field of history, primary sources frequently include documents that were created around the same time period that they were describing, and most often produced by someone who had direct experience or knowledge of the subject matter. In contrast, secondary sources present the ideas and viewpoints of other authors about the primary sources; in history, for example, these can include books and other written works about the particular historical periods or eras in which the primary sources were produced. Primary sources pertinent in history include diaries, letters, statistics, government information, and original journal articles and books. In literature, a primary source might be a literary novel, a poem or book of poems, or a play. Secondary sources addressing primary sources may be criticism, dissertations, theses, and journal articles. Tertiary sources, typically reference works referring to primary and secondary sources, include encyclopedias, bibliographies, handbooks, abstracts, and periodical indexes.

In scientific fields, when scientists conduct laboratory experiments to answer specific research questions and test hypotheses, lab reports and reports of research results constitute examples of primary sources. When researchers produce statistics to support or refute hypotheses, those statistics are primary sources. When a scientist is studying some subject longitudinally or conducting a case study, they may keep a journal or diary. For example, Charles Darwin kept diaries of extensive notes on his studies during sea voyages on the *Beagle*, visits to the Galápagos Islands, etc.; Jean Piaget kept journals of observational notes for case studies of children's learning behaviors. Many scientists, particularly in past centuries, shared and discussed discoveries, questions, and ideas with colleagues through letters, which also constitute primary sources. When a scientist seeks to replicate another's experiment, the reported results, analysis, and commentary on the original work is a secondary source, as is a student's dissertation if it analyzes or discusses others' work rather than reporting original research or ideas.

Reliable and Unreliable Sources

Understanding whether or not a source of information is reliable or unreliable is a critical component of writing factual, credible, and validated literature. Reliable sources are especially important when writing research papers and persuasive papers but can also play a large part in fiction, as writers often research real events from which to inspire their stories. **Reliable sources** are those that are evidence based (such as papers written with information presented in peer-reviewed journals), authored by someone who is a credible expert in the topic (e.g., a Michelin-star chef who writes a book about the benefits of using locally sourced ingredients), or a documented report from someone who experienced an event firsthand (such as a survivor of a historical event). Common reliable sources include journal papers, memoirs, and books published by well-known publishing companies. Online pages from these sources, as well as academic institutions and government institutions, are generally considered reliable resources also.

Unreliable sources are those that publish information that cannot necessarily be proven, hold a partial or biased viewpoint, or have not been reviewed by other credible sources (such as self-published literature). Common examples of unreliable sources include personal blogs (unless they draw from reliable sources) and social media. It is also important to understand the intention behind the publication of a piece of literature and the purpose for which it is being used. For example, a private academic institution with strong religious leanings may publish internal literature that is in line with the religious beliefs; this piece of literature is an inherently biased and subjective point of view. While it may seem like an unreliable literature source for someone who is writing a research paper that presents evidence-based information, it can be a reliable resource for a speech at a church that belongs to that same religion.

Paraphrasing and Plagiarizing

Paraphrasing refers to discussing sourced information in a unique way. While a paraphrase of the sourced information may cover the same topics, the author who is paraphrasing must add something new to the discussion (such as a personal analysis or viewpoint). Lifting information word for word from an original source or lifting information that is simply too similar in idea and presentation is considered **plagiarism**. Plagiarism can be avoided by putting information taken directly from the original source in quotation marks and/or attributing full credit to the original source through citations, such as an endnote, footnote, or comprehensive bibliography. Students should consider adding citations even when paraphrasing an original source, as it is always safer to cite when it is unnecessary than to inappropriately miss a citation. Some terms are considered "shared language" and cannot be expressed in any other way so do not need to be referenced. For example, a list of pharmaceuticals that cause similar side effects can only be presented in so many different ways. A number of online tools exist to ensure and check that literature has not been plagiarized. These tools work by scanning students' work and comparing them against available online sources and can be a valuable aid for teachers.

How to Locate and Cite Credible Print and Digital Sources

Books as Resources
When a student has an assignment to research and write a paper, one of the first steps after determining the topic is to select research sources. The student may begin by conducting an Internet or library search of the topic, may refer to a reading list provided by the instructor, or may use an annotated bibliography of works related to the topic. To evaluate the worth of the book for the research paper, the student first considers the book title to get an idea of its content. Then the student can scan the book's table of contents for chapter titles and topics to get further ideas of their applicability to the topic. The student may also turn to the end of the book to look for an alphabetized index. Most academic textbooks and scholarly works have these; students can look up key topic terms to see how many are included and how many pages are devoted to them.

Journal Articles
Like books, journal articles are primary or secondary sources the student may need to use for researching any topic. To assess whether a journal article will be a useful source for a particular paper topic, a student can first get some idea about the content of the article by reading its title and subtitle, if any exists. Many journal articles, particularly scientific ones, include abstracts. These are brief summaries of the content. The student should read the abstract to get a more specific idea of whether the experiment, literature review, or other work documented is applicable to the paper topic. Students should also check the references at the end of the article, which today often contain links to related works for exploring the topic further.

Encyclopedias and Dictionaries
Dictionaries and encyclopedias are both reference books for looking up information alphabetically. Dictionaries are more exclusively focused on vocabulary words. They include each word's correct spelling, pronunciation, variants, part(s) of speech, definitions of one or more meanings, and examples used in a sentence. Some dictionaries provide illustrations of certain words when these inform the meaning. Some dictionaries also offer synonyms, antonyms, and related words under a word's entry. Encyclopedias, like dictionaries, often provide word pronunciations and definitions. However, they have broader scopes: one can look up entire subjects in encyclopedias, not just words, and find comprehensive, detailed information about historical events, famous people, countries, disciplines of study, and many other things. Dictionaries

are for finding word meanings, pronunciations, and spellings; encyclopedias are for finding breadth and depth of information on a variety of topics.

Card Catalogs

A card catalog is a means of organizing, classifying, and locating the large numbers of books found in libraries. Without being able to look up books in library card catalogs, it would be virtually impossible to find them on library shelves. Card catalogs may be on traditional paper cards filed in drawers, or electronic catalogs accessible online; some libraries combine both. Books are shelved by subject area; subjects are coded using formal classification systems—standardized sets of rules for identifying and labeling books by subject and author. These assign each book a call number: a code indicating the classification system, subject, author, and title. Call numbers also function as bookshelf "addresses" where books can be located. Most public libraries use the Dewey Decimal Classification System. Most university, college, and research libraries use the Library of Congress Classification. Nursing students will also encounter the National Institute of Health's National Library of Medicine Classification System, which major collections of health sciences publications utilize.

Databases

A database is a collection of digital information organized for easy access, updating, and management. Users can sort and search databases for information. One way of classifying databases is by content, i.e. full-text, numerical, bibliographical, or images. Another classification method used in computing is by organizational approach. The most common approach is a relational database, which is tabular and defines data so they can be accessed and reorganized in various ways. A distributed database can be reproduced or interspersed among different locations within a network. An object-oriented database is organized to be aligned with object classes and subclasses defining the data. Databases usually collect files like product inventories, catalogs, customer profiles, sales transactions, student bodies, and resources. An associated set of application programs is a database management system or database manager. It enables users to specify which reports to generate, control access to reading and writing data, and analyze database usage. Structured Query Language (SQL) is a standard computer language for updating, querying, and otherwise interfacing with databases.

Language

Parts of Speech

Possessives

Possessive forms indicate possession, i.e. that something belongs to or is owned by someone or something. As such, the most common parts of speech to be used in possessive form are adjectives, nouns, and pronouns. The rule for correctly spelling/punctuating possessive nouns and proper nouns is with - *'s*, like "the woman's briefcase" or "Frank's hat." With possessive adjectives, however, apostrophes are not used: these include *my, your, his, her, its, our*, and *their*, like "my book," "your friend," "his car," "her house," "its contents," "our family," or "their property." Possessive pronouns include *mine, yours, his, hers, its, ours,* and *theirs*. These also have no apostrophes. The difference is that possessive adjectives take direct objects, whereas possessive pronouns replace them. For example, instead of using two possessive adjectives in a row, as in "I forgot my book, so Blanca let me use her book," which reads monotonously, replacing the second one with a possessive pronoun reads better: "I forgot my book, so Blanca let me use hers."

Pronouns

There are three pronoun cases: subjective case, objective case, and possessive case. Pronouns as subjects are pronouns that replace the subject of the sentence, such as *I, you, he, she, it, we, they* and *who*. Pronouns as objects replace the object of the sentence, such as *me, you, him, her, it, us, them*, and *whom*. Pronouns that show possession are *mine, yours, hers, its, ours, theirs*, and *whose*. The following are examples of different pronoun cases:

- Subject pronoun: *She* ate the cake for her birthday. *I* saw the movie.
- Object pronoun: You gave *me* the card last weekend. She gave the picture to *him*.
- Possessive pronoun: That bracelet you found yesterday is *mine*. *His* name was Casey.

Adjectives

Adjectives are descriptive words that modify nouns or pronouns. They may occur before or after the nouns or pronouns they modify in sentences. For example, in "This is a big house," *big* is an adjective modifying or describing the noun *house*. In "This house is big," the adjective is at the end of the sentence rather than preceding the noun it modifies.

A rule of punctuation that applies to adjectives is to separate a series of adjectives with commas. For example, "Their home was a large, rambling, old, white, two-story house." A comma should never separate the last adjective from the noun, though.

Adverbs

Whereas adjectives modify and describe nouns or pronouns, adverbs modify and describe adjectives, verbs, or other adverbs. Adverbs can be thought of as answers to questions in that they describe when, where, how, how often, how much, or to what extent.

Many (but not all) adjectives can be converted to adverbs by adding *–ly*. For example, in "She is a quick learner," *quick* is an adjective modifying *learner*. In "She learns quickly," *quickly* is an adverb modifying *learns*. One exception is *fast*. *Fast* is an adjective in "She is a fast learner." However, *–ly* is never added to the word *fast*; it retains the same form as an adverb in "She learns fast."

Verbs

A verb is a word or phrase that expresses action, feeling, or state of being. Verbs explain what their subject is *doing*. Three different types of verbs used in a sentence are action verbs, linking verbs, and helping verbs.

Action verbs show a physical or mental action. Some examples of action verbs are *play, type, jump, write, examine, study, invent, develop,* and *taste*. The following example uses an action verb:

Kat *imagines* that she is a mermaid in the ocean.

The verb *imagines* explains what Kat is doing: she is imagining being a mermaid.

Linking verbs connect the subject to the predicate without expressing an action. The following sentence shows an example of a linking verb:

The mango *tastes* sweet.

The verb *tastes* is a linking verb. The mango doesn't *do* the tasting, but the word *taste* links the mango to its predicate, sweet. Most linking verbs can also be used as action verbs, such as *smell, taste, look, seem, grow,* and *sound*. Saying something *is* something else is also an example of a linking verb. For example, if we were to say, "Peaches is a dog," the verb *is* would be a linking verb in this sentence, since it links the subject to its predicate.

Helping verbs are verbs that help the main verb in a sentence. Examples of helping verbs are *be, am, is, was, have, has, do, did, can, could, may, might, should,* and *must,* among others. The following are examples of helping verbs:

> Jessica *is* planning a trip to Hawaii.

> Brenda *does* not like camping.

> Xavier *should* go to the dance tonight.

Notice that after each of these helping verbs is the main verb of the sentence: *planning, like,* and *go.* Helping verbs usually show an aspect of time.

Errors in Usage, Mechanics, and Spelling

Subject-Verb Agreement
Lack of subject-verb agreement is a very common grammatical error. One of the most common instances is when people use a series of nouns as a compound subject with a singular instead of a plural verb. Here is an example:

> Identifying the best books, locating the sellers with the lowest prices, and paying for them *is* difficult

instead of saying "*are* difficult." Additionally, when a sentence subject is compound, the verb is plural:

> He and his cousins *were* at the reunion.

However, if the conjunction connecting two or more singular nouns or pronouns is "or" or "nor," the verb must be singular to agree:

> That pen or another one like it is in the desk drawer.

If a compound subject includes both a singular noun and a plural one, and they are connected by "or" or "nor," the verb must agree with the subject closest to the verb: "Sally or her sisters go jogging daily"; but "Her sisters or Sally goes jogging daily."

Simply put, singular subjects require singular verbs and plural subjects require plural verbs. A common source of agreement errors is not identifying the sentence subject correctly. For example, people often write sentences incorrectly like, "The group of students *were* complaining about the test." The subject is not the plural "students" but the singular "group." Therefore, the correct sentence should read, "The group of students *was* complaining about the test." The converse also applies, for example, in this incorrect sentence: "The facts in that complicated court case *is* open to question." The subject of the sentence is not the singular "case" but the plural "facts." Hence the sentence would correctly be written: "The facts in that complicated court case *are* open to question." New writers should not be misled by the distance between the subject and verb, especially when another noun with a different number intervenes as in these examples. The verb must agree with the subject, not the noun closest to it.

Pronoun-Antecedent Agreement

Pronouns within a sentence must refer specifically to one noun, known as the **antecedent**. Sometimes, if there are multiple nouns within a sentence, it may be difficult to ascertain which noun belongs to the pronoun. It's important that the pronouns always clearly reference the nouns in the sentence so as not to confuse the reader. Here's an example of an unclear pronoun reference:

> After Catherine cut Libby's hair, David bought her some lunch.

The pronoun in the examples above is *her*. The pronoun could either be referring to *Catherine* or *Libby*. Here are some ways to write the above sentence with a clear pronoun reference:

> After Catherine cut Libby's hair, David bought Libby some lunch.

> David bought Libby some lunch after Catherine cut Libby's hair.

But many times the pronoun will clearly refer to its antecedent, like the following:

> After David cut Catherine's hair, he bought her some lunch.

Homophones

Homophones are words that have different meanings and spellings but sound the same. These can be confusing for English Language Learners (ELLs) and beginning students, but even native English-speaking adults can find them problematic unless informed by context. Whereas listeners must rely entirely on context to **differentiate** spoken homophone meanings, readers with good spelling knowledge have a distinct advantage since homophones are spelled differently. For instance, *their* means belonging to them; *there* indicates location; and *they're* is a contraction of *they are*, despite different meanings, they all sound the same. *Lacks* can be a plural noun or a present-tense, third-person singular verb; either way it refers to absence—*deficiencies* as a plural noun and *is deficient in* as a verb. But *lax* is an adjective that means loose, slack, relaxed, uncontrolled, or negligent. These two spellings, derivations, and meanings are completely different. With speech, listeners cannot know spelling and must use context; but with print, readers with spelling knowledge can differentiate them with or without context.

Homonyms, Homophones, and Homographs

Homophones are words that sound the same in speech but have different spellings and meanings. For example, *to, too,* and *two* all sound alike, but have three different spellings and meanings. Homophones with different spellings are also called heterographs. Homographs are words that are spelled identically but have different meanings. If they also have different pronunciations, they are heteronyms. For instance, *tear* pronounced one way means a drop of liquid formed by the eye; pronounced another way, it means to rip. Homophones that are also homographs are homonyms. For example, *bark* can mean the outside of a tree or a dog's vocalization; both meanings have the same spelling. *Stalk* can mean a plant stem or to pursue and/or harass somebody; these are spelled and pronounced the same. *Rose* can mean a flower or the past tense of *rise*. Many non-linguists confuse things by using "homonym" to mean sets of words that are homophones but not homographs, and also those that are homographs but not homophones.

The word *row* can mean to use oars to propel a boat; a linear arrangement of objects or print; or an argument. It is pronounced the same with the first two meanings, but differently with the third. Because it is spelled identically regardless, all three meanings are homographs. However, the two meanings pronounced the same are homophones, whereas the one with the different pronunciation is a heteronym. By contrast, the word *read* means to peruse language, whereas the word *reed* refers to a marsh plant. Because these are pronounced the same way, they are homophones; because they are spelled differently, they are heterographs. Homonyms are both homophones and homographs—pronounced and spelled identically, but with different meanings. One distinction between homonyms is of those with separate, unrelated etymologies, called "true" homonyms, e.g. *skate* meaning a fish or *skate* meaning to glide over ice/water. Those with common origins are called polysemes or polysemous homonyms, e.g. the *mouth* of an animal/human or of a river.

Irregular Plurals

One type of irregular English plural involves words that are spelled the same whether they are singular or plural. These include *deer, fish, salmon, trout, sheep, moose, offspring, species, aircraft*, etc. The spelling rule for making these words plural is simple: they do not change. Another type of irregular English plurals does change from singular to plural form, but it does not take regular English *–s* or *–es* endings. Their irregular plural endings are largely derived from grammatical and spelling conventions in the other languages of their origins, like Latin, German, and vowel shifts and other linguistic mutations. Some examples of these words and their irregular plurals include *child* and *children; die* and *dice; foot* and *feet; goose* and *geese; louse* and *lice; man* and *men; mouse* and *mice; ox* and *oxen; person* and *people; tooth* and *teeth;* and *woman* and *women.*

Contractions

Contractions are formed by joining two words together, omitting one or more letters from one of the component words, and replacing the omitted words with an apostrophe. An obvious yet often forgotten rule for spelling contractions is to place the apostrophe where the letters were omitted; for example, spelling errors like *did'nt* for *didn't. Didn't* is a contraction of *did not.* Therefore, the apostrophe replaces the "o" that is omitted from the "not" component. Another common error is confusing contractions with possessives because both include apostrophes, e.g. spelling the possessive *its* as "it's," which is a contraction of "it is"; spelling the possessive *their* as "they're," a contraction of "they are"; spelling the possessive *whose* as "who's," a contraction of "who is"; or spelling the possessive *your* as "you're," a contraction of "you are."

Frequently Misspelled Words

One source of spelling errors is not knowing whether to drop the final letter *e* from a word when its form is changed by adding an ending to indicate the past tense or progressive participle of a verb, converting an adjective to an adverb, a noun to an adjective, etc. Some words retain the final *e* when another syllable is added; others lose it. For example, *true* becomes *truly; argue* becomes *arguing; come* becomes *coming; write* becomes *writing;* and *judge* becomes *judging.* In these examples, the final *e* is dropped before adding the ending. But *severe* becomes *severely; complete* becomes *completely; sincere* becomes *sincerely; argue* becomes *argued;* and *care* becomes *careful.* In these instances, the final *e* is retained before adding the ending. Note that some words, like *argue* in these examples, drops the final *e* when the *–ing* ending is added to indicate the participial form; but the regular past tense ending of *–ed* makes it *argued,* in effect replacing the final *e* so that *arguing* is spelled without an *e* but *argued* is spelled with one.

Some English words contain the vowel combination of *ei,* while some contain the reverse combination of *ie.* Many people confuse these. Some examples include these:

> *ceiling, conceive, leisure, receive, weird, their, either, foreign, sovereign, neither, neighbors, seize, forfeit, counterfeit, height, weight, protein,* and *freight*

Words with *ie* include *piece, believe, chief, field, friend, grief, relief, mischief, siege, niece, priest, fierce, pierce, achieve, retrieve, hygiene, science,* and *diesel.* A rule that also functions as a mnemonic device is "I before E except after C, or when sounded like A as in 'neighbor' or 'weigh'." However, it is obvious from the list above that many exceptions exist.

Many people often misspell certain words by confusing whether they have the vowel *a, e,* or *i,* frequently in the middle syllable of three-syllable words or beginning the last syllables that sound the same in different words. For example, in the following correctly spelled words, the vowel in boldface is the one people typically get wrong by substituting one or either of the others for it:

> cem**e**tery, quant**i**ties, ben**e**fit, priv**i**lege, unpleas**a**nt, sep**a**rate, independ**e**nt, excell**e**nt, cat**e**gories, indispens**a**ble, and irrelev**a**nt

The words with final syllables that sound the same when spoken but are spelled differently include *unpleasant, independent, excellent,* and *irrelevant.* Another source of misspelling is whether or not to double consonants when adding suffixes. For example, we double the last consonant before *–ed* and *–ing* endings in *controlled, beginning, forgetting, admitted, occurred, referred,* and *hopping;* but we do not double the last consonant before the suffix in *shining, poured, sweating, loving, hating, smiling,* and *hoping.*

One way in which people misspell certain words frequently is by failing to include letters that are silent. Some letters are articulated when pronounced correctly but elided in some people's speech, which then transfers to their writing. Another source of misspelling is the converse: people add extraneous letters. For example, some people omit the silent *u* in *guarantee,* overlook the first *r* in *surprise,* leave out the *z* in *realize,* fail to double the *m* in *recommend,* leave out the middle *i* from *aspirin,* and exclude the *p* from *temperature.* The converse error, adding extra letters, is common in words like *until* by adding a second *l* at the end; or by inserting a superfluous syllabic *a* or *e* in the middle of *athletic,* reproducing a common mispronunciation.

Rules of Capitalization
The first word of any document, and of each new sentence, is capitalized. Proper nouns, like names and adjectives derived from proper nouns, should also be capitalized. Here are some examples:

- Grand Canyon
- Pacific Palisades
- Golden Gate Bridge
- Freudian slip
- Shakespearian, Spenserian, or Petrarchan sonnet
- Irish song

Some exceptions are adjectives, originally derived from proper nouns, which through time and usage are no longer capitalized, like *quixotic, herculean,* or *draconian.* Capitals draw attention to specific instances of people, places, and things. Some categories that should be capitalized include the following:

- brand names
- companies
- weekdays
- months
- governmental divisions or agencies
- historical eras
- major historical events
- holidays

- institutions
- famous buildings
- ships and other manmade constructions
- natural and manmade landmarks
- territories
- nicknames
- epithets
- organizations
- planets
- nationalities
- tribes
- religions
- names of religious deities
- roads
- special occasions, like the Cannes Film Festival or the Olympic Games

Exceptions

Related to American government, capitalize the noun Congress but not the related adjective congressional. Capitalize the noun U.S. Constitution, but not the related adjective constitutional. Many experts advise leaving the adjectives federal and state in lowercase, as in federal regulations or state water board, and only capitalizing these when they are parts of official titles or names, like Federal Communications Commission or State Water Resources Control Board. While the names of the other planets in the solar system are capitalized as names, Earth is more often capitalized only when being described specifically as a planet, like Earth's orbit, but lowercase otherwise since it is used not only as a proper noun but also to mean *land, ground, soil*, etc.

Names of animal species or breeds are not capitalized unless they include a proper noun. Then, only the proper noun is capitalized. Antelope, black bear, and yellow-bellied sapsucker are not capitalized. However, Bengal tiger, German shepherd, Australian shepherd, French poodle, and Russian blue cat are capitalized.

Other than planets, celestial bodies like the sun, moon, and stars are not capitalized. Medical conditions like tuberculosis or diabetes are lowercase; again, exceptions are proper nouns, like Epstein-Barr syndrome, Alzheimer's disease, and Down syndrome. Seasons and related terms like winter solstice or autumnal equinox are lowercase. Plants, including fruits and vegetables, like poinsettia, celery, or avocados, are not capitalized unless they include proper names, like Douglas fir, Jerusalem artichoke, Damson plums, or Golden Delicious apples.

Titles and Names

When official titles precede names, they should be capitalized, except when there is a comma between the title and name. But if a title follows or replaces a name, it should not be capitalized. For example, "the president" without a name is not capitalized, as in "The president addressed Congress." But with a name it is capitalized, like "President Obama addressed Congress." Or, "Chair of the Board Janet Yellen was appointed by President Obama." One exception is that some publishers and writers nevertheless capitalize President, Queen, Pope, etc., when these are not accompanied by names to show respect for these high offices. However, many writers in America object to this practice for violating democratic principles of equality. Occupations before full names are not capitalized, like owner Mark Cuban, director Martin Scorsese, or coach Roger McDowell.

Some universal rules for capitalization in composition titles include capitalizing the following:

- The first and last words of the title
- Forms of the verb *to be* and all other verbs
- Pronouns
- The word *not*

Universal rules for NOT capitalizing include the articles *the, a,* or *an,* the conjunctions *and, or,* or *nor,* and the preposition *to,* or *to* as part of the infinitive form of a verb. The exception to all of these is UNLESS any of them is the first or last word in the title, in which case they are capitalized. Other words are subject to differences of opinion and differences among various stylebooks or methods. These include *as, but, if,* and *or,* which some capitalize and others do not. Some authorities say no preposition should ever be capitalized; some say prepositions five or more letters long should be capitalized. The *Associated Press Stylebook* advises capitalizing prepositions longer than three letters (like *about, across,* or *with*).

Sentence Types

Incomplete Sentences
Four types of incomplete sentences are sentence fragments, run-on sentences, subject-verb and/or pronoun-antecedent disagreement, and non-parallel structure.

Sentence fragments are caused by absent subjects, absent verbs, or dangling/uncompleted dependent clauses. Every sentence must have a subject and a verb to be complete. An example of a fragment is "Raining all night long," because there is no subject present. "It was raining all night long" is one correction. Another example of a sentence fragment is the second part in "Many scientists think in unusual ways. Einstein, for instance." The second phrase is a fragment because it has no verb. One correction is "Many scientists, like Einstein, think in unusual ways." Finally, look for "cliffhanger" words like *if, when, because,* or *although* that introduce dependent clauses, which cannot stand alone without an independent clause. For example, to correct the sentence fragment "If you get home early," add an independent clause: "If you get home early, we can go dancing."

Run-On Sentences
A run-on sentence combines two or more complete sentences without punctuating them correctly or separating them. For example, a run-on sentence caused by a lack of punctuation is the following:

> There is a malfunction in the computer system however there is nobody available right now who knows how to troubleshoot it.

One correction is, "There is a malfunction in the computer system; however, there is nobody available right now who knows how to troubleshoot it." Another is, "There is a malfunction in the computer system. However, there is nobody available right now who knows how to troubleshoot it."

An example of a comma splice of two sentences is the following:

> Jim decided not to take the bus, he walked home.

Replacing the comma with a period or a semicolon corrects this. Commas that try and separate two independent clauses without a contraction are considered comma splices.

Parallel Sentence Structures

Parallel structure in a sentence matches the forms of sentence components. Any sentence containing more than one description or phrase should keep them consistent in wording and form. Readers can easily follow writers' ideas when they are written in parallel structure, making it an important element of correct sentence construction. For example, this sentence lacks parallelism: "Our coach is a skilled manager, a clever strategist, and works hard." The first two phrases are parallel, but the third is not. Correction: "Our coach is a skilled manager, a clever strategist, and a hard worker." Now all three phrases match in form. Here is another example:

Fred intercepted the ball, escaped tacklers, and a touchdown was scored.

This is also non-parallel. Here is the sentence corrected:

Fred intercepted the ball, escaped tacklers, and scored a touchdown.

Varieties of English

Varieties and subsets of English, such as local dialects, registers, and colloquialisms, can provide additional descriptive imagery, historical and cultural context, and details that add to the overall meaning of the literature. This is a way to document various manifestations of a single language as presented by different groups of people. A character that utilizes the dialect of his or her region provides a certain authenticity that can draw the reader further into the setting, culture, and character interactions of the story. However, this practice can prove to be somewhat difficult and controversial, as it depicts the author's perspective of the English variety that is being used, as well as may indicate certain intolerant biases the author may have (such as racial-, ethnic-, or class-based views). However, when dialects are researched from reliable sources and utilized in a respectful, well-intentioned manner, it can benefit both the author and the reader. It allows the author to examine and work with a new creative realm (which can expand their general writing capabilities) and allows the reader to potentially better understand and experience the nuances of a character to which the reader may not otherwise be able to relate. The use of dialect in a literary text may also cause readers to question their own assumptions and beliefs about certain groups of people that may have otherwise gone unnoticed. Some linguistic experts have noted, though, that when people read written dialect that is intended to be associated with their own race, culture, class, geographical region, or some other categorization, they typically do not relate or respond favorably. Comparatively, a number of linguistic experts also argue that the use of dialects, registers, and colloquialisms are best used in stage dramas or films, as this ensures they are used in the manner intended by the writer and can be fairly critiqued. Additionally, many readers state that reading dialect is difficult for them and requires a much slower pace of reading, as if they were reading a completely different language.

Context, Syntax, and Knowledge of Roots and Affixes

By learning some of the etymologies of words and their parts, readers can break new words down into components and analyze their combined meanings. For example, the root word *soph* is Greek for wise or knowledge. Knowing this informs the meanings of English words including *sophomore, sophisticated,* and *philosophy*. Those who also know that *phil* is Greek for love will realize that *philosophy* means the love of knowledge. They can then extend this knowledge of *phil* to understand *philanthropist* (one who loves people), *bibliophile* (book lover), *philharmonic* (loving harmony), *hydrophilic* (water-loving), and so on. In addition, *phob-* derives from the Greek *phobos,* meaning fear. This informs all words ending with it as meaning fear of various things: *acrophobia* (fear of heights), *arachnophobia* (fear of spiders), *claustrophobia* (fear of enclosed spaces), *ergophobia* (fear of work), and *hydrophobia* (fear of water), among others.

Some English word origins from other languages, like ancient Greek, are found in large numbers and varieties of English words. An advantage of the shared ancestry of these words is that once readers recognize the meanings of some Greek words or word roots, they can determine or at least get an idea of what many different English words mean. As an example, the Greek word *métron* means to measure, a measure, or something used to measure; the English word meter derives from it. Knowing this informs many other English words, including *altimeter, barometer, diameter, hexameter, isometric,* and *metric.* While readers must know the meanings of the other parts of these words to decipher their meaning fully, they already have an idea that they are all related in some way to measures or measuring.

While all English words ultimately derive from a proto-language known as Indo-European, many of them historically came into the developing English vocabulary later, from sources like the ancient Greeks' language, the Latin used throughout Europe and much of the Middle East during the reign of the Roman Empire, and the Anglo-Saxon languages used by England's early tribes. In addition to classic revivals and native foundations, by the Renaissance era other influences included French, German, Italian, and Spanish. Today we can often discern English word meanings by knowing common roots and affixes, particularly from Greek and Latin.

The following is a list of common prefixes and their meanings:

Prefix	Definition	Examples
a-	without	atheist, agnostic
ad-	to, toward	advance
ante-	before	antecedent, antedate
anti-	opposing	antipathy, antidote
auto-	self	autonomy, autobiography
bene-	well, good	benefit, benefactor
bi-	two	bisect, biennial
bio-	life	biology, biosphere
chron-	time	chronometer, synchronize
circum-	around	circumspect, circumference
com-	with, together	commotion, complicate
contra-	against, opposing	contradict, contravene
cred-	belief, trust	credible, credit
de-	from	depart
dem-	people	demographics, democracy
dis-	away, off, down, not	dissent, disappear
equi-	equal, equally	equivalent
ex-	former, out of	extract
for-	away, off, from	forget, forswear
fore-	before, previous	foretell, forefathers
homo-	same, equal	homogenized
hyper-	excessive, over	hypercritical, hypertension
in-	in, into	intrude, invade
inter-	among, between	intercede, interrupt

mal-	bad, poorly, not	malfunction
micr-	small	microbe, microscope
mis-	bad, poorly, not	misspell, misfire
mono-	one, single	monogamy, monologue
mor-	die, death	mortality, mortuary
neo-	new	neolithic, neoconservative
non-	not	nonentity, nonsense
omni-	all, everywhere	omniscient
over-	above	overbearing
pan-	all, entire	panorama, pandemonium
para-	beside, beyond	parallel, paradox
phil-	love, affection	philosophy, philanthropic
poly-	many	polymorphous, polygamous
pre-	before, previous	prevent, preclude
prim-	first, early	primitive, primary
pro-	forward, in place of	propel, pronoun
re-	back, backward, again	revoke, recur
sub-	under, beneath	subjugate, substitute
super-	above, extra	supersede, supernumerary
trans-	across, beyond, over	transact, transport
ultra-	beyond, excessively	ultramodern, ultrasonic, ultraviolet
un-	not, reverse of	unhappy, unlock
vis-	to see	visage, visible

The following is a list of common suffixes and their meanings:

Suffix	Definition	Examples
-able	likely, able to	capable, tolerable
-ance	act, condition	acceptance, vigilance
-ard	one that does excessively	drunkard, wizard
-ation	action, state	occupation, starvation
-cy	state, condition	accuracy, captaincy
-er	one who does	teacher
-esce	become, grow, continue	convalesce, acquiesce
-esque	in the style of, like	picturesque, grotesque
-ess	feminine	waitress, lioness
-ful	full of, marked by	thankful, zestful
-ible	able, fit	edible, possible, divisible
-ion	action, result, state	union, fusion
-ish	suggesting, like	churlish, childish
-ism	act, manner, doctrine	barbarism, socialism
-ist	doer, believer	monopolist, socialist
-ition	action, result, state,	sedition, expedition
-ity	quality, condition	acidity, civility
-ize	cause to be, treat with	sterilize, mechanize, criticize

-less	lacking, without	hopeless, countless
-like	like, similar	childlike, dreamlike
-ly	like, of the nature of	friendly, positively
-ment	means, result, action	refreshment, disappointment
-ness	quality, state	greatness, tallness
-or	doer, office, action	juror, elevator, honor
-ous	marked by, given to	religious, riotous
-some	apt to, showing	tiresome, lonesome
-th	act, state, quality	warmth, width
-ty	quality, state	enmity, activity

Figurative Language

Not meant to be taken literal, figurative language is useful when the author of a text wants to produce an emotional effect in the reader or add a heightened complexity to the meaning of the text. Figurative language is used more heavily in texts such as literary fiction, poetry, critical theory, and speeches. Figurative language goes beyond literal language, allowing readers to form associations they wouldn't normally form with literal language. Using language in a figurative sense appeals to the imagination of the reader. It is important to remember that words themselves are signifiers of objects and ideas, and not the objects and ideas themselves. Figurative language can highlight this detachment by creating multiple associations, but also points to the fact that language is fluid and capable of creating a world full of linguistic possibilities. Figurative language, it can be argued, is the heart of communication even outside of fiction and poetry. People connect through humor, metaphors, cultural allusions, puns, and symbolism in their everyday rhetoric. The following are terms associated with figurative language:

Simile
A simile is a comparison of two things using *like*, *than*, or *as*. A simile usually takes objects that have no apparent connection, such as a mind and an orchid, and compares them:

> His mind was as complex and rare as a field of ghost orchids.

Similes encourage a new, fresh perspective on objects or ideas that wouldn't otherwise occur. Similes are different than metaphors. Metaphors do not use *like*, *than*, or *as*. So, a metaphor from the above example would be:

> His mind was a field of ghost orchids.

Thus, similes highlight the comparison by focusing on the figurative side of the language, elucidating more the author's intent: a field of ghost orchids is something complex and rare, like the mind of a genius. With the metaphor, however, we get a beautiful yet somewhat equivocal comparison.

Metaphor
A popular use of figurative language, metaphors compare objects or ideas directly, asserting that something *is* a certain thing, even if it isn't. The following is an example of a metaphor used by writer Virginia Woolf:

> Books are the mirrors of the soul.

Metaphors have a vehicle and a tenor. The tenor is "books" and the vehicle is "mirrors of the soul." That is, the tenor is what is meant to be described, and the vehicle is that which carries the weight of the comparison. In this metaphor, perhaps the author means to say that written language (books) reflect a person's most inner thoughts and desires.

There are also dead metaphors, which means that the phrases have been so overused to the point where the figurative meaning becomes literal, like the phrase "What you're saying is crystal clear." The phrase compares "what's being said" to something "crystal clear." However, since the latter part of the phrase is in such popular use, the meaning seems literal ("I understand what you're saying") even when it's not.

Finally, an extended metaphor is a metaphor that goes on for several paragraphs, or even an entire text. John Keats' poem "On First Looking into Chapman's Homer" begins, "Much have I travell'd in the realms of gold," and goes on to explain the first time he hears Chapman's translation of Homer's writing. We see the extended metaphor begin in the first line. Keats is comparing travelling into "realms of gold" and exploration of new lands to the act of hearing a certain kind of literature for the first time. The extended metaphor goes on until the end of the poem where Keats stands "Silent, upon a peak in Darien," having heard the end of Chapman's translation. Keats has gained insight into new lands (new text) and is the richer for it.

The following are brief definitions and examples of popular figurative language:

Onomatopoeia: A word that, when spoken, imitates the sound to which it refers. Ex: "We heard a loud *boom* while driving to the beach yesterday."

Personification: When human characteristics are given to animals, inanimate objects, or abstractions. An example would be in William Wordsworth's poem "Daffodils" where he sees a "crowd . . . / of golden daffodils . . . / Fluttering and dancing in the breeze." Dancing is usually a characteristic attributed solely to humans, but Wordsworth personifies the daffodils here as a crowd of people dancing.

Juxtaposition: Juxtaposition is placing two objects side by side for comparison. In literature, this might look like placing two characters side by side for contrasting effect, like God and Satan in Milton's "Paradise Lost."

Paradox: A paradox is a statement that is self-contradictory but will be found nonetheless true. One example of a paradoxical phrase is when Socrates said "I know one thing; that I know nothing." Seemingly, if Socrates knew nothing, he wouldn't know that he knew nothing. However, it is one thing he knows: that true wisdom begins with casting all presuppositions one has about the world aside.

Hyperbole: A hyperbole is an exaggeration. Ex: "I'm so tired I could sleep for centuries."

Allusion: An allusion is a reference to a character or event that happened in the past. An example of a poem littered with allusions is T.S. Eliot's "The Waste Land." An example of a biblical allusion manifests when the poet says, "I will show you fear in a handful of dust," creating an ominous tone from Genesis 3:19 "For you are dust, and to dust you shall return."

Pun: Puns are used in popular culture to invoke humor by exploiting the meanings of words. They can also be used in literature to give hints of meaning in unexpected places. One example of a pun is when Mercutio is giving his monologue after he is stabbed by Tybalt in "Romeo and Juliet" and says, "look for me tomorrow and you will find me a grave man."

Imagery: This is a collection of images given to the reader by the author. If a text is rich in imagery, it is easier for the reader to imagine themselves in the author's world. One example of a poem that relies on imagery is William Carlos Williams' "The Red Wheelbarrow":

> so much depends
> upon
>
> a red wheel
> barrow
>
> glazed with rain
> water
>
> beside the white
> chickens

The starkness of the imagery and the placement of the words in the poem, to some readers, throw the poem into a meditative state where, indeed, the world of this poem is made up solely of images of a purely simple life. This poem tells a story in sixteen words by using imagery.

Symbolism: A symbol is used to represent an idea or belief system. For example, poets in Western civilization have been using the symbol of a rose for hundreds of years to represent love. In Japan, poets have used the firefly to symbolize passionate love, and sometimes even spirits of those who have died. Symbols can also express powerful political commentary and can be used in propaganda.

Irony: There are three types of irony. Verbal irony is when a person states one thing and means the opposite. For example, a person is probably using irony when they say, "I can't wait to study for this exam next week." Dramatic irony occurs in a narrative and happens when the audience knows something that the characters do not. In the modern TV series *Hannibal*, we as an audience know that Hannibal Lecter is a serial killer, but most of the main characters do not. This is dramatic irony. Finally, situational irony is when one expects something to happen, and the opposite occurs. For example, we can say that a fire station burning down would be an instance of situational irony.

Word Choice and Tone

Context Clues

Readers can often figure out what unfamiliar words mean without interrupting their reading to look them up in dictionaries by examining context. Context includes the other words or sentences in a passage. One common context clue is the root word and any affixes (prefixes/suffixes). Another common context clue is a synonym or definition included in the sentence. Sometimes both exist in the same sentence. Here's an example:

> Scientists who study birds are *ornithologists*.

Many readers may not know the word *ornithologist*. However, the example contains a definition (scientists who study birds). The reader may also have the ability to analyze the suffix (-*logy*, meaning the study of) and root (*ornitho*-, meaning bird).

Another common context clue is a sentence that shows differences. Here's an example:

> Birds *incubate* their eggs outside of their bodies, unlike mammals.

Some readers may be unfamiliar with the word *incubate*. However, since we know that "unlike mammals," birds incubate their eggs outside of their bodies, we can infer that *incubate* has something to do with keeping eggs warm outside the body until they are hatched.

In addition to analyzing the etymology of a word's root and affixes and extrapolating word meaning from sentences that contrast an unknown word with an antonym, readers can also determine word meanings from sentence context clues based on logic. Here's an example:

Birds are always looking out for predators that could attack their young.

The reader who is unfamiliar with the word *predator* could determine from the context of the sentence that predators usually prey upon baby birds and possibly other young animals. Readers might also use the context clue of etymology here, as *predator* and *prey* have the same root.

Denotation and Connotation

Denotation refers to a word's explicit definition, like that found in the dictionary. Denotation is often set in comparison to connotation. Connotation is the emotional, cultural, social, or personal implication associated with a word. Denotation is more of an objective definition, whereas connotation can be more subjective, although many connotative meanings of words are similar for certain cultures. The denotative meanings of words are usually based on facts, and the connotative meanings of words are usually based on emotion. Here are some examples of words and their denotative and connotative meanings in Western culture:

Word	Denotative Meaning	Connotative Meaning
Home	A permanent place where one lives, usually as a member of a family.	A place of warmth; a place of familiarity; comforting; a place of safety and security. "Home" usually has a positive connotation.
Snake	A long reptile with no limbs and strong jaws that moves along the ground; some snakes have a poisonous bite.	An evil omen; a slithery creature (human or nonhuman) that is deceitful or unwelcome. "Snake" usually has a negative connotation.
Winter	A season of the year that is the coldest, usually from December to February in the northern hemisphere and from June to August in the southern hemisphere.	Circle of life, especially that of death and dying; cold or icy; dark and gloomy; hibernation, sleep, or rest. Winter can have a negative connotation, although many who have access to heat may enjoy the snowy season from their homes.

Transitional Words and Phrases

In connected writing, some sentences naturally lead to others, whereas in other cases, a new sentence expresses a new idea. We use transitional phrases to connect sentences and the ideas they convey. This makes the writing coherent. Transitional language also guides the reader from one thought to the next. For example, when pointing out an objection to the previous idea, starting a sentence with "However," "But," or "On the other hand" is transitional. When adding another idea or detail, writers use "Also," "In addition," "Furthermore," "Further," "Moreover," "Not only," etc. Readers have difficulty perceiving connections between ideas without such transitional wording.

Three Tiers of Vocabulary

The three tiers of vocabulary are based off of a developmental model that classifies how young students organize and integrate types of words into their personal usage. **Tier one** words are considered the simplest words that are relatively short, have a singular meaning, and are both frequently used in conversation as well as in written literature. It is believed these words are learned and absorbed through routine observation and interactions that take place as a young child grows. Tier one words may include common first words for children, such as *mommy, daddy, dog, ball, hi, up,* and other words related to children's home environments, primary caregivers, and daily experiences. **Tier two** words consist of more complex vocabulary that make up mature conversations and meaningful literary texts yet may not regularly be utilized in routine conversation. However, some researchers argue that this tier of words is where concentrated instruction should fall and moving toward using tier two in regular interpersonal communication is a worthy linguistic goal. Expanding this tier encourages students to have a wider array of words with which to not only communicate among themselves and relate better to one another but to also understand acclaimed literary texts and, consequently, the world in which they exist. **Tier three** vocabulary words are highly specialized, technical words that are usually specific to a topic, field, or industry. For grade-school students, tier three words may only be utilized in regard to a specific class to fit a specific function (e.g., the word *isosceles* will likely only be used in a student's geometry class to discuss triangles).

Word Choice, Order, and Punctuation

Word Choice
Words can be very powerful. When written words are used with the intent to make an argument or support a position, the words used—and the way in which they are arranged—can have a dramatic effect on the readers. Clichés, colloquialisms, run-on sentences, and misused words are all examples of the ways word choice can negatively affect writing quality. Unless the writer carefully considers word choice, a written work stands to lose credibility.

If a writer's overall intent is to provide a clear meaning on a subject, they must consider not only the exact words to use, but also their placement, repetition, and suitability. Academic writing should be intentional and clear, and it should be devoid of awkward or vague descriptions that can easily lead to misunderstandings. When readers find themselves reading and rereading just to gain a clear understanding of the writer's intent, there may be an issue with word choice. Although the words used in academic writing are different from those used in a casual conversation, they shouldn't necessarily be overly academic either. It may be relevant to employ key words that are associated with the subject but struggling to inject these words into a paper just to sound academic may defeat the purpose. If the message cannot be clearly understood the first time, word choice may be the culprit.

Word choice also conveys the author's attitude and sets a tone. Although each word in a sentence carries a specific denotation, it might also carry positive or negative connotations—and it is the connotations that set the tone and convey the author's attitude. Consider the following similar sentences:

It was the same old routine that happens every Saturday morning—eat, exercise, chores.

The Saturday morning routine went off without a hitch—eat, exercise, chores.

The first sentence carries a negative connotation with the author's "same old routine" word choice. The feelings and attitudes associated with this phrase suggest that the author is bored or annoyed at the Saturday morning routine. Although the second sentence carries the same topic—explaining the Saturday morning routine—the choice to use the expression "without a hitch" conveys a positive or cheery attitude.

An author's writing style can likewise be greatly affected by word choice. When writing for an academic audience, for example, it is necessary for the author to consider how to convey the message by carefully considering word choice. If the author interchanges between third-person formal writing and second-person informal writing, the author's writing quality and credibility are at risk. Formal writing involves complex sentences, an objective viewpoint, and the use of full words as opposed to the use of a subjective viewpoint, contractions, and first or second-person usage commonly found in informal writing.

Content validity, the author's ability to support the argument, and the audience's ability to comprehend the written work are all affected by the author's word choice.

Order

For fluent composition, writers must use a variety of sentence types and structures, and also ensure that they smoothly flow together when they are read. To accomplish this, they must first be able to identify fluent writing when they read it. This includes being able to distinguish among simple, compound, complex, and compound-complex sentences in text; to observe variations among sentence types, lengths, and beginnings; and to notice figurative language and understand how it augments sentence length and imparts musicality. Once students/writers recognize superior fluency, they should revise their own writing to be more readable and fluent. They must be able to apply acquired skills to revisions before being able to apply them to new drafts.

One strategy for revising writing to increase its sentence fluency is flipping sentences. This involves rearranging the word order in a sentence without deleting, changing, or adding any words. For example, the student or other writer who has written the sentence, "We went bicycling on Saturday" can revise it to, "On Saturday, we went bicycling." Another technique is using appositives. An appositive is a phrase or word that renames or identifies another adjacent word or phrase. Writers can revise for sentence fluency by inserting main phrases/words from one shorter sentence into another shorter sentence, combining them into one longer sentence, e.g. from "My cat Peanut is a gray and brown tabby. He loves hunting rats." to "My cat Peanut, a gray and brown tabby, loves hunting rats." Revisions can also connect shorter sentences by using conjunctions and commas and removing repeated words: "Scott likes eggs. Scott is allergic to eggs" becomes "Scott likes eggs, but he is allergic to them."

One technique for revising writing to increase sentence fluency is "padding" short, simple sentences by adding phrases that provide more details specifying why, how, when, and/or where something took place. For example, a writer might have these two simple sentences: "I went to the market. I purchased a cake." To revise these, the writer can add the following informative dependent and independent clauses and prepositional phrases, respectively: "Before my mother woke up, I sneaked out of the house and went to the supermarket. As a birthday surprise, I purchased a cake for her." When revising sentences to make them longer, writers must also punctuate them correctly to change them from simple sentences to compound, complex, or compound-complex sentences.

Skills Writers Can Employ to Increase Fluency

One way writers can increase fluency is by varying the beginnings of sentences. Writers do this by starting most of their sentences with different words and phrases rather than monotonously repeating the same ones across multiple sentences. Another way writers can increase fluency is by varying the lengths of sentences. Since run-on sentences are incorrect, writers make sentences longer by also converting them from simple to compound, complex, and compound-complex sentences. The coordination and subordination involved in these also give the text more variation and interest, hence more fluency. Here are a few more ways writers can increase fluency:

- Varying the transitional language and conjunctions used makes sentences more fluent.
- Writing sentences with a variety of rhythms by using prepositional phrases.
- Varying sentence structure adds fluency.

Punctuation
Ellipses
Ellipses (. . .) signal omitted text when quoting. Some writers also use them to show a thought trailing off, but this should not be overused outside of dialogue. An example of an ellipsis would be if someone is quoting a phrase out of a professional source but wants to omit part of the phrase that isn't needed: "Dr. Skim's analysis of pollen inside the body is clearly a myth . . . that speaks to the environmental guilt of our society."

Commas
Commas separate words or phrases in a series of three or more. The Oxford comma is the last comma in a series. Many people omit this last comma, but many times it causes confusion. Here is an example:

I love my sisters, the Queen of England and Madonna.

This example without the comma implies that the "Queen of England and Madonna" are the speaker's sisters. However, if the speaker was trying to say that they love their sisters, the Queen of England, as well as Madonna, there should be a comma after "Queen of England" to signify this.

Commas also separate two coordinate adjectives ("big, heavy dog") but not cumulative ones, which should be arranged in a particular order for them to make sense ("beautiful ancient ruins").

A comma ends the first of two independent clauses connected by conjunctions. Here is an example:

I ate a bowl of tomato soup, and I was hungry very shortly after.

Here are some brief rules for commas:

- Commas follow introductory words like *however, furthermore, well, why,* and *actually,* among others.
- Commas go between city and state: Houston, Texas.
- If using a comma between a surname and Jr. or Sr. or a degree like M.D., also follow the whole name with a comma: "Martin Luther King, Jr., wrote that."
- A comma follows a dependent clause beginning a sentence: "Although she was very small, . . ."
- Nonessential modifying words/phrases/clauses are enclosed by commas: "Wendy, who is Peter's sister, closed the window."
- Commas introduce or interrupt direct quotations: "She said, 'I hate him.' 'Why,' I asked, 'do you hate him?'"

Semicolons
Semicolons are used to connect two independent clauses but should never be used in the place of a comma. They can replace periods between two closely connected sentences: "Call back tomorrow; it can

wait until then." When writing items in a series and one or more of them contains internal commas, separate them with semicolons, like the following:

> People came from Springfield, Illinois; Alamo, Tennessee; Moscow, Idaho; and other locations.

Hyphens

Here are some rules concerning hyphens:

- Compound adjectives like state-of-the-art or off-campus are hyphenated.
- Original compound verbs and nouns are often hyphenated, like "throne-sat," "video-gamed," "no-meater."
- Adjectives ending in *–ly* are often hyphenated, like "family-owned" or "friendly-looking."
- "Five years old" is not hyphenated, but singular ages like "five-year-old" are.
- Hyphens can clarify. For example, in "stolen vehicle report," "stolen-vehicle report" clarifies that "stolen" modifies "vehicle," not "report."
- Compound numbers twenty-one through ninety-nine are spelled with hyphens.
- Prefixes before proper nouns/adjectives are hyphenated, like "mid-September" and "trans-Pacific."

Parentheses

Parentheses enclose information such as an aside or more clarifying information: "She ultimately replied (after deliberating for an hour) that she was undecided." They are also used to insert short, in-text definitions or acronyms: "His FBS (fasting blood sugar) was higher than normal." When parenthetical information ends the sentence, the period follows the parentheses: "We received new funds ($25,000)." Only put periods within parentheses if the whole sentence is inside them: "Look at this. (You'll be astonished.)" However, this can also be acceptable as a clause: "Look at this (you'll be astonished)." Although parentheses appear to be part of the sentence subject, they are not, and do not change subject-verb agreement: "Will (and his dog) was there."

Quotation Marks

Quotation marks are typically used when someone is quoting a direct word or phrase someone else writes or says. Additionally, quotation marks should be used for the titles of poems, short stories, songs, articles, chapters, and other shorter works. When quotations include punctuation, periods and commas should *always* be placed inside of the quotation marks.

When a quotation contains another quotation inside of it, the outer quotation should be enclosed in double quotation marks and the inner quotation should be enclosed in single quotation marks. For example: "Timmy was begging, 'Don't go! Don't leave!'" When using both double and single quotation marks, writers will find that many word-processing programs may automatically insert enough space between the single and double quotation marks to be visible for clearer reading. But if this is not the case, the writer should write/type them with enough space between to keep them from looking like three single quotation marks. Additionally, non-standard usages, terms used in an unusual fashion, and technical terms are often clarified by quotation marks. Here are some examples:

> My "friend," Dr. Sims, has been micromanaging me again.

> This way of extracting oil has been dubbed "fracking."

Apostrophes

One use of the apostrophe is followed by an *s* to indicate possession, like *Mrs. White's home* or *our neighbor's dog*. When using the *'s* after names or nouns that also end in the letter *s,* no single rule applies: some experts advise adding both the apostrophe and the *s*, like "the Jones's house," while others prefer using only the apostrophe and omitting the additional *s*, like "the Jones' house." The wisest expert advice is to pick one formula or the other and then apply it consistently. Newspapers and magazines often use *'s* after common nouns ending with *s*, but add only the apostrophe after proper nouns or names ending with *s*. One common error is to place the apostrophe before a name's final *s* instead of after it: "Ms. Hasting's book" is incorrect if the name is Ms. Hastings.

Plural nouns should not include apostrophes (e.g. "apostrophe's"). Exceptions are to clarify atypical plurals, like verbs used as nouns: "These are the do's and don'ts." Irregular plurals that do not end in *s* always take apostrophe-*s*, not *s*-apostrophe—a common error, as in "childrens' toys," which should be "children's toys." Compound nouns like mother-in-law, when they are singular and possessive, are followed by apostrophe-*s*, like "your mother-in-law's coat." When a compound noun is plural and possessive, the plural is formed before the apostrophe-*s*, like "your sisters-in-laws' coats." When two people named possess the same thing, use apostrophe-*s* after the second name only, like "Dennis and Pam's house."

Speaking and Listening

Communicating for a Variety of Purposes with Diverse Partners

Effective communication in multiple settings with different kinds of people is a necessary skill in today's highly global world. The way people communicate with others is shaped by a multitude of factors, including, but not limited to, the society and culture in which they were raised, the society and culture in which their parents were raised, their home environment, their peer group, and the types of exposure and interactions experienced with both strangers and acquaintances. Additionally, nonverbal communication is a large part of interpersonal interactions; it also varies based on social norms, culture, upbringing, and personal experiences. In general, an effective baseline technique for effective communication is to treat the other person professionally, kindly, and respectfully.

Regardless of the topic at hand, these behaviors are more likely to set the tone for productive and thoughtful communication than rude or aggressive communication. If possible, one should learn what they can about the person with whom he or she will be communicating. Understanding the other person's background and expectations and anticipating concerns can be useful techniques to foster positive communication. Additionally, discussing commonalities and shared end goals for the interaction can benefit both participants (e.g., what does each person hope to gain from the interaction; what are next action items for when the conversation ends). If it is known that a person is from a different culture (e.g., a student who immigrates from another country), researching cultural norms can help understand that person's nonverbal communication and other actions. However, it is important to note that not all individuals from a culture may identify with its beliefs or norms, so assumptions should not be made. Instead, encouraging others to directly share more about themselves and their beliefs can provide the context for communication.

Active Listening

Active listening is a skill that allows the person who is speaking to feel valued and acknowledged. Additionally, this skill helps the listener truly understand what the speaker intends to communicate. Active listening is characterized by focused, undistracted attention in which the listener concentrates not only on the words the speaker is saying but also on the speaker's nonverbal cues and body language. Active listeners will ensure they are receiving the intended communication by asking clarifying and engaging questions. This practice shows they listened to the words being spoken, interpreted them for meaning, and then checked that their perception of the communication matches what the speaker intended to relay. This technique is useful in most interpersonal relationships but especially beneficial in high-conflict or high-pressure situations (such as discussing a problem with a supervisor or talking with a child who is struggling to learn a lesson), tutoring (to ensure the student who is receiving tutoring is comprehending what is being taught), counseling (to better support and empower someone who is having a mental or emotional crisis), and during interviews (to ensure the person being interviewed is represented fairly). When both parties involved in a conversation utilize active listening skills, it allows for a more productive and objective interaction of an issue rather than an emotionally charged one.

Oral Presentations

Public speaking is commonly listed as a top fear for most individuals; however, learning the elements of what defines an engaging oral presentation and diligently applying them can help alleviate some of the apprehension. In addition to the content presented, the speaker's behaviors play a key role in how a presentation is received by the intended audience.

Engaging oral presentations should be clearly organized and practiced beforehand so the presenter is able to transition seamlessly from one topic to the next. If the presenter appears unprepared, the audience may feel as though he or she is incompetent, lose confidence in the presenter, or lose interest altogether. If using visual aids, such as a slide deck, the presenter should avoid reading directly off the slides. Instead, the presenter should consider highlighting key components on the visual aid and providing additional, applicable details during their speech. These ideas should remain concise in an oral presentation so as to respect the audience's attention span.

The introduction of the presentation should be a powerful attention grabber for the audience; this first impression sets the tone and level of interest for the remainder of the presentation. The introduction could provide shock value to the audience, hold their attention by introducing something of high value to them, or cause a memorable emotional reaction. As the presentation progresses, the speaker should ensure he or she remains engaged with the audience throughout (e.g., asking interactive questions, involving the audience in other ways, making regular eye contact), speaks loudly and clearly, and avoids nervous rambling to fill breaks in the presentation. If the presenter does become nervous or fumbles during a presentation, a pause is often more effective in mentally resetting and moving forward. It is also less noticeable for the audience than stuttering or rambling.

Finally, as the presentation comes to a close, the presenter should end on a note that not only summarizes the main points but also clearly emphasizes the overall value of the presentation to the audience. The ending of a presentation often gives justification to why the audience provided undivided attention to the presenter for the preceding minutes. For example, a presentation on investment planning options could conclude with an exercise where the audience mentally visualizes how they want to experience their retirement years and what tools they could use to financially achieve their goals.

Practice Questions

1. Which of these is NOT a good way to improve writing style through grammar?
    a. Alternating among different sentence structures
    b. Using fewer words instead of unnecessary words
    c. Consistently using one-subject and one-verb sentences
    d. Writing in the active voice more than passive voice

2. Of the following statements, which is most accurate about topic sentences?
    a. They are always first in a paragraph.
    b. They are always last in a paragraph.
    c. They are only found once in every essay.
    d. They are explicit or may be implicit.

3. Which of the following is considered criteria for a good paragraph topic sentence?
    a. Clear
    b. Subtle
    c. Lengthy
    d. Ambiguous

4. "We don't go out as much because babysitters, gasoline, and parking is expensive." Which grammatical error does this sentence demonstrate?
    a. It contains a misplaced modifier.
    b. It lacks subject-verb agreement.
    c. It introduces a dangling participle.
    d. It does not have a grammar error.

5. Which of the following versions of a sentence has correct pronoun-antecedent agreement?
    a. Every student must consult their advisor first.
    b. All students must talk with their advisors first.
    c. All students must consult with his advisor first.
    d. Every student must consult their advisors first.

6. Which version of this sentence is grammatically correct?
    a. Give it to Shirley and I.
    b. Both Choices *C* and *D*.
    c. Give it to Shirley and me.
    d. Give it to me and Shirley.

7. What parts of speech are modified by adjectives?
    a. Verbs
    b. Nouns
    c. Pronouns
    d. Both Choices *B* and *C*

8. What part(s) of speech do adverbs modify?
    a. Verbs
    b. Adverbs
    c. Adjectives
    d. All of the above ←

9. What accurately reflects expert advice for beginning writers regarding topic sentences?
    a. They should use topic sentences in every two to three paragraphs.
    b. They should vary topic sentence positioning in paragraphs.
    → c. They should include a topic sentence in every paragraph.
    d. They should make each topic sentence broad and general.

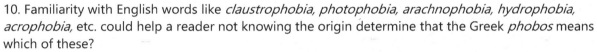

10. Familiarity with English words like *claustrophobia, photophobia, arachnophobia, hydrophobia, acrophobia,* etc. could help a reader not knowing the origin determine that the Greek *phobos* means which of these?
    a. Love
    b. Fear
    c. Hate
    d. Know

Questions 11 and 12 are based off the following passage:

> Rehabilitation, rather than punitive justice, is becoming much more popular in prisons around the world. Prisons in America, especially, where the recidivism rate is 67 percent, would benefit from mimicking prison tactics in Norway, which has a recidivism rate of only 20 percent. In Norway, the idea is that a rehabilitated prisoner is much less likely to offend than one harshly punished. Rehabilitation includes proper treatment for substance abuse, psychotherapy, health and dental care, and education programs.

11. Which of the following best captures the author's purpose?
    a. To show the audience one of the effects of criminal rehabilitation by comparison
    b. To persuade the audience to donate to American prisons for education programs
    c. To convince the audience of the harsh conditions of American prisons
    d. To inform the audience of the incredibly lax system of Norway prisons

12. Which of the following describes the word *recidivism* as it is used in the passage?
    a. The lack of violence in the prison system.
    b. The opportunity of inmates to receive therapy in prison.
    c. The event of a prisoner escaping the compound.
    d. The likelihood of a convicted criminal to reoffend.

Questions 13–15 are based off the following passage from Virginia Woolf's Mrs. Dalloway:

> What a lark! What a plunge! For so it had always seemed to her, when, with a little squeak of the hinges, which she could hear now, she had burst open the French windows and plunged at Bourton into the open air. How fresh, how calm, stiller than this of course, the air was in the early morning; like the flap of a wave; the kiss of a wave; chill and sharp and yet (for a girl of eighteen as she then was) solemn, feeling as she did, standing there at the open window, that something awful was about to happen; looking at the flowers, at the trees with the smoke winding off them and the rooks rising, falling; standing and looking until Peter Walsh said, "Musing among the

vegetables?"—was that it?—"I prefer men to cauliflowers"—was that it? He must have said it at breakfast one morning when she had gone out on to the terrace—Peter Walsh. He would be back from India one of these days, June or July, she forgot which, for his letters were awfully dull; it was his sayings one remembered; his eyes, his pocket-knife, his smile, his grumpiness and, when millions of things had utterly vanished—how strange it was!—a few sayings like this about cabbages.

13. The passage is reflective of which of the following types of writing?
    a. Persuasive
    b. Expository
    c. Technical
    d. Narrative

14. What was the narrator feeling right before Peter Walsh's voice distracted her?
    a. A spark of excitement for the morning
    b. Anger at the larks
    c. A sense of foreboding
    d. Confusion at the weather

15. What is the main point of the passage?
    a. To present the events leading up to a party
    b. To show the audience that the narrator is resentful towards Peter
    c. To introduce Peter Walsh back into the narrator's memory
    d. To reveal what mornings are like in the narrator's life

Question 16 is based on the following passage from The Federalist No. 78 *by Alexander Hamilton:*

According to the plan of the convention, all judges who may be appointed by the United States are to hold their offices *during good behavior*, which is conformable to the most approved of the State constitutions and among the rest, to that of this State. Its propriety having been drawn into question by the adversaries of that plan, is no light symptom of the rage for objection, which disorders their imaginations and judgments. The standard of good behavior for the continuance in office of the judicial magistracy, is certainly one of the most valuable of the modern improvements in the practice of government. In a monarchy, it is an excellent barrier to the despotism of the prince; in a republic, it is a no less excellent barrier to the encroachments and oppressions of the representative body. And it is the best expedient that can be devised in any government, to secure a steady, upright, and impartial administration of the laws.

16. What is Hamilton's point in this excerpt?
    a. To show the audience that despotism within a monarchy is no longer the standard practice in the states
    b. To convince the audience that judges holding their positions based on good behavior is a practical way to avoid corruption
    c. To persuade the audience that having good behavior should be the primary characteristic of a person in a government body and their voting habits should reflect this
    d. To convey the position that judges who serve for a lifetime will not be perfect, and therefore we must forgive them for their bad behavior when it arises

Questions 17–19 are based on the passage from Many Marriages *by Sherwood Anderson:*

There was a man named Webster who lived in a town of twenty-five thousand people in the state of Wisconsin. He had a wife named Mary and a daughter named Jane and he was himself a fairly prosperous manufacturer of washing machines. When the thing happened of which I am about to write, he was thirty-seven or thirty-eight years old and his one child, the daughter, was seventeen. Of the details of his life up to the time a certain revolution happened within him it will be unnecessary to speak. He was however a rather quiet man inclined to have dreams which he tried to crush out of himself in order that he function as a washing machine manufacturer; and no doubt, at odd moments, when he was on a train going some place or perhaps on Sunday afternoons in the summer when he went alone to the deserted office of the factory and sat several hours looking out at a window and along a railroad track, he gave way to dreams.

17. What does the author mean by the following sentence?
"Of the details of his life up to the time a certain revolution happened within him it will be unnecessary to speak."

    a. The details of his external life don't matter; only the details of his internal life matter.
    b. Whatever happened in his life before he had a certain internal change is irrelevant.
    c. He had a traumatic experience earlier in his life that rendered it impossible for him to speak.
    d. Before the revolution, he was a lighthearted man who always wished to speak to others no matter who they were.

18. From what Point Of View is this narrative told?
    a. First person limited
    b. First person omniscient
    c. Second person
    d. Third person

19. What did Webster do for a living?
    a. Washing machine manufacturer
    b. Train operator
    c. Leader of the revolution
    d. Stay-at-home husband

Questions 20–22 are based on the following passage from the biography Queen Victoria *by E. Gordon Browne, M.A.:*

The old castle soon proved to be too small for the family, and in September 1853 the foundation-stone of a new house was laid. After the ceremony, the workmen were entertained at dinner, which was followed by Highland games and dancing in the ballroom.

Two years later, they entered the new castle, which the Queen described as "charming; the rooms delightful; the furniture, papers, everything perfection."

The Prince was untiring in planning improvements, and in 1856 the Queen wrote: "Every year my heart becomes more fixed in this dear Paradise, and so much more so now, that *all* has become my dearest Albert's *own* creation, own work, own building, own laying out as at Osborne; and his great taste, and the impress of his dear hand, have been stamped everywhere. He was very busy today, settling and arranging many things for next year."

20. This excerpt is considered which of the following?
    a. Primary source
    b. Secondary source
    c. Tertiary source
    d. None of these

21. How many years did it take for the new castle to be built?
    a. One year
    b. Two years
    c. Three years
    d. Four years

22. What does the word *impress* mean in the third paragraph?
    a. To affect strongly in feeling
    b. To urge something to be done
    c. To impose a certain quality upon
    d. To press a thing onto something else

Questions 23–25 are based on the following passage from The Life, Crime, and Capture of John Wilkes Booth *by George Alfred Townsend:*

> Having completed these preparations, Mr. Booth entered the theater by the stage door; summoned one of the scene shifters, Mr. John Spangler, emerged through the same door with that individual, leaving the door open, and left the mare in his hands to be held until he (Booth) should return. Booth who was even more fashionably and richly dressed than usual, walked thence around to the front of the theater, and went in. Ascending to the dress circle, he stood for a little time gazing around upon the audience and occasionally upon the stage in his usual graceful manner. He was subsequently observed by Mr. Ford, the proprietor of the theater, to be slowly elbowing his way through the crowd that packed the rear of the dress circle toward the right side, at the extremity of which was the box where Mr. and Mrs. Lincoln and their companions were seated. Mr. Ford casually noticed this as a slightly extraordinary symptom of interest on the part of an actor so familiar with the routine of the theater and the play.

23. How is the above passage organized?
    a. Chronological
    b. Cause and effect
    c. Problem to solution
    d. Main idea with supporting details

24. Based on your knowledge of history, what is about to happen?
    a. An asteroid is about to hit the earth.
    b. The best opera of all times is about to premiere.
    c. A playhouse is about to be burned to the ground.
    d. A president is about to be assassinated.

25. What does the author mean by the last two sentences?
   a. Mr. Ford was suspicious of Booth and assumed he was making his way to Mr. Lincoln's box.
   b. Mr. Ford assumed Booth's movement throughout the theater was due to being familiar with the theater.
   c. Mr. Ford thought that Booth was making his way to the theater lounge to find his companions.
   d. Mr. Ford thought that Booth was elbowing his way to the dressing room to get ready for the play.

26. Which of the following English words is derived from a Greek source?
   a. Move
   b. Motor
   c. Moron
   d. Mobile

27. Homophones are defined as which of these?
   a. They have the same sounds.
   b. They have the same spelling.
   c. They have the same meaning.
   d. They have the same roots.

28. The word *tear*, pronounced one way, means a drop of eye fluid; pronounced another way, it means to rip. What is this type of word called?
   a. A homograph
   b. A heteronym
   c. A homonym
   d. Both *A* and *B*

29. Which of these words is considered a plural?
   a. Cactus
   b. Bacteria
   c. Criterion
   d. Elf

30. Which of these words has an irregular plural that is the same as its singular form?
   a. Louse
   b. Goose
   c. Mouse
   d. Moose

31. Of the following words with irregular plurals, which one has a plural ending *most* different from those of the others?
   a. Ox
   b. Child
   c. Person
   d. Woman

32. Which of the following sentences uses the apostrophe(s) correctly?
   a. Please be sure to bring you're invitation to the event.
   b. All of your friends' invitations were sent the same day.
   c. All of your friends parked they're cars along the street.
   d. Who's car is parked on the street with it's lights on?

33. Of the following, which word is spelled correctly?
    a. Wierd
    b. Forfeit
    c. Beleive
    d. Concieve

34. Which of these words has the correct spelling?
    a. Insolent
    b. Irrelevent
    c. Independant
    d. Indispensible

35. Exceptions and variations in rules for capitalization are accurately reflected in which of these?
    a. *Congress* is capitalized and so is *Congressional.*
    b. *Constitution* is capitalized as well as *Constitutional.*
    c. *Caucasian* is capitalized, but *white,* referring to race, is not.
    d. *African-American* and *Black* as a race are both capitalized.

36. Which of the following statements is true about the Oxford comma?
    a. It is the first comma in a series of three or more items.
    b. It is the last comma in a series before *or,* or before *and.*
    c. It is any comma separating items in series of three or more.
    d. It is frequently omitted because it does not serve a purpose.

37. In the following sentence, which version has the correct punctuation?
    a. Delegates attended from Springfield; Illinois, Alamo; Tennessee, Moscow; Idaho, and other places.
    b. Delegates attended from Springfield Illinois, Alamo Tennessee, Moscow Idaho, and other places.
    c. Delegates attended from Springfield, Illinois; Alamo, Tennessee; Moscow, Idaho; and other places.
    d. Delegates attended from Springfield, Illinois, Alamo, Tennessee, Moscow, Idaho, and other places.

38. Of the following phrases, which correctly applies the rules for hyphenation?
    a. Finely-tuned
    b. Family owned
    c. Friendly looking
    d. Fraudulent-ID claim

39. What is the rule for using quotation marks with a quotation inside of a quotation?
    a. Single quotation marks around the outer quotation, double quotation marks around the inner one
    b. Double quotation marks to enclose the outer quotation and also to enclose the inner quotation
    c. Single quotation marks that enclose the outer quotation as well as the inner quotation
    d. Double quotation marks around the outer quotation, single quotation marks around the inner one

40. Which of the following phrases correctly uses apostrophes?
    a. Dennis and Pam's house
    b. Dennis's and Pam's house
    c. Dennis' and Pam's house
    d. Dennis's and Pam house

41. Which of these correctly applies the rule to make irregular plural nouns possessive?
    a. Geeses' honks
    b. Childrens' toys
    c. Teeths' enamel
    d. Women's room

42. Which of the following is a writing technique recommended for attaining sentence fluency?
    a. Varying the endings of sentences
    b. Making sentence lengths uniform
    c. Using consistent sentence rhythm
    d. Varying sentence structures used ←

43. Among elements of an effective paragraph, the element of coherence is reflected by which of these?
    a. Focus on one main point throughout
    b. The use of logical and verbal bridges ←
    c. A sentence identifying the main idea
    d. Data, examples, illustrations, analysis

44. What is the subject of the sentence: "Don't drink and drive."?
    a. Drink
    b. Drive
    c. Don't
    d. Understood *you*

45. The above sentence is an example of what type of sentence?
    a. Declarative
    b. Imperative ←
    c. Interrogative
    d. Exclamatory

Questions 46–50 are based on the following passage from The Story of Germ Life *by Herbert William Conn:*

> When we study more carefully the effect upon the milk of the different species of bacteria found in the dairy, we find that there is a great variety of changes which they produce when they are allowed to grow in milk. The dairyman experiences many troubles with his milk. It sometimes curdles without becoming acid. Sometimes it becomes bitter, or acquires an unpleasant "tainted" taste, or, again, a "soapy" taste. Occasionally a dairyman finds his milk becoming slimy, instead of souring and curdling in the normal fashion. At such times, after a number of hours, the milk becomes so slimy that it can be drawn into long threads. Such an infection proves very troublesome, for many a time it persists in spite of all attempts made to remedy it. Again, in other cases the milk will turn blue, acquiring about the time it becomes sour a beautiful sky-blue colour. Or it may become red, or occasionally yellow. All of these troubles the dairyman owes to the presence in his milk of unusual species of bacteria which grow there abundantly.

46. What is the author's purpose in writing this passage?
    a. To show the readers that dairymen have difficult jobs
    b. To show the readers different ways their milk might go bad
    c. To show some of the different effects of milk on bacteria
    d. To show some of the different effects of bacteria on milk

47. What is the tone of this passage?
   a. Excitement
   b. Anger
   c. Neutral
   d. Sorrowful

48. Which of the following reactions does NOT occur in the above passage when bacteria infect the milk?
   a. It can have a soapy taste.
   b. The milk will turn black.
   c. It can become slimy.
   d. The milk will turn blue.

49. What is the meaning of "curdle" as depicted in the following sentence?
"Occasionally a dairyman finds his milk becoming slimy, instead of souring and curdling in the normal fashion."
   a. Lumpy
   b. Greasy
   c. Oily
   d. Slippery

50. Why, according to the passage, does an infection with slimy threads prove very troublesome?
   a. Because it is impossible to get rid of.
   b. Because it can make the milk-drinker sick.
   c. Because it turns the milk a blue color.
   d. Because it makes the milk taste bad.

Questions 51–54 are based on the following passage. It is from Oregon, Washington, and Alaska. Sights and Scenes for the Tourist, *written by E.L. Lomax in 1890:*

Portland is a very beautiful city of 60,000 inhabitants, and situated on the Willamette river twelve miles from its junction with the Columbia. It is perhaps true of many of the growing cities of the West, that they do not offer the same social advantages as the older cities of the East. But this is principally the case as to what may be called boom cities, where the larger part of the population is of that floating class which follows in the line of temporary growth for the purposes of speculation, and in no sense applies to those centers of trade whose prosperity is based on the solid foundation of legitimate business. As the metropolis of a vast section of country, having broad agricultural valleys filled with improved farms, surrounded by mountains rich in mineral wealth, and boundless forests of as fine timber as the world produces, the cause of Portland's growth and prosperity is the trade which it has as the center of collection and distribution of this great wealth of natural resources, and it has attracted, not the boomer and speculator, who find their profits in the wild excitement of the boom, but the merchant, manufacturer, and investor, who seek the surer if slower channels of legitimate business and investment. These have come from the East, most of them within the last few years. They came as seeking a better and wider field to engage in the same occupations they had followed in their Eastern homes, and bringing with them all the love of polite life which they had acquired there, have established here a new society, equaling in all respects that which they left behind. Here are as fine churches, as complete a system of schools, as fine residences, as great a love of music and art, as can be found at any city of the East of equal size.

51. What is a characteristic of a "boom city," as indicated by the passage?
    a. A city that is built on solid business foundation of mineral wealth and farming
    b. An area of land on the west coast that quickly becomes populated by residents from the east coast
    c. A city that, due to the hot weather and dry climate, catches fire frequently, resulting in a devastating population drop
    d. A city whose population is made up of people who seek quick fortunes rather than building a solid business foundation

52. The author would classify Portland as which of the following?
    a. A boom city
    b. A city on the east coast
    c. An industrial city
    d. A city of legitimate business ⟵

53. What type of passage is this?
    a. A business proposition
    b. A travel guide ⟵
    c. A journal entry
    d. A scholarly article

54. What does the word *metropolis* mean in the middle of the passage?
    a. Farm
    b. Country
    c. City
    d. Valley

Questions 55–56 are based on the excerpt from The Golden Bough *by Sir James George Frazer:*

> The other of the minor deities at Nemi was Virbius. Legend had it that Virbius was the young Greek hero Hippolytus, chaste and fair, who learned the art of venery from the centaur Chiron, and spent all his days in the greenwood chasing wild beasts with the virgin huntress Artemis (the Greek counterpart of Diana) for his only comrade.

55. Based on a prior knowledge of literature, the reader can infer this passage is taken from which of the following?
    a. A eulogy
    b. A myth
    c. A historical document
    d. A technical document

56. What is the meaning of the word *comrade* as the last word in the passage?
    a. Friend
    b. Enemy
    c. Brother
    d. Pet

Questions 57–59 are based on Poems by Alexander Pushkin *by Ivan Panin:*

> I do not believe there are as many as five examples of deviation from the literalness of the text. Once only, I believe, have I transposed two lines for convenience of translation; the other deviations are (*if* they are such) a substitution of an *and* for a comma in order to make now and then the reading of a line musical. With these exceptions, I have sacrificed *everything* to faithfulness of rendering. My object was to make Pushkin himself, without a prompter, speak to English readers. To make him thus speak in a foreign tongue was indeed to place him at a disadvantage; and music and rhythm and harmony are indeed fine things, but truth is finer still. I wished to present not what Pushkin would have said, or should have said, if he had written in English, but what he does say in Russian. That, stripped from all ornament of his wonderful melody and grace of form, as he is in a translation, he still, even in the hard English tongue, soothes and stirs, is in itself a sign that through the individual soul of Pushkin sings that universal soul whose strains appeal forever to man, in whatever clime, under whatever sky.

57. What is meant by the last sentence of the passage?
a. That the artistic beauty of Pushkin's poetry runs so deep that it is retained in translations to any language
b. That the artistic beauty of Pushkin's poetry is lost in the hard English tone
c. That Pushkin's poetry should not be translated because it strips it of its artistic beauty and meaning
d. That Pushkin's poetry is written in a universal language, so it does not need to be translated

58. Where would you most likely find this passage in a text?
a. Appendix
b. Table of contents
c. First chapter
d. Preface

59. According to the author, what is the most important aim of translation work?
a. To retain the beauty of the work.
b. To retain the truth of the work.
c. To retain the melody of the work.
d. To retain the form of the work.

Questions 60–63 are based on the following passage from Variation of Animals and Plants *by Charles Darwin:*

> Peach (Amygdalus persica)—In the last chapter I gave two cases of a peach-almond and a double-flowered almond which suddenly produced fruit closely resembling true peaches. I have also given many cases of peach-trees producing buds, which, when developed into branches, have yielded nectarines. We have seen that no less than six named and several unnamed varieties of the peach have thus produced several varieties of nectarine. I have shown that it is highly improbable that all these peach-trees, some of which are old varieties, and have been propagated by the million, are hybrids from the peach and nectarine, and that it is opposed to all analogy to attribute the occasional production of nectarines on peach-trees to the direct action of pollen from some neighbouring nectarine-tree. Several of the cases are highly remarkable, because, firstly, the fruit thus produced has sometimes been in part a nectarine and in part a peach; secondly, because nectarines thus suddenly produced have reproduced themselves by seed; and thirdly, because nectarines are produced from peach-trees from seed as well as from buds. The seed of the nectarine, on the other hand, occasionally produces peaches; and we have seen in one

instance that a nectarine-tree yielded peaches by bud-variation. As the peach is certainly the oldest or primary variety, the production of peaches from nectarines, either by seeds or buds, may perhaps be considered as a case of reversion. Certain trees have also been described as indifferently bearing peaches or nectarines, and this may be considered as bud-variation carried to an extreme degree.

60. Which of the following statements is NOT a detail from the passage?
    a. At least six named varieties of the peach have produced several varieties of nectarine.
    b. It is not probable that all of the peach trees mentioned are hybrids from the peach and nectarine.
    c. An unremarkable case is the fact that nectarines are produced from peach trees from seeds as well as from buds.
    d. The production of peaches from nectarines might be considered a case of reversion.

61. *After*, *since*, and *whereas* are all examples of which of the following?
    a. Coordinate conjunctions
    b. Coordinate adjectives
    c. Demonstrative adjectives
    d. Subordinating conjunctions ←———

62. All EXCEPT which of the following words or phrases are interjections?
    a. Good gracious
    b. Oh
    c. Ahh
    d. Running

63. An *independent clause* can be defined as which of the following?
    a. A sentence without a subject
    b. A sentence without a verb
    c. A sentence with a subject and verb that expresses a complete thought
    d. A sentence that is combined by a conjunction and preposition

64. *Beyond the wall*, *beside the car*, and *under the floor* are examples of which of the following?
    a. Prepositional phrases
    b. Occupational phrases
    c. Auxiliary phrases
    d. Dual phrases

65. *This*, *that*, and *those* can be used as both of which of the following?
    a. Demonstrative pronouns and adjectives
    b. Demonstrative adjectives and adverbs
    c. Clauses and compound sentences
    d. Prepositions and adjectives

66. The word *not* is which of the following?
    a. Adverb
    b. Adjective
    c. Noun
    d. Pronoun

67. A *complex sentence* can be defined as which of the following?
    a. A sentence that contains no prepositional phrases
    b. A sentence that contains an indefinite pronoun
    c. A sentence that contains two independent clauses
    d. A sentence that contains at least one independent clause and at least one dependent clause

68. Choose the sentence that contains a comma splice.
    a. The boys never met; they were strangers.
    b. The boys never met: they were strangers.
    c. The boys never met, they were strangers.
    d. The boys, never met; they were strangers.

69. Subjective case can also be called which of the following?
    a. Objective case
    b. Possessive case
    c. Adjective case
    d. Nominative case

70. The underlined portion of the following sentence contains an example of which grammatical convention?
    The woman behind you is my <u>mother</u>.
    a. Pronoun
    b. Predicate nominative
    c. Adjective
    d. Prepositional phrase

71. *Comparative* and *superlative* are types of which of the following?
    a. Nouns
    b. Adjectives and adverbs
    c. Verbs
    d. Pronouns

72. The underlined portion of the following sentence contains an example of which verb form?
    Sandy <u>will have finished</u> by the end of the second semester.
    a. Present
    b. Past perfect
    c. Future perfect
    d. Present progressive

73. Fill in the blank. Gerund phrases function as _____ in a sentence.
    a. Adjectives
    b. Adverbs
    c. Conjunctions
    d. Nouns

74. Which of the following sentences contains an example of passive voice?
    a. The poem was written by a student.
    b. The poem contained two metaphors and a simile.
    c. A student wrote the poem.
    d. A student decided to write a poem yesterday.

76

75. All EXCEPT which of the following words are examples of relative pronouns?
    a. Who
    b. Whom
    c. That
    d. These

76. Fill in the blank. A(n) _____ refers to whom or for whom the action of the verb is being done.
    a. Direct object
    b. Indirect object
    c. Subject object
    d. Object subject

77. "I like writing, playing soccer, and eating" is an example of which grammatical convention?
    a. Appositive
    b. Complement
    c. Verbal
    d. Parallelism

78. Transition words can be used for all EXCEPT which of the following purposes?
    a. To explain
    b. To compare
    c. As conjunctions
    d. To replace a verb

79. Run-on or fused sentences *must* contain two or more of which of the following?
    a. Dependent phrases
    b. Independent phrases
    c. Sentences with passive voice
    d. Independent clauses

80. Fill in the blank. Collective nouns are paired with _____ in a sentence.
    a. Collective verbs
    b. Singular verbs
    c. Singular nouns
    d. Plural verbs

Answer Explanations

1. C: Good ways to improve writing style through grammatical choices include alternating among simple, complex, compound, and compound-complex sentence structures (Choice *A*) to prevent monotony and ensure variety; using fewer words when more words are unnecessary (Choice *B*); NOT writing all simple sentences with only one subject and one verb each (Choice *C*); and writing in the active voice more often than in the passive voice (Choice *D*). Active voice uses fewer words and also emphasizes action more strongly.

2. D: The topic sentence of a paragraph is often at or near the beginning, but not always, so Choice *A* is incorrect. Some topic sentences are at the ends of paragraphs, but not always. Therefore, Choice *B* is incorrect. There is more than one topic sentence in an essay, especially if the essay is built on multiple paragraphs, so Choice *C* is incorrect. The topic sentence in a paragraph may be stated explicitly, or it may only be implied, requiring the reader to infer what the topic is rather than identify it as an overt statement. Thus, Choice *D* is correct.

3. A: Criteria for a good paragraph topic sentence include clarity, emphasis rather than subtlety, brevity rather than length, and straightforwardness rather than ambiguousness. Therefore, Choices *B, C,* and *D* are incorrect.

4. B: The sentence lacks subject-verb agreement. Three nouns require plural "are," not singular "is." A misplaced modifier (Choice *A*) is incorrectly positioned, modifying the wrong part. For example, in Groucho Marx's famous joke, "One morning I shot an elephant in my pajamas. How he got into my pajamas I don't know" (*Animal Crackers,* 1930), he refers in the second sentence to the misplaced modifier in the first. A dangling participle (Choice *C*) leaves a verb participle hanging by omitting the subject it describes; e.g. "Walking down the street, the house was on fire."

5. B: Choice *A* lacks pronoun-antecedent agreement: "Every student" is singular but "their" is plural. Choice *B* correctly combines plural "All students" with plural "their advisors." Choice *C* has plural "All students" but singular "his advisor." Choice *D* has singular "Every student" but plural "their advisors."

6. B: When compounding subjects by adding nouns including proper nouns (names) to pronouns, the pronoun's form should not be changed by the addition. Since "Give it to me" is correct, not "Give it to I," we would not write "Give it to Shirley and I" (Choice *A*). "Shirley" and "me" are correct in either position in Choices *C* and *D*. "Give it to" requires an object. Only "me," "us," "him," "her," and "them" can be objects; "I," "we," "he," "she," and "they" are used as subjects, but never as objects.

7. D: Adjectives modify nouns (Choice *B*) or pronouns (Choice *C*) by describing them. For example, in the phrase "a big, old, red house," the noun "house" is modified and described by the adjectives "big," "old," and "red." Adjectives do not modify verbs, adverbs do; therefore, Choice *A* is incorrect.

8. D: Adverbs modify verbs (Choice *A*), other adverbs (Choice *B*), or adjectives (Choice *C*). For example, in "She slept soundly," the verb is "slept" and the adverb modifying it is "soundly." In "He finished extremely quickly," the adverb "especially" modifies the adverb "quickly." In "She was especially enthusiastic," the adverb "especially" modifies the adjective "enthusiastic."

9. C: Experts advise students/beginning writers to include a topic sentence in every paragraph. Although professional writers do not always do this, beginners should, to learn how to write good topic sentences and paragraphs, rather than include a topic sentence in only every second or third paragraph, so Choice *A* is incorrect. Although experienced writers can also vary the positioning of topic sentences within paragraphs, experts advise new/learning writers to start paragraphs with topic sentences; therefore, Choice *B* is wrong. A topic sentence should be narrow and restricted, not broad and general; thus, Choice *D* is incorrect.

10. B: *Phobos* means "fear" in Greek. From it, English has derived the word *phobia*, meaning an abnormal or exaggerated fear; and a multitude of other words ending in *-phobia*, whose beginnings specify the object of the fear, as in the examples given. Another ubiquitous English word part deriving from Greek is *phil* as a prefix or suffix, meaning love (Choice *A*), such as *philosophy, hydrophilic, philanthropist,* and *philharmonic*. The Greek word for hate (Choice *C*) is *miseo,* found in English words like *misogyny* and *misanthrope*. The Greek word meaning wise or knowledge (Choice *D*) is *sophos,* found in English *sophisticated* and *philosophy*.

11. A: The author's purpose is to show the audience one of the effects of criminal rehabilitation by comparison. Choice *B* is incorrect because although it is obvious the author favors rehabilitation, the author never asks for donations from the audience. Choices *C* and *D* are also incorrect. We can infer from the passage that American prisons are probably harsher than Norway prisons. However, the best answer that captures the author's purpose is Choice *A*, because we see an effect by the author (recidivism rate of each country) comparing Norwegian and American prisons.

12. D: The likelihood of a convicted criminal to reoffend. The passage explains how a Norwegian prison, due to rehabilitation, has a smaller rate of recidivism. Thus, we can infer that recidivism is probably not a positive attribute. Choices *A* and *B* are both positive attributes—the lack of violence and the opportunity of inmates to receive therapy—so Norway would probably not have a lower rate of these two things. Choice *C* is possible, but it does not make sense in context, because the author does not talk about tactics in which to keep prisoners inside the compound, but ways in which to rehabilitate criminals so that they can live as citizens when they get out of prison.

13. D: The passage is reflective of a narrative. A narrative is used to tell a story, as we see the narrator trying to do so in this passage by using memory and dialogue. Choice *A*, persuasive writing, uses rhetorical devices to try and convince the audience of something, and there is no persuasion or argument within this passage. Choice *B*, expository, is a type of writing used to inform the reader. Choice *C*, technical writing, is usually used within business communications and uses technical language to explain procedures or concepts to someone within the same technical field.

14. C: The narrator was feeling a sense of foreboding. The narrator, after feeling excitement for the morning, feels "that something awful was about to happen," which is considered foreboding. The narrator mentions larks and weather in the passage, but there is no proof of anger or confusion at either of them.

15. C: The main point of the passage is to introduce Peter Walsh back into the narrator's memory. Choice *A* is incorrect because, although the novel *Mrs. Dalloway* is about events leading up to a party, the passage does not mention anything about a party. Choice *B* is incorrect; the narrator calls Peter *dull* at one point, but the rest of her memories of him are more positive. Choice *D* is incorrect; although morning is described within the first few sentences of the passage, the passage quickly switches to a description of Peter Walsh and the narrator's memories of him.

16. B: The point is to convince the audience that judges holding their positions based on good behavior is a practical way to avoid corruption.

17. B: The sentence is best taken to mean that whatever happened in his life before he had a certain internal change is irrelevant. Choices *A, C,* and *D* use some of the same language as the original passage, like "revolution," "speak," and "details," but they do not capture the meaning of the statement. The statement is saying the details of his previous life are not going to be talked about—that he had some kind of epiphany, and moving forward in his life is what the narrator cares about.

18. B: It is told in first-person omniscient. This is the best guess with the information we have. In the world of the passage, the narrator is first-person, because we see them use the "I," but they also know the actions and thoughts of the protagonist, a character named "Webster." First-person limited tells their own story, making Choice *A* incorrect. Choice *C* is incorrect; second person uses "you" to tell the story. Third person uses "them," "they," etc., and would not fall into use of the "I" in the narrative, making Choice *D* incorrect.

19. A: Webster is a washing machine manufacturer. This question assesses reading comprehension. We see in the second sentence that Webster "was a fairly prosperous manufacturer of washing machines," making Choice A the correct answer.

20. B: This excerpt is considered a secondary source because it actively interprets primary sources. We see direct quotes from the queen, which would be considered a primary source. But since we see those quotes being interpreted and analyzed, the excerpt becomes a secondary source. Choice *C,* tertiary source, is an index of secondary and primary sources, like an encyclopedia or Wikipedia.

21. B: It took two years for the new castle to be built. It states this in the first sentence of the second paragraph. In the third year, we see the Prince planning improvements, and arranging things for the fourth year.

22. C: In this context, *impress* means to impose a certain quality upon. The sentence states that "the impress of his dear hand [has] been stamped everywhere," regarding the quality of his tastes and creations on the house. Choice *A* is one definition of *impress*, but this definition is used more as a verb than a noun: "She impressed us as a songwriter." Choice *B* is incorrect because it is also used as a verb: "He impressed the need for something to be done." Choice *D* is incorrect because it is part of a physical act: "the businessman impressed his mark upon the envelope." The phrase in the passage is figurative, since the workmen did most of the physical labor, not the Prince.

23. A: The passage presents us with a sequence of events that happens in chronological order. Choice *B* is incorrect. Cause and effect organization would usually explain why something happened or list the effects of something. Choice *C* is incorrect because problem and solution organization would detail a problem and then present a solution to the audience, and there is no solution presented here. Finally, Choice *D* is incorrect. We are entered directly into the narrative without any main idea or any kind of argument being delivered.

24. D: A president is about to be assassinated. The context clues in the passage give hints to what is about to happen. The passage mentions John Wilkes Booth as "Mr. Booth," the man who shot Abraham Lincoln. The passage also mentions a "Mr. Ford," and we know that Lincoln was shot in Ford's theater. Finally, the passage mentions Mr. and Mrs. Lincoln. By adding all these clues up and layering them on our prior knowledge of history, the assassination of President Lincoln by Booth in Ford's theater is probably the next thing that is going to happen.

25. B: Mr. Ford assumed Booth's movement throughout the theater was due to being familiar with the theater. Choice *A* is incorrect; although Booth does eventually make his way to Lincoln's box, Mr. Ford does not make this distinction in this part of the passage. Choice *C* is incorrect; although the passage mentions "companions," it mentions Lincoln's companions rather than Booth's companions. Finally, Choice *D* is incorrect; the passage mentions "dress circle," which means the first level of the theater, but this is different from a "dressing room."

26. C: The English word *moron* is derived from the Greek *mor-* meaning dull or foolish. *Sophomore* also combines *soph* from Greek *sophos*, meaning wise, with *mor*—i.e. literally "wise fool." The words *move* (Choice *A*), *motor* (Choice *B*), *mobile* (Choice *D*), and many others are all derived from the Latin *mot-* or *mov-*, from the Latin words *movere*, to move and *motus*, motion.

27. A: Homophones are words that are pronounced the same way, but are spelled differently and have different meanings. For example, *lax* and *lacks* are homophones. Words spelled the same (Choice *B*) but with different meanings are homographs. Words with the same meaning (Choice *C*) are synonyms, which are spelled and pronounced differently.

28. D: Words that are spelled the same way are homographs (Choice *A*); if they are pronounced differently, they are heteronyms (Choice *B*). The example given fits both definitions. But homonyms (Choice *C*) are spelled the same way (i.e. homographs) AND also pronounced the same way (i.e. homophones), NOT differently. Therefore, Choices *A* and *B* both correctly describe *tear*, but Choice *C* does not.

29. B: Bacteria is considered a plural word. The singular word for "bacteria" is "bacterium." Cactus, criterion, and elf are all considered singular words, making Choices *A, C,* and *D* incorrect.

30. D: *Moose* is both the singular and plural form of the word. Other words that do not change from singular to plural include *deer, fish,* and *sheep*. *Louse* (Choice *A*) has an irregular plural, but it is *lice*, not the same as the singular. *Goose* (Choice *B*) has the irregular plural *geese*, also not the same as the singular. *Mouse* (Choice *C*), like *louse*, has the irregular plural *mice*, also different from its singular form.

31. C: The irregular plural of *ox* (Choice *A*) is *oxen*. The irregular plural of *child* (Choice *B*) is *children*. The irregular plural of *woman* (Choice *D*) is *women*. These irregular plurals all end in *–en*. However, *person* (Choice *C*) has the irregular plural of *people*, which has a different ending than the others. It can also be pluralized as *persons;* but this is a regular plural, not an irregular one.

32. B: The plural possessive noun *friends'* is correctly punctuated with an apostrophe following the plural -*s* ending. *Friend's* would indicate a singular possessive noun, like something belonging to one friend. *Friends* would indicate a plural noun not possessing anything. In Choice *A*, the second-person possessive is *your*, NOT "you're," a contraction of "you are." In Choice *C*, the third-person plural possessive is *their*, NOT "they're," a contraction of "they are." There are two errors in Choice *D*. The first possessive is *whose*, NOT "who's," a contraction of "who is;" the second is *its*, NOT "it's," a contraction of "it is."

33. B: *Forfeit* is spelled correctly. Choice *A* is misspelled and should be *weird*. Choice *C* is misspelled and should be *believe*. Choice *D* is misspelled and should be *conceive*. Many people confuse the spellings of words with *ie* and *ei* combinations. Some rules that apply to most English words, with 22 exceptions, are: I before E except after C; except after C and before L, P, T, or V; when sounding like *A* as in weight; when sounding like *I* as in height; or when an *ei* combination is formed by a prefix or a suffix.

34. A: *Insolent* is correctly spelled. Many people misspell words that sound the same but are spelled differently by confusing the vowels *a, e,* and *i*. For example, Choice *B* is correctly spelled *irrelevant;* Choice *C* is correctly spelled *independent;* and the correct spelling of Choice *D* is *indispensable*. Confusion is increased by these variations: Choices *B* and *C* sound the same but end with *-ant* and *-ent*, respectively; and while Choice *D* ends with *-able*, other words like *irrepressible* and *gullible* correctly end with *-ible*, which is incorrect in *indispensable*.

35. C: While terms like *Caucasian* and *African-American* are capitalized, the words *white* (Choice *C*) and *black* (Choice *D*) when referring to race should NOT be capitalized. While the name *Congress* is capitalized, the adjective *congressional* should NOT be capitalized (Choice *A*). Although the name of the U.S. *Constitution* is capitalized, the related adjective *constitutional* is NOT capitalized (Choice *B*).

36. B: The Oxford comma is the last comma following the last item in a series and preceding the word *or* or *and*. It is NOT the first (Choice *A*), or any comma separating items in a series (Choice *C*) other than the last. While it is true that many people omit this comma, it is NOT true that it serves no purpose (Choice *D*). It can prevent confusion when series include compound nouns.

37. C: A city and its state should always be separated by a comma. When items in a series contain internal commas, they should be separated by semicolons. City and state are never separated by a semicolon (Choice *A*). The city and its state are never named without punctuation between them (Choice *B*). The reason it is incorrect to use all commas, both between each city and its state and also between city-state pairs (Choice *D*), is obvious: some of the names used can refer to multiple places, causing serious confusion without different punctuation marks to identify them.

38. D: One rule for using hyphens is to clarify meaning: without the hyphen in this phrase, a reader could interpret it to mean that the claim is fraudulent; the hyphen makes it clear that it is the ID that is fraudulent. Another rule is that adverbs with *–ly* endings are not hyphenated, so (Choice *A*) should be *finely tuned*. However, an additional rule is that adjectives with *–ly* endings are hyphenated; hence Choice *B* should be *family-owned* and Choice *C* should be *friendly-looking*.

39. D: The rule for writing a quotation with another quotation inside it is to use double quotation marks to enclose the outer quotation, and use single quotation marks to enclose the inner quotation. Here is an example: "I don't think he will attend, because he said, 'I am extremely busy.'" The correct usage is reversed in Choice *A*. Choices *B* and *C* are incorrect, as this would not distinguish one quotation from the other.

40. A: When two people are named and both possess the same object, the apostrophe-*s* indicating possession should be placed ONLY after the second name, NOT after both names, making Choices *B* and *C* incorrect. It is also incorrect to use the apostrophe-*s* after the first name instead of the second (Choice *D*).

41. D: Irregular plurals that do not end in *–s* are always made possessive by adding apostrophe-*s*. A common error people make is to add *–s*-apostrophe instead of vice versa, as in the other three choices. *Geese* (Choice *A*), *children* (Choice *B*) and *teeth* (Choice *C*) are already plural, so adding an *s* before the apostrophe constitutes a double plural. Adding the *–s* after the apostrophe (i.e. *geese's, children's,* and *teeth's*) correctly makes these plurals possessive.

42. D: Some writing techniques recommended for attaining sentence fluency include varying the beginnings of sentences, making Choice *A* incorrect; varying sentence lengths rather than making them all uniform, making Choice *B* incorrect; varying sentence rhythms rather than consistently using the same rhythm, making Choice *C* incorrect; and varying sentence structures among simple, compound, complex, and compound-complex, making Choice *D* correct.

43. B: Four elements of an effective paragraph are unity, coherence, a topic sentence, and development. Focusing on one main point throughout (Choice *A*) the paragraph reflects the element of unity. Using logical and verbal bridges (Choice *B*) between/across sentences reflects the element of coherence. A sentence identifying the main idea (Choice *C*) of the paragraph reflects the element of a topic sentence. Citing data, giving examples, including illustrations, and analyzing (Choice *D*) the topic all reflect the element of developing the paragraph sufficiently.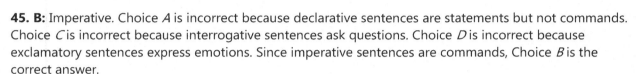

44. D: Understood *you*. Choices *A*, *B*, and *C* are all verbs, so they cannot be the subject of the sentence. Choice *D* is the correct answer because commands often necessitate an understood *you*.

45. B: Imperative. Choice *A* is incorrect because declarative sentences are statements but not commands. Choice *C* is incorrect because interrogative sentences ask questions. Choice *D* is incorrect because exclamatory sentences express emotions. Since imperative sentences are commands, Choice *B* is the correct answer.

46. D: The passage explains the different ways bacteria can affect milk by detailing the color and taste of different infections. Choices *A* and *B* might be true, but they are not the main purpose of the passage as detailed in the first sentence. Choice *C* is incorrect, since milk does not have an effect on bacteria in this particular passage.

47. C: The tone of this passage is neutral, since it is written in an academic/informative voice. It is important to look at the author's word choice to determine the tone of a passage. We have no indication that the author is excited, angry, or sorrowful at the effects of bacteria on milk, so Choices *A*, *B*, and *D* are incorrect.

48. B: The milk will turn black is not a reaction mentioned in the passage. The passage does state, however, that the milk may get "soapy," that it can become "slimy," and that it may turn out to be a "beautiful sky-blue colour," making Choices *A*, *C*, and *D* incorrect.

49. A: In the sentence, we know that the word "curdle" means the opposite of "slimy." The words greasy, oily, and slippery are all very similar to the word slimy, making Choices *B*, *C*, and *D* incorrect. "Lumpy" means clotted, chunky, or thickened.

50. A: It is troublesome because it is impossible to get rid of. The passage mentions milk turning blue or tasting bad, and milk could possibly even make a milk-drinker sick if it has slimy threads. However, we know for sure that the slimy threads prove troublesome because they can become impossible to get rid of from this sentence: "Such an infection proves very troublesome, for many a time it persists in spite of all attempts made to remedy it."

51. D: A "boom city" is a city whose population is made up of people who seek quick fortunes rather than building a solid business foundation. Choice *A* is a characteristic of Portland, but not that of a boom city. Choice *B* is close—a boom city is one that becomes quickly populated, but it is not necessarily always populated by residents from the east coast. Choice *C* is incorrect because a boom city is not one that catches fire frequently, but one made up of people who are looking to make quick fortunes from the resources provided on the land.

52. D: The author would classify Portland as a city of legitimate business. We can see the proof in this sentence: "the cause of Portland's growth and prosperity is the trade which it has as the center of collection and distribution of this great wealth of natural resources, and it has attracted, not the boomer and speculator . . . but the merchant, manufacturer, and investor, who seek the surer if slower channels of legitimate business and investment." Choices *A*, *B*, and *C* are not mentioned in the passage and are incorrect.

53. B: This passage is part of a travel guide. Our first hint is in the title: *Oregon, Washington, and Alaska. Sights and Scenes for the Tourist.* Although the passage talks about business, there is no proposition included, which makes Choice *A* incorrect. Choice *C* is incorrect because the style of the writing is more informative and formal rather than personal and informal. Choice *D* is incorrect; this could possibly be a scholarly article, but the best choice is that it is a travel guide, due to the title and the details of what the city has to offer at the very end.

54. C: *Metropolis* means city. Portland is described as having agricultural valleys, but it is not solely a "farm" or "valley," making Choices *A* and *D* incorrect. We know from the description of Portland that it is more representative of a city than a countryside or country, making Choice *B* incorrect.

55. B: The passage is taken from a myth. Look for the key words that give away the type of passage this is, such as "deities," "Greek hero," "centaur," and the names of demigods like Artemis. A eulogy is typically a speech given at a funeral, making Choice *A* incorrect. Choices *C* and *D* are incorrect, as "virgin huntresses" and "centaurs" are typically not found in historical or professional documents.

56. A: Based on the context of the passage, we can see that Hippolytus was a friend to Artemis because he "spent all his days in the greenwood chasing wild beasts" with her. The other choices are incorrect.

57. A: The author is saying that the artistic beauty of Pushkin's poetry runs so deep that it is retained even in its translation to the "hard English tongue" or to any language. He says that even though translating the work out of its original Russian form removes its "wonderful melody and grace of form," the poetry is so universal that it will "appeal forever to man, in whatever clime, under whatever sky." This means the author believes Pushkin's poetry is so beautiful that it will appeal to readers all over the world (in different climes (climates) and skies (locations)) and throughout time.

58. D: You would most likely find this in the preface. A preface to a text usually explains what the author has done or aims to do with the work. An appendix is usually found at the end of a text and does not talk about what the author intends to do to the work, making Choice *A* incorrect. A table of contents does not contain prose, but bullet points listing chapters and sections found in the text, making Choice *B* incorrect. Choice *C* is incorrect; the first chapter would include the translation work (here, poetry), and not the author's intentions.

59. B: The most important aim, according to the author, is to retain the truth of the work. The author says that "music and rhythm and harmony are indeed fine things, but truth is finer still," which means that the author stuck to a literal translation instead of changing up any words that might make the English language translation sound better.

60. C: Choice *C* is correct because the word *unremarkable* should be changed to *remarkable* to be consistent with the details of the passage. This question requires close attention to the passage. Choice *A* is incorrect; it can be found where the passage says, "no less than six named and several unnamed varieties of the peach have thus produced several varieties of nectarine." Choice *B* is incorrect; it can be found where the passage says, "it is highly improbable that all these peach-trees . . . are hybrids from the peach and nectarine." Choice *D* is incorrect because we see in the passage that "the production of peaches from nectarines, either by seeds or buds, may perhaps be considered as a case of reversion."

61. D: Subordinating conjunctions. Choices *B* and *C, coordinate adjectives* and *demonstrative adjectives,* are incorrect because *after, since,* and *whereas* are not adjectives. Choice *A, coordinate conjunctions,* is incorrect because coordinating conjunctions are placed between words when the writer wants to give equal emphasis to each word, like *and* or *but.* Choice *D* is correct because subordinating conjunctions such as *after, since,* and *whereas* are often used at the beginning of subordinating clauses.

62. D: Running. Choices *A, B,* and *C* are incorrect because interjections are used to express emotion. Choice *D* is correct because the word *running* is most commonly used as a verb or noun, not an interjection.

63. C: A sentence with a subject and verb that expresses a complete thought. Choices *A* and *B* are incorrect because they describe the characteristics of a phrase. Choice *D* is incorrect because a sentence cannot be combined by a preposition. Choice *C* is correct because an independent clause must contain a subject and verb and express a complete thought.

64. A: Prepositional phrases. Choices *B, C,* and *D* are not related. Choice *A* is correct because prepositional phrases are composed of prepositions and their objects.

65. A: Demonstrative pronouns and adjectives. Choices *C* and *D* are incorrect. Choice *B* is incorrect because the words are not adverbs. Choice *A* is correct because the words can be used as adjectives when they are used to describe nouns, or pronouns when they are used to replace nouns.

66. A: Adverb. Choices *B, C,* and *D* are incorrect. Choice *A* is correct because the word *not* can be used to modify an adjective, a verb, or another adverb.

67. D: A sentence that contains at least one independent clause and at least one dependent clause. Choices *A* and *B* are incorrect because the number of prepositional phrases or indefinite pronouns has no bearing on whether a sentence is considered complex. Choice *C* is incorrect because a sentence with two independent clauses is a compound sentence.

68. C: The boys never met, they were strangers. Choices *A* and *B* are not possibilities because they don't contain commas. Choice *D* is incorrect because a comma splice occurs when a comma is used to incorrectly join two independent clauses. Therefore, Choice *C* is correct.

69. D: Nominative case. Choices *A, B,* and *C* are incorrect. The objective case is commonly used as a form of noun or pronoun used in object complements, direct objects, subject of the infinitive, and object of a preposition. The possessive case is used to show possession. The adjective case does not occur within the English language. Therefore, Choice *D* is correct.

70. B: Predicate nominative. Choices *A, C,* and *D* are incorrect. The word *mother* is not a pronoun, adjective, or prepositional phrase. Choice *B* is correct because a predicate nominative occurs when a noun that refers to the subject appears in the predicate of the sentence.

71. B: Adjectives and adverbs. Choices *A, C,* and *D* are incorrect. There are no comparative or superlatives nouns, pronouns, or verbs. Therefore, Choice *B* is correct, since adjectives and adverbs are used to describe nouns or modify adjectives, verbs, and other adverbs.

72. C: Future perfect. Choices *A, B,* and *D* are incorrect. Choice *C* is correct because the word *will* in the verb phrase *will have finished* denotes that the action will occur in the future.

73. D: Nouns. Choices *A*, *B*, and *C* are incorrect. Choice *D* is correct because gerund phrases contain gerunds, which are verbs that function as nouns in a sentence.

74. A: The poem was written by a student. Choices *B, C*, and *D* are incorrect. Choice *A* is correct because passive voice occurs when the subject is acted upon by the verb.

75. D: These. Choices *A*, *B*, and *C* are relative pronouns. Relative pronouns are used to join a clause or phrase to a noun or pronoun. Therefore, Choice *D* is the correct answer.

76. B: Indirect object. Choices *C* and *D* are not related. Choice *A* is incorrect because a direct object receives the action of the verb. Choice *B* is correct because an indirect object refers to whom or for whom the action of the verb is being done.

77. D: Parallelism. Choices *A*, *B*, and *C* are all unrelated. Choice *D* is correct because parallelism refers to the state of being the same or congruent. The present participles *writing, playing,* and *eating* are congruent parts of speech within a list and are thus parallel.

78. D: To replace a verb. Choices *A*, *B*, and *C* are incorrect. Choice *D* is correct. Transition words cannot be used to replace a verb.

79. D: Independent clauses. Choices *A* and *B* are unrelated and incorrect. Choice *C* is incorrect because passive voice has no bearing on whether a sentence is a run-on or a fused sentence. Choice *D* is correct because a run-on or fused sentence occurs when two independent clauses are joined incorrectly.

80. B: Collective nouns, such as team, family, and band, describe a group of individuals, animals, or things. They are paired with singular verbs. For example, "the family moved to Greece." Collective verbs, Choice *A*, do not exist. Collective nouns are not necessarily paired with singular nouns in the subject of a sentence, and are not paired with plural verbs, so Choices *C* and *D* are incorrect.

Mathematics

Numbers and Operations

Writing Numbers Using Base-10 Numerals, Number Names, and Expanded Form

The **base-10 number system** is also called the **decimal system of naming numbers**. There is a decimal point that sets the value of numbers based on their position relative to the decimal point. The order from the decimal point to the right is the tenths place, then hundredths place, then thousandths place. From the decimal point to the left, the place value is ones, tens, hundreds, etc. The number 2,356 can be described in words as "two thousand three hundred fifty-six." In expanded form, it can be written as:

$$(2 \times 1{,}000) + (3 \times 100) + (5 \times 10) + (6 \times 1)$$

The expanded form shows the value each number holds in its place. The number 3,093 can be written in words as "three thousand ninety-three." In expanded form, it can be expressed as:

$$(3 \times 1{,}000) + (0 \times 100) + (9 \times 10) + (3 \times 1)$$

Notice that the zero is added in the expanded form as a place holder. There are no hundreds in the number, so a zero is written in the hundreds place.

Composing and Decomposing Multidigit Numbers

Composing and decomposing numbers reveals the place value held by each number 0 through 9 in each position. For example, the number 17 is read as "seventeen." It can be decomposed into the numbers 10 and 7. It can be described as 1 group of ten and 7 ones. The one in the tens place represents one set of ten. The seven in the ones place represents seven sets of one. Added together, they make a total of seventeen. The number 48 can be written in words as "forty-eight." It can be decomposed into the numbers 40 and 8, where there are 4 groups of ten and 8 groups of one. The number 296 can be decomposed into 2 groups of one hundred, 9 groups of ten, and 6 groups of one. There are two hundreds, nine tens, and six ones. Decomposing and composing numbers lays the foundation for visually picturing the number and its place value, and adding and subtracting multiple numbers with ease.

Identifying the Place and Value of a Digit

Each number in the base-10 system is made of the numbers 0—9, located in different places relative to the decimal point. Based on where the numbers fall, the value of a digit changes. For example, the number 7,509 has a seven in the thousands place. This means there are seven groups of one thousand. The number 457 has a seven in the ones place. This means there are seven groups of one. Even though there is a seven in both numbers, the place of the seven tells the value of the digit. A practice question may ask the place and value of the 4 in 3,948. The four is found in the tens place, which means four represents the number 40, or four groups of ten. Another place value may be on the opposite side of the decimal point. A question may ask the place and value of the 8 in the number 203.80. In this case, the eight is in the tenths place because it is in the first place to the right of the decimal point. It holds a value of eight-tenths, or eight groups of one-tenth.

Recognizing Relative Value of a Digit Given Its Place

The value of a digit is found by recognizing its place relative to the rest of the number. For example, the number 569.23 contains a 6. The position of the 6 is two places to the left of the decimal, putting it in the tens place. The tens place gives it a value of 60, or six groups of ten. The number 39.674 has a 4 in it. The number 4 is located three places to the right of the decimal point, placing it in the thousandths place. The value of the 4 is four-thousandths, because of its position relative to the other numbers and to the decimal. It can be described as 0.004 by itself, or four groups of one-thousandths. The numbers 100 and 0.1 are both made up of ones and zeros. The first number, 100, has a 1 in the hundreds place, giving it a value of one hundred. The second number, 0.1, has a 1 in the tenths place, giving that 1 a value of one-tenth. The place of the number gives it the value.

Using Whole-Number Exponents to Denote Powers of 10

Numbers can also be written using exponents. The number 7,000 can be written as $7 \times 1,000$ because 7 is in the thousands place. It can also be written as 7×10^3 because $1,000 = 10^3$. Another number that can use this notation is 500. It can be written as 5×100, or 5×10^2, because $100 = 10^2$. The number 30 can be written as 3×10, or 3×10^1, because $10 = 10^1$. Notice that each one of the exponents of 10 is equal to the number of zeros in the number. Seven is in the thousands place, with three zeros, and the exponent on ten is 3. The five is in the hundreds place, with two zeros, and the exponent on the ten is 2. A question may give the number 40,000 and ask for it to be rewritten using exponents with a base of ten. Because the number has a four in the ten-thousands place and four zeros, it can be written using an exponent of four: 4×10^4.

Rounding Multidigit Numbers to Any Place Value

Numbers can be rounded by recognizing the place value where the rounding takes place, then looking at the number to the right. If the number to the right is five or greater, the number to be rounded goes up one. If the number to the right is four or less, the number to be rounded stays the same. For example, the number 438 can be rounded to the tens place. The number 3 is in the tens place and the number to the right is 8. Because the 8 is 5 or greater, the 3 then rounds up to a 4. The rounded number is 440. Another number, 1,394, can be rounded to the thousands place. The number in the thousands place is 1, and the number to the right is 3. As the 3 is 4 or less, it means the 1 stays the same and the rounded number is 1,000. Rounding is also a form of estimating. The number 9.58 can be rounded to the tenths place. The number 5 is in the tenths place, and the number 8 is to the right of it. Because 8 is 5 or greater, the 5 changes to a 6. The rounded number becomes 9.6.

Solving Multistep Mathematical and Real-World Problems Using Addition, Subtraction, Multiplication, and Division

One-step problems take only one mathematical step to solve. For example, solving the equation $5x = 45$ is a one-step problem because the one step of dividing both sides of the equation by 5 is the only step necessary to obtain the solution $x = 9$. The **multiplication principle of equality** is the one step used to isolate the variable. The equation is of the form $ax = b$, where a and b are rational numbers. Similarly, the **addition principle of equality** could be the one step needed to solve a problem. In this case, the equation would be of the form $x + a = b$ or $x - a = b$, for real numbers a and b.

A **multi-step problem** involves more than one step to find the solution, or it could consist of solving more than one equation. An equation that involves both the addition principle and the multiplication principle is a two-step problem, and an example of such an equation is:

$$2x - 4 = 5$$

Solving involves adding 4 to both sides and then dividing both sides by 2. An example of a two-step problem involving two separate equations is $y = 3x$:

$$2x + y = 4$$

The two equations form a system of two equations that must be solved together in two variables. The system can be solved by the substitution method. Since y is already solved for in terms of x, plug $3x$ in for y into the equation:

$$2x + y = 4$$

resulting in

$$2x + 3x = 4$$

Therefore, $5x = 4$ and $x = \frac{4}{5}$. Because there are two variables, the solution consists of a value for both x and for y. Substitute $x = \frac{4}{5}$ into either original equation to find y. The easiest choice is $y = 3x$. Therefore:

(x,y) and

$$y = 3 \times \frac{4}{5} = \frac{12}{5}$$ ordered pair *

The solution can be written as the ordered pair $\left(\frac{4}{5}, \frac{12}{5}\right)$.

Real-world problems can be translated into both one-step and multi-step problems. In either case, the word problem must be translated from the verbal form into mathematical expressions and equations that can be solved using algebra. An example of a one-step real-world problem is the following: A cat weighs half as much as a dog living in the same house. If the dog weighs 14.5 pounds, how much does the cat weigh? To solve this problem, an equation can be used. In any word problem, the first step must be defining variables that represent the unknown quantities. For this problem, let x be equal to the unknown weight of the cat. Because two times the weight of the cat equals 14.5 pounds, the equation to be solved is: $2x = 14.5$. Use the multiplication principle to divide both sides by 2. Therefore, $x = 7.25$. The cat weighs 7.25 pounds.

Most of the time, real-world problems are more difficult than this one and consist of multi-step problems. The following is an example of a multi-step problem: The sum of two consecutive page numbers is equal to 437. What are those page numbers? First, define the unknown quantities. If x is equal to the first page number, then $x + 1$ is equal to the next page number because they are consecutive integers. Their sum is equal to 437, and this statement translates to the equation:

$$x + x + 1 = 437$$

To solve, first collect like terms to obtain:

$$2x + 1 = 437$$

Then, subtract 1 from both sides and then divide by 2. The solution to the equation is $x = 218$. Therefore, the two consecutive page numbers that satisfy the problem are 218 and 219. It is always important to make sure that answers to real-world problems make sense. For instance, it should be a red flag if the solution to this same problem resulted in decimals, which would indicate the need to check the work. Page numbers are whole numbers; therefore, if decimals are found to be answers, the solution process should be double-checked to see where mistakes were made.

Identifying Different Problem Situations for the Operations

The four basic operations include addition, subtraction, multiplication, and division. The result of addition is a sum, the result of subtraction is a difference, the result of multiplication is a product, and the result of division is a quotient. Each type of operation can be used when working with rational numbers; however, the basic operations need to be understood first while using simpler numbers before working with fractions and decimals.

Performing these operations should first be learned using whole numbers. Addition needs to be done column by column. To add two whole numbers, add the ones column first, then the tens columns, then the hundreds, etc. If the sum of any column is greater than 9, a one must be carried over to the next column. For example, the following is the result of 482 + 924:

$$
\begin{array}{r}
1 \\
482 \\
+924 \\
\hline
1406
\end{array}
$$

Notice that the sum of the tens column was 10, so a one was carried over to the hundreds column. Subtraction is also performed column by column. Subtraction is performed in the ones column first, then the tens, etc. If the number on top is less than the number below, a one must be borrowed from the column to the left.

For example, the following is the result of 5,424 − 756:

$$
\begin{array}{r}
4\ 13\ 11\ 14 \\
5\ \ 4\ \ 2\ \ 4 \\
-\ 7\ \ 5\ \ 6 \\
\hline
4\ \ 6\ \ 6\ \ 8
\end{array}
$$

Notice that a one is borrowed from the tens, hundreds, and thousands place. After subtraction, the answer can be checked through addition. A check of this problem would be to show that 756 + 4,668 = 5,424.

Multiplication of two whole numbers is performed by writing one on top of the other. The number on top is known as the **multiplicand**, and the number below is the **multiplier**. Perform the multiplication by multiplying the multiplicand by each digit of the multiplier. Make sure to place the ones value of each result under the multiplying digit in the multiplier. Each value to the right is then a 0. The product is found by adding each product. For example, the following is the process of multiplying 46 times 37 where 46 is the multiplicand and 37 is the multiplier:

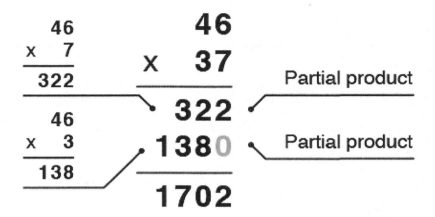

Finally, division can be performed using long division. When dividing a number by another number, the first number is known as the **dividend**, and the second is the **divisor**. For example, with $a \div b = c$, a is the dividend, b is the divisor, and c is the quotient. For long division, place the dividend within the division symbol and the divisor on the outside. For example, with $8{,}764 \div 4$, refer to the first problem in the diagram below. First, there are 2 4's in the first digit, 8. This number 2 gets written above the 8. Then, multiply 4 times 2 to get 8, and that product goes below the 8. Subtract to get 8, and then carry down the 7. Continue the same steps.

$$7 \div 4 = 1 \text{ R3}$$

so 1 is written above the 7. Multiply 4 times 1 to get 4 and write it below the 7. Subtract to get 3 and carry the 6 down next to the 3. Resulting steps give a 9 and a 1. The final subtraction results in a 0, which means that 8,764 is divisible by 4. There are no remaining numbers.

The second example shows that:

$$4{,}536 \div 216 = 21$$

The steps are a little different because 216 cannot be contained in 4 or 5, so the first step is placing a 2 above the 3 because there are 2 216's in 453. Finally, the third example shows that $546 \div 31 = 17 \text{ R19}$.

The 19 is a remainder. Notice that the final subtraction does not result in a 0, which means that 546 is not divisible by 31. The remainder can also be written as a fraction over the divisor to say that:

$$546 \div 31 = 17\frac{19}{31}$$

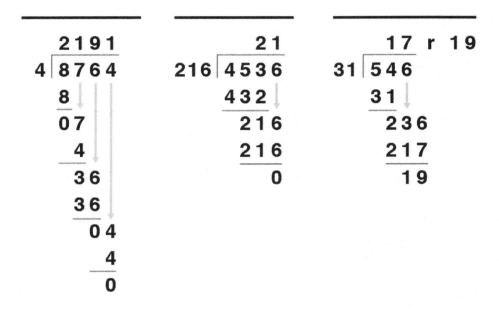

If a division problem relates to a real-world application, and a remainder does exist, it can have meaning. For example, consider the third example:

$$546 \div 31 = 17 \text{ R}19$$

Let's say that we had $546 to spend on calculators that cost $31 each, and we wanted to know how many we could buy. The division problem would answer this question. The result states that 17 calculators could be purchased, with $19 left over. Notice that the remainder will never be greater than or equal to the divisor.

Once the operations are understood with whole numbers, they can be used with integers. There are many rules surrounding operations with negative numbers. First, consider addition with integers. The sum of two numbers can first be shown using a number line. For example, to add $-5 + (-6)$, plot the point -5 on the number line. Then, because a negative number is being added, move 6 units to the left. This process results in landing on -11 on the number line, which is the sum of -5 and -6. If adding a positive number, move to the right. Visualizing this process using a number line is useful for understanding; however, it is not efficient. A quicker process is to learn the rules. When adding two numbers with the same sign, add the absolute values of both numbers, and use the common sign of both numbers as the sign of the sum. For example, to add $-5 + (-6)$, add their absolute values $5 + 6 = 11$. Then, introduce a negative number because both addends are negative. The result is -11. To add two integers with unlike signs, subtract the lesser absolute value from the greater absolute value, and apply the sign of the number with the greater absolute value to the result. For example, the sum $-7 + 4$ can be computed by finding the difference $7 - 4 = 3$ and then applying a negative because the value with the larger absolute value is negative. The result is -3. Similarly, the sum $-4 + 7$ can be found by computing the same difference but leaving it as a positive result because the addend with the larger absolute value is positive. Also, recall that any number plus 0 equals that number. This is known as the **Addition Property of 0**.

Subtracting two integers can be computed by changing to addition to avoid confusion. The rule is to add the first number to the opposite of the second number. The opposite of a number is the number on the other side of 0 on the number line, which is the same number of units away from 0. For example, -2 and 2 are opposites. Consider $4 - 8$. Change this to adding the opposite as follows: $4 + (-8)$. Then, follow the rules of addition of integers to obtain -4. Secondly, consider $-8 - (-2)$. Change this problem to adding the opposite as $-8 + 2$, which equals -6. Notice that subtracting a negative number functions the same as adding a positive number.

Multiplication and division of integers are actually less confusing than addition and subtraction because the rules are simpler to understand. If two factors in a multiplication problem have the same sign, the result is positive. If one factor is positive and one factor is negative, the result, known as the **product**, is negative. For example, $(-9)(-3) = 27$ and $9(-3) = -27$. Also, any number times 0 always results in 0. If a problem consists of more than a single multiplication, the result is negative if it contains an odd number of negative factors, and the result is positive if it contains an even number of negative factors. For example:

$$(-1)(-1)(-1)(-1) = 1$$

and

$$(-1)(-1)(-1)(-1)(-1) = 1$$

These two examples of multiplication also bring up another concept. Both are examples of repeated multiplication, which can be written in a more compact notation using exponents. The first example can be written as $(-1)^4 = 1$, and the second example can be written as $(-1)^5 = -1$. Both are exponential expressions, -1 is the base in both instances, and 4 and 5 are the respective exponents. Note that a negative number raised to an odd power is always negative, and a negative number raised to an even power is always positive. Also, $(-1)^4$ is not the same as -1^4. In the first expression, the negative is included in the parentheses, but it is not in the second expression. The second expression is found by evaluating 1^4 first to get 1 and then by applying the negative sign to obtain -1.

A similar theory applies within division. First, consider some vocabulary. When dividing 14 by 2, it can be written in the following ways: $14 \div 2 = 7$ or $\frac{14}{2} = 7$. 14 is the **dividend**, 2 is the **divisor**, and 7 is the **quotient**. If two numbers in a division problem have the same sign, the quotient is positive. If two numbers in a division problem have different signs, the quotient is negative. For example:

$$14 \div (-2) = -7$$

and

$$-14 \div (-2) = 7$$

To check division, multiply the quotient times the divisor to obtain the dividend. Also, remember that 0 divided by any number is equal to 0. However, any number divided by 0 is undefined. It just does not make sense to divide a number by 0 parts.

If more than one operation is to be completed in a problem, follow the Order of Operations. The mnemonic device, PEMDAS, for the order of operations states the order in which addition, subtraction, multiplication, and division need to be done. It also includes when to evaluate operations within grouping symbols and when to incorporate exponents. PEMDAS, which some remember by thinking "please excuse my dear Aunt Sally," refers to parentheses, exponents, multiplication, division, addition, and subtraction. First, within an expression, complete any operation that is within parentheses, or any other grouping symbol like brackets, braces, or absolute value symbols. Note that this does not refer to the case when parentheses are used to represent multiplication like $(2)(5)$. An operation is not within parentheses like it is in (2×5). Then, any exponents must be computed. Next, multiplication and division are performed from left to right. Finally, addition and subtraction are performed from left to right.

The following is an example in which the operations within the parentheses need to be performed first, so the order of operations must be applied to the exponent, subtraction, addition, and multiplication within the grouping symbol:

$$9 - 3(3^2 - 3 + 4 \cdot 3)$$

$$9 - 3(3^2 - 3 + 4 \cdot 3) \quad \text{Work within the parentheses first}$$

$$= 9 - 3(9 - 3 + 12)$$

$$= 9 - 3(18)$$

$$= 9 - 54$$

$$= -45$$

Once the rules for integers are understood, move on to learning how to perform operations with fractions and decimals. Recall that a rational number can be written as a fraction and can be converted to a decimal through division. If a rational number is negative, the rules for adding, subtracting, multiplying, and dividing integers must be used. If a rational number is in fraction form, performing addition, subtraction, multiplication, and division is more complicated than when working with integers. First, consider addition. To add two fractions having the same denominator, add the numerators and then reduce the fraction. When an answer is a fraction, it should always be in lowest terms. **Lowest terms** means that every common factor, other than 1, between the numerator and denominator is divided out. For example:

$$\frac{2}{8} + \frac{4}{8} = \frac{6}{8} = \frac{6 \div 2}{8 \div 2} = \frac{3}{4}$$

Both the numerator and denominator of $\frac{6}{8}$ have a common factor of 2, so 2 is divided out of each number to put the fraction in lowest terms. If denominators are different in an addition problem, the fractions must be converted to have common denominators. The **least common denominator (LCD)** of all the given denominators must be found, and this value is equal to the **least common multiple (LCM)** of the denominators. This non-zero value is the smallest number that is a multiple of both denominators. Then, rewrite each original fraction as an equivalent fraction using the new denominator. Once in this form, apply the process of adding with like denominators. For example, consider:

$$\frac{1}{3} + \frac{4}{9}$$

[handwritten: $\frac{3}{9} + \frac{4}{9} = \frac{7}{9}$]

The LCD is 9 because it is the smallest multiple of both 3 and 9. The fraction $\frac{1}{3}$ must be rewritten with 9 as its denominator. Therefore, multiply both the numerator and denominator times 3. Multiplying times $\frac{3}{3}$ is the same as multiplying times 1, which does not change the value of the fraction. Therefore, an equivalent fraction is $\frac{3}{9}$, and:

$$\frac{1}{3} + \frac{4}{9} = \frac{3}{9} + \frac{4}{9} = \frac{7}{9}$$

which is in lowest terms. Subtraction is performed in a similar manner; once the denominators are equal, the numerators are then subtracted. The following is an example of addition of a positive and a negative fraction:

$$-\frac{5}{12} + \frac{5}{9} = -\frac{5 \times 3}{12 \times 3} + \frac{5 \times 4}{9 \times 4} = -\frac{15}{36} + \frac{20}{36} = \frac{5}{36}$$

Common denominators are not used in multiplication and division. To multiply two fractions, multiply the numerators together and the denominators together. Then, write the result in lowest terms. For example:

$$\frac{2}{3} \times \frac{9}{4} = \frac{18}{12} = \frac{3}{2}$$

[handwritten: multiply left to right]

Alternatively, the fractions could be factored first to cancel out any common factors before performing the multiplication. For example:

$$\frac{2}{3} \times \frac{9}{4} = \frac{2}{3} \times \frac{3 \times 3}{2 \times 2} = \frac{3}{2}$$

This second approach is helpful when working with larger numbers, as common factors might not be obvious. Multiplication and division of fractions are related because the division of two fractions is changed into a multiplication problem. This means that dividing a fraction by another fraction is the same as multiplying the first fraction by the reciprocal of the second fraction, so that second fraction must be inverted, or "flipped," to be in reciprocal form. For example:

$$\frac{11}{15} \div \frac{3}{5} = \frac{11}{15} \times \frac{5}{3} = \frac{55}{45} = \frac{11}{9}$$

[handwritten: division changes to multiplication]

The fraction $\frac{5}{3}$ is the reciprocal of $\frac{3}{5}$. It is possible to multiply and divide numbers containing a mix of integers and fractions. In this case, convert the integer to a fraction by placing it over a denominator of 1. For example, a division problem involving an integer and a fraction is:

$$3 \div \frac{1}{2} = \frac{3}{1} \times \frac{2}{1} = \frac{6}{1} = 6$$

Finally, when performing operations with rational numbers that are negative, the same rules apply as when performing operations with integers. For example, a negative fraction times a negative fraction results in a positive value, and a negative fraction subtracted from a negative fraction results in a negative value.

Operations can be performed on rational numbers in decimal form. Recall that to write a fraction as an equivalent decimal expression, divide the numerator by the denominator. For example:

$$\frac{1}{8} = 1 \div 8 = 0.125$$

With the case of decimals, it is important to keep track of place value. To add decimals, make sure the decimal places are in alignment so that the numbers are lined up with their decimal points and add vertically. If the numbers do not line up because there are extra or missing place values in one of the numbers, then zeros may be used as placeholders. For example, $0.123 + 0.23$ becomes:

$$\begin{array}{r} 0.123 \\ + \underline{0.230} \\ 0.353 \end{array}$$

Subtraction is done the same way. Multiplication and division are more complicated. To multiply two decimals, place one on top of the other as in a regular multiplication process and do not worry about lining up the decimal points. Then, multiply as with whole numbers, ignoring the decimals. Finally, in the solution, insert the decimal point as many places to the left as there are total decimal values in the original problem. Here is an example of a decimal multiplication problem:

$$\begin{array}{r} 0.52 \quad \textit{2 decimal places} \\ \times \underline{\ 0.2} \quad \textit{1 decimal place} \\ 0.104 \quad \textit{3 decimal places} \end{array}$$

The answer to 52 times 2 is 104, and because there are three decimal values in the problem, the decimal point is positioned three units to the left in the answer.

The decimal point plays an integral role throughout the whole problem when dividing with decimals. First, set up the problem in a long division format. If the divisor is not an integer, the decimal must be moved to the right as many units as needed to make it an integer. The decimal in the dividend must be moved to the right the same number of places to maintain equality. Then, division is completed normally. Here is an example of long division with decimals:

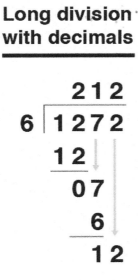

Long division with decimals

Because the decimal point is moved two units to the right in the divisor of 0.06 to turn it into the integer 6, it is also moved two units to the right in the dividend of 12.72 to make it 1,272. The result is 212, and remember that a division problem can always be checked by multiplying the answer times the divisor to see if the result is equal to the dividend.

Sometimes it is helpful to round answers that are in decimal form. First, find the place to which the rounding needs to be done. Then, look at the digit to the right of it. If that digit is 4 or less, the number in the place value to its left stays the same, and everything to its right becomes a 0. This process is known as **rounding down**. If that digit is 5 or higher, round up by increasing the place value to its left by 1, and every number to its right becomes a 0. If those 0's are in decimals, they can be dropped. For example, 0.145 rounded to the nearest hundredth place would be rounded up to 0.15, and 0.145 rounded to the nearest tenth place would be rounded down to 0.1.

Another operation that can be performed on rational numbers is the square root. Dealing with real numbers only, the positive square root of a number is equal to one of the two repeated positive factors of that number. For example:

$$\sqrt{49} = \sqrt{7 \times 7} = 7$$

A **perfect square** is a number that has a whole number as its square root. Examples of perfect squares are 1, 4, 9, 16, 25, etc. If a number is not a perfect square, an approximation can be used with a calculator. For example, $\sqrt{67} = 8.185$, rounded to the nearest thousandth place. The square root of a fraction involving perfect squares involves breaking up the problem into the square root of the numerator separate from the square root of the denominator. For example:

$$\frac{\sqrt{16}}{\sqrt{25}} \qquad \frac{\sqrt{16}}{\sqrt{25}} = \frac{4}{5} \qquad\qquad \frac{\sqrt{2}}{\sqrt{5}}$$

If the fraction does not contain perfect squares, a calculator can be used. Therefore, $\sqrt{\frac{2}{5}} = 0.632$, rounded to the nearest thousandth place. A common application of square roots involves the Pythagorean theorem. Given a right triangle, the sum of the squares of the two legs equals the square of the hypotenuse. For example, consider the following right triangle:

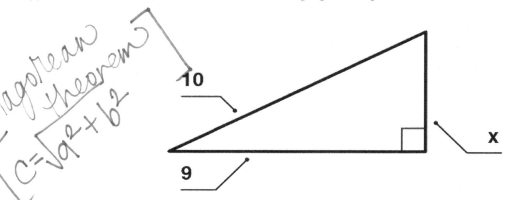

(handwritten: Pythagorean theorem $c = \sqrt{a^2 + b^2}$; triangle labeled h, b)

The missing side, x, can be found using the Pythagorean theorem. Since:

$$\qquad 9^2 + x^2 = 10^2$$

$$\qquad 81 + x^2 = 100$$

(handwritten: $10^2 = a^2 + b^2$ $a^2 + b^2 = c^2$ $9^2 + x^2 = 10^2$ $81 + x^2 = 100$)

which gives $x^2 = 19$. To solve for x, take the square root of both sides. Therefore, $x = \sqrt{19} = 4.36$, which has been rounded to two decimal places.

(handwritten: $\sqrt{x^2} = \sqrt{19}$)

In addition to the square root, the cube root is another operation. If a number is a **perfect cube**, the cube root of that number is equal to one of the three repeated factors. For example:

$$\sqrt[3]{27} = \sqrt[3]{3 \times 3 \times 3} = 3$$

Also, unlike square roots, a negative number has a cube root. The result is a negative number. For example:

$$\sqrt[3]{-27} = \sqrt[3]{(-3)(-3)(-3)} = -3$$

(handwritten: negative numbers have cube roots)

Similar to square roots, if the number is not a perfect cube, a calculator can be used to find an approximation. Therefore:

$$\sqrt[3]{\frac{2}{3}} = 0.873$$

rounded to the nearest thousandth place.

Higher-order roots also exist. The number relating to the root is known as the **index**. Given the following root, $\sqrt[3]{64}$, 3 is the index, and 64 is the **radicand**. The entire expression is known as the **radical**. Higher-order roots exist when the index is larger than 3. They can be broken up into two groups: even and odd roots. Even roots, when the index is an even number, follow the properties of square roots. A negative number does not have an even root, and an even root is found by finding the single factor that is repeated the same number of times as the index in the radicand. For example, the fifth root of 32 is equal to 2 because:

$$\sqrt[5]{32} = \sqrt[5]{2 \times 2 \times 2 \times 2 \times 2} = 2$$

Odd roots, when the index is an odd number, follow the properties of cube roots. A negative number has an odd root. Similarly, an odd root is found by finding the single factor that is repeated that many times to obtain the radicand. For example, the 4th root of 81 is equal to 3 because $3^4 = 81$. This radical is written as:

$3 \cdot 3 \cdot 3 \cdot 3$

$$\sqrt[4]{81} = 3$$

Higher-order roots can also be evaluated on fractions and decimals, for example, because:

$$\left(\frac{2}{7}\right)^4 = \frac{16}{2,401}$$

$$\sqrt[4]{\frac{16}{2,401}} = \frac{2}{7}$$

Because:

$$(0.1)^5 = 0.00001, \sqrt[5]{0.00001} = 0.1$$

When performing operations in rational numbers, sometimes it might be helpful to round the numbers in the original problem to get a rough check of what the answer should be. For example, if you walked into a grocery store and had a $20 bill, your approach might be to round each item to the nearest dollar and add up all the items to make sure that you will have enough money when you check out. This process involves obtaining an estimation of what the exact total would be. In other situations, it might be helpful to round to the nearest $10 amount or $100 amount. **Front-end rounding** might be helpful as well in many situations. In this type of rounding, each number is rounded to the highest possible place value. Therefore, all digits except the first digit become 0. Consider a situation in which you are at the furniture store and want to estimate your total on three pieces of furniture that cost $434.99, $678.99, and $129.99.

Front-end rounding would round these three amounts to $400, $700, and $100. Therefore, the estimate of your total would be:

$$\$400 + \$700 + \$100 = \$1,200$$

compared to the exact total of $1,243.97. In this situation, the estimate is not that far off the exact answer. Rounding is useful in both approximating an answer when an exact answer is not needed and for comparison when an exact answer is needed. For instance, if you had a complicated set of operations to complete and your estimate was $1,000, if you obtained an exact answer of $100,000, something is off. You might want to check your work to see if a mistake was made because an estimate should not be that different from an exact answer. Estimates can also be helpful with square roots. If a square root of a number is not known, the closest perfect square can be found for an approximation. For example, $\sqrt{50}$ is not equal to a whole number, but 50 is close to 49, which is a perfect square, and $\sqrt{49} = 7$. Therefore, $\sqrt{50}$ is a little bit larger than 7. The actual approximation, rounded to the nearest thousandth, is 7.071.

Using Inverse Operations to Solve Problems

Inverse operations can be used to solve problems where there is a missing value. The area for a rectangle may be given, along with the length, but the width may be unknown. This situation can be modeled by the equation:

$$\text{Area} = \text{Length} \times \text{Width}$$

The area is 40 square feet and the length is 10 feet. The equation becomes:

$$40 = 10 \times w$$

In order to find the w, we recognize that some number multiplied by 10 yields the number 40. The inverse operation to multiplication is division, so the 10 can be divided on both sides of the equation. This operation cancels out the 10 and yields an answer of 4 for the width. The following equation shows the work:

$$40 = 10 \times w$$

$$\frac{40}{10} = \frac{10 \times w}{10}$$

$$4 = w$$

Other inverse operations can be used to solve problems as well. The following equation can be solved for b:

$$b + 4 = 9$$

Because 4 is added to b, it can be subtracted on both sides of the equal sign to cancel out the four and solve for b, as follows:

$$b + 4 - 4 = 9 - 4$$

$$b = 5$$

Whatever operation is used in the equation, the inverse operation can be used and applied to both sides of the equals sign to solve for an unknown value.

Interpreting Remainders in Division Problems

Understanding remainders begins with understanding the division problem. The problem $24 \div 7$ can be read as "twenty-four divided by seven." The problem is asking how many groups of 7 will fit into 24. Counting by seven, the multiples are 7, 14, 21, 28. Twenty-one, which is three groups of 7, is the closest to 24. The difference between 21 and 24 is 3, which is called the remainder. This is a remainder because it is the number that is left out after the three groups of seven are taken from 24. The answer to this division problem can be written as 3 with a remainder 3, or $3\frac{3}{7}$. The fraction $\frac{3}{7}$ can be used because it shows the part of the whole left when the division is complete. Another division problem may have the following numbers: $36 \div 5$. This problem is asking how many groups of 5 will fit evenly into 36. When counting by multiples of 5, the following list is generated: 5, 10, 15, 20, 25, 30, 35, 40. As seen in the list, there are seven groups of five that make 35. To get to the total of 36, there needs to be one additional number. The answer to the division problem would be:

$$36 \div 5 = 7 \text{ R1}$$

or $7\frac{1}{5}$. The fractional part represents the number that cannot make up a whole group of five.

Various Strategies and Algorithms Used to Perform Operations on Rational Numbers

Rational numbers are any numbers that can be written as a fraction of integers. Operations to be performed on rational numbers include adding, subtracting, multiplying, and dividing. Essentially, this refers to performing these operations on fractions. Adding and subtracting fractions must be completed by first finding the least common denominator. For example, the problem:

$$\frac{3}{5} + \frac{6}{7}$$

requires that the common multiple be found between 5 and 7. The smallest number that divides evenly by 5 and 7 is 35. For the denominators to become 35, they must be multiplied by 7 and 5 respectively. The fraction $\frac{3}{5}$ can be multiplied by 7 on the top and bottom to yield the fraction $\frac{21}{35}$. The fraction $\frac{6}{7}$ can be multiplied by 5 to yield the fraction $\frac{30}{35}$. Now that the fractions have the same denominator, the numerators can be added. The answer to the addition problem becomes:

$$\frac{3}{5} + \frac{6}{7} = \frac{21}{35} + \frac{30}{35} = \frac{51}{35}$$

The same technique can be used for subtraction of rational numbers. The operations multiplication and division may seem easier to perform because finding common denominators is unnecessary. If the problems reads

$$\frac{1}{3} \times \frac{4}{5}$$

then the numerators and denominators are multiplied by each other and the answer is found to be $\frac{4}{15}$. For division, the problem must be changed to multiplication before performing operations. The following words can be used to remember to leave, change, and flip before multiplying. If the problems reads:

$$\frac{3}{7} \div \frac{3}{4}$$

then the first fraction is *left* alone, the operation is *changed* to multiplication, and then the last fraction is *flipped*. The problem becomes:

$$\frac{3}{7} \times \frac{4}{3} = \frac{12}{21}$$

Rational numbers can also be negative. When two negative numbers are added, the result is a negative number with an even greater magnitude. When a negative number is added to a positive number, the result depends on the value of each addend. For example:

$$-4 + 8 = 4$$

because the positive number is larger than the negative number. For multiplying two negative numbers, the result is positive. For example:

$$-4 \times -3 = 12$$

where the negatives cancel out and yield a positive answer.

Recognizing Concepts of Rational Numbers and Their Operations

Rational numbers can be whole or negative numbers, fractions, or repeating decimals because these numbers can all be written as fractions. Whole numbers can be written as fractions; for example, 25 and 17 can be written as $\frac{25}{1}$ and $\frac{17}{1}$. One way of interpreting these fractions is to say that they are **ratios**, or comparisons of two quantities. The fractions given may represent 25 students to 1 classroom, or 17 desks to 1 computer lab. Repeating decimals can also be written as fractions of integers, such as 0.3333 and 0.6666667. These repeating decimals can be written as the fractions $\frac{1}{3}$ and $\frac{2}{3}$. Fractions can be described as having a part-to-whole relationship. The fraction $\frac{1}{3}$ may represent 1 piece of pizza out of the whole cut into 3 pieces. The fraction $\frac{2}{3}$ may represent 2 pieces of the same whole pizza. Adding the fractions $\frac{1}{3}$ and $\frac{2}{3}$ is as simple as adding the numerators, 1 and 2, because the denominator on both fractions is 3. This means the numbers in the numerators are referring to multiples of the same size piece of pizza. When adding these fractions, the result is $\frac{3}{3}$, or 1. Both of these numbers are rational and represent a whole, or in this problem, a whole pizza.

Other than fractions, rational numbers also include whole numbers and negative integers. When whole numbers are added, other than zero, the result is always greater than the addends. For example, the equation:

$$4 + 18 = 22$$

shows 4 increased by 18, with a result of 22. When subtracting rational numbers, sometimes the result is a negative number. For example, the equation:

$$5 - 12 = -7$$

shows that taking 12 away from 5 results in a negative answer because 5 is smaller than 12. The difference is -7 because the starting number is smaller than the number taken away. For multiplication and division, similar results are found. Multiplying rational numbers may look like the following equation:

$$5 \times 7 = 35$$

where both numbers are positive and whole, and the result is a larger number than the factors. The number 5 is counted 7 times, which results in a total of 35. Sometimes, the equation looks like:

$$-4 \times 3 = -12$$

so the result is negative because a positive number times a negative number gives a negative answer. The rule is that any time a negative number and a positive number are multiplied or divided, the result is negative.

Examples Where Multiplication Does Not Result in a Product Greater than Both Factors and Division Does Not Result in a Quotient Smaller than the Dividend

A common misconception of multiplication is that it always results in a value greater than the beginning number, or factors. This is not always the case. When working with fractions, multiplication may be used to take part of another number. For example, $\frac{1}{2} \times \frac{1}{4}$ can be read as "one-half times one-fourth," or taking one-half of one-fourth. The latter translation makes it easier to understand the concept. Taking half of one-fourth will result in a smaller number that one-fourth. It will result in one-eighth. The same happens with multiplying two-thirds times three-fifths, or $\frac{2}{3} \times \frac{3}{5}$. The concept of taking two-thirds, which is a part, of three-fifths, means that there will be an even smaller part as the result. Multiplication of these two fractions yields the answer $\frac{6}{15}$, or $\frac{2}{5}$.

In the same way, another misconception is that division always has results smaller than the beginning number or dividend. When working with whole numbers, division asks how many times a whole goes into another whole. This result will always be smaller than the dividend, where $6 \div 2 = 3$ and $20 \div 5 = 4$. When working with fractions, the number of times a part goes into another part depends on the value of each fraction. For example, three-fourths divided by one-fourth, or $\frac{3}{4} \div \frac{1}{4}$, asks to find how many times $\frac{1}{4}$ will go into $\frac{3}{4}$. Because these have the same denominator, the numerators can be compared as is, without needing to convert the fractions. The result is easily found to be 3 because one goes into three 3 times.

Composing and Decomposing Fractions

Fractions are ratios of whole numbers and their negatives. Fractions represent parts of wholes, whether pies, or money, or work. The number on top, or numerator, represents the part, and the bottom number, or denominator, represents the whole. The number $\frac{1}{2}$ represents half of a whole. Other ways to represent one-half are $\frac{2}{4}, \frac{3}{6}$, and $\frac{5}{10}$. These are fractions not written in simplest form, but the numerators are all halves of the denominators. The fraction $\frac{1}{4}$ represents 1 part to a whole of 4 parts. This can be modeled by the quarter's value in relation to the dollar. One quarter is $\frac{1}{4}$ of a dollar. In the same way, 2 quarters make up $\frac{1}{2}$ of a dollar, so 2 fractions of $\frac{1}{4}$ make up a fraction of $\frac{1}{2}$. Three quarters make up three-fourths of a dollar. The three fractions of $\frac{1}{4} + \frac{1}{4} + \frac{1}{4}$ are equal to $\frac{3}{4}$ of a whole. This illustration can be seen using the bars below divided into one whole, then two halves, then three sections of one-third, then four sections of one-fourth. Based on the size of the fraction, different numbers of each fraction are needed to make up a whole.

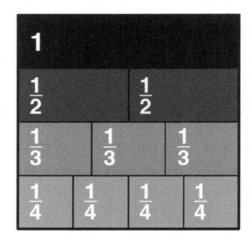

Recognizing That the Value of a Unit Fraction Decreases as the Value of the Denominator Increases

A **unit fraction** is a fraction where the numerator has a value of one. The fractions one-half, one-third, one-seventh, and one-tenth are all examples of unit fractions. Nonexamples of unit fractions include three-fourths, four-fifths, and seven-twelfths. The value of unit fractions changes as the denominator changes, because the numerator is always one. The unit fraction one-half requires two parts to make a whole. The unit fraction one-third requires three parts to make a whole. In the same way, if the unit fraction changes to one-thirteenth, then the number of parts required to make a whole becomes thirteen. An illustration of this is seen in the figure below. As the denominator increases, the size of the parts for each fraction decreases. As the bar goes from one-fourth to one-fifth, the size of the bars decreases, but

unit fraction = $\frac{1}{X}$

104

the size of the denominator increases to five. This pattern continues down the diagram as the bars, or value of the fraction, get smaller, the denominator gets larger.

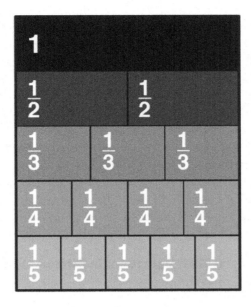

Using the Same Whole When Comparing Fractions

Comparing fractions requires the use of a common denominator. This necessity can be seen by the two pies below. The first pie has a shaded value of $\frac{2}{10}$ because two pieces are shaded out of the total of ten equal pieces. The second pie has a shaded value of $\frac{2}{7}$ because two pieces are shaded out of a total of seven equal pieces. These two fractions, two-tenths and two-sevenths, have the same numerator and so a misconception may be that they are equal. By looking at the shaded region in each pie, it is apparent that the fractions are not equal. The numerators are the same, but the denominators are not. Two parts of a whole are not equivalent unless the whole is broken into the same number of parts. To compare the shaded regions, the denominators seven and ten must be made equal. The lowest number that the two denominators will both divide evenly into is 70, which is the lowest common denominator. Then the numerators must be converted by multiplying by the opposite denominator. These operations result in the two fractions $\frac{14}{70}$ and $\frac{20}{70}$. Now that these two have the same denominator, the conclusion can be made that $\frac{2}{7}$ represents a larger portion of the pie, as seen in the figure below.

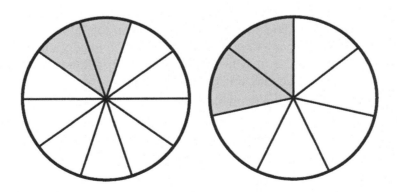

PEMDAS → left to right for add & sub.

Solving Problems Using the Order of Operations

The **order of operations** refers to the order in which problems are to be solved, from parenthesis or grouping, to addition and subtraction. A common way of remembering the order of operations is PEMDAS, or "Please Excuse My Dear Aunt Sally." The letters stand for parenthesis, or grouping, exponents, multiply/divide, and add/subtract. The first step is to complete any operations inside the grouping symbols, or parenthesis. The next step is to simplify all exponents. After exponents, the operations of multiplication and division are performed in the order they appear from left to right. The last operations are addition and subtraction, also performed from left to right. The following problem requires the use of order of operations to be solved: $2(3^3 + 5) - 8$. The first step is to perform the operations inside the grouping symbols, or parenthesis. Inside the parenthesis, the exponent would be performed first, then the addition of $(3^3 + 5)$ which is $(27 + 5)$ or (32). These operations lead to the next step of $2(32) - 8$, where the multiplication can be performed between 2 and 8. This step leads to the problem $64 - 8$, where the answer is 56. The order of operations is important because if solved in a different order, the resulting number would not be 56. A common of when the order of operations can be used is when a store is having a sale and customers may use coupons. Other places may be at a restaurant, for the check, or the gas station when using a card to pay.

Representing Rational Numbers and Their Operations in Different Ways

Rational numbers can be written as fractions, but also as a percent or decimal. For example, three-fourths is a fraction written as three divided by four or $\frac{3}{4}$. It represents three parts out of a whole of four parts. By dividing three by four, the decimal of 0.75 is found. This decimal represents the same part to whole relationship as three-fourths. Seventy-five is in the hundredths place, so it can be read as 75 out of 100, the same ratio as 3 to 4. The decimal 0.75 is the same as 75 out of 100, or 75%. The rational number three-fourths represents the same portion as the decimal 0.75 and the percentage 75%. Because there are different ways to represent rational numbers, the operations used to manipulate rational numbers can look different also. For the operation of multiplication, the problem can use a dot, an "x," or simply writing two variables side by side to indicate the need to find the product. Division can be represented by the line in a fraction or a division symbol. When adding or subtracting, the form of rational numbers is important and can be changed. Sometimes it is simpler to work with fractions, while sometimes decimals are easier to manipulate, depending on the operation. When comparing portion size, it may be easier to see each number as a percent, so it is important to understand the different ways rational numbers can be represented.

Representing Rational Numbers and Sums and Differences of Rational Numbers on a Number Line

A **number line** is a tool used to compare numbers by showing where they fall in relation to one another. Labeling a number line with integers is simple because they have no fractional component and the values are easier to understand. The number line may start at -3 and go up to -2, then -1, then 0, and 1, 2, 3. This order shows that number 2 is larger than -1 because it falls further to the right on the number line. When positioning rational numbers, the process may take more time because it requires that they all be in the same form. If they are percentages, fractions, and decimals, then conversions will have to be made to put them in the same form. For example, if the numbers $\frac{5}{4}$, 45%, and 2.38 need to be put in order on a number line, the numbers must first be transformed into one single form. Decimal form is an easy common ground because fractions can be changed by simply dividing and percentages can be changed by moving the decimal point. After conversions are made, the list becomes 1.25, 0.45, and 2.38 respectively. Now the list is easier to arrange. The number line with the list in order is shown in the top half of the graphic below in the order 0.45, 1.25, and 2.38.

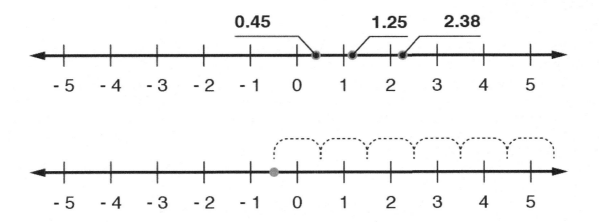

The sums and differences of rational numbers can be found using a number line after the rational numbers are put into the same form. This method is especially helpful when understanding the addition and subtraction of negative numbers. For example, the rational number six can be added to negative one-half using the number line. The following expression represents the problem: $-\frac{1}{2} + 6$. First, the original number $-\frac{1}{2}$ can be labeled as in the lower half of the graphic above, by the dot. Then 6 can be added by counting by whole numbers on the number line. The arcs on the graph represent the addition. The final answer is positive $5\frac{1}{2}$.

Illustrating and Explaining Multiplication and Division Problems Using Equations, Rectangular Arrays, and Area Models

Multiplication and division can be represented by equations. These equations show the numbers involved and the operation. For example, "eight multiplied by six equals forty-eight" is seen in the following equation: $8 \times 6 = 48$. This operation can be modeled by rectangular arrays where one factor, 8, is the number of rows, and the other factor, 6, is the number of columns, as follows:

Array of 8 x 6 = 48

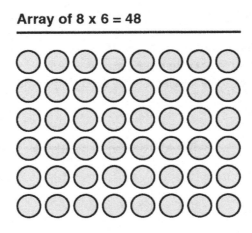

Rectangular arrays show what happens with the concept of multiplication. As one row of dots is drawn, that represents the first factor in the problem. Then the second factor is used to add the number of columns. The final model includes six rows of eight columns which results in forty-eight dots. These rectangular arrays show how multiplication of whole numbers will result in a number larger than the factors.

Division can also be represented by equations and area models. A division problem such as "twenty-four divided by three equals eight" can be written as the following equation: $24 \div 8 = 3$. The object below shows an area model to represent the equation. As seen in the model, the whole box represents 24 and the 3 sections represent the division by 3. In more detail, there could be 24 dots written in the whole box and each box could have 8 dots in it. Division shows how numbers can be divided into groups. For the example problem, it is asking how many numbers will be in each of the 3 groups that together make 24. The answer is 8 in each group.

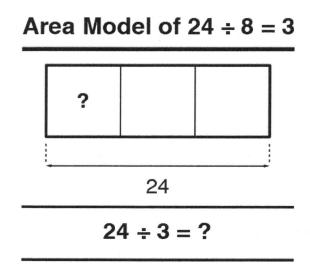

Area Model of $24 \div 8 = 3$

$$24 \div 3 = ?$$

Comparing, Classifying, and Ordering Rational Numbers

Whole numbers are the numbers 0, 1, 2, 3, ... Examples of other whole numbers would be 413 and 8,431. Notice that numbers such as 4.13 and $\frac{1}{4}$ are not included in whole numbers. **Counting numbers**, also known as **natural numbers**, consist of all whole numbers except for the zero. In set notation, the natural numbers are the set $\{1, 2, 3, ...\}$. The entire set of whole numbers and negative versions of those same numbers comprise the set of numbers known as integers. Therefore, in set notation, the integers are $\{..., -3, -2, -1, 0, 1, 2, 3, ...\}$. Examples of other integers are $-4,981$ and $90,131$. A number line is a great way to visualize the integers. Integers are labeled on the following number line:

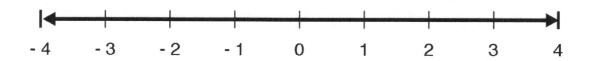

numerator
denominator

The arrows on the right- and left-hand sides of the number line show that the line continues indefinitely in both directions.

Fractions also exist on the number line as parts of a whole. For example, if an entire pie is cut into two pieces, each piece is half of the pie, or $\frac{1}{2}$. The top number in any fraction, known as the **numerator**, defines how many parts there are. The bottom number, known as the **denominator**, states how many pieces the whole is divided into. Fractions can also be negative or written in their corresponding decimal form.

A **decimal** is a number that uses a decimal point and numbers to the right of the decimal point representing the part of the number that is less than 1. For example, 3.5 is a decimal and is equivalent to the fraction $\frac{7}{2}$ or mixed number $3\frac{1}{2}$. The decimal is found by dividing 2 into 7. Other examples of fractions are $\frac{2}{7}, \frac{-3}{14},$ and $\frac{14}{27}$.

Any number that can be expressed as a fraction is known as a **rational number**. Basically, if a and b are any integers and $b \neq 0$, then $\frac{a}{b}$ is a rational number. Any integer can be written as a fraction where the denominator is 1, so therefore the rational numbers consist of all fractions and all integers.

Any number that is not rational is known as an irrational number. Consider the number $\pi =$ 3.141592654 .... The decimal portion of that number extends indefinitely. In that situation, a number can never be written as a fraction. Another example of an irrational number is $\sqrt{2} = 1.414213662$ .... Again, this number cannot be written as a ratio of two integers.

Together, the set of all rational and irrational numbers makes up the real numbers. The number line contains all real numbers. To graph a number other than an integer on a number line, it needs to be plotted between two integers. For example, 3.5 would be plotted halfway between 3 and 4.

Even numbers are integers that are divisible by 2. For example, 6, 100, 0, and −200 are all even numbers. Odd numbers are integers that are not divisible by 2. If an odd number is divided by 2, the result is a fraction. For example, −5, 11, and −121 are odd numbers.

Prime numbers consist of natural numbers greater than 1 that are not divisible by any other natural numbers other than themselves and 1. For example, 3, 5, and 7 are prime numbers. If a natural number is not prime, it is known as a composite number. 8 is a composite number because it is divisible by both 2 and 4, which are natural numbers other than itself and 1.

The **absolute value** of any real number is the distance from that number to 0 on the number line. The absolute value of a number can never be negative. For example, the absolute value of both 8 and −8 is 8 because they are both 8 units away from 0 on the number line. This is written as $|8| = |-8| = 8$.

Ordering and Comparing Rational Numbers
Ordering rational numbers is a way to compare two or more different numerical values. Determining whether two amounts are equal, less than, or greater than is the basis for comparing both positive and negative numbers. Also, a group of numbers can be compared by ordering them from the smallest amount to the largest amount. A few symbols are necessary to use when ordering rational numbers. The equals sign, =, shows that the two quantities on either side of the symbol have the same value. For example, $\frac{12}{3} = 4$ because both values are equivalent. Another symbol that is used to compare numbers is <, which represents "less than." With this symbol, the smaller number is placed on the left and the larger

number is placed on the right. Always remember that the symbol's "mouth" opens up to the larger number. When comparing negative and positive numbers, it is important to remember that the number occurring to the left on the number line is always smaller and is placed to the left of the symbol. This idea might seem confusing because some values could appear to be larger, even though they are not. For example, $-5 < 4$ is read "negative 5 is less than 4." Here is an image of a number line for help:

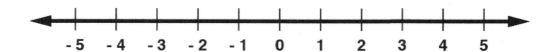

The symbol $\leq$ represents "less than or equal to," and it joins $<$ with equality. Therefore, both $-5 \leq 4$ and $-5 \leq -5$ are true statements and "-5 is less than or equal to both 4 and -5." Other symbols are $>$ and $\geq$, which represent "greater than" and "greater than or equal to." Both $4 \geq -1$ and $-1 \geq -1$ are correct ways to use these symbols.

Here is a chart of these four inequality symbols:

Symbol	Definition
<	less than
≤	less than or equal to
>	greater than
≥	greater than or equal to

Comparing integers is a straightforward process, especially when using the number line, but the comparison of decimals and fractions is not as obvious. When comparing two non-negative decimals, compare digit by digit, starting from the left. The larger value contains the first larger digit. For example, 0.1456 is larger than 0.1234 because the value 4 in the hundredths place in the first decimal is larger than the value 2 in the hundredths place in the second decimal. When comparing a fraction with a decimal, convert the fraction to a decimal and then compare in the same manner. Finally, there are a few options when comparing fractions. If two non-negative fractions have the same denominator, the fraction with the larger numerator is the larger value. If they have different denominators, they can be converted to equivalent fractions with a common denominator to be compared, or they can be converted to decimals to be compared. When comparing two negative decimals or fractions, a different approach must be used. It is important to remember that the smaller number exists to the left on the number line. Therefore, when comparing two negative decimals by place value, the number with the larger first place value is smaller due to the negative sign. Whichever value is closer to 0 is larger. For instance, -0.456 is larger than -0.498 because of the values in the hundredth places. If two negative fractions have the same denominator, the fraction with the larger numerator is smaller because of the negative sign.

Converting Between Fractions, Decimals, and Percents

Within the number system, different forms of numbers can be used. It is important to be able to recognize each type, as well as work with, and convert between, the given forms. The **real number system** comprises natural numbers, whole numbers, integers, rational numbers, and irrational numbers. Natural numbers, whole numbers, integers, and irrational numbers typically are not represented as fractions, decimals, or percentages. Rational numbers, however, can be represented as any of these three forms. A **rational number** is a number that can be written in the form $\frac{a}{b}$, where a and b are integers, and b is not equal to zero. In other words, rational numbers can be written in a fraction form. The value a is the **numerator**, and b is the **denominator**.

If the numerator is equal to zero, the entire fraction is equal to zero. Non-negative fractions can be less than 1, equal to 1, or greater than 1. Fractions are less than 1 if the numerator is smaller (less than) than the denominator. For example, $\frac{3}{4}$ is less than 1. A fraction is equal to 1 if the numerator is equal to the denominator. For instance, $\frac{4}{4}$ is equal to 1. Finally, a fraction is greater than 1 if the numerator is greater than the denominator: the fraction $\frac{11}{4}$ is greater than 1.

When the numerator is greater than the denominator, the fraction is called an **improper fraction**. An improper fraction can be converted to a mixed number, a combination of both a whole number and a fraction. To convert an improper fraction to a mixed number, divide the numerator by the denominator. Write down the whole number portion, and then write any remainder over the original denominator. For example, $\frac{11}{4}$ is equivalent to $2\frac{3}{4}$. Conversely, a mixed number can be converted to an improper fraction by multiplying the denominator by the whole number and adding that result to the numerator.

Fractions can be converted to decimals. With a calculator, a fraction is converted to a decimal by dividing the numerator by the denominator. For example:

$$\frac{2}{5} = 2 \div 5 = 0.4$$

Sometimes, rounding might be necessary. Consider:

$$\frac{2}{7} = 2 \div 7 = 0.28571429$$

This decimal could be rounded for ease of use, and if it needed to be rounded to the nearest thousandth, the result would be 0.286. If a calculator is not available, a fraction can be converted to a decimal manually. First, find a number that, when multiplied by the denominator, has a value equal to 10, 100, 1,000, etc. Then, multiply both the numerator and denominator times that number. The decimal form of the fraction is equal to the new numerator with a decimal point placed as many place values to the left as there are zeros in the denominator. For example, to convert $\frac{3}{5}$ to a decimal, multiply both the numerator and denominator times 2, which results in $\frac{6}{10}$. The decimal is equal to 0.6 because there is one zero in the denominator, and so the decimal place in the numerator is moved one unit to the left. In the case where rounding would be necessary while working without a calculator, an approximation must be found. A number close to 10, 100, 1,000, etc. can be used. For example, to convert $\frac{1}{3}$ to a decimal, the numerator and denominator can be multiplied by 33 to turn the denominator into approximately 100, which makes for an easier conversion to the equivalent decimal. This process results in $\frac{33}{99}$ and an approximate decimal of 0.33. Once in decimal form, the number can be converted to a percentage. Multiply the decimal by 100 and then place a percent sign after the number. For example, 0.614 is equal to 61.4%. In other words, move the decimal place two units to the right and add the percentage symbol.

Applying the Concepts of Ratios and Unit Rates to Describe Relationships Between Two Quantities

Recall that a ratio is the comparison of two different quantities. Comparing 2 apples to 3 oranges results in the ratio 2:3, which can be expressed as the fraction $\frac{2}{5}$. Note that order is important when discussing ratios. The number mentioned first is the antecedent, and the number mentioned second is the consequent. Note that the consequent of the ratio and the denominator of the fraction are *not* the same. When there are 2 apples to 3 oranges, there are five fruit total; two fifths of the fruit are apples, while three fifths are oranges. The ratio 2:3 represents a different relationship that the ratio 3:2. Also, it is important to make sure that when discussing ratios that have units attached to them, the two quantities use the same units. For example, to think of 8 feet to 4 yards, it would make sense to convert 4 yards to feet by multiplying by 3. Therefore, the ratio would be 8 feet to 12 feet, which can be expressed as the fraction $\frac{8}{20}$. Also, note that it is proper to refer to ratios in lowest terms. Therefore, the ratio of 8 feet to 4 yards is equivalent to the fraction $\frac{2}{5}$.

Many real-world problems involve ratios. Often, problems with ratios involve proportions, as when two ratios are set equal to find the missing amount. However, some problems involve deciphering single ratios. For example, consider an amusement park that sold 345 tickets last Saturday. If 145 tickets were sold to adults and the rest of the tickets were sold to children, what would the ratio of the number of adult tickets to children's tickets be? A common mistake would be to say the ratio is 145:345. However, 345 is the total number of tickets sold, not the number of children's tickets. There were $345 - 145 = 200$ tickets sold to children. The correct ratio of adult to children's tickets is 145:200. As a fraction, this expression is written as $\frac{145}{345}$, which can be reduced to $\frac{29}{69}$.

While a ratio compares two measurements using the same units, rates compare two measurements with different units. Examples of rates would be $200 for 8 hours of work, or 500 miles traveled per 20 gallons. Because the units are different, it is important to always include the units when discussing rates. Rates can be easily seen because if they are expressed in words, the two quantities are usually split up using one of the following words: *for, per, on, from, in.* Just as with ratios, it is important to write rates in lowest terms. A common rate that can be found in many real-life situations is cost per unit. This quantity describes how much one item or one unit costs. This rate allows the best buy to be determined, given a couple of different sizes of an item with different costs. For example, if 2 quarts of soup was sold for $3.50 and 3 quarts was sold for $4.60, to determine the best buy, the cost per quart should be found. $\frac{\$3.50}{2 \text{ qt}} = \$1.75$ per quart, and $\frac{\$4.60}{3 \text{ qt}} = \$1.53$ per quart. Therefore, the better deal would be the 3-quart option.

Rate of change problems involve calculating a quantity per some unit of measurement. Usually the unit of measurement is time. For example, meters per second is a common rate of change. To calculate this measurement, find the amount traveled in meters and divide by total time traveled. The calculation is an average of the speed over the entire time interval. Another common rate of change used in the real world is miles per hour. Consider the following problem that involves calculating an average rate of change in temperature. Last Saturday, the temperature at 1:00 a.m. was 34 degrees Fahrenheit, and at noon, the temperature had increased to 75 degrees Fahrenheit. What was the average rate of change over that time interval? The average rate of change is calculated by finding the change in temperature and dividing by the total hours elapsed.

112

Therefore, the rate of change was equal to:

$$\frac{75-34}{12-1} = \frac{41}{11} \text{ degrees per hour}$$

This quantity rounded to two decimal places is equal to 3.72 degrees per hour.

A common rate of change that appears in algebra is the slope calculation. Given a linear equation in one variable, $y = mx + b$, the *slope, m,* is equal to $\frac{rise}{run}$ or $\frac{change\ in\ y}{change\ in\ x}$. In other words, slope is equivalent to the ratio of the vertical and horizontal changes between any two points on a line. The vertical change is known as the *rise*, and the horizontal change is known as the *run*. Given any two points on a line (x_1, y_1) and (x_2, y_2), slope can be calculated with the formula:

$$m = \frac{y_2 - y_1}{x_2 - x_1} = \frac{\Delta y}{\Delta x}$$

Common real-world applications of slope include determining how steep a staircase should be, calculating how steep a road is, and determining how to build a wheelchair ramp.

Many times, problems involving rates and ratios involve proportions. A proportion states that two ratios (or rates) are equal. The property of cross products can be used to determine if a proportion is true, meaning both ratios are equivalent. If $\frac{a}{b} = \frac{c}{d}$, then to clear the fractions, multiply both sides by the least common denominator, bd. This results in $ad = bc$, which is equal to the result of multiplying along both diagonals. For example, $\frac{4}{40} = \frac{1}{10}$ grants the cross product $4 \times 10 = 40 \times 1$, which is equivalent to $40 = 40$ and shows that this proportion is true. Cross products are used when proportions are involved in real-world problems.

Consider the following: If 3 pounds of fertilizer will cover 75 square feet of grass, how many pounds are needed for 375 square feet? To solve this problem, a proportion can be set up using two ratios. Let x equal the unknown quantity, pounds needed for 375 feet. Then, the equation found by setting the two given ratios equal to one another is $\frac{3}{75} = \frac{x}{375}$. Cross-multiplication gives:

$$3 \times 375 = 75x$$

Therefore, $1,125 = 75x$. Divide both sides by 75 to get $x = 15$. Therefore, 15 pounds of fertilizer are needed to cover 375 square feet of grass.

Another application of proportions involves similar triangles. If two triangles have the same measurement as two triangles in another triangle, the triangles are said to be **similar**. If two are the same, the third pair of angles are equal as well because the sum of all angles in a triangle is equal to 180 degrees. Each pair of equivalent angles are known as **corresponding angles**. **Corresponding sides** face the corresponding angles, and it is true that corresponding sides are in proportion. For example, consider the following set of similar triangles:

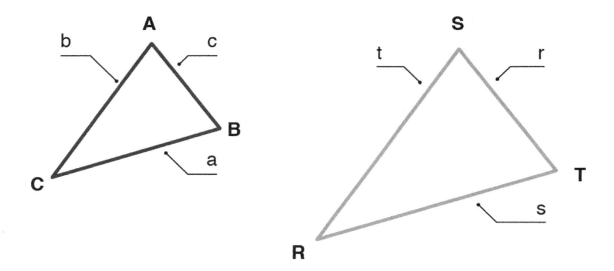

Angles A and S have the same measurement, angles C and R have the same measurement, and angles B and T have the same measurement. Therefore, the following proportion can be set up from the sides:

$$\frac{c}{r} = \frac{a}{s} = \frac{b}{t}$$

This proportion can be helpful in finding missing lengths in pairs of similar triangles. For example, if the following triangles are similar, a proportion can be used to find the missing side lengths, a and b.

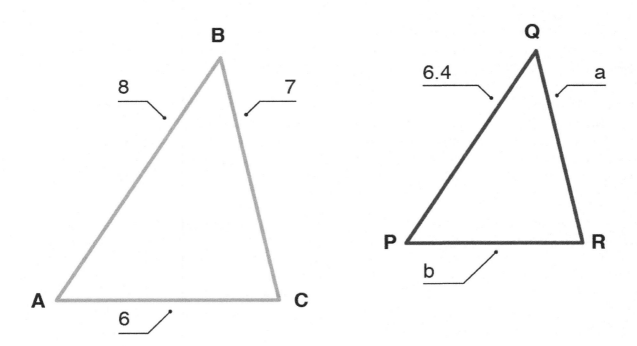

The proportions $\frac{8}{6.4} = \frac{6}{b}$ and $\frac{8}{6.4} = \frac{7}{a}$ can both be cross multiplied and solved to obtain $a = 5.6$ and $b = 4.8$.

A real-life situation that uses similar triangles involves measuring shadows to find heights of unknown objects. Consider the following problem: A building casts a shadow that is 120 feet long, and at the same time, another building that is 80 feet high casts a shadow that is 60 feet long. How tall is the first building? Each building, together with the sun rays and shadows casted on the ground, forms a triangle. They are similar because each building forms a right angle with the ground, and the sun rays form equivalent angles. Therefore, these two pairs of angles are both equal. Because all angles in a triangle add up to 180 degrees, the third angles are equal as well. Both shadows form corresponding sides of the triangle, the buildings form corresponding sides, and the sun rays form corresponding sides. Therefore, the triangles are similar, and the following proportion can be used to find the missing building length:

$$\frac{120}{x} = \frac{60}{80}$$

Cross-multiply to obtain the cross products, $9600 = 60x$. Then, divide both sides by 60 to obtain $x = 160$. This solution means that the other building is 160 feet high.

Understanding Percent as a Rate per 100

Percentages are defined to be parts per one hundred. To convert a decimal to a percentage, move the decimal point two units to the right and place the percent sign after the number. Percentages appear in many scenarios in the real world. It is important to make sure the statement containing the percentage is translated to a correct mathematical expression. Be aware that it is extremely common to make a mistake when working with percentages within word problems.

An example of a word problem containing a percentage is the following: 35% of people speed when driving to work. In a group of 5,600 commuters, how many would be expected to speed on the way to their place of employment? The answer to this problem is found by finding 35% of 5,600. First, change the percentage to the decimal 0.35. Then compute the product: $0.35 \times 5,600 = 1,960$. Therefore, it would be expected that 1,960 of those commuters would speed on their way to work based on the data given. In this situation, the word "of" signals to use multiplication to find the answer. Another way percentages are used is in the following problem: Teachers work 8 months out of the year. What percent of the year do they work? To answer this problem, find what percent of 12 the number 8 is, because there are 12 months in a year. Divide 8 by 12 and convert that number to a percentage: $\frac{8}{12} = \frac{2}{3} = 0.66\overline{6}$. The percentage rounded to the nearest tenth place tells us that teachers work 66.7% of the year. Percentages also appear in real-world application problems involving finding missing quantities like in the following question: 60% of what number is 75? To find the missing quantity, an equation can be used. Let x be equal to the missing quantity. Therefore, $0.60x = 75$. Divide each side by 0.60 to obtain 125. Therefore, 60% of 125 is equal to 75.

Sales tax is an important application relating to percentages because tax rates are usually given as percentages. For example, a city might have an 8% sales tax rate. Therefore, when an item is purchased with that tax rate, the real cost to the customer is 1.08 times the price in the store. For example, a $25 pair of jeans costs the customer $25 \times 1.08 = 27. Sales tax rates can also be determined if they are unknown when an item is purchased. If a customer visits a store and purchases an item for $21.44, but the price in the store was $19, they can find the tax rate by first subtracting $21.44 - $19 to obtain $2.44, the sales tax amount. The sales tax is a percentage of the in-store price. Therefore, the tax rate is $\frac{2.44}{19} = 0.128$, which has been rounded to the nearest thousandths place. In this scenario, the actual sales tax rate given as a percentage is 12.8%.

Solving Unit Rate Problems

A **unit rate** is a rate with a denominator of one. It is a comparison of two values with different units where one value is equal to one. Examples of unit rates include 60 miles per hour and 200 words per minute. Problems involving unit rates may require some work to find the unit rate. For example, if Mary travels 360 miles in 5 hours, what is her speed, expressed as a unit rate? The rate can be expressed as the following fraction: $\frac{360 \ miles}{5 \ hours}$. The denominator can be changed to one by dividing by five. The numerator will also need to be divided by five to follow the rules of equality. This division turns the fraction into $\frac{72 \ miles}{1 \ hour}$, which can now be labeled as a unit rate because one unit has a value of one. Another type question involves the use of unit rates to solve problems. For example, if Trey needs to read 300 pages and his average speed is 75 pages per hour, will he be able to finish the reading in 5 hours? The unit rate is 75 pages per hour, so the total of 300 pages can be divided by 75 to find the time. After the division, the time it takes to read is four hours. The answer to the question is yes, Trey will finish the reading within 5 hours.

Using Proportional Relationships to Solve Ratio and Percent Problems

Fractions appear in everyday situations, and in many scenarios, they appear in the real-world as ratios and in proportions. A **ratio** is formed when two different quantities are compared. For example, in a group of 50 people, if there are 33 females and 17 males, the ratio of females to males is 33 to 17. This expression can be written in the fraction form as $\frac{33}{50}$, where the denominator is the sum of females and males, or by using the ratio symbol, 33:17. The order of the number matters when forming ratios. In the same setting, the ratio of males to females is 17 to 33, which is equivalent to $\frac{17}{50}$ or 17:33. A **proportion** is an equation involving two ratios. The equation $\frac{a}{b} = \frac{c}{d}$, or $a:b = c:d$ is a proportion, for real numbers a, b, c, and d. Usually, in one ratio, one of the quantities is unknown, and cross-multiplication is used to solve for the unknown. Consider $\frac{1}{4} = \frac{x}{5}$. To solve for x, cross-multiply to obtain $5 = 4x$. Divide each side by 4 to obtain the solution $x = \frac{5}{4}$. It is also true that percentages are ratios in which the second term is 100 minus the first term. For example, 65% is 65:35 or $\frac{65}{100}$. Therefore, when working with percentages, one is also working with ratios.

Real-world problems frequently involve proportions. For example, consider the following problem: If 2 out of 50 pizzas are usually delivered late from a local Italian restaurant, how many would be late out of 235 orders? The following proportion would be solved with x as the unknown quantity of late pizzas: $\frac{2}{50} = \frac{x}{235}$. Cross multiplying results in $470 = 50x$. Divide both sides by 50 to obtain $x = \frac{470}{50}$, which in lowest terms is equal to $\frac{47}{5}$. In decimal form, this improper fraction is equal to 9.4. Because it does not make sense to answer this question with decimals (portions of pizzas do not get delivered) the answer must be rounded. Traditional rounding rules would say that 9 pizzas would be expected to be delivered late. However, to be safe, rounding up to 10 pizzas out of 235 would probably make more sense.

Prime and Composite Numbers

A **prime number** is a whole number greater than 1 that can only be divided by 1 and itself. Examples are 2, 3, 5, 7, and 11. A **composite number** can be evenly divided by a number other than 1 and itself. Examples of composite numbers are 4 and 9. Four can be divided evenly by 1, 2, and 4. Nine can be divided evenly by 1, 3, and 9. When given a list of numbers, one way to determine which ones are prime or composite is to find the **prime factorization** of each number. For example, a list of numbers may include 13 and 24. The prime factorization of 13 is 1 and 13 because those are the only numbers that go into it evenly, so it is a prime number. The prime factorization of 24 is $2 \times 2 \times 2 \times 3$ because those are the prime numbers that multiply together to get 24. This also shows that 24 is a composite number because 2 and 3 are factors along with 1 and 24.

Finding Factors and Multiples of Numbers

Factorization is the process of breaking up a mathematical quantity, such as a number or polynomial, into a product of two or more factors. For example, a factorization of the number 16 is $16 = 8 \times 2$. If multiplied out, the factorization results in the original number. A **prime factorization** is a specific factorization when the number is factored completely using prime numbers only. For example, the prime factorization of 16 is:

$$16 = 2 \times 2 \times 2 \times 2$$

A factor tree can be used to find the prime factorization of any number. Within a factor tree, pairs of factors are found until no other factors can be used, as in the following factor tree of the number 84:

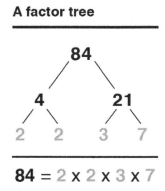

A factor tree

84 = 2 x 2 x 3 x 7

It first breaks 84 into 21×4, which is not a prime factorization. Then, both 21 and 4 are factored into their primes. The final numbers on each branch consist of the numbers within the prime factorization. Also, a factorization of an algebraic expression can be found. Throughout the process, a more complicated expression can be decomposed into products of simpler expressions. To factor a polynomial, first determine if there is a greatest common factor. If there is, factor it out. For example, $2x^2 + 8x$ has a greatest common factor of $2x$ and can be written as $2x(x + 4)$. Once the greatest common monomial factor is factored out, if applicable, count the number of terms in the polynomial. If there are two terms, is it a difference of squares, a sum of cubes, or a difference of cubes? If so, the following rules can be used:

$$a^2 - b^2 = (a + b)(a - b)$$

$$a^3 + b^3 = (a + b)(a^2 - ab + b^2)$$

$$a^3 - b^3 = (a - b)(a^2 + ab + b^2)$$

If there are three terms, and if the trinomial is a perfect square trinomial, it can be factored into the following:

$$a^2 + 2ab + b^2 = (a + b)^2$$

$$a^2 - 2ab + b^2 = (a - b)^2$$

If not, try factoring into a product of two binomials by trial and error into a form of $(x + p)(x + q)$. For example, to factor $x^2 + 6x + 8$, determine what two numbers have a product of 8 and a sum of 6. Those numbers are 4 and 2, so the trinomial factors into $(x + 2)(x + 4)$.

Finally, if there are four terms, try factoring by grouping. First, group terms together that have a common monomial factor. Then, factor out the common monomial factor from the first two terms. Next, look to see if a common factor can be factored out of the second set of two terms that results in a common binomial factor.

Finally, factor out the common binomial factor of each expression, for example:

$$xy - x + 5y - 5$$

$$x(y - 1) + 5(y - 1)$$

$$(y - 1)(x + 5)$$

After the expression is completely factored, check to see if the factorization is correct by multiplying to try to obtain the original expression. Factorizations are helpful in solving equations that consist of a polynomial set equal to 0. If the product of two algebraic expressions equals 0, then at least one of the factors is equal to 0. Therefore, factor the polynomial within the equation, set each factor equal to 0, and solve. For example, $x^2 + 7x - 18 = 0$ can be solved by factoring into:

$$(x + 9)(x - 2) = 0$$

Set each factor equal to 0, and solve to obtain $x = -9$ and $x = 2$.

A **multiple** of a number is the result of multiplying that number by an integer. For example, some multiples of 3 are 6, 9, 12, 15, and 18. These multiples are found by multiplying 3 by 2, 3, 4, 5, and 6, respectively. Some multiples of 5 include 5, 10, 15, and 20. This also means that 5 is a factor of 5, 10, 15, and 20. Some questions may ask which numbers in a list are multiples of a given number. For example, find and circle the multiples of 12 in the following list: 136, 144, 312, 400. If a number is evenly divisible by 12, then it is a multiple of 12. The numbers 144 and 312 are multiples of 12 because 12 times 12 is 144, and 12 times 26 is 312. The other numbers, 136 and 400, are not multiples because they yield a number with a fractional component when divided by 12.

The Reasonableness of Results Within the Context of a Given Problem

The reasonableness of an answer found in a math problem gives evidence to the accuracy of the work. If the answer is not reasonable, the work can be redone in order to find the error and correct the problem. Problems that involve fractions and decimals are good places to use reasonableness to check answers. For example, Karen has $63.75 to spend on sodas for her family gathering. If each soda costs $1.50, how many can she buy? The answer can be found by division, but because there are decimals, an estimate can be found by rounding the two numbers and doing easy division. The money can round to $64 and the sodas can round to $2. An estimate is 32 sodas. When the actual division is done, the answer should be close to 32. If not, it is a sign that there is an error in the math.

Using Mental Math, Estimation, and Rounding Strategies to Solve Problems and Determine Reasonableness of Results

Sometimes it is helpful to find an estimated answer to a problem rather than working out an exact answer. An estimation might be much quicker to find, and given the scenario, an estimation might be all that is required. For example, if Aria goes grocery shopping and has only a $100 bill to cover all of her purchases, it might be appropriate for her to estimate the total of the items she is purchasing to determine if she has enough money to cover them. Also, an estimation can help determine if an answer makes sense. For instance, if an answer in the 100s is expected, but the result is a fraction less than 1, something is probably wrong in the calculation.

The first type of estimation involves rounding. As mentioned, *rounding* consists of expressing a number in terms of the nearest decimal place like the tenth, hundredth, or thousandth place, or in terms of the nearest whole number unit like tens, hundreds, or thousands place. When rounding to a specific place value, look at the digit to the right of the place. If it is 5 or higher, round the number to its left up to the next value, and if it is 4 or lower, keep that number at the same value. For instance, 1,654.2674 rounded to the nearest thousand is 2,000, and the same number rounded to the nearest thousandth is 1,654.267. Rounding can be used in the scenario when grocery totals need to be estimated. Items can be rounded to the nearest dollar. For example, a can of corn that costs $0.79 can be rounded to $1.00, and then all other items can be rounded in a similar manner and added together. When working with larger numbers, it might make more sense to round to higher place values. For example, when estimating the total value of a dealership's car inventory, it would make sense to round the car values to the nearest thousands place.

The price of a car that is on sale for $15,654 can be estimated at $16,000. All other cars on the lot could be rounded in the same manner, and then their sum can be found. Depending on the situation, it might make sense to calculate an over-estimate. For example, to make sure Aria has enough money at the grocery store, rounding up every time for each item would ensure that she will have enough money when it comes time to pay. A $0.40 item rounded up to $1.00 would ensure that there is a dollar to cover that item. Traditional rounding rules would round $0.40 to $0, which does not make sense in this particular real-world setting. Aria might not have a dollar available at checkout to pay for that item if she uses traditional rounding. It is up to the customer to decide the best approach when estimating.

Estimating is also very helpful when working with measurements. Bryan is updating his kitchen and wants to retile the floor. Again, an over-measurement might be useful. Also, rounding to nearest half-unit might be helpful. For instance, one side of the kitchen might have an exact measurement of 14.32 feet, and the most useful measurement needed to buy tile could be estimating this quantity to be 14.5 feet. If the kitchen was rectangular and the other side measured 10.9 feet, Bryan might round the other side to 11 feet. Therefore, Bryan would find the total tile necessary according to the following area calculation: $14.5 \times 11 = 159.5$. square feet. To make sure he purchases enough tile, Bryan would probably want to purchase at least 160 square feet of tile. This is a scenario in which an estimation might be more useful than an exact calculation. Having more tile than necessary is better than having an exact amount, in case any tiles are broken or otherwise unusable.

Finally, estimation is helpful when exact answers are necessary. Consider a situation in which Sabina has many operations to perform on numbers with decimals, and she is allowed a calculator to find the result. Even though an exact result can be obtained with a calculator, there is always a possibility that Sabina could make an error while inputting the data. For example, she could miss a decimal place, or misuse a parenthesis, causing a problem with the actual order of operations. In this case, a quick estimation at the beginning would be helpful to make sure the final answer is given with the correct number of units. Sabina has to find the exact total of 10 cars listed for sale at the dealership. Each price has two decimal places included to account for both dollars and cents. If one car is listed at $21,234.43 but Sabina incorrectly inputs into the calculator the price of $2,123.443, this error would throw off the final sum by almost $20,000. A quick estimation at the beginning, by rounding each price to the nearest thousands place and finding the sum of the prices, would give Sabina an amount to compare the exact amount to. This comparison would let Sabina see if an error was made in her exact calculation.

Algebraic Thinking

Differentiating Between Algebraic Expressions and Equations

An **algebraic expression** is a mathematical phrase that may contain numbers, variables, and mathematical operations. An expression represents a single quantity. For example, $3x + 2$ is an algebraic expression.

An **algebraic equation** is a mathematical sentence with two expressions that are equal to each other. That is, an equation must contain an equals sign, as in $3x + 2 = 17$. This statement says that the value of the expression on the left side of the equals sign is equivalent to the value of the expression on the right side. In an expression, there are not two sides because there is no equals sign. The equals sign ($=$) is the difference between an expression and an equation.

To distinguish an expression from an equation, just look for the equals sign.

Example: Determine whether each of these is an expression or an equation.

- $16 + 4x = 9x - 7$ Solution: Equation

- $-27x - 42 + 19y$ Solution: Expression

- $4 = x + 3$ Solution: Equation

Adding and Subtracting Linear Algebraic Expressions

To add and subtract linear algebra expressions, you must combine like terms. **Like terms** are described as those terms that have the same variable with the same exponent. In the following example, the x-terms can be added because the variable is the same and the exponent on the variable of one is also the same. These terms add to be $9x$. The other like terms are called *constants* because they have no variable component.

These terms will add to be nine.

Example: Add $(3x - 5) + (6x + 14)$

$3x - 5 + 6x + 14$ Rewrite without parentheses

$3x + 6x - 5 + 14$ Commutative property of addition

$9x + 9$ Combine like terms

$$(3x - 5) + (6x + 14)$$
$$3x - 5 + 6x + 14$$
$$9x + 9$$
$$9x = -9$$
$$x = -1$$

When subtracting linear expressions, be careful to add the opposite when combining like terms. Do this by distributing -1, which is multiplying each term inside the second parenthesis by negative one. Remember that distributing -1 changes the sign of each term.

121

Example: Subtract $(17x + 3) - (27x - 8)$

$17x + 3 - 27x + 8$ Distributive Property

$17x - 27x + 3 + 8$ Commutative property of addition

$-10x + 11$ Combine like terms

Example: Simplify by adding or subtracting:

$(6m + 28z - 9) + (14m + 13) - (-4z + 8m + 12)$

$6m + 28z - 9 + 14m + 13 + 4z - 8m - 12$ Distributive Property

$6m + 14m - 8m + 28z + 4z - 9 + 13 - 12$ Commutative Property of

Addition

$12m + 32z - 8$ Combine like terms

Using the Distributive Property to Generate Equivalent Linear Algebraic Expressions

The Distributive Property: $a(b + c) = ab + ac$

The **distributive property** is a way of taking a factor and multiplying it through a given expression in parentheses. Each term inside the parentheses is multiplied by the outside factor, eliminating the parentheses. The following example shows how to distribute the number 3 to all the terms inside the parentheses.

Example: Use the distributive property to write an equivalent algebraic expression:

$3(2x + 7y + 6)$

$3(2x) + 3(7y) + 3(6)$ Distributive property

$6x + 21y + 18$ Simplify

Because $a - b$ can be written $a + (-b)$, the distributive property can be applied in the example below.

Example: Use the distributive property to write an equivalent algebraic expression.

$7(5m - 8)$

$7[5m + (-8)]$ Rewrite subtraction as addition of -8

$7(5m) + 7(-8)$ Distributive property

$35m - 56$ Simplify

$3(2x + 7y + 6)$
$6x + 21y + 18$

122

In the following example, note that the factor of 2 is written to the right of the parentheses but is still distributed as before.

Example: Use the distributive property to write an equivalent algebraic expression:

$(3m + 4x - 10)2$

$(3m)2 + (4x)2 + (-10)2$ Distributive property

$6m + 8x - 20$ Simplify

Example: $-(-2m + 6x)$

In this example, the negative sign in front of the parentheses can be interpreted as $-1(-2m + 6x)$

$-1(-2m + 6x)$

$-1(-2m) + (-1)(6x)$ Distributive property

$2m - 6x$ Simplify

Evaluating Simple Algebraic Expressions for Given Values of Variables

To evaluate an algebra expression for a given value of a variable, replace the variable with the given value. Then perform the given operations to simplify the expression.

Example: Evaluate $12 + x$ for $x = 9$

$12 + (9)$ Replace x with the value of 9 as given in the problem. It is a good idea to always use parentheses when substituting this value. This will be particularly important in the following examples.

21 Add

Now see that when x is 9, the value of the given expression is 21.

Example: Evaluate $4x + 7$ for $x = 3$

$4(3) + 7$ Replace the x in the expression with 3

$12 + 7$ Multiply (remember order of operations)

19 Add

Therefore, when x is 3, the value of the given expression is 19.

Example: Evaluate $-7m - 3r - 18$ for $m = 2$ and $r = -1$

$-7(2) - 3(-1) - 18$ Replace m with 2 and r with -1

$-14 + 3 - 18$ Multiply

-29 Add

123

So, when m is 2 and r is -1, the value of the given expression is -29.

Using Mathematical Terms to Identify Parts of Expressions and Describe Expressions

A **variable** is a symbol used to represent a number. Letters, like x, y, and z, are often used as variables in algebra.

A **constant** is a number that cannot change its value. For example, 18 is a constant.

A **term** is a constant, variable, or the product of constants and variables. In an expression, terms are separated by $+$ and $-$ signs. Examples of terms are $24x$, -32, and $15xyz$.

Like terms are terms that contain the same variables. For example, $6z$ and $-8z$ are like terms, and $9xy$ and $17xy$ are like terms. Constants, like 23 and 51, are like terms as well.

A **factor** is something that is multiplied by something else. A factor may be a constant, a variable, or a sum of constants or variables.

A **coefficient** is the numerical factor in a term that has a variable. In the term $16x$, the coefficient is 16.

Example: Given the expression, $6x - 12y + 18$, answer the following questions.

    a.   How many terms are in the expression?

    a.   Solution: 3

    b.   Name the terms.

    b.   Solution: $6x$, $-12y$, and 18 *(Notice that the minus sign preceding the 12 is interpreted to represent negative 12)*

    c.   Name the factors.

    c.   Solution: 6, x, -12, y

    d.   What are the coefficients in this expression?

    d.   Solution: 6 and -12

    e.   What is the constant in this expression?

    e.   Solution: 18

Translating Between Verbal Statements and Algebraic Expressions or Equations

When presented with a real-world problem that must be solved, the first step is always to determine what the unknown quantity is that must be solved for. Use a variable, such as x or t, to represent that unknown quantity. Sometimes there can be two or more unknown quantities. In this case, either choose an additional variable, or if a relationship exists between the unknown quantities, express the other quantities in terms of the original variable. After choosing the variables, form algebraic expressions and/or equations that represent the verbal statement in the problem. The following table shows examples of vocabulary used to represent the different operations.

Addition	Sum, plus, total, increase, more than, combined, in all
Subtraction	Difference, less than, subtract, reduce, decrease, fewer, remain
Multiplication	Product, multiply, times, part of, twice, triple
Division	Quotient, divide, split, each, equal parts, per, average, shared

The combination of operations and variables form both mathematical expression and equations. The difference between expressions and equations is that there are no equals signs in an expression, and that expressions are **evaluated** to find an unknown quantity, while equations are **solved** to find an unknown quantity. Also, inequalities can exist within verbal mathematical statements. Instead of a statement of equality, expressions state quantities are *less than*, *less than or equal to*, *greater than*, or *greater than or equal to*. Another type of inequality is when a quantity is said to be *not equal to* another quantity. The symbol used to represent "not equal to" is $\neq$.

The steps for solving inequalities in one variable are the same steps for solving equations in one variable. The addition and multiplication principles are used. However, to maintain a true statement when using the $<, \leq, >$, and $\geq$ symbols, if a negative number is either multiplied times both sides of an inequality or divided from both sides of an inequality, the sign must be flipped. For instance, consider the following inequality: $3 - 5x \leq 8$. First, 3 is subtracted from each side to obtain $-5x \leq 5$. Then, both sides are divided by -5, while flipping the sign, to obtain $x \geq -1$. Therefore, any real number greater than or equal to -1 satisfies the original inequality.

Using Formulas to Determine Unknown Quantities

Given the formula for the area of a rectangle $A = lw$, with A = area, l = length, and w = width, the area of a rectangle can be determined, given the length and the width.

For example, if the length of a rectangle is 7 cm and the width is 10 cm, find the area of the rectangle.

Solution: Just as when evaluating expressions, replace the variables with the given values.

Given $\quad A = lw$, l = 7 and w = 10.

$\quad\quad A = (7)(10)$ $\quad\quad\quad\quad\quad\quad\quad$ Replace l with 7 and w with 10

$\quad\quad A = 70$ $\quad\quad\quad\quad\quad\quad\quad\quad\quad$ Multiply

Therefore, the area of the rectangle is 70 cm^2.

Example: The formula for perimeter of a rectangle, $P = 2l + 2w$, where P is perimeter, l is length, and w is width. If the length of a rectangle is 12 inches and the width is 9 inches, find the perimeter.

Solution: $\quad\quad\quad P = 2l + 2w$

$\quad\quad\quad\quad\quad\quad P = 2(12) + 2(9)$ $\quad\quad\quad\quad\quad$ Replace l with 12 and w with 9

$\quad\quad\quad\quad\quad\quad P = 24 + 18$ $\quad\quad\quad\quad\quad\quad$ Use correct order of operations; multiply first

$\quad\quad\quad\quad\quad\quad P = 42$ $\quad\quad\quad\quad\quad\quad\quad\quad$ Add

The perimeter of this rectangle is 42 inches.

When solving equations, it is important to note which quantity must be solved for. This quantity can be referred to as the **quantity of interest**. The goal of solving is to isolate the variable in the equation using logical mathematical steps. The **addition property of equality** states that the same real number can be added to both sides of an equation and equality is maintained. Also, the same real number can be subtracted from both sides of an equation to maintain equality. Second, the **multiplication property of equality** states that the same nonzero real number can multiply both sides of an equation, and still, equality is maintained. Because division is the same as multiplying times a reciprocal, an equation can be divided by the same number on both sides as well.

When solving inequalities, the same ideas are used. However, when multiplying by a negative number on both sides of an inequality, the inequality symbol must be flipped in order to maintain the logic. The same is true when dividing both sides of an inequality by a negative number.

Basically, in order to isolate a quantity of interest in either an equation or inequality, the same thing must be done to both sides of the equals sign, or inequality symbol, to keep everything mathematically correct.

Differentiating Between Dependent and Independent Variables in Formulas

Independent variables are independent, meaning they are not changed by other variables within the context of the problem. **Dependent variables** are dependent, meaning they may change depending on how other variables change in the problem. For example, in the formula for the perimeter of a fence, the length and width are the independent variables and the perimeter is the dependent variable. The formula is shown below.

$$P = 2l + 2w$$

As the width or the length changes, the perimeter may also change. The first variables to change are the length and width, which then result in a change in perimeter. The change does not come first with the perimeter and then with length and width. When comparing these two types of variables, it is helpful to ask which variable causes the change and which variable is affected by the change.

Another formula to represent this relationship is the formula for circumference show below.

$$C = \pi \times d$$

The C represents circumference and the d represents diameter. The pi symbol is approximated by the fraction $\frac{22}{7}$, or 3.14. In this formula, the diameter of the circle is the independent variable. It is the portion of the circle that changes, which changes the circumference as a result. The circumference is the variable that is being changed by the diameter, so it is called the dependent variable. It depends on the value of the diameter.

Another place to recognize independent and dependent variables can be in experiments. A common experiment is one where the growth of a plant is tested based on the amount of sunlight it receives. Each plant in the experiment is given a different amount of sunlight, but the same amount of other nutrients like light and water. The growth of the plants is measured over a given time period and the results show how much sunlight is best for plants. In this experiment, the independent variable is the amount of sunlight that each plant receives. The dependent variable is the growth of each plant. The growth depends on the amount of sunlight, which gives reason for the distinction between independent and dependent variables.

Solving Multistep One-Variable Linear Equations and Inequalities

An **equation in one variable** is a mathematical statement where two algebraic expressions in one variable, usually x, are set equal. To solve the equation, the variable must be isolated on one side of the equals sign. The addition and multiplication principles of equality are used to isolate the variable. The **addition principle of equality** states that the same number can be added to or subtracted from both sides of an equation. Because the same value is being used on both sides of the equals sign, equality is maintained. For example, the equation $2x = 5x$ is equivalent to both $2x + 3 = 5x + 3$, and $2x - 5 = 5x - 5$. This principle can be used to solve the following equation: $x + 5 = 4$. The variable x must be isolated, so to move the 5 from the left side, subtract 5 from both sides of the equals sign.

Therefore:

$$x + 5 - 5 = 4 - 5$$

So, the solution is $x = -1$. This process illustrates the idea of an **additive inverse** because subtracting 5 is the same as adding -5. Basically, add the opposite of the number that must be removed to both sides of the equals sign. The **multiplication principle of equality** states that equality is maintained when a number is either multiplied times both expressions on each side of the equals sign, or when both expressions are divided by the same number. For example, $4x = 5$ is equivalent to both $16x = 20$ and $x = \frac{5}{4}$. Multiplying both sides times 4 and dividing both sides by 4 maintains equality. Solving the equation $6x - 18 = 5$ requires the use of both principles. First, apply the addition principle to add 18 to both sides of the equals sign, which results in $6x = 23$. Then use the multiplication principle to divide both sides by 6, giving the solution $x = \frac{23}{6}$. Using the multiplication principle in the solving process is the same as involving a multiplicative inverse. A **multiplicative inverse** is a value that, when multiplied by a given number, results in 1. Dividing by 6 is the same as multiplying by $\frac{1}{6}$, which is both the reciprocal and multiplicative inverse of 6.

When solving a linear equation in one variable, checking the answer shows if the solution process was performed correctly. Plug the solution into the variable in the original equation. If the result is a false statement, something was done incorrectly during the solution procedure. Checking the example above gives the following:

$$6 \times \frac{23}{6} - 18 = 23 - 18 = 5$$

Therefore, the solution is correct.

Some equations in one variable involve fractions or the use of the distributive property. In either case, the goal is to obtain only one variable term and then use the addition and multiplication principles to isolate that variable. Consider the equation $\frac{2}{3}x = 6$. To solve for x, multiply each side of the equation by the reciprocal of $\frac{2}{3}$, which is $\frac{3}{2}$. This step results in $\frac{3}{2} \times \frac{2}{3}x = \frac{3}{2} \times 6$, which simplifies into the solution $x = 9$. Now consider the equation:

$$3(x + 2) - 5x = 4x + 1$$

Use the distributive property to clear the parentheses. Therefore, multiply each term inside the parentheses by 3. This step results in:

$$3x + 6 - 5x = 4x + 1$$

Next, collect like terms on the left-hand side. **Like terms** are terms with the same variable or variables raised to the same exponent(s). Only like terms can be combined through addition or subtraction. After collecting like terms, the equation is:

$$-2x + 6 = 4x + 1$$

Finally, apply the addition and multiplication principles. Add $2x$ to both sides to obtain $6 = 6x + 1$. Then, subtract 1 from both sides to obtain $5 = 6x$. Finally, divide both sides by 6 to obtain the solution $\frac{5}{6} = x$.

Two other types of solutions can be obtained when solving an equation in one variable. The final result could be that there is either no solution or that the solution set contains all real numbers. Consider the equation:

$$4x = 6x + 5 - 2x$$

First, the like terms can be combined on the right to obtain:

$$4x = 4x + 5$$

Next, subtract $4x$ from both sides. This step results in the false statement $0 = 5$. There is no value that can be plugged into x that will ever make this equation true. Therefore, there is no solution. The solution procedure contained correct steps, but the result of a false statement means that no value satisfies the equation. The symbolic way to denote that no solution exists is $\emptyset$. Next, consider the equation:

$$5x + 4 + 2x = 9 + 7x - 5$$

Combining the like terms on both sides results in:

$$7x + 4 = 7x + 4$$

The left-hand side is exactly the same as the right-hand side. Using the addition principle to move terms, the result is $0 = 0$, which is always true. Therefore, the original equation is true for any number, and the solution set is all real numbers. The symbolic way to denote such a solution set is $\mathbb{R}$, or in interval notation, $(-\infty, \infty)$.

Interpreting Solutions of Multistep One-Variable Linear Equations and Inequalities

Multistep one-variable equations involve the use of one variable in an equation with many operations. For example, the equation $2x + 4 = 10$ involves one variable, x, and multiple steps to solve for the value of x. The first step is to move the four to the opposite side of the equation by subtracting 4. The next step is to divide by 2. The final answer yields a value of 3 for the variable x.

The steps for this process are shown below.

$$2x + 4 = 10$$

$$-4 \quad -4 \qquad \text{Subtract 4 on both sides}$$

$$2x = 6$$

$$\div 2 \quad \div 2 \qquad \text{Divide by 2 on both sides}$$

$$x = 3$$

When the result is found, the value of the variable must be interpreted. For this problem, a value of 3 can be understood as the number that can be doubled and then increased by 4 to yield a value of 10.

Inequalities can also be interpreted in much the same way. The following inequality can be solved to find the value of b:

$$\frac{b}{7} - 8 \geq 7$$

This inequality models the amount of money a group of friends earned for cleaning up a neighbor's yard, b. There were 7 friends, so the money had to be split seven times. Then $8 was taken away from each friend to pay for materials they bought to help clean the yard. All these things needed to be less than or equal to seven for the friends to each receive at least $7. The first step is to add 8 to both sides of the inequality. Then, both sides can be multiplied by 7 to get rid of the denominator on the left side. The resulting inequality is $b \geq 105$. Because the answer is not only an equals sign, the value for b is not a single number. In this problem, the answer communicates that the value of b must be greater than or equal to $105 in order for each friend to make at least $7 for their work. The number for b, what they are paid, can be more than 105 because that would mean they earned more money. They do not want it to be less than 105 because their profit will drop below $7 apiece.

Using Linear Relationships Represented by Equations, Tables, and Graphs to Solve Problems

A **linear function that models a linear relationship between two quantities** is of the form $y = mx + b$, or in function form $f(x) = mx + b$. In a linear function, the value of y depends on the value of x, and y increases or decreases at a constant rate as x increases. Therefore, the independent variable is x, and the dependent variable is y. The graph of a linear function is a line, and the constant rate can be seen by looking at the steepness, or slope, of the line. If the line increases from left to right, the slope is positive. If the line slopes downward from left to right, the slope is negative. In the function, m represents slope. Each point on the line is an **ordered pair** (x, y), where x represents the x-coordinate of the point and y represents the y-coordinate of the point. The point where $x = 0$ is known as the y-intercept, and it is the place where the line crosses the y-axis. If $x = 0$ is plugged into $f(x) = mx + b$, the result is $f(0) = b$, so therefore, the point $(0, b)$ is the y-intercept of the line. The derivative of a linear function is its slope.

Consider the following situation. A taxicab driver charges a flat fee of $2 per ride and $3 a mile. This statement can be modeled by the function $f(x) = 3x + 2$ where x represents the number of miles and $f(x) = y$ represents the total cost of the ride. The total cost increases at a constant rate of $2 per mile, and that is why this situation is a linear relationship. The slope $m = 3$ is equivalent to this rate of change. The flat fee of $2 is the y-intercept. It is the place where the graph crosses the x-axis, and it represents the cost when $x = 0$, or when no miles have been traveled in the cab. The y-intercept in this situation represents the flat fee.

Graphs, equations, and tables are three different ways to represent linear relationships. The following graph shows a linear relationship because the relationship between the two variables is constant. As the distance increases by 25 miles, the time lapses by 1 hour. This pattern continues for the rest of the graph. The line represents a constant rate of 25 miles per hour. This graph can also be used to solve problems involving predictions for a future time. After 8 hours of travel, the rate can be used to predict the distance covered. Eight hours of travel at 25 miles per hour covers a distance of 200 miles. The equation at the top of the graph corresponds to this rate also. The same prediction of distance in a given time can be found using the equation. For a time of 10 hours, the distance would be 250 miles, as the equation yields:

$$d = 25 \times 10 = 250$$

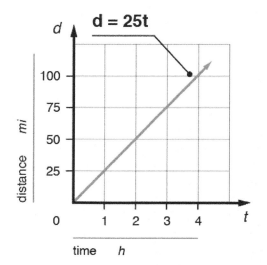

Another representation of a linear relationship can be seen in a table. The first thing to observe from the table is that the y-values increase by the same amount of 3 each time. As the x-values increase by 1, the y-values increase by 3. This pattern shows that the relationship is linear. If this table shows the money earned, y-value, for the hours worked, x-value, then it can be used to predict how much money will be earned for future hours. If 6 hours are worked, then the pay would be $19. For further hours and money to be determined, it would be helpful to have an equation that models this table of values. The equation will show the relationship between x and y. The y-value can each time be determined by multiplying the x-value by 3, then adding 1. The following equation models this relationship:

$$y = 3x + 1$$

Now that there is an equation, any number of hours, x, can be substituted into the equation to find the amount of money earned, y.

$y = 3x + 1$	
x	**y**
0	1
1	4
2	7
4	13
5	16

Algebraically Solving Linear Equations or Inequalities in One Variable

A **linear equation in one variable** can be solved using the following steps:

1. Simplify the algebraic expressions on both sides of the equals sign by removing all parentheses, using the distributive property, and then collecting all like terms.

2. Collect all variable terms on one side of the equals sign and all constant terms on the other side by adding the same quantity to both sides of the equals sign, or by subtracting the same quantity from both sides of the equals sign.

3. Isolate the variable by either dividing both sides of the equation by the same number, or by multiplying both sides by the same number.

4. Check the answer.

The only difference between solving linear inequalities versus equations is that when multiplying by a negative number or dividing by a negative number, the direction of the inequality symbol must be reversed.

If an equation contains multiple fractions, it might make sense to clear the equation of fractions first by multiplying all terms by the least common denominator. Also, if an equation contains several decimals, it might make sense to clear the decimals as well by multiplying times a factor of 10. If the equation has decimals in the hundredths place, multiply every term in the equation by 100.

Interpreting the Variables and Constants in Expressions for Linear Functions within the Context Presented

A **linear function of the form** $f(x) = mx + b$ has two important quantities: m and b. The quantity m represents the slope of the line, and the quantity b represents the y-intercept of the line. When the function represents an actual real-life situation, or mathematical model, these two quantities are very meaningful. The slope, m, represents the rate of change, or the amount y increases or decreases given an increase in x. If m is positive, the rate of change is positive, and if m is negative, the rate of change is negative. The y-intercept, b, represents the amount of the quantity y when x is 0. In many applications, if the x-variable is never a negative quantity, the y-intercept represents the initial amount of the quantity y. Often the x-variable represents time, so it makes sense that the x-variable is never negative.

Consider the following example. These two equations represent the cost, C, of t-shirts, x, at two different printing companies:

$$C(x) = 7x$$

$$C(x) = 5x + 25$$

The first equation represents a scenario that shows the cost per t-shirt is $7. In this equation, x varies directly with y. There is no y-intercept, which means that there is no initial cost for using that printing company. The rate of change is 7, which is price per shirt. The second equation represents a scenario that has both an initial cost and a cost per t-shirt. The slope 5 shows that each shirt is $5. The y-intercept 25 shows that there is an initial cost of using that company. Therefore, it makes sense to use the first company at $7 a shirt when only purchasing a small number of t-shirts. However, any large orders would be cheaper by going with the second company because eventually that initial cost will be negligible.

Identifying, Extending, Describing, and Generating Number and Shape Patterns

Patterns in math are those sets of numbers or shapes that follow a rule. Given a set of values, patterns allow the question of "what's next?" to be answered. In the following set there are two types of shapes, a white rectangle and a gray circle. The set contains a pattern because every odd-placed shape is a white rectangle and every even-placed spot is taken by a gray circle. This is a pattern because there is a rule of white rectangle, then gray circle, that is followed to find the set.

A set of numbers can also be described as having a pattern if there is a rule that can be followed to reproduce the set. The following set of numbers has a rule of adding 3 each time. It begins with zero and increases by 3 each time. By following this rule and pattern, the number after 12 is found to be 15. Further extending the pattern, the numbers are 18, 21, 24, 27. The pattern of increasing by multiples of three can describe this pattern.

$$0 \quad 3 \quad 6 \quad 9 \quad 12 \quad \boxed{} \quad \dots$$

A pattern can also be generated from a given rule. Starting with zero, the rule of adding 5 can be used to produce a set of numbers. The following list will result from using the rule: 0, 5, 10, 15, 20. Describing this pattern can include words such as "multiples" of 5 and an "increase" of 5. Any time this pattern needs to be extended, the rule can be applied to find more numbers. Patterns are identified by the rules they follow. This rule should be able to generate new numbers or shapes, while also applying to the given numbers or shapes.

Making Conjectures, Predictions, and Generalizations Based on Patterns

Given a certain pattern, future numbers or shapes can be found. Pascal's triangle is an example of a pattern of numbers. Questions can be asked of the triangle, such as, "what comes next?" and "what values determine the next line?" By examining the different parts of the triangle, conjectures can be made about how the numbers are generated. For the first few rows of numbers, the increase is small. Then the numbers begin to increase more quickly. By looking at each row, a conjecture can be made that the sum of the first row determines the second row's numbers. The second row's numbers can be added to find the third row. To test this conjecture, two numbers can be added, and the number found directly between and below them should be that sum. For the third row, the middle number is 2, which is the sum of the two 1s above it. For the fifth row, the 1 and 3 can be added to find a sum of 4, the same number below the 1 and 3.

This pattern continues throughout the triangle. Once the pattern is confirmed to apply throughout the triangle, predictions can be made for future rows. The sums of the bottom row numbers can be found and then added to the bottom of the triangle. In more general terms, the diagonal rows have patterns as well. The outside numbers are always 1. The second diagonal rows are in counting order. The third diagonal row increases each time by one more than the previous. It is helpful to generalize patterns because it makes the pattern more useful in terms of applying it. Pascal's triangle can be used to predict the tossing of a coin, predicting the chances of heads or tails for different numbers of tosses. It can also be used to show the Fibonacci Sequence, which is found by adding the diagonal numbers together.

Pascal's Triangle

```
                            1
                         1     1
                      1     2     1
                   1     3     3     1
                1     4     6     4     1
             1     5    10    10     5     1
          1     6    15    20    15     6     1
       1     7    21    35    35    21     7     1
    1     8    28    56    70    56    28     8     1
 1     9    36    84   126   126    84    36     9     1
1    10    45   120   200   252   200   120    45    10    1
```

Identifying Relationships Between the Corresponding Terms of Two Numerical Patterns

Sets of numerical patterns can be found by starting with a number and following a given rule. If two sets are generated, the corresponding terms in each set can be found to relate to one another by one or more operations. For example, the following table shows two sets of numbers that each follow their own pattern. The first column shows a pattern of numbers increasing by 1. The second column shows the numbers increasing by 4. Because the numbers are lined up, corresponding numbers are side by side for the two sets. A question to ask is, "How can the number in the first column be turned into the number in the second column?"

1	4
2	8
3	12
4	16
5	20

This answer will lead to the relationship between the two sets. By recognizing the multiples of 4 in the right column and the counting numbers in order in the left column, the relationship of multiplying by four is determined. The first set is multiplied by 4 to get the second set of numbers. To confirm this relationship, each set of corresponding numbers can be checked. For any two sets of numerical patterns, the corresponding numbers can be lined up to find how each one relates to the other. In some cases, the relationship is simply addition or subtraction, multiplication or division. In other relationships, these operations are used in conjunction with each together. As seen in the following table, the relationship uses multiplication and addition. The following expression shows this relationship: $3x + 2$. The x represents the numbers in the first column.

1	5
2	8
3	11
4	14

Geometry and Measurement, Data, Statistics, and Probability

Using Definitions to Identify Lines, Rays, Line Segments, Parallel Lines, and Perpendicular Lines

Geometric figures can be identified by matching the definition with the object. For example, a **line segment** is made up of two endpoints and the line drawn between them. A **ray** is made up of one endpoint and one extending side that goes on forever. A **line** has no endpoints and two sides that extend on forever. These three geometric figures are shown below. What happens at A and B determines the name of each figure.

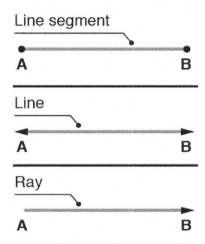

Parallel and perpendicular lines are made up of two lines, like the second figure above. They are distinguished from each other by how the two lines interact. **Parallel** lines run alongside one another, but they never intersect. **Perpendicular** lines intersect at a 90-degree, or a right, angle. An example of these two sets of lines is shown below. Also shown in the figure are nonexamples of these two types of lines. Because the first set of lines, in the top left corner, will eventually intersect if they continue, they are not parallel. In the second set, the lines run in the same direction and will never intersect, making them parallel. The third set, in the bottom left corner, intersect at an angle that is not right, or not 90 degrees. The fourth set is perpendicular because the lines intersect at exactly a right angle.

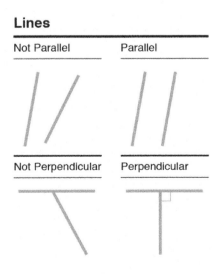

135

Classifying Angles Based on Their Measure

When two rays are joined together at their endpoints, an **angle** is formed. Angles can be described based on their measure. An angle whose measure is 90 degrees is described as a right angle, just as with perpendicular lines. Ninety degrees is a standard to which other angles are compared. If an angle is less than ninety degrees, it is an **acute** angle. If it is greater than ninety degrees, it is **obtuse**. If an angle is equal to twice a right angle, or 180 degrees, it is a **straight** angle. Examples of these types of angles are shown below:

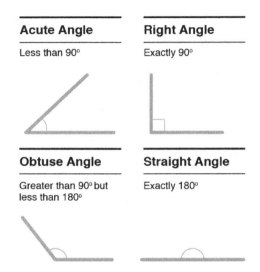

Acute Angle

Less than 90°

Right Angle

Exactly 90°

Obtuse Angle

Greater than 90° but less than 180°

Straight Angle

Exactly 180°

A **straight angle** is equal to 180 degrees, or a straight line. If the line continues through the **vertex**, or point where the rays meet, and does not change direction, then the angle is straight. This is shown in Figure 1 below. The second figure shows an obtuse angle. Its measure is greater than ninety degrees, but less than that of a straight angle. An estimate for its measure may be 175 degrees. Figure 3 shows acute angles. The first is just less than that of a right angle. Its measure may be estimated to be 80 degrees. The second acute angle has a measure that is much smaller, at approximately 35 degrees, but it is still classified as acute because it is between zero and 90 degrees.

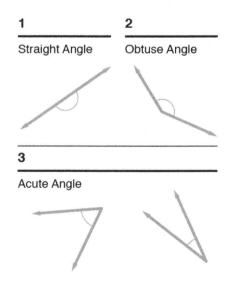

1

Straight Angle

2

Obtuse Angle

3

Acute Angle

136

Composing and Decomposing Two- and Three-Dimensional Shapes

Basic shapes are those polygons that are made up of straight lines and angles and can be described by their number of sides and concavity. Some examples of those shapes are rectangles, triangles, hexagons, and pentagons. These shapes have identifying characteristics on their own, but they can also be decomposed into other shapes. For example, the following can be described as one hexagon, as see in the first figure. It can also be decomposed into six equilateral triangles. The last figure shows how the hexagon can be decomposed into three rhombuses.

Decomposing a Hexagon

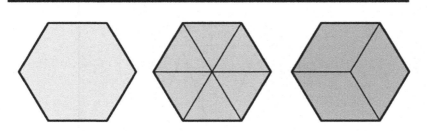

More complex shapes can be formed by combining basic shapes or lining them up side by side. Below is an example of a house. This house is one figure all together but can be decomposed into seven different shapes. The chimney is a parallelogram and the roof is made up of two triangles. The bottom of the house is a square alongside three triangles. There are many other ways of decomposing this house. Different shapes can be used to line up together and form one larger shape. The area for the house can be calculated by finding the individual areas for each shape, then adding them all together. For this house, there would be the area of four triangles, one square, and one parallelogram. Adding these all together would result in the area of the house as a whole. Decomposing and composing shapes is commonly done with a set of tangrams. A **tangram** is a set of shapes that includes different size triangles, rectangles, and parallelograms.

A Tangram of a House

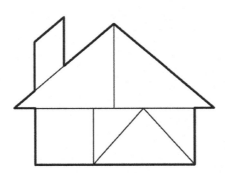

Using Attributes to Classify or Draw Polygons and Solids

Shapes are defined by their angles and number of sides. A shape with one continuous side, where all points on that side are equidistant from a center point is called a **circle**. A shape made with three straight line segments is a **triangle**. A shape with four sides is called a **quadrilateral**, but more specifically a **square, rectangle, parallelogram,** or **trapezoid**, depending on the interior angles. These shapes are two-dimensional and only made up of straight lines and angles. **Solids** can be formed by combining these shapes and forming three-dimensional figures. These figures have another dimension because they add one more direction. Examples of solids may be prisms or spheres. There are four figures below that can be described based on their sides and dimensions. Figure 1 is a cone because it has three dimensions, where the bottom is a circle and the top is formed by the sides combining to one point. Figure 2 is a triangle because it has two dimensions, made up of three line segments. Figure 3 is a cylinder made up of two base circles and a rectangle to connect them in three dimensions. Figure 4 is an oval because it is one continuous line in two dimensions, not equidistant from the center.

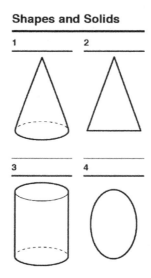

Figure 5 below is made up of squares in three dimensions, combined to make a cube. Figure 6 is a rectangle because it has four sides that intersect at right angles. More specifically, it can be described as a square because the four sides have equal measures. Figure 7 is a pyramid because the bottom shape is a square and the sides are all triangles. These triangles intersect at a point above the square. Figure 8 is a circle because it is made up of one continuous line where the points are all equidistant from one center point.

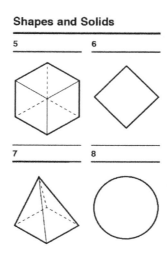

Representing Three-Dimensional Figures with Nets

The **net of a figure** is the resulting two-dimensional shapes when a three-dimensional shape is broken down. For example, the net of a cone is shown below. The base of the cone is a circle, shown at the bottom. The rest of the cone is a quarter of a circle. The bottom is the circumference of the circle, while the top comes to a point. If the cone is cut down the side and laid out flat, these would be the resulting shapes.

The Net of a Cone

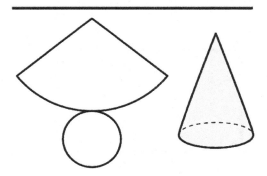

A net for a pyramid is shown in the figure below. The base of the pyramid is a square. The four shapes coming off the pyramid are triangles. When built up together, folding the triangles to the top results in a pyramid.

The Net of a Pyramid

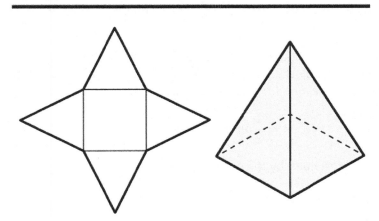

One other net for a figure is the one shown below for a cylinder. When the cylinder is broken down, the bases are circles and the side is a rectangle wrapped around the circles. The circumference of the circle turns into the length of the rectangle.

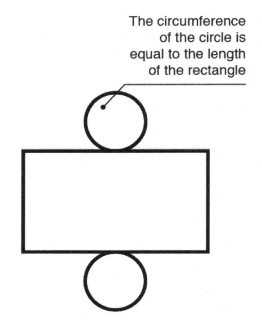

The circumference
of the circle is
equal to the length
of the rectangle

Nets can be used in calculating different values for given shapes. One useful way to calculate surface area is to find the net of the object, then find the area of each of the shapes and add them together. Nets are also useful in composing shapes and decomposing objects so as to view how objects connect and can be used in conjunction with each other.

Using Nets Made of Rectangles and Triangles to Determine the Surface Area of Three-Dimensional Figures

Surface area of three-dimensional figures is the total area of each of the faces of the figures. Nets are used to lay out each face of an object. On the following page, the dimensions are labeled for each of the faces of the triangular prism. The area for each of the two triangles can be determined by the formula:

$$A = \frac{1}{2}bh = \frac{1}{2} \times 8 \times 9 = 36 \text{ cm}^2$$

The rectangle areas can be described by the equation:

$$A = lw = 8 \times 5 + 9 \times 5 + 10 \times 5$$

$$40 + 45 + 50 = 135 \text{ cm}^2$$

The area for the triangles can be multiplied by two, then added to the rectangle areas to yield a total surface area of 207 cm².

A Triangular Prism and Its Net

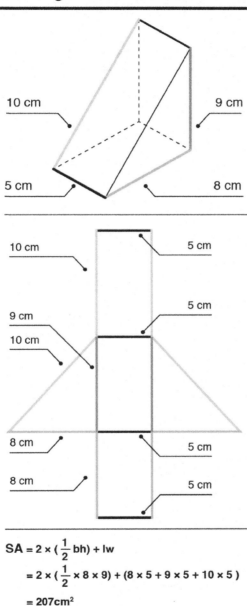

$$SA = 2 \times (\tfrac{1}{2}bh) + lw$$

$$= 2 \times (\tfrac{1}{2} \times 8 \times 9) + (8 \times 5 + 9 \times 5 + 10 \times 5)$$

$$= 207 \text{cm}^2$$

Other figures that have rectangles or triangles in their nets include pyramids, rectangular prisms, and cylinders. When the shapes of these three-dimensional objects are found, and areas are calculated, the sum will result in the surface area. The following picture shows the net for a rectangular prism. The dimensions for each of the shapes that make up the prism are shown to the right. As a formula, the surface area is the sum of each shape added together. The following equation shows the formula:

$$SA = 5 \times 10 + 5 \times 6 + 6 \times 10 + 5 \times 6 + 5 \times 10 + 6 \times 10$$

$$SA = 50 + 30 + 60 + 30 + 50 + 60 = 280 \text{ m}^2$$

A Rectangular Prism and its Net

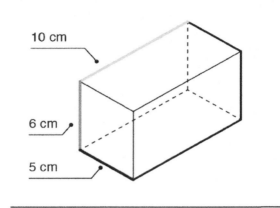

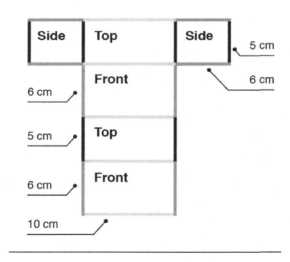

SA = 5×10 + 5×6 + 6×10 + 5×6 + 5×10 + 6×10

= 50 + 30 + 60 + 30 + 50 + 60

= 280cm²

Finding the Area and Perimeter of Polygons, Including Those with Fractional Side Lengths

Perimeter and area are two commonly used geometric quantities that describe objects. **Perimeter** is the distance around an object. The perimeter of an object can be found by adding the lengths of all sides. Perimeter may be used in problems dealing with lengths around objects such as fences or borders. It may also be used in finding missing lengths or working backwards. If the perimeter is given, but a length is missing, use subtraction to find the missing length. Given a square with side length s, the formula for perimeter is $P = 4s$. Given a rectangle with length l and width w, the formula for perimeter is $P = 2l + 2w$. The perimeter of a triangle is found by adding the three side lengths, and the perimeter of a trapezoid is found by adding the four side lengths. The units for perimeter are always the original units of length, such as meters, inches, miles, etc. When discussing a circle, the distance around the object is referred to as its circumference, not perimeter. The formula for circumference of a circle is $C = 2\pi r$, where r represents the radius of the circle. This formula can also be written as $C = d\pi$, where d represents the diameter of the circle.

Area is the two-dimensional space covered by an object. These problems may include the area of a rectangle, a yard, or a wall to be painted. Finding the area may be a simple formula, or it may require multiple formulas to be used together. The units for area are square units, such as square meters, square inches, and square miles. Given a square with side length s, the formula for its area is $A = s^2$. Formulas for common shapes are shown below:

Shape	Formula	Graphic
Rectangle	$Area = length \times width$	
Triangle	$Area = \dfrac{1}{2} \times base \times height$	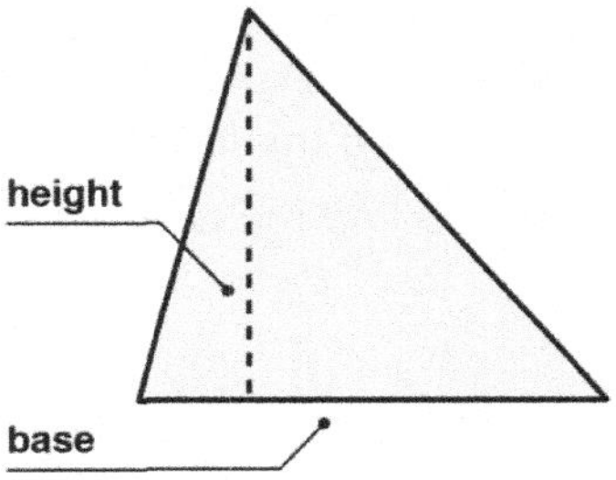
Circle	$Area = \pi \times radius^2$	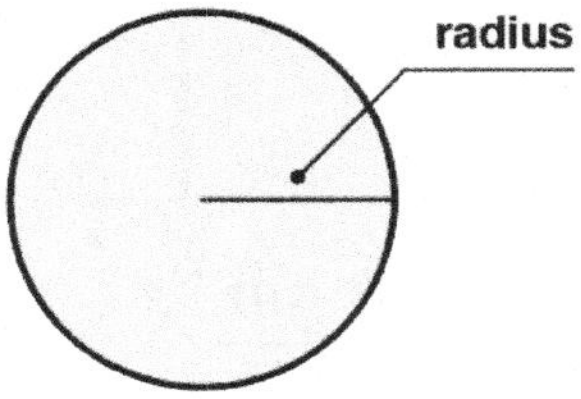

The following formula, not as widely used as those shown above, but very important, is the area of a trapezoid:

Area of a Trapezoid

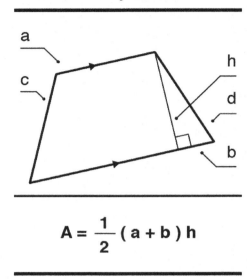

$$A = \frac{1}{2}(a + b)h$$

To find the area of the shapes above, use the given dimensions of the shape in the formula. Complex shapes might require more than one formula. To find the area of the figure below, break the figure into two shapes. The rectangle has dimensions 6 cm by 7 cm. The triangle has dimensions 6 cm by 6 cm. Plug the dimensions into the rectangle formula: $A = 6 \times 7$. Multiplication yields an area of 42 cm². The triangle area can be found using the formula $A = \frac{1}{2} \times 4 \times 6$. Multiplication yields an area of 12 cm². Add the areas of the two shapes to find the total area of the figure, which is 54 cm².

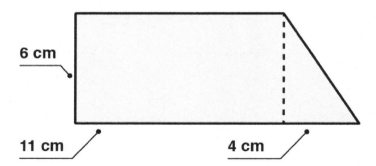

Instead of combining areas, some problems may require subtracting them, or finding the difference.

To find the area of the shaded region in the figure below, determine the area of the whole figure. Then subtract the area of the circle from the whole.

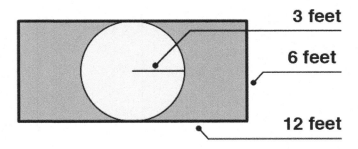

The following formula shows the area of the outside rectangle: $A = 12 \times 6 = 72$ ft^2. The area of the inside circle can be found by the following formula: $A = \pi(3)^2 = 9\pi = 28.3$ ft^2. As the shaded area is outside the circle, the area for the circle can be subtracted from the area of the rectangle to yield an area of 43.7 ft^2.

While some geometric figures may be given as pictures, others may be described in words. If a rectangular playing field with dimensions 95 meters long by 50 meters wide is measured for perimeter, the distance around the field must be found. The perimeter includes two lengths and two widths to measure the entire outside of the field. This quantity can be calculated using the following equation: $P = 2(95) + 2(50) = 290\ m$. The distance around the field is 290 meters.

Finding the Volume and Surface Area of Right Rectangular Prisms, Including Those with Fractional Edge Lengths

Perimeter and area are two-dimensional descriptions; volume is three-dimensional. **Volume** describes the amount of space that an object occupies, but it's different from area because it has three dimensions instead of two. The units for volume are cubic units, such as cubic meters, cubic inches, and cubic miles. Volume can be found by using formulas for common objects such as cylinders and boxes.

The following chart shows a diagram and formula for the volume of two objects.

Shape	Formula	Diagram
Rectangular Prism (box)	$V = length \times width \times height$	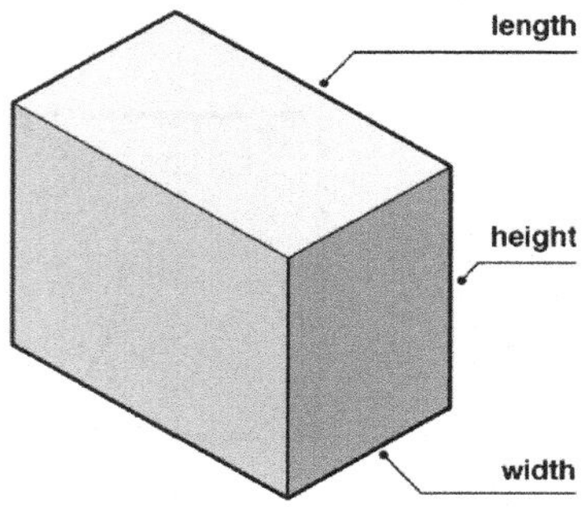
Cylinder	$V = \pi \times radius^2 \times height$	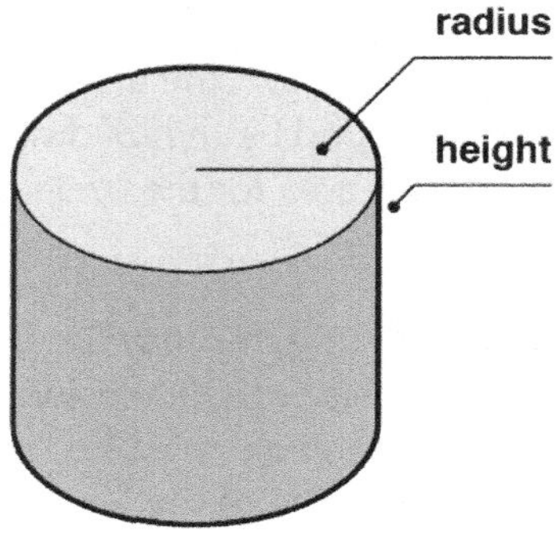

Volume formulas of these two objects are derived by finding the area of the bottom two-dimensional shape, such as the circle or rectangle, and then multiplying times the height of the three-dimensional shape. Other volume formulas include the volume of a cube with side length s: $V = s^3$; the volume of a sphere with radius r: $V = \frac{4}{3}\pi r^3$; and the volume of a cone with radius r and height h: $V = \frac{1}{3}\pi r^2 h$.

If a soda can has a height of 5 inches and a radius on the top of 1.5 inches, the volume can be found using one of the given formulas. A soda can is a cylinder. Knowing the given dimensions, the formula can be completed as follows:

$$V = \pi (radius)^2 \times height$$

$$\pi (1.5 \text{ in})^2 \times 5 \text{ in} = 35.325 \text{ in}^3$$

Notice that the units for volume are inches cubed because it refers to the number of cubic inches required to fill the can.

With any geometric calculations, it's important to determine what dimensions are given and what quantities the problem is asking for. If a connection can be made between them, the answer can be found.

Other geometric quantities can include angles inside a triangle. The sum of the measures of three angles in any triangle is 180 degrees. Therefore, if only two angles are known inside a triangle, the third can be found by subtracting the sum of the two known quantities from 180. Two angles whose sum is equal to 90 degrees are known as **complementary angles**. For example, angles measuring 72 and 18 degrees are complementary, and each angle is a complement of the other. Finally, two angles whose sum is equal to 180 degrees are known as **supplementary angles**. To find the supplement of an angle, subtract the given angle from 180 degrees. For example, the supplement of an angle that is 50 degrees is $180 - 50 = 130$ degrees.

These terms involving angles can be seen in many types of word problems. For example, consider the following problem: The measure of an angle is 60 degrees less than two times the measure of its complement. What is the angle's measure? To solve this, let x be the unknown angle. Therefore, its complement is $90 - x$. The problem gives that:

$$x = 2(90 - x) - 60$$

To solve for x, distribute the 2, and collect like terms. This process results in:

$$x = 120 - 2x$$

Then, use the addition property to add $2x$ to both sides to obtain $3x = 120$. Finally, use the multiplication properties of equality to divide both sides by 3 to get $x = 40$. Therefore, the angle measures 40 degrees. Also, its complement measures 50 degrees.

Right rectangular prisms are those prisms in which all sides are rectangles and all angles are right, or equal to 90 degrees. The volume for these objects can be found by multiplying the length by the width by the height. The formula is $V = lwh$. For the following prism, the volume formula is:

$$V = 6\frac{1}{2} \times 3 \times 9$$

When dealing with fractional edge lengths, it is helpful to convert the length to an improper fraction. The length $6\frac{1}{2}$ cm becomes $\frac{13}{2}$ cm. Then the formula becomes:

$$V = \frac{13}{2} \times 3 \times 9$$

$$\frac{13}{2} \times \frac{3}{1} \times \frac{9}{1} = \frac{351}{2}$$

This value for volume is better understood when turned into a mixed number, which would be $175\frac{1}{2}$ cm³.

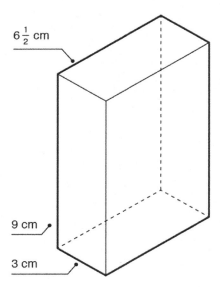

When dimensions for length are given with fractional parts, it can be helpful to turn the mixed number into an improper fraction, then multiply to find the volume, then convert back to a mixed number. When finding surface area, this conversion to improper fractions can also be helpful. The surface area can be found for the same prism above by breaking down the figure into basic shapes. These shapes are rectangles, made up of the two bases, two sides, and the front and back.

The formula for the surface area uses the area for each of these shapes for the terms in the following equation:

$$SA = 6\frac{1}{2} \times 3 + 6\frac{1}{2} \times 3 + 3 \times 9 + 3 \times 9 + 6\frac{1}{2} \times 9 + 6\frac{1}{2} \times 9$$

Because there are so many terms in a surface area formula and because this formula contains a fraction, it can be simplified by combining groups that are the same. Each set of numbers is used twice, to represent areas for the opposite sides of the prism. The formula can be simplified to:

$$SA = 2\left(6\frac{1}{2} \times 3\right) + 2(3 \times 9) + 2\left(6\frac{1}{2} \times 9\right)$$

$$2\left(\frac{13}{2} \times 3\right) + 2(27) + 2\left(\frac{13}{2} \times 9\right)$$

$$2\left(\frac{39}{2}\right) + 54 + 2\left(\frac{117}{2}\right)$$

$$39 + 54 + 117$$

$$210 \text{ cm}^2$$

Surface Area

Surface area is defined as the area of the surface of a figure. A **pyramid** has a surface made up of four triangles and one square. To calculate the surface area of a pyramid, the areas of each individual shape are calculated. Then the areas are added together. This method of decomposing the shape into two-dimensional figures to find area, then adding the areas, can be used to find surface area for any figure. Once these measurements are found, the area is described with square units. For example, the following figure shows a rectangular prism. The figure beside it shows the rectangular prism broken down into two-dimensional shapes, or rectangles. The area of each rectangle can be calculated by multiplying the length by the width. The area for the six rectangles can be represented by the following expression:

$$5 \times 6 + 5 \times 10 + 5 \times 6 + 6 \times 10 + 5 \times 10 + 6 \times 10$$

The total for all these areas added together is 280 m^2, or 280 square meters. This measurement represents the surface area because it is the area of all six surfaces of the rectangular prism.

The Net of a Rectangular Prism

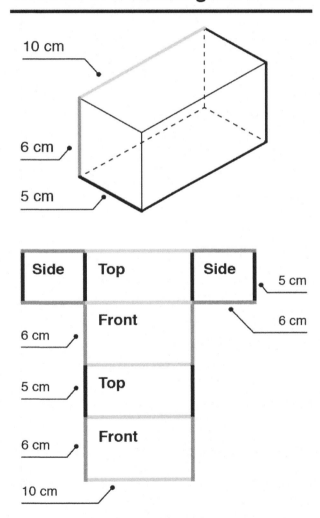

Another shape that has a surface area is a cylinder. The shapes used to make up the **cylinder** are two circles and a rectangle wrapped around between the two circles. A common example of a cylinder is a can. The two circles that make up the bases are obvious shapes. The rectangle can be more difficult to see, but the label on a can will help illustrate it. When the label is removed from a can and laid flat, the shape is a rectangle. When the areas for each shape are needed, there will be two formulas. The first is the area for the circles on the bases. This area is given by the formula $A = \pi r^2$. There will be two of these areas. Then the area of the rectangle must be determined. The width of the rectangle is equal to the height of the can, h. The length of the rectangle is equal to the circumference of the base circle, $2\pi r$. The area for the rectangle can be found by using the formula $A = 2\pi r \times h$. By adding the two areas for the bases and the area of the rectangle, the surface area of the cylinder can be found, described in units squared.

Determining How Changes to Dimensions Change Area and Volume

When the dimensions of an object change, the area and volume are also subject to change. For example, the following rectangle has an area of 98 square centimeters ($A = 7 \times 14 = 98$ cm^2). If the length is increased by 2, to be 16 cm, then the area becomes $A = 7 \times 16 = 112$ cm^2. The area increased by 14 cm, or twice the width because there were two more widths of 7 cm.

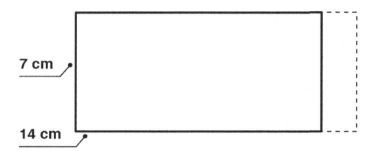

For the volume of an object, there are three dimensions. The given prism has a volume of:

$$V = 4 \times 12 \times 3 = 144 \text{ m}^3$$

If the height is increased by 3, the volume becomes:

$$V = 4 \times 12 \times 6 = 288 \text{ m}^3$$

The increase of 3 for the height, or doubling of the height, resulted in a volume that was doubled. From the original, if the width was doubled, the volume would be:

$$V = 8 \times 12 \times 3 = 288 \text{ m}^3$$

When the width doubled, the volume was doubled also. The same increase in volume would result if the length was doubled.

Identifying the x-axis, the y-axis, the Origin, and the Four Quadrants in the Coordinate Plane

The coordinate plane is a way of identifying the position of a point in relation to two axes. The **coordinate plane** is made up of two intersecting lines, the x-axis and the y-axis. These lines intersect at a right angle, and their intersection point is called the origin. The points on the coordinate plane are labeled based on their position in relation to the origin. If a point is found 4 units to the right and 2 units up from the origin, the location is described as (4, 2). These numbers are the x- and y-coordinates, always written in the order (x, y). This point is also described as lying in the first quadrant. Every point in the first quadrant has a location that is positive in the x and y directions.

The following figure shows the coordinate plane with examples of points that lie in each quadrant:

The Coordinate Plane

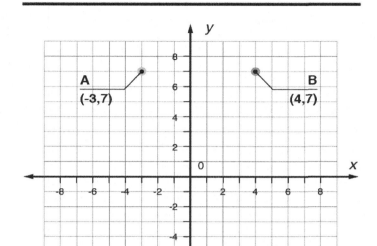

Point B lies in the first quadrant, described with positive x- and y-values, above the x-axis and to the right of the y-axis. Point A lies in the second quadrant, where the x-value is negative and the y-value is positive. This quadrant is above the x-axis and to the left of the y-axis. Point D lies in the third quadrant, where both the x- and y-values are negative. Points in this quadrant are described as being below the x-axis and to the left of the y-axis. Point C is in the fourth quadrant, where the x-value is positive and the y-value is negative.

Solving Problems Involving Elapsed Time, Money, Length, Volume, and Mass

To solve problems, follow these steps: identify the variables that are known, decide which equation should be used, substitute the numbers, and solve. To solve an equation for the amount of time that has elapsed since an event, use the equation $T = L - E$ where T represents the elapsed time, L represents the later time, and E represents the earlier time. For example, the Minnesota Vikings have not appeared in the Super Bowl since 1976. If the year is now 2017, how long has it been since the Vikings were in the Super Bowl? The later time, L, is 2017, E = 1976 and the unknown is T. Substituting these numbers, the equation is $T = 2017 - 1976$, and so T = 41. It has been 41 years since the Vikings have appeared in the Super Bowl. Questions involving total cost can be solved using the formula, $C = I + T$ where C represents the total cost, I represents the cost of the item purchased, and T represents the tax amount. To find the length of a rectangle given the area = 32 square inches and width = 8 inches, the formula $A = L \times W$ can be used. Substitute 32 for A and substitute 8 for w, giving the equation $32 = L \times 8$. This equation is solved by dividing both sides by 8 to find that the length of the rectangle is 4. The formula for volume of a rectangular prism is given by the equation $V = L \times W \times H$. If the length of a rectangular juice box is 4 centimeters, the width is 2 centimeters, and the height is 8 centimeters, what is the volume of this box? Substituting in the formula we find $V = 4 \times 2 \times 8$, so the volume is 64 cubic centimeters. In a similar fashion as those previously shown, the mass of an object can be calculated given the formula, Mass = Density × Volume.

Measuring and Comparing Lengths of Objects Using Standard Tools

Lengths of objects can be measured using tools such as rulers, yard sticks, meter sticks, and tape measures. Typically, a ruler measures 12 inches, or one foot. For this reason, a ruler is normally used to measure lengths smaller than or just slightly more than 12 inches. Rulers may represent centimeters instead of inches. Some rulers have inches on one side and centimeters on the other. Be sure to recognize what units you are measuring in. The standard ruler measurements are divided into units of 1 inch and normally broken down to $\frac{1}{2}, \frac{1}{4}, \frac{1}{8}$, and even $\frac{1}{16}$ of an inch for more precise measurements. If measuring in centimeters, the centimeter is likely divided into tenths. To measure the size of a picture, for purposes of buying a frame, a ruler is helpful. If the picture is very large, a yardstick, which measures 3 feet and normally is divided into feet and inches, might be useful. Using metric units, the meter stick measures 1 meter and is divided into 100 centimeters. To measure the size of a window in a home, either a yardstick or meter stick would work. To measure the size of a room, though, a tape measure would be the easiest tool to use. Tape measures can measure up to 10 feet, 25 feet, or more.

Comparing Relative Sizes of U.S. Customary Units and Metric Units

Measuring length in United States customary units is typically done using inches, feet, yards, and miles. When converting among these units, remember that 12 inches = 1 foot, 3 feet = 1 yard, and 5280 feet = 1 mile. Common customary units of weight are ounces and pounds. The conversion needed is 16 ounces = 1 pound. For customary units of volume ounces, cups, pints, quarts, and gallons are typically used. For conversions, use 8 ounces = 1 cup, 2 cups = 1 pint, 2 pints = 1 quart, and 4 quarts = 1 gallon. For measuring lengths in metric units, know that 100 centimeters = 1 meter, and 1000 meters = 1 kilometer. For metric units of measuring weights, grams and kilograms are often used. Know that 1000 grams = 1 kilogram when making conversions. For metric measures of volume, the most common units are milliliters and liters. Remember that 1000 milliliters = 1 liters.

Converting Units within Both the United States Customary System and the Metric System

When working with dimensions, sometimes the given units don't match the formula, and conversions must be made. The metric system has base units of meter for length, kilogram for mass, and liter for liquid volume. This system expands to three places above the base unit and three places below. These places correspond with prefixes with a base of 10.

The following table shows the conversions:

kilo-	hecto-	deka-	base	deci-	centi-	milli-
1,000 times the base	100 times the base	10 times the base		1/10 times the base	1/100 times the base	1/1000 times the base

To convert between units within the metric system, values with a base ten can be multiplied. The decimal can also be moved in the direction of the new unit by the same number of zeros on the number. For example, 3 meters is equivalent to 0.003 kilometers. The decimal moved three places (the same number of zeros for kilo-) to the left (the same direction from base to kilo-). Three meters is also equivalent to 3,000

152

millimeters. The decimal is moved three places to the right because the prefix milli- is three places to the right of the base unit.

The English Standard system used in the United States has a base unit of foot for length, pound for weight, and gallon for liquid volume. These conversions aren't as easy as the metric system because they aren't a base ten model. The following table shows the conversions within this system.

Length	Weight	Capacity
1 foot (ft) = 12 inches (in) 1 yard (yd) = 3 feet 1 mile (mi) = 5280 feet 1 mile = 1760 yards	1 pound (lb) = 16 ounces (oz) 1 ton = 2000 pounds	1 tablespoon (tbsp) = 3 teaspoons (tsp) 1 cup (c) = 16 tablespoons 1 cup = 8 fluid ounces (oz) 1 pint (pt) = 2 cups 1 quart (qt) = 2 pints 1 gallon (gal) = 4 quarts

When converting within the English Standard system, most calculations include a conversion to the base unit and then another to the desired unit. For example, take the following problem: 3 qt = ___ c. There is no straight conversion from quarts to cups, so the first conversion is from quarts to pints. There are 2 pints in 1 quart, so there are 6 pints in 3 quarts. This conversion can be solved as a proportion:

$$\frac{3 \text{ qt}}{x} = \frac{1 \text{ qt}}{2 \text{ pt}}$$

It can also be observed as a ratio 2:1, expanded to 6:3. Then the 6 pints must be converted to cups. The ratio of pints to cups is 1:2, so the expanded ratio is 6:12. For 6 pints, the measurement is 12 cups. This problem can also be set up as one set of fractions to cancel out units. It begins with the given information and cancels out matching units on top and bottom to yield the answer. Consider the following expression:

$$\frac{3 \text{ qt}}{1} \times \frac{2 \text{ pt}}{1 \text{ qt}} \times \frac{2 \text{ c}}{1 \text{ pt}}$$

It's set up so that units on the top and bottom cancel each other out:

$$\frac{3 \ \cancel{\text{qt}}}{1} \times \frac{2 \ \cancel{\text{pt}}}{1 \ \cancel{\text{qt}}} \times \frac{2 \text{ c}}{1 \ \cancel{\text{pt}}}$$

The numbers can be calculated as $3 \times 2 \times 2$ on the top and 1 on the bottom. It still yields an answer of 12 cups.

This process of setting up fractions and canceling out matching units can be used to convert between standard and metric systems. A few common equivalent conversions are 2.54 cm = 1 in, 3.28 ft = 1 m, and 2.205 lb = 1 kg. Writing these as fractions allows them to be used in conversions. For the fill-in-the-blank problem 5 m = ___ ft, an expression using conversions starts with the expression $\frac{5 \text{ m}}{1} \times \frac{3.28 \text{ ft}}{1 \text{ m}}$, where the units of meters will cancel each other out and the final unit is feet. Calculating the numbers yields 16.4 feet. This problem only required two fractions. Others may require longer expressions, but the underlying rule stays the same. When there's a unit on the top of the fraction that's the same as the unit on the bottom, then they cancel each other out. Using this logic and the conversions given above, many units can be converted between and within the different systems.

The conversion between Fahrenheit and Celsius is found in a formula:

$$°C = (°F - 32) \times \frac{5}{9}$$

For example, to convert 78°F to Celsius, the given temperature would be entered into the formula:

$$°C = (78 - 32) \times \frac{5}{9}$$

Solving the equation, the temperature comes out to be 25.56°C. To convert in the other direction, the formula becomes:

$$°F = °C \times \frac{9}{5} + 32$$

Remember the order of operations when calculating these conversions.

Solving Problems by Plotting Points and Drawing Polygons in the Coordinate Plane

Shapes can be plotted on the coordinate plane to identify the location of each vertex and the length of each side. The original shape is seen in the figure below in the first quadrant. The length is 6 and the width is 4. The reflection of this rectangle is in the fourth quadrant. A reflection across the y-axis can be found by determining each point's distance to the y-axis and moving it that same distance on the opposite side. For example, the point C is located at (2, 1). The reflection of this point moves to (–2, 1) when reflected across the y-axis. The original point A is located at (2, 5), and the reflection across the y-axis is located at (–2, 5). It is evident that the reflection across the y-axis changes the sign of the x-coordinate. A reflection across the x-axis changes the sign on the y-coordinate, as seen in the reflected figure below. Other translations can be found using the coordinate plane, such as rotations around the origin and reflections across the y-axis.

Identifying Statistical Questions

Statistics is the branch of mathematics that deals with the collection, organization, and analysis of data. A statistical question is one that can be answered by collecting and analyzing data. When collecting data, expect variability. For example, "How many pets does Yanni own?" is not a statistical question because it can be answered in one way. "How many pets do the people in a certain neighborhood own?" is a statistical question because, to determine this answer, one would need to collect data from each person in the neighborhood, and it is reasonable to expect the answers to vary.

Identify these as statistical or not statistical:

1. How old are you?

2. What is the average age of the people in your class?

3. How tall are the students in Mrs. Jones' sixth grade class?

4. Do you like Brussels sprouts?

5. Do the people in your family like Brussels sprouts?

Recognizing which Measure of Center Best Describes a Set of Data

One way information can be interpreted from tables, charts, and graphs is through statistics. The three most common calculations for a set of data are the mean, median, and mode. These three are called measures of central tendency. Measures of central tendency are helpful in comparing two or more different sets of data. The **mean** refers to the average and is found by adding up all values and dividing the total by the number of values. In other words, the mean is equal to the sum of all values divided by the number of data entries. For example, if you bowled a total of 532 points in 4 bowling games, your mean score was $\frac{532}{4} = 133$ points per game. A common application of mean useful to students is calculating what he or she needs to receive on a final exam to receive a desired grade in a class.

The **median** is found by lining up values from least to greatest and choosing the middle value. If there's an even number of values, then the mean of the two middle amounts must be calculated to find the median. For example, the median of the set of dollar amounts $5, $6, $9, $12, and $13 is $9. The median of the set of dollar amounts $1, $5, $6, $8, $9, $10 is $7, which is the mean of $6 and $8. The **mode** is the value that occurs the most. The mode of the data set {1, 3, 1, 5, 5, 8, 10} actually refers to two numbers: 1 and 5. In this case, the data set is bimodal because it has two modes. A data set can have no mode if no amount is repeated. Another useful statistic is range. The **range** for a set of data refers to the difference between the highest and lowest value.

In some cases, some numbers in a list of data might have weights attached to them. In that case, a weighted mean can be calculated. A common application of a weighted mean is GPA. In a semester, each class is assigned a number of credit hours, its weight, and at the end of the semester each student receives a grade. To compute GPA, an A is a 4, a B is a 3, a C is a 2, a D is a 1, and an F is a 0. Consider a student that takes a 4-hour English class, a 3-hour math class, and a 4-hour history class and receives all B's. The weighted mean, GPA, is found by multiplying each grade times its weight, number of credit hours, and dividing by the total number of credit hours. Therefore, the student's GPA is:

$$\frac{3 \times 4 + 3 \times 3 + 3 \times 4}{11} = \frac{33}{1} = 3.0.$$

The following bar chart shows how many students attend a cycle class on each day of the week. To find the mean attendance for the week, each day's attendance can be added together, $10 + 7 + 6 + 9 + 8 + 14 + 4 = 58$, and the total divided by the number of days, $58 \div 7 = 8.3$. The mean attendance for the week was 8.3 people. The median attendance can be found by putting the attendance numbers in order from least to greatest: 4, 6, 7, 8, 9, 10, 14, and choosing the middle number: 8 people. The mode for attendance is none for this set of data because no numbers repeat. The range is 10, which is found by finding the difference between the lowest number, 4, and the highest number, 14.

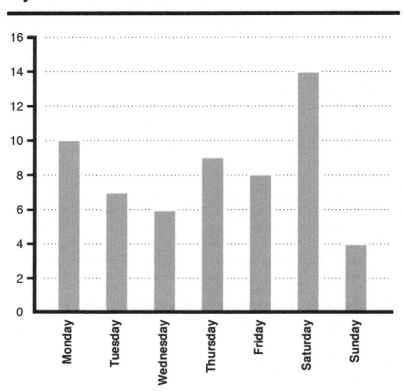

Cycle class attendance

A **histogram** is a bar graph used to group data into "bins" that cover a range on the horizontal, or x-axis. Histograms consist of rectangles whose height is equal to the frequency of a specific category. The horizontal axis represents the specific categories. Because they cover a range of data, these bins have no gaps between bars, unlike the bar graph above. In a histogram showing the heights of adult golden retrievers, the bottom axis would be groups of heights, and the y-axis would be the number of dogs in each range. Evaluating this histogram would show the height of most golden retrievers as falling within a certain range. It also provides information to find the average height and range for how tall golden retrievers may grow.

The following is a histogram that represents exam grades in a given class. The horizontal axis represents ranges of the number of points scored, and the vertical axis represents the number of students. For example, approximately 33 students scored in the 60 to 70 range.

Results of the exam

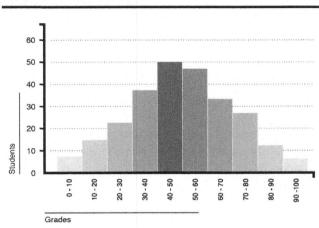

Measures of central tendency can be discussed using a histogram. If the points scored were shown with individual rectangles, the tallest rectangle would represent the mode. A bimodal set of data would have two peaks of equal height. Histograms can be classified as having data *skewed to the left, skewed to the right,* or *normally distributed,* which is also known as **bell-shaped**. These three classifications can be seen in the following chart:

Measures of central tendency images

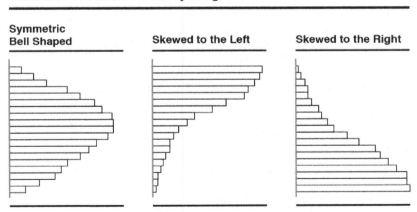

When the data is normal, the mean, median, and mode are all very close. They all represent the most typical value in the data set. The mean is typically used as the best measure of central tendency in this case because it does include all data points. However, if the data is skewed, the mean becomes less meaningful. The median is the best measure of central tendency because it is not affected by any outliers, unlike the mean. When the data is skewed, the mean is dragged in the direction of the skew. Therefore, if the data is not normal, it is best to use the median as the measure of central tendency.

The measures of central tendency and the range may also be found by evaluating information on a line graph.

In the line graph from a previous example that showed the daily high and low temperatures, the average high temperature can be found by gathering data from each day on the triangle line. The days' highs are 82, 78, 75, 65, and 70. The average is found by adding them together to get 370, then dividing by 5 (because there are 5 temperatures). The average high for the five days is 74. If 74 degrees is found on the graph, then it falls in the middle of the values on the triangle line. The m low temperature can be found in the same way.

Given a set of data, the correlation coefficient, r, measures the association between all the data points. If two values are correlated, there is an association between them. However, correlation does not necessarily mean causation, or that one value causes the other. There is a common mistake made that assumes correlation implies causation. Average daily temperature and number of sunbathers are both correlated and have causation. If the temperature increases, that change in weather causes more people to want to catch some rays. However, wearing plus-size clothing and having heart disease are two variables that are correlated but do not have causation. The larger someone is, the more likely he or she is to have heart disease. However, being overweight does not cause someone to have the disease.

The value of the correlation coefficient is between −1 and 1, where −1 represents a perfect negative linear relationship, 0 represents no relationship between the two data sets, and 1 represents a perfect positive linear relationship. A negative linear relationship means that as x values increase, y values decrease. A positive linear relationship means that as x values increase, y values increase. The formula for computing the correlation coefficient is:

$$r = \frac{n\sum xy - (\sum x)(\sum y)}{\sqrt{n(\sum x^2) - (\sum x)^2}\sqrt{n(\sum y^2) - (y)^2}}$$

n is the number of data points

The closer r is to 1 or −1, the stronger the correlation. A correlation can be seen when plotting data. If the graph resembles a straight line, there is a correlation.

Determining How Changes in Data Affect Measures of Center or Range

An **outlier** is a data point that lies an unusual distance from other points in the data set. Removing an outlier from a data set will change the measures of center. Removing a large outlier from a data set will decrease both the mean and the median. Removing a small outlier from a data set will increase both the mean and the median. For example, in data set {3, 6, 8, 12, 13, 14, 60}, the data point 60, is an outlier because it is unusually far from the other points. In this data set the mean is 16.6. Notice that this mean number is even larger than all other data points in the set except for 60. Removing the outlier, the mean changes to 9.3 and the median becomes 10. Removing an outlier will also decrease the range. In the data set above, the range is 57 when the outlier is included, but decreases to 11 when the outlier is removed.

Adding an outlier to a data set will affect the centers of measure as well. When a larger outlier is added to a data set, the mean and median increase. When a small outlier is added to a data set, the mean and median decrease. Adding an outlier to a data set will increase the range.

This does not seem to provide an appropriate measure of center when considering this data set. What will happen if that outlier is removed? Removing the extremely large data point, 60, is going to reduce the mean to 9.3. The mean decreased dramatically because 60 was much larger than any of the other data points. What would happen with an extremely low value in a data set like this one, {12, 87, 90, 95, 98, 100}? The mean of the given set is 80. When the outlier, 12, is removed, the mean should increase and should fit more closely to the other data points. Removing 12 and recalculating the mean shows that this is correct. The mean after removing 12 is 94. So, removing a large outlier will decrease the mean while removing a small outlier will increase the mean.

Describing a Set of Data

Independent and dependent are two types of variables that describe how they relate to each other. The **independent variable** is the variable controlled by the experimenter. It stands alone and isn't changed by other parts of the experiment. This variable is normally represented by x and is found on the horizontal, or x-axis, of a graph. The **dependent variable** changes in response to the independent variable. It reacts to, or depends on, the independent variable. This variable is normally represented by y and is found on the vertical, or y-axis of the graph.

The relationship between two variables, x and y, can be seen on a scatterplot.

The following scatterplot shows the relationship between weight and height. The graph shows the weight as x and the height as y. The first dot on the left represents a person who is 45 kg and approximately 150 cm tall. The other dots correspond in the same way. As the dots move to the right and weight increases, height also increases. A line could be drawn through the middle of the dots to move from bottom left to top right. This line would indicate a **positive correlation** between the variables. If the variables had a **negative correlation**, then the dots would move from the top left to the bottom right.

Height and Weight

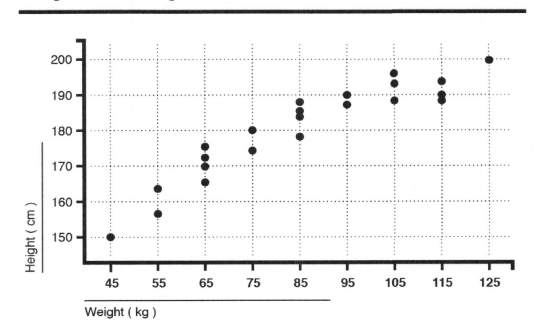

A **scatterplot** is useful in determining the relationship between two variables, but it's not required. Consider an example where a student scores a different grade on his math test for each week of the month. The independent variable would be the weeks of the month. The dependent variable would be the grades, because they change depending on the week. If the grades trended up as the weeks passed, then the relationship between grades and time would be positive. If the grades decreased as the time passed, then the relationship would be negative. (As the number of weeks went up, the grades went down.)

The relationship between two variables can further be described as strong or weak. The relationship between age and height shows a strong positive correlation because children grow taller as they grow up. In adulthood, the relationship between age and height becomes weak, and the dots will spread out. People stop growing in adulthood, and their final heights vary depending on factors like genetics and health. The closer the dots on the graph, the stronger the relationship. As they spread apart, the relationship becomes weaker. If they are too spread out to determine a correlation up or down, then the variables are said to have no correlation.

Variables are values that change, so determining the relationship between them requires an evaluation of who changes them. If the variable changes because of a result in the experiment, then it's dependent. If the variable changes before the experiment, or is changed by the person controlling the experiment, then it's the independent variable. As they interact, one is manipulated by the other. The manipulator is the independent, and the manipulated is the dependent. Once the independent and dependent variable are determined, they can be evaluated to have a positive, negative, or no correlation.

Interpreting Various Displays of Data

Tables, charts, and graphs can be used to convey information about different variables. They are all used to organize, categorize, and compare data, and they all come in different shapes and sizes. Each type has its own way of showing information, whether it is in a column, shape, or picture. To answer a question relating to a table, chart, or graph, some steps should be followed. First, the problem should be read thoroughly to determine what is being asked to determine what quantity is unknown. Then, the title of the table, chart, or graph should be read. The title should clarify what data is actually being summarized in the table. Next, look at the key and labels for both the horizontal and vertical axes, if they are given. These items will provide information about how the data is organized. Finally, look to see if there is any more labeling inside the table. Taking the time to get a good idea of what the table is summarizing will be helpful as it is used to interpret information.

Tables are a good way of showing a lot of information in a small space. The information in a table is organized in columns and rows. For example, a table may be used to show the number of votes each candidate received in an election. By interpreting the table, one may observe which candidate won the election and which candidates came in second and third. In using a bar chart to display monthly rainfall amounts in different countries, rainfall can be compared between counties at different times of the year. Graphs are also a useful way to show change in variables over time, as in a line graph, or percentages of a whole, as in a pie graph.

The table below relates the number of items to the total cost. The table shows that 1 item costs $5. By looking at the table further, 5 items cost $25, 10 items cost $50, and 50 items cost $250. This cost can be extended for any number of items. Since 1 item costs $5, then 2 items would cost $10. Though this information isn't in the table, the given price can be used to calculate unknown information.

Number of Items	1	5	10	50
Cost ($)	5	25	50	250

A bar graph is a graph that summarizes data using bars of different heights. It is useful when comparing two or more items or when seeing how a quantity changes over time. It has both a horizontal and vertical axis. Interpreting **bar graphs** includes recognizing what each bar represents and connecting that to the two variables. The bar graph below shows the scores for six people on three different games. The color of the bar shows which game each person played, and the height of the bar indicates their score for that game. William scored 25 on game 3, and Abigail scored 38 on game 3. By comparing the bars, it's obvious that Williams scored lower than Abigail.

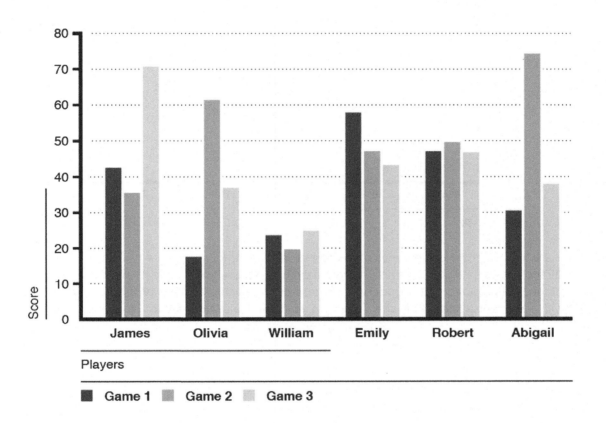

A line graph is a way to compare two variables. Each variable is plotted along an axis, and the graph contains both a horizontal and a vertical axis. On a **line graph**, the line indicates a continuous change. The change can be seen in how the line rises or falls, known as its slope, or rate of change. Often, in line graphs, the horizontal axis represents a variable of time. Audiences can quickly see if an amount has grown or decreased over time. The bottom of the graph, or the x-axis, shows the units for time, such as days, hours, months, etc. If there are multiple lines, a comparison can be made between what the two lines represent. For example, the following line graph shows the change in temperature over five days. The top line represents the high, and the bottom line represents the low for each day. Looking at the top line alone, the high decreases for a day, then increases on Wednesday. Then it decreased on Thursday and increases again on Friday. The low temperatures have a similar trend, shown in bottom line. The range in temperatures each day can also be calculated by finding the difference between the top line and bottom line on a particular day. On Wednesday, the range was 14 degrees, from 62 to 76° F.

Daily Temperatures

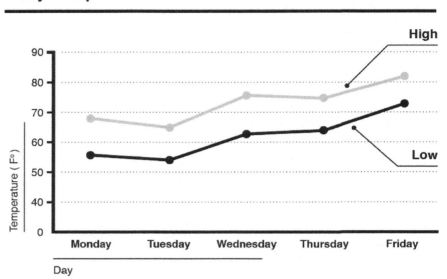

Pie charts are used to show percentages of a whole, as each category is given a piece of the pie, and together all the pieces make up a whole. They are a circular representation of data which are used to highlight numerical proportion. It is true that the arc length of each pie slice is proportional to the amount it individually represents. When a pie chart is shown, an audience can quickly make comparisons by comparing the sizes of the pieces of the pie. They can be useful for comparison between different categories. The following pie chart is a simple example of three different categories shown in comparison to each other.

Light gray represents cats, dark gray represents dogs, and the gray between those two represents other pets. As the pie is cut into three equal pieces, each value represents just more than 33 percent, or $\frac{1}{3}$ of the whole. Values 1 and 2 may be combined to represent $\frac{2}{3}$ of the whole. In an example where the total pie represents 75,000 animals, then cats would be equal to $\frac{1}{3}$ of the total, or 25,000. Dogs would equal 25,000 and other pets also equal 25,000.

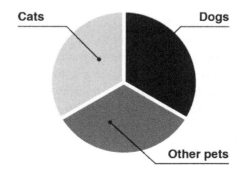

The fact that a circle is 360 degrees is used to create a pie chart. Because each piece of the pie is a percentage of a whole, that percentage is multiplied times 360 to get the number of degrees each piece represents. In the example above, each piece is $\frac{1}{3}$ of the whole, so each piece is equivalent to 120 degrees. Together, all three pieces add up to 360 degrees.

Stacked bar graphs, also used fairly frequently, are used when comparing multiple variables at one time. They combine some elements of both pie charts and bar graphs, using the organization of bar graphs and the proportionality aspect of pie charts. The following is an example of a stacked bar graph that represents the number of students in a band playing drums, flute, trombone, and clarinet. Each bar graph is broken up further into girls and boys.

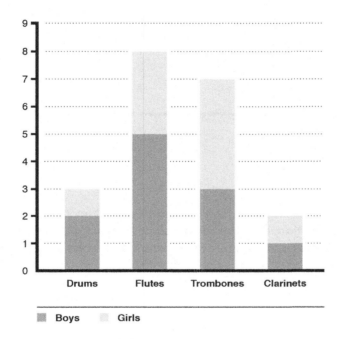

To determine how many boys play trombone, refer to the darker portion of the trombone bar, resulting in 3 students.

A **scatterplot** is another way to represent paired data. It uses Cartesian coordinates, like a line graph, meaning it has both a horizontal and vertical axis. Each data point is represented as a dot on the graph.

The dots are never connected with a line. For example, the following is a scatterplot showing people's age versus height.

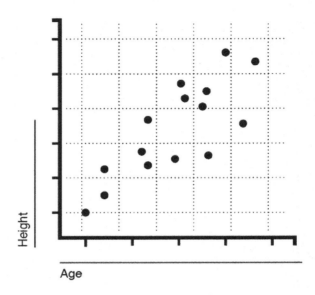

A scatterplot, also known as a **scattergram**, can be used to predict another value and to see if an association, known as a **correlation**, exists between a set of data. If the data resembles a straight line, the data is **associated**. The following is an example of a scatterplot in which the data does not seem to have an association:

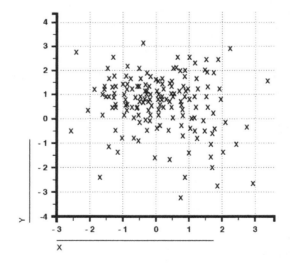

Sets of numbers and other similarly organized data can also be represented graphically. Venn diagrams are a common way to do so. A Venn diagram represents each set of data as a circle. The circles overlap, showing that each set of data is overlapping. A Venn diagram is also known as a **logic diagram** because it visualizes all possible logical combinations between two sets. Common elements of two sets are represented by the area of overlap. The following is an example of a Venn diagram of two sets A and B:

Parts of the Venn Diagram

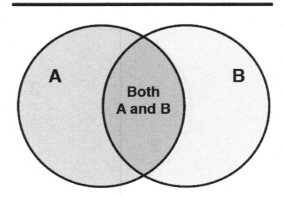

Another name for the area of overlap is the **intersection**. The intersection of A and B, $A \cap B$, contains all elements that are in both sets A and B. The union of A and B, $A \cup B$, contains all elements that are in either set A or set B. Finally, the complement of $A \cup B$ is equal to all elements that are not in either set A or set B. These elements are placed outside of the circles.

The following is an example of a Venn diagram in which 30 students were surveyed asking which type of siblings they had: brothers, sisters, or both. Ten students only had a brother, 7 students only had a sister, and 5 had both a brother and a sister. This number 5 is the intersection and is placed where the circles overlap. Two students did not have a brother or a sister. Two is therefore the complement and is placed outside of the circles.

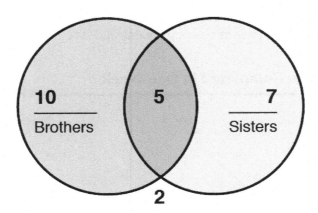

Venn diagrams can have more than two sets of data. The more circles, the more logical combinations are represented by the overlapping. The following is a Venn diagram that represents a different situation. Now, there were 30 students surveyed about the color of their socks. The innermost region represents those students that have green, pink, and blue socks on (perhaps a striped pattern). Therefore, 2 students had all three colors on their socks. In this example, all students had at least one of the three colors on their socks, so no one exists in the complement.

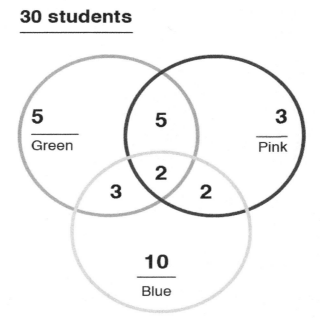

30 students

5
___
Green

5

3
___
Pink

2

3

2

10
___
Blue

Venn diagrams are typically not drawn to scale, but if they are and their area is proportional to the amount of data it represents, it is known as an **area-proportional** Venn diagram.

Identifying, Constructing, and Completing Graphs That Correctly Represent Given Data

Data is often displayed with a line graph, bar graph, or pie chart.

The line graph below shows the number of push-ups that a student did over one week.

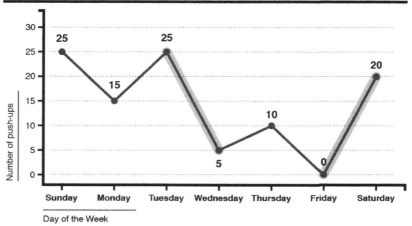

Push-Ups Completed in One Week

166

Notice that the horizontal axis displays the day of the week and the vertical axis displays the number of push-ups. A point is placed above each day of the week to show how many push-ups were done each day. For example, on Sunday the student did 25 push-ups. The line that connects the points shows how much the number of push-ups fluctuated throughout the week.

The bar graph below compares number of people who own various types of pets.

What kind of pet do you own?

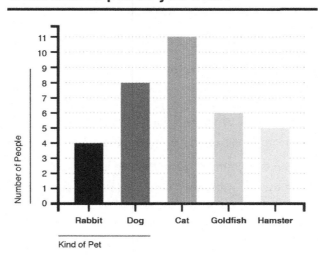

On the horizontal axis, the kind of pet is displayed. On the vertical axis, the number of people is displayed. Bars are drawn to show the number of people who own each type of pet. With the bar graph, it can quickly be determined that the fewest number of people own a rabbit and the greatest number of people own a cat.

The pie graph below displays students in a class who scored A, B, C, or D. Each slice of the pie is drawn to show the portion of the whole class that is represented by each letter grade. For example, the smallest portion represents students who scored a D. This means that the smallest number of students scored a D.

Student Grades

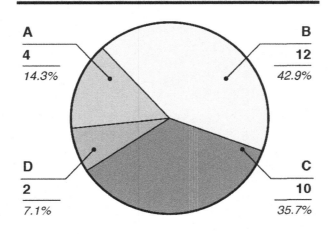

Choosing Appropriate Graphs to Display Data

Data may be displayed with a line graph, bar graph, or pie chart.

- A line graph is used to display data that changes continuously over time.

- A bar graph is used to compare data from different categories or groups and is helpful for recognizing relationships.

- A pie chart is used when the data represents parts of a whole.

Interpreting Probabilities Relative to Likelihood of Occurrence

Probability describes how likely it is that an event will occur. Probabilities are always a number from zero to 1. If an event has a high likelihood of occurrence, it will have a probability close to 1. If there is only a small chance that an event will occur, the likelihood is close to zero. A fair six-sided die has one of the numbers 1, 2, 3, 4, 5, and 6 on each side. When this die is rolled there is a one in six chance that it will land on 2. This is because there are six possibilities and only one side has a 2 on it. The probability then is $\frac{1}{6}$ or 0.167. The probability of rolling an even number from this die is three in six, which is $\frac{1}{2}$ or 0.5. This is because there are three sides on the die with even numbers (2, 4, 6), and there are six possible sides. The probability of rolling a number less than 10 is one because every side of the die has a number less than 6, so this is certain to occur. On the other hand, the probability of rolling a number larger than 20 is zero. There are no numbers greater than 20 on the die, so it is certain that this will not occur, thus the probability is zero.

If a teacher says that the probability of anyone passing her final exam is 0.2, is it highly likely that anyone will pass? No, the probability of anyone passing her exam is low because 0.2 is closer to zero than to 1. If another teacher is proud that the probability of students passing his class is 0.95, how likely is it that a student will pass? It is highly likely that a student will pass because the probability, 0.95, is very close to 1.

A **two-way frequency table** displays categorical data with two variables, and it highlights relationships that exist between those two variables. Such tables are used frequently to summarize survey results and are also known as **contingency tables**. Each cell shows a count pertaining to that individual variable paring, known as a **joint frequency**, and the totals of each row and column also are in the table.

Consider the following two-way frequency table:

Distribution of the Residents of a Particular Village

	70 or older	69 or younger	Totals
Women	20	40	60
Men	5	35	40
Total	25	75	100

Table 1 shows the breakdown of ages and sexes of 100 people in a particular village. The total number of people in the data is shown in the bottom right corner. Each total is shown at the end of each row or column, as well. For instance, there were 25 people age 70 or older and 60 women in the data. The 20 in the first cell shows that out of 100 total villagers, 20 were women aged 70 or older. The 5 in the cell below shows that out of 100 total villagers, 5 were men aged 70 or older.

A two-way table can also show relative frequencies. If instead of the count, the percentage of people in each category was placed into the cells, the two-way table would show relative frequencies. If each frequency is calculated over the entire total of 100, the first cell would be 20% or 0.2. However, the relative frequencies can also be calculated over row or column totals. If row totals were used, the first cell would be:

$$\frac{20}{60} = 0.333 = 33.3\%$$

If column totals were used, the first cell would be:

$$\frac{20}{25} = 0.8 = 80\%$$

Such tables can be used to calculate **conditional probabilities**, which are probabilities that an event occurs, given another event. Consider a randomly selected villager. The probability of selecting a male 70 years old or older is $\frac{5}{100} = 0.05$ because there are 5 males over the age of 70 and 100 total villagers.

Practice Questions

1. What is $\frac{12}{60}$ converted to a percentage?

   a. 0.20

   b. 20%

   c. 25%

   d. 12%

$$\frac{12}{60} = \frac{x}{100}$$

2. Which of the following is the correct decimal form of the fraction $\frac{14}{33}$ rounded to the nearest hundredth place?

   a. 0.420

   b. 0.42

   c. 0.424

   d. 0.140

$$\frac{14}{33} = \frac{x}{100}$$

3. Which of the following represents the correct sum of $\frac{14}{15}$ and $\frac{2}{5}$?

   a. $\frac{20}{15}$

   b. $\frac{4}{3}$

   c. $\frac{16}{20}$

   d. $\frac{4}{5}$

$$\frac{6}{15} + \frac{14}{15} = \frac{20}{15}$$

4. What is the product of $\frac{5}{14}$ and $\frac{7}{20}$?

   a. $\frac{1}{8}$

   b. $\frac{35}{280}$

   c. $\frac{12}{34}$

   d. $\frac{1}{2}$

$$\frac{5}{14} \times \frac{7}{20} \qquad \frac{35}{280} \qquad \frac{35}{280}$$

5. What is the result of dividing 24 by $\frac{8}{5}$?

   a. $\frac{5}{3}$

   b. $\frac{3}{5}$

   c. $\frac{120}{8}$

   d. 15

$$24 \div \frac{8}{5} \qquad \frac{24}{1} \times \frac{5}{8} \qquad \frac{120}{8}$$

6. Subtract $\frac{5}{14}$ from $\frac{5}{24}$. Which of the following is the correct result?

   a. $\frac{25}{168}$

   b. 0

   c. $-\frac{25}{168}$

   d. $\frac{1}{10}$

$\frac{5}{24} - \frac{5}{14}$

$\frac{35}{128}$

$\frac{35}{168} - \frac{60}{168} = \frac{-25}{168}$

7. Which of the following is a correct mathematical statement?

   a. $\frac{1}{3} < -\frac{4}{3}$

   b. $-\frac{1}{3} > \frac{4}{3}$

   c. $\frac{1}{3} > -\frac{4}{3}$

   d. $-\frac{1}{3} \geq \frac{4}{3}$

$\frac{1}{3} < -\frac{4}{3}$

$-\frac{1}{3} > \frac{4}{3}$

$\frac{1}{3} > -\frac{4}{3}$ ✓

8. Which of the following is incorrect?

   a. $-\frac{1}{5} < \frac{4}{5}$ ✓

   b. $\frac{4}{5} > -\frac{1}{5}$ ✓

   c. $-\frac{1}{5} > \frac{4}{5}$ ✗

   d. $\frac{1}{5} > -\frac{4}{5}$ ✓

9. What is the solution to the equation $3(x + 2) = 14x - 5$?

   a. $x = 1$

   b. No solution

   c. $x = 0$

   d. All real numbers

$11 = 14x - 3x$

$11 = 11x$

$x = 1$

$3(x+2) = 14x - 5$

$3x + 6 = 14x - 5$

$10 - 0 + 2 = 0 + 12 - 0$

10. What is the solution to the equation $10 - 5x + 2 = 7x + 12 - 12x$?

   a. $x = 12$

   b. No solution

   c. $x = 0$

   d. All real numbers

$10 - 5x + 2 = 7x + 12 - 12x$

$12 - 12 =$

$12x + 12 - 12x$

$0 = 0x$

PEMDAS ?

11. Which of the following is the result when solving the equation $4(x + 5) + 6 = 2(2x + 3)$?

   a. Any real number is a solution.

   b. There is no solution.

   c. $x = 6$ is the solution.

   d. $x = 26$ is the solution.

$4(x+5) + 6 = 2(2x+3)$

$4x + 20 + 6 = 4x + 6$

$-4x \qquad -4x$

$20 + 6 = 0$?

12. How many cases of cola can Lexi purchase if each case is $3.50 and she has $40?
    a. 10
    b. 12
    c. 11.4
    d. 11

13. Two consecutive integers exist such that the sum of three times the first and two less than the second is equal to 411. What are those integers?
    a. 103 and 104
    b. 104 and 105
    c. 102 and 103
    d. 100 and 101

14. In a neighborhood, 15 out of 80 of the households have children under the age of 18. What percentage of the households have children?
    a. 0.1875%
    b. 18.75%
    c. 1.875%
    d. 15%

15. Gina took an algebra test last Friday. There were 35 questions, and she answered 60% of them correctly. How many correct answers did she have?
    a. 35
    b. 20
    c. 21
    d. 25

16. Paul took a written driving test, and he got 12 of the questions correct. If he answered 75% of the total questions correctly, how many problems were there in the test?
    a. 25
    b. 16
    c. 20
    d. 18

17. If a car is purchased for $15,395 with a 7.25% sales tax, how much is the total price?
    a. $15,395.07
    b. $16,511.14
    c. $16,411.13
    d. $15,402

18. A car manufacturer usually makes 15,412 SUVs, 25,895 station wagons, 50,412 sedans, 8,123 trucks, and 18,312 hybrids a month. About how many cars are manufactured each month?
    a. 120,000
    b. 200,000
    c. 300,000
    d. 12,000

19. Each year, a family goes to the grocery store every week and spends $105. About how much does the family spend annually on groceries?

    a. $10,000
    b. $50,000
    c. $500
    d. $5,000

20. Bindee is having a barbeque on Sunday and needs 12 packets of ketchup for every 5 guests. If 60 guests are coming, how many packets of ketchup should she buy?

    a. 100
    b. 12
    c. 144
    d. 60

21. A grocery store sold 48 bags of apples in one day, and 9 of the bags contained Granny Smith apples. The rest contained Red Delicious apples. What is the ratio of bags of Granny Smith to bags of Red Delicious that were sold?

    a. 48:9
    b. 39:9
    c. 9:48
    d. 9:39

9:39

22. If Oscar's bank account totaled $4,000 in March and $4,900 in June, what was the rate of change in his bank account total over those three months?

    a. $900 a month
    b. $300 a month
    c. $4,900 a month
    d. $100 a month

23. Erin and Katie work at the same ice cream shop. Together, they always work less than 21 hours a week. In a week, if Katie worked two times as many hours as Erin, how many hours could Erin work?

    a. Less than 7 hours
    b. Less than or equal to 7 hours
    c. More than 7 hours
    d. Less than 8 hours

< 21

6×2=12 + 6 = 18
7×2=14 + 7 = 21

24. From the chart below, which two are preferred by more men than women?

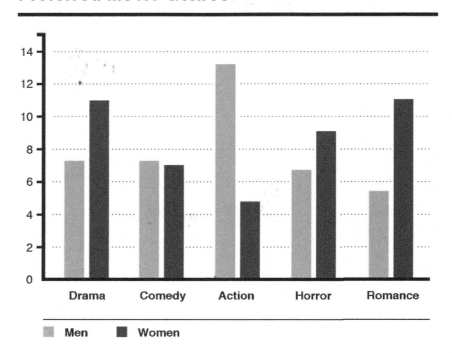

Preferred Movie Genres

Men, Women — Drama, Comedy, Action, Horror, Romance

a. Comedy and Action
b. Drama and Comedy
c. Action and Horror
d. Action and Romance

25. Which type of graph best represents a continuous change over a period of time?
    a. Bar graph
    b. Line graph
    c. Pie graph
    d. Histogram

174

26. Using the graph below, what is the mean number of visitors for the first 4 hours?

Museum Visitors

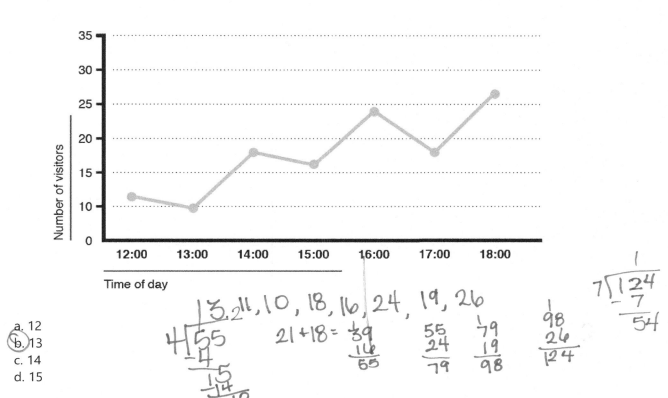

Time of day

a. 12
b. 13
c. 14
d. 15

27. What is the mode for the grades shown in the chart below?

Science Grades	
Jerry	65
Bill	95
Anna	80
Beth	95
Sara	85
Ben	72
Jordan	98

a. 65
b. 33
c. 95
d. 90

28. What type of relationship is there between age and attention span as represented in the graph below?

Attention Span

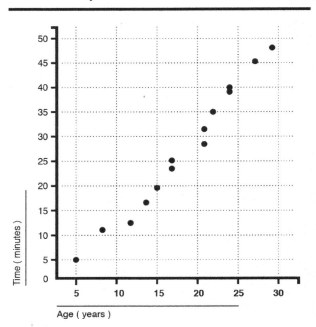

Age (years)

a. No correlation
b. Positive correlation
c. Negative correlation
d. Weak correlation

29. What is the area of the shaded region?

$\frac{1}{2}b \times h$

$\frac{1}{2}3$

$\frac{1}{2} \times \frac{3}{1}$ $\frac{3}{2} \times \frac{2}{1}$ $\frac{6}{2} = 3m^2$

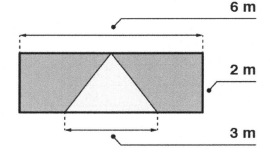

6 m

2 m

3 m

a. 9 m²
b. 12 m²
c. 6 m²
d. 8 m²

$6 \times 2 = 12m^2$

30. What is the volume of the cylinder below?

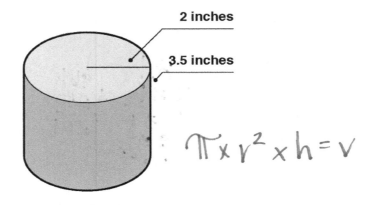

2 inches

3.5 inches

$\pi \times r^2 \times h = v$

a. 18.84 in^3
b. 45.00 in^3
c. 70.43 in^3
d. 43.96 in^3

$3.14 \times 4 \times 3.5 = v$

$3.14 \times 4 = 12.56$

$\begin{array}{r} 3.14 \\ \times 4 \\ \hline 12.56 \end{array}$

$\begin{array}{r} 12.56 \\ \times 3.5 \\ \hline \end{array}$

31. How many kiloliters are in 6 liters?
a. 6,000
b. 600
c. 0.006
d. 0.0006

32. How many centimeters are in 3 feet? (Note: 2.54 cm = 1 in)
a. 0.635
b. 91.44
c. 14.17
d. 7.62

$\begin{array}{r} 2.54 \\ \times 12 \\ \hline 508 \\ 2540 \\ \hline 3048 \end{array}$ $\times 3$

33. Which of the following relations is a function?
a. {(1, 4), (1, 3), (2, 4), (5, 6)}
b. {(-1, -1), (-2, -2), (-3, -3), (-4, -4)}
c. {(0, 0), (1, 0), (2, 0), (1, 1)}
d. {(1, 0), (1, 2), (1, 3), (1, 4)}

A

34. Find the indicated function value:

$$f(5) \text{ for } f(x) = x^2 - 2x + 1$$

a. 16
b. 1
c. 5
d. Does not exist

$25 - 10 + 1$

$15 + 1 = 16$

35. What is the domain of:

$$f(x) = 4x^2 + 2x - 1$$

a. $(0, \infty)$
b. $(-\infty, 0)$
c. $(-\infty, \infty)$

$-1 \quad 4 - 2 - 1$

$2 - 1 = 1$

d. $(-1, 4)$

36. The function $f(x) = 3.1x + 240$ models the total U.S. population, in millions, x years after the year 1980. Use this function to answer the following question: What is the total U.S. population in 2011? Round to the nearest million.
  a. 336 people
  b. 336 million people
  c. 6,474 people
  d. 647 million people

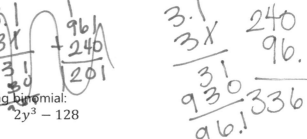

37. Find the correct factorization of the following binomial:
$$2y^3 - 128$$

  a. $2(y + 8)(y - 8)$
  b. $2(y - 4)(y^2 + 4y + 16)$
  c. $2(y - 4)(y + 4)^2$
  d. $2(y - 4)^3$

38. What is the simplified form of $(4y^3)^4(3y^7)^2$?
  a. $12y^{26}$
  b. $2,304y^{16}$
  c. $12y^{14}$
  d. $2,304y^{26}$

39. The following set represents the test scores from a university class: {35, 79, 80, 87, 87, 90, 92, 95, 95, 98, 99}. If the outlier is removed from this set, which of the following is TRUE?
  a. The mean and the median will decrease.
  b. The mean and the median will increase.
  c. The mean and the mode will increase.
  d. The mean and the mode will decrease.

40. The number of members of the House of Representatives varies directly with the total population in a state. If the state of New York has 19,800,000 residents and has 27 total representatives, how many should Ohio have with a population of 11,800,000?
  a. 10
  b. 16
  c. 11
  d. 5

41. Which of the statements below is a statistical question?
  a. What was your grade on the last test?
  b. What were the grades of the students in your class on the last test?
  c. What kind of car do you drive?
  d. What was Sam's time in the marathon?

42. Eva Jane is practicing for an upcoming 5K run. She has recorded the following times (in minutes):

25, 18, 23, 28, 30, 22.5, 23, 33, 20

Use the above information to answer the next three questions to the closest minute. What is Eva Jane's mean time?

a. 26 minutes
b. 19 minutes
c. 25 minutes
d. 23 minutes

43. What is the mode of Eva Jane's time?

a. 16 minutes
b. 20 minutes
c. 23 minutes
d. 33 minutes

44. What is Eva Jane's median time?

a. 23 minutes
b. 17 minutes
c. 28 minutes
d. 19 minutes

45. Given the linear function $g(x) = \frac{1}{4}x - 2$, which domain value corresponds to a range value of $\frac{1}{8}$?

a. $\frac{17}{2}$
b. $-\frac{63}{32}$
c. 0
d. $\frac{2}{17}$

46. A ball is thrown up from a building that is 800 feet high. Its position s in feet above the ground is given by the function $s = -32t^2 + 90t + 800$, where t is the number of seconds since the ball was thrown. How long will it take for the ball to come back to its starting point? Round your answer to the nearest tenth of a second.

a. 0 seconds
b. 2.8 seconds
c. 3 seconds
d. 8 seconds

47. The population of coyotes in the local national forest has been declining since 2000. The population can be modeled by the function $y = -(x - 2)^2 + 1600$, where y represents number of coyotes and x represents the number of years past 2000. When will there be no more coyotes?

a. 2020
b. 2040
c. 2012
d. 2042

179

48. What is the volume of the given figure?

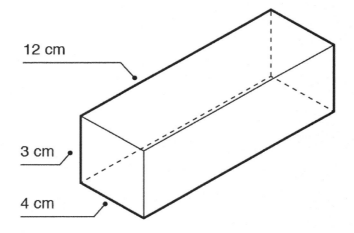

12 cm

3 cm

4 cm

    a. 38 units^3
    b. 144 units^3
    c. 72 units^3
    d. 36 units^3

49. Which equation correctly shows how to find the surface area of a cylinder?

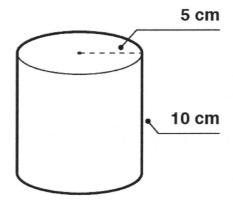

5 cm

10 cm

    a. $SA = 2\pi \times 5 \times 10 + 2(\pi 5^2)$
    b. $SA = 5 \times 2\pi \times 5$
    c. $SA = 2\pi 5^2$
    d. $SA = 2\pi \times 10 + \pi 5^2$

50. Which shapes could NOT be used to compose a hexagon?

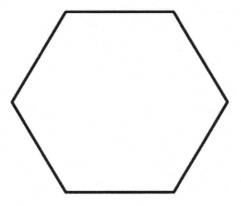

     a. Six triangles
     b. One rectangle and two triangles
     c. Two rectangles
     d. Two trapezoids

Answer Explanations

1. B: The fraction $\frac{12}{60}$ can be reduced to $\frac{1}{5}$, in lowest terms. First, it must be converted to a decimal. Dividing 1 by 5 results in 0.2. Then, to convert to a percentage, move the decimal point two units to the right and add the percentage symbol. The result is 20%.

2. B: If a calculator is used, divide 33 into 14 and keep two decimal places. If a calculator is not used, multiply both the numerator and denominator times 3. This results in the fraction $\frac{42}{99}$, and hence a decimal of 0.42.

3. B: Common denominators must be used. The LCD is 15, and $\frac{2}{5} = \frac{6}{15}$. Therefore, $\frac{14}{15} + \frac{6}{15} = \frac{20}{15}$, and in lowest terms, the answer is $\frac{4}{3}$. A common factor of 5 was divided out of both the numerator and denominator.

4. A: A product is found by multiplication. Multiplying two fractions together is easier when common factors are cancelled first to avoid working with larger numbers.

$$\frac{5}{14} \times \frac{7}{20}$$

$$\frac{5}{2 \times 7} \times \frac{7}{5 \times 4}$$

$$\frac{1}{2} \times \frac{1}{4} = \frac{1}{8}$$

5. D: Division is completed by multiplying times the reciprocal. Therefore:

$$24 \div \frac{8}{5}$$

$$\frac{24}{1} \times \frac{5}{8}$$

$$\frac{3 \times 8}{1} \times \frac{5}{8}$$

$$\frac{15}{1} = 15$$

6. C: Common denominators must be used. The LCD is 168, so each fraction must be converted to have 168 as the denominator.

$$\frac{5}{24} - \frac{5}{14}$$

$$\frac{5}{24} \times \frac{7}{7} - \frac{5}{14} \times \frac{12}{12}$$

$$\frac{35}{168} - \frac{60}{168}$$

$$-\frac{25}{168}$$

7. C: The correct mathematical statement is the one in which the smaller of the two numbers is on the "less than" side of the inequality symbol. It is written in Choice C that $\frac{1}{3} > -\frac{4}{3}$, which is the same as $-\frac{4}{3} < \frac{1}{3}$, a correct statement.

8. C: $-\frac{1}{5} > \frac{4}{5}$ is incorrect. The expression on the left is negative, which means that it is smaller than the expression on the right. As it is written, the inequality states that the expression on the left is greater than the expression on the right, which is not true.

9. A: First, the distributive property must be used on the left side. This results in:

$$3x + 6 = 14x - 5$$

The addition property is then used to add 5 to both sides, and then to subtract $3x$ from both sides, resulting in $11 = 11x$. Finally, the multiplication property is used to divide each side by 11. Therefore, $x = 1$ is the solution.

10. D: First, like terms are collected to obtain:

$$12 - 5x = -5x + 12$$

Then, if the addition principle is used to move the terms with the variable, $5x$ is added to both sides and the mathematical statement $12 = 12$ is obtained. This is always true; therefore, all real numbers satisfy the original equation.

11. B: The distributive property is used on both sides to obtain:

$$4x + 20 + 6 = 4x + 6$$

Then, like terms are collected on the left, resulting in $4x + 26 = 4x + 6$. Next, the addition principle is used to subtract $4x$ from both sides, and this results in the false statement $26 = 6$. Therefore, there is no solution.

12. D: This is a one-step real-world application problem. The unknown quantity is the number of cases of cola to be purchased. Let x be equal to this amount. Because each case costs \$3.50, the total number of cases multiplied by \$3.50 must equal \$40. This translates to the mathematical equation $3.5x = 40$. Divide both sides by 3.5 to obtain $x = 11.4286$, which has been rounded to four decimal places. Because cases are sold whole, and there is not enough money to purchase 12 cases, 11 cases is the correct answer.

13. A: First, the variables have to be defined. Let x be the first integer; therefore, $x + 1$ is the second integer. This is a two-step problem. The sum of three times the first and two less than the second is translated into the following expression:

$$3x + (x + 1 - 2)$$

This expression is set equal to 411 to obtain:

$$3x + (x + 1 - 2) = 411$$

The left-hand side is simplified to obtain:

$$4x - 1 = 411$$

The addition and multiplication properties are used to solve for x. First, add 1 to both sides and then divide both sides by 4 to obtain $x = 103$. The next consecutive integer is 104.

14. B: First, the information is translated into the ratio $\frac{15}{80}$. To find the percentage, translate this fraction into a decimal by dividing 15 by 80. The corresponding decimal is 0.1875. Move the decimal point two units to the right to obtain the percentage 18.75%.

15. C: Gina answered 60% of 35 questions correctly; 60% can be expressed as the decimal 0.60. Therefore, she answered $0.60 \times 35 = 21$ questions correctly.

16. B: The unknown quantity is the number of total questions on the test. Let x be equal to this unknown quantity. Therefore, $0.75x = 12$. Divide both sides by 0.75 to obtain $x = 16$.

17. B: If sales tax is 7.25%, the price of the car must be multiplied times 1.0725 to account for the additional sales tax. Therefore:

$$15{,}395 \times 1.0725 = 16{,}511.1375$$

This amount is rounded to the nearest cent, which is $16,511.14.

18. A: Rounding can be used to find the best approximation. All of the values can be rounded to the nearest thousand. 15,412 SUVs can be rounded to 15,000. 25,815 station wagons can be rounded to 26,000. 50,412 sedans can be rounded to 50,000. 8,123 trucks can be rounded to 8,000. Finally, 18,312 hybrids can be rounded to 18,000. The sum of the rounded values is 117,000, which is closest to 120,000.

19. D: There are 52 weeks in a year, and if the family spends $105 each week, that amount is close to $100. A good approximation is $100 a week for 50 weeks, which is found through the product $50 \times 100 = \$5{,}000$.

20. C: This problem involves ratios and percentages. If 12 packets are needed for every 5 people, this statement is equivalent to the ratio $\frac{12}{5}$. The unknown amount x is the number of ketchup packets needed for 60 people. The proportion $\frac{12}{5} = \frac{x}{60}$ must be solved. Cross-multiply to obtain $12 \times 60 = 5x$. Therefore, $720 = 5x$. Divide each side by 5 to obtain $x = 144$.

21. D: There were 48 total bags of apples sold. If 9 bags were Granny Smith and the rest were Red Delicious, then $48 - 9 = 39$ bags were Red Delicious. Therefore, the ratio of Granny Smith to Red Delicious is 9:39.

22. B: The average rate of change is found by calculating the difference in dollars over the elapsed time. Therefore, the rate of change is equal to ($4,900 − $4,000) ÷ 3 months, which is equal to $900 ÷ 3 or $300 per month.

23. A: Let x be the unknown, the number of hours Erin can work. We know Katie works $2x$, and the sum of all hours is less than 21. Therefore, $x + 2x < 21$, which simplifies into $3x < 21$. Solving this results in the inequality $x < 7$ after dividing both sides by 3. Therefore, Erin can work less than 7 hours.

24. A: The chart is a bar chart showing how many men and women prefer each genre of movies. The dark gray bars represent the number of women, while the light gray bars represent the number of men. The light gray bars are higher and represent more men than women for the genres of Comedy and Action.

25. B: A line graph represents continuous change over time. The line on the graph is continuous and not broken, as on a scatter plot. A bar graph may show change but isn't necessarily continuous over time. A pie graph is better for representing percentages of a whole. Histograms are best used in grouping sets of data in bins to show the frequency of a certain variable.

26. C: The mean for the number of visitors during the first 4 hours is 14. The mean is found by calculating the average for the four hours. Adding up the total number of visitors during those hours gives $12 + 10 + 18 + 16 = 56$. Then $56 ÷ 4 = 14$.

27. C: The mode for a set of data is the value that occurs the most. The grade that appears the most is 95. It's the only value that repeats in the set.

28. B: The relationship between age and time for attention span is a positive correlation because the general trend for the data is up and to the right. As the age increases, so does attention span.

29. A: The area of the shaded region is calculated in a few steps. First, the area of the rectangle is found using the formula:

$$A = length \times width = 6 \text{ m} \times 2 \text{ m} = 12 \text{ m}^2$$

Second, the area of the triangle is found using the formula:

$$A = \frac{1}{2} \times base \times height = \frac{1}{2} \times 3 \text{ m} \times 2 \text{ m} = 3 \text{ m}^2$$

The last step is to take the rectangle area and subtract the triangle area. The area of the shaded region is:

$$A = 12 \text{ m}^2 - 3 \text{ m}^2 = 9 \text{ m}^2$$

30. D: The volume for a cylinder is found by using the formula:

$$V = \pi r^2 h = \pi (2 \text{ in})^2 \times 3.5 \text{ in} = 43.96 \text{ in}^3$$

31. C: There are 0.006 kiloliters in 6 liters because 1 liter is 0.001 kiloliters. The conversion comes from the chart where the prefix kilo- is found three places to the left of the base unit.

32. B: The conversion between feet and centimeters requires a middle term. As there are 2.54 centimeters in 1 inch, the conversion between inches and feet must be found. As there are 12 inches in a foot, the fractions can be set up as follows:

$$3 \text{ ft} \times \frac{12 \text{ in}}{1 \text{ ft}} \times \frac{2.54 \text{ cm}}{1 \text{ in}}$$

The feet and inches cancel out to leave only centimeters for the answer. The numbers are calculated across the top and bottom to yield:

$$\frac{3 \times 12 \times 2.54}{1 \times 1} = 91.44$$

The number and units used together form the answer of 91.44 cm.

33. B: The only relation in which every x-value corresponds to exactly one y-value is the relation given in B, making it a function. The other relations have the same first component paired up to different second components, which goes against the definition of functions.

34. A: To find a function value, plug in the number given for the variable and evaluate the expression, using the order of operations (parentheses, exponents, multiplication, division, addition, subtraction). The function given is a polynomial function:

$$f(5) = 5^2 - 2 \times 5 + 1$$

$$f(5) = 25 - 10 + 1 = 16$$

35. C: The function given is a polynomial function. Anything can be plugged into a polynomial function to get an output. Therefore, its domain is all real numbers, which is expressed in interval notation as $(-\infty, \infty)$.

36. B: The variable x represents the number of years after 1980. The year 2011 was 31 years after 1980, so plug 31 into the function to obtain:

$$f(31) = 3.1 \times 31 + 240 = 336.1$$

This value rounds to 336 and represents 336 million people.

37. B: First, the common factor 2 can be factored out of both terms, resulting in:

$$2(y^3 - 64)$$

The resulting binomial is a difference of cubes that can be factored using the rule:

$$a^3 - b^3 = (a - b)(a^2 + ab + b^2)$$

with $a = y$ and $b = 4$. Therefore, the result is:

$$2(y - 4)(y^2 + 4y + 16)$$

38. D: The exponential rules $(ab)^m = a^m b^m$ and $(a^m)^n = a^{mn}$ can be used to rewrite the expression as:

$$4^4 y^{12} \times 3^2 y^{14}$$

The coefficients are multiplied together and the exponential rule $a^m a^n = a^{m+n}$ is then used to obtain the simplified form $2{,}304y^{26}$.

39. B: The outlier is 35. When a small outlier is removed from a data set, the mean and the median increase. The first step in this process is to identify the outlier, which is the number that lies away from the given set. Once the outlier is identified, the mean and median can be recalculated. The mean will be affected because it averages all of the numbers. The median will be affected because it finds the middle number, which is subject to change because a number is lost. The mode will most likely not change because it is the number that occurs the most, which will not be the outlier if there is only one outlier.

40. B: The number of representatives varies directly with the population, so the equation necessary is $N = k \times P$, where N is number of representatives, k is the variation constant, and P is total population in millions. Plugging in the information for New York allows k to be solved for. This process gives $27 = k \times 19.8$, so $k = 1.36$. Therefore, the formula for number of representatives given total population in millions is $N = 1.36 \times P$. Plugging in $P = 11.8$ for Ohio results in $N = 16.05$, which rounds to 16 total representatives.

41. B: This is a statistical question because to determine this answer one would need to collect data from each person in the class and it is expected the answers would vary. The other answers do not require data to be collected from multiple sources, therefore the answers will not vary.

42. C: The mean is found by adding all the times together and dividing by the number of times recorded.

$$25 + 18 + 23 + 28 + 30 + 22.5 + 23 + 33 + 20 = 222.5, \text{ divided by } 9 = 24.7$$

Rounding to the nearest minute, the mean is 25.

43. C: The mode is the time from the data set that occurs most often. The number 23 occurs twice in the data set, while all others occur only once, so the mode is 23.

44. A: To find the median of a data set, you must first list the numbers from smallest to largest, and then find the number in the middle. If there are two numbers in the middle, add the two numbers in the middle together and divide by 2. Putting this list in order from smallest to greatest yields 18, 20, 22.5, 23, 23, 25, 28, 30, and 33, where 23 is the middle number, so 23 minutes is the median.

45. A: The range value is given, and this is the output of the function. Therefore, the function must be set equal to $\frac{1}{8}$ and solved for x. Thus, $\frac{1}{8} = \frac{1}{4}x - 2$ needs to be solved. The fractions can be cleared by multiplying times the LCD 8. This results in $1 = 2x - 16$. Add 16 to both sides and divide by 2 to obtain $x = \frac{17}{2}$.

46. C: The ball is back at the starting point when the function is equal to 800 feet. Therefore, this results in solving the equation:

$$800 = -32t^2 + 90t + 800$$

Subtract 800 off of both sides and factor the remaining terms to obtain:

$$0 = 2t(-16 + 45t)$$

Setting both factors equal to 0 results in $t = 0$, which is when the ball was thrown up initially, and:

$$t = \frac{45}{16} = 2.8 \text{ seconds}$$

Therefore, it will take the ball 2.8 seconds to come back down to its staring point.

47. D: There will be no more coyotes when the population is 0, so set y equal to 0 and solve the quadratic equation:

$$0 = -(x - 2)^2 + 1600$$

Subtract 1600 from both sides and divide through by -1. This results in $1600 = (x - 2)^2$. Then, take the square root of both sides. This process results in the following equation:

$$\pm 40 = x - 2$$

Adding 2 to both sides results in two solutions: $x = 42$ and $x = -38$. Because the problem involves years after 2000, the only solution that makes sense is 42. Add 42 to 2000, so therefore in 2042 there will be no more coyotes.

48. B: The volume of a rectangular prism is found by multiplying the length by the width by the height. This formula yields an answer of 144 cubic units. The answer must be in cubic units because volume involves all three dimensions. Each of the other answers have only two dimensions that are multiplied, and one dimension is forgotten, as in D, where 12 and 3 are multiplied.

49. A: The surface area for a cylinder is the sum of the two circle bases and the rectangle formed on the side. This is easily seen in the net of a cylinder.

The Net of a Cylinder

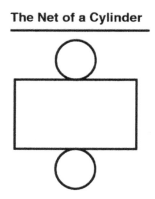

The area of a circle is found by multiplying pi times the radius squared. The rectangle's area is found by multiplying the circumference of the circle by the height. The equation $SA = 2\pi \times 5 \times 10 + 2(\pi 5^2)$ shows the area of the rectangle as $2\pi \times 5 \times 10$, which yields 314. The area of the bases is found by $\pi 5^2$, which yields 78.5, then multiplied by 2 for the two bases.

50. C: A hexagon can be formed by any combination of the given shapes except for two rectangles. There are no two rectangles that can make up a hexagon.

Social Studies

United States History, Government, and Citizenship

European Exploration and Colonization

In what's referred to as the "Age of Exploration," Europeans began exploring overseas regions they'd never seen before. The Age of Exploration started in the early 15th century and lasted until the late 18th century, and in practice, it represents the earliest stage of globalization. Technological innovation facilitated European exploration, like the *caravel* (a smaller and more maneuverable ship first used by the Portuguese to explore West Africa), the *astrolabe* (used to measure the inclined position in the sky of a celestial body), and the *quadrant* (an instrument used to take angular measurements of altitude in astronomy and navigation), which increased navigators' accuracy.

European monarchies hired explorers primarily to expand trade routes, particularly to increase access to the Indian spice markets. There were other motivating factors, however, such as the desire to spread Christianity and pursue glory.

As exploration increased, European powers adopted the policies of mercantilism and colonialism. **Mercantilism** is an economic policy that prioritizes the wealth, trade, and accumulation of resources for the sole benefit of the nation. Colonization was an outgrowth of mercantilism that involved establishing control over foreign people and territories. Unsurprisingly, mercantilism and colonialism were a major source of conflict between native people, colonists, and colonizers.

In 1492, Christopher Columbus arrived in the Caribbean, though he initially and mistakenly believed he'd landed in India. Over the next two centuries, European powers established several colonies in North America to extract the land's resources and prevent their rivals from doing the same. In 1565, Spain established the first European colony in North America at St. Augustine in present-day Florida. Along with building a South and Central American empire, Spain colonized Mexico and much of the present-day American southwest, southeast, and heartland (Louisiana Territory). Sweden colonized the mid-Atlantic region of the present-day United States in 1638, but the Netherlands conquered these colonies in 1655. France colonized Canada, Hudson's Bay, Acadia (near present-day Maine), and Newfoundland. In 1717, France assumed control over the Louisiana Territory from Spain.

In 1607, England established its first colony at Jamestown. Six years later, Jamestown colonists imported the first slaves to North America. During the rest of the 17th century, British separatist Puritans (Pilgrims) arrived on the **Mayflower** in Cape Cod, Massachusetts. Great Britain conquered New Netherlands (New York) in 1674, effectively driving the Dutch out of North America.

England's North American holdings expanded into the Thirteen Colonies—Connecticut, Delaware, Georgia, Maryland, Massachusetts, New Hampshire, New Jersey, New York, North Carolina, Pennsylvania, Rhode Island, South Carolina, and Virginia. Some colonies were royal colonies, while others were chartered to business corporations or proprietary local governments. The chartered colonies allowed for more self-government, but the Crown withdrew the charters and placed all thirteen colonies under direct royal control by the second half of the 18th century.

The American Revolution

The aftermath of the French and Indian War (1756–1763) set the stage for a conflict between the American colonists and Great Britain. After defeating France and her Native American allies, England passed a series of controversial laws. First, the Proclamation of 1763 barred the colonists from settling west of the Appalachian Mountains in an effort to appease Native Americans. Second, the Quebec Act of 1774 granted protections to their recently acquired French-Canadian colonies. Third, England passed a series of taxes on the colonists to pay their war debt, including the Sugar Act (1764), Quartering Act (1765), Stamp Act (1765), Townshend Acts (1767), Tea Act (1773), and the Intolerable Acts (1774).

To the colonists, it appeared as if England was rewarding the combatants of the French and Indian War and punishing the colonists who fought for England. As a result, protests erupted, especially in New England. The most significant were those surrounding the Boston Massacre (1770) and the Boston Tea Party (1773). Colonists organized the First Continental Congress in 1774 to request the repeal of the Intolerable Acts and affirm their loyalty to the Crown. When King George III refused, the crisis escalated in April 1775 at the Battle of Lexington and Concord, the first armed conflict between British troops and colonial militias. A Second Continental Congress then met in Philadelphia, and the delegates issued Thomas Jefferson's Declaration of Independence on July 4, 1776. The Declaration of Independence declared that all people enjoyed basic rights, specifically the right to life, liberty, and the pursuit of happiness, and accused King George III of violating colonists' rights, which justified the American revolution.

The Continental Army lost its first major offensive campaign in Quebec City in December 1775, but victories at Trenton and Saratoga boosted morale. The tides of war turned against England when the Americans and France signed the Treaty of Alliance in 1778. France sent resources and troops to support the Americans, and the Marquis de Lafayette served as a combat commander at the final decisive battle at Yorktown. On September 3, 1783, the Treaty of Paris secured American independence.

Founding of the United States

Enacted during the American Revolution, the Articles of Confederation was the original governing document of the United States. However, the Articles of Confederation was ineffective due to its weak central government. The government didn't include a president or judiciary branch, and Congress didn't have the power to tax or raise money for an army. The final straw was the Articles of Confederation's failure to handle the Shays' Rebellion (1786–1787). In May 1787, the Founding Fathers convened the Constitutional Convention in Philadelphia. George Washington served as the Convention's president, and James Madison wrote the draft that was the basis for the Constitution.

Slavery challenged the Constitutional Convention from the outset, foreshadowing the American Civil War. The South wanted slaves to count for representation, even though slaves couldn't vote, but not taxes, while the North advocated for the opposite. The Three-Fifths Compromise settled the issue by counting slaves as three-fifths of a person for taxation and representation. In addition, the delegates agreed to a compromise that allowed slave owners to capture escaped slaves in exchange for ending the international slave trade by 1808.

The delegates also debated representation in Congress. The New Jersey Plan proposed a single legislative body with one vote per state. In contrast, the Virginia Plan proposed two legislative bodies with representation decided by the states' populations. The delegates agreed to the Connecticut Compromise—two legislative bodies with one house based on population (House of Representatives) and the other granting each state two votes (Senate). Two other branches, the judiciary and executive, were also included in the final document, and a series of checks and balances divided power between all three branches. The Constitution also expressly addressed issues from the Articles of Confederation by providing for a significantly stronger central government.

The Constitution, including its interpretation by the Supreme Court of the United States, divided the powers as follows:

Exclusive federal government powers
- Coin money
- Declare war
- Establish lower federal courts
- Sign foreign treaties
- Expand territories and admit new states
- Regulate immigration
- Regulate interstate commerce

Exclusive state government powers
- Establish local government
- Hold and regulate elections ✳
- Implement welfare and benefit programs
- Create and oversee public education
- Establish licensing requirements
- Regulate state corporations
- Regulate commerce within the state

Concurrent powers (shared)
- Levy taxes
- Borrow money
- Charter corporations

Federalists in FAVOR of Constitution —

Anti-Federalists wanted Bill of Rights

Nine of the thirteen states needed to ratify the Constitution before it became law, and a heated debate over the Constitution spread throughout the nation. Those in favor of the Constitution, called the Federalists, produced and distributed the **Federalist Papers**, which James Madison, Alexander Hamilton, and John Jay wrote under the pseudonym "Publius." Thomas Jefferson and Patrick Henry led the Anti-Federalists and called for the inclusion of a bill of rights. The Constitution was ratified on June 21, 1778, and three years later, the Bill of Rights was added. The Bill of Rights is the first ten amendments to the Constitution ratified together in December 1791.

Bill of Rights
- First Amendment: freedom of speech, freedom of press, free exercise of religion, and the right to assemble peacefully and petition the government
- Second Amendment: the right to bear arms
- Third Amendment: the right to refuse to quarter (house) soldiers
- Fourth Amendment: prohibits unreasonable searches and seizures and requires a warrant based on probable cause

- Fifth Amendment: protects due process, requires a grand jury indictment for certain felonies, protects against the government seizing property without compensation, protects against self-incrimination, and prohibits double jeopardy
- Sixth Amendment: the right to a fair and speedy criminal trial, the right to view criminal accusations, the right to present witnesses, and the right to counsel in criminal trials
- Seventh Amendment: the right to a trial by jury in civil cases
- Eighth Amendment: prohibits cruel and unusual punishment
- Ninth Amendment: establishes the existence of unnamed rights and grants them to citizens
- Tenth Amendment: reserves all non-specified powers to the states or people

The Founding Fathers created a decentralized federal system to protect against tyranny. The Tenth Amendment is what enshrines the principle of federalism—the separation of power between federal, state, and local government. In general, the federal government can limit or prohibit the states from enacting certain policies, and state governments exercise exclusive control over local government.

The rights enjoyed by Americans are rooted in the Bill of Rights, but no right is unconditional. In some specific circumstances, the government can restrict citizens' rights. The government is especially powerful during wartime. For example, President Abraham Lincoln suspended the right to due process during the Civil War. This is a major reason why the present War on Terror is controversial, as it creates a permanent state of war. Other common limits are defamation laws and limits on "fighting words."

Following the Civil War, the concept of civil rights was added to rights enjoyed by Americans. The Thirteenth, Fourteenth, and Fifteen Amendments prohibited slavery, provided for due process and equal protection under the law, and protected the right to vote based on race, color, or previous condition of servitude, respectively. Inspired by the Civil Rights Movement, activists have fought for equal rights and protection under the law based on gender and sexuality, culminating in the landmark Supreme Court decision *United States v. Windsor* (2013), which established the right to same-sex marriage.

Americans also have responsibilities. First and foremost, Americans are expected to obey the civil and criminal justice system, or else they will face what can be severe punishment. The United States imprisons more of its citizens, in both the total prison population and per capita, than any other country in the world by a wide margin. Civil disobedience has been used in the United States to great effect, but there's typically strong pushback from the establishment and the public. Despite being fondly remembered, Martin Luther King, Jr. was opposed by the majority of the country for his entire life.

The other major responsibility for citizens is to participate in the political system. Although voting, donating to candidates, running for office, and other forms of participation are not legally mandated, the United States is a representative democracy, and a lack of public participation undermines the government's legitimacy. Yet, voter turnout is low in the United States. Approximately 55 percent of registered Americans vote in presidential elections, and local elections have even lower turnout.

Growth and Expansion of the United States

Shortly after gaining independence, the United States rapidly expanded based on **manifest destiny**—the belief that Americans hold special virtues, America has a duty to spread those virtues westward, and success is a certainty.

In 1803, President Thomas Jefferson purchased the Louisiana territory from France. The Louisiana Purchase included 828,000 square miles of land west of the Mississippi River. Unsure of what he had purchased, Jefferson organized several expeditions to explore the new territory, including the famous Lewis and Clark Expedition. To consolidate the eastern seaboard under American control, President James Monroe purchased New Spain (present-day Florida) in the Adams-Onís Treaty of 1819.

Conflict with Native Americans was constant and brutal. Great Britain allied with Native American tribes in the present-day Midwest, using them as a buffer to protect her Canadian colonies. Britain's support for Native American raids on American colonies ignited tensions and led to the War of 1812. Two years later, Great Britain and the United States signed the Treaty of Ghent, ending the war with a neutral resolution, and British support for the Native Americans evaporated. The Supreme Court's decision in *Worcester v. Georgia* (1832) later established the concept of tribal sovereignty; however, President Andrew Jackson refused to enforce the Court's decision. Consequently, Americans continued to colonize Native American land at will. President Jackson also passed the first of several Indian Removal Acts, forcing native tribes westward on the Trail of Tears.

Tensions on the American-Mexican border worsened after President John Tyler annexed Texas in 1845. That same year, James K. Polk succeeded Tyler after winning the election of 1844 on a platform of manifest destiny. President Polk ordered General Zachary Taylor to march his army into the disputed territory, which ignited the Mexican-American War. The United States dominated the conflict and annexed the present-day American southwest and California through the 1848 Treaty of Guadalupe Hidalgo. Polk also settled the Oregon Country dispute with Britain, establishing the British-American boundary at the 49th parallel.

The United States purchased Alaska from Russia in 1867, and Hawaii was annexed in 1898 to complete what would become the fifty states.

The migration of settlers into these new territories was facilitated by technological innovation and legislation. Steamships allowed the settlers to navigate the nation's many winding rivers, and railroads exponentially increased the speed of travel and transportation of supplies to build settlements. Canals were also important for connecting the eastern seaboard to the Midwest. Thus, the fastest growing settlements were typically located near a major body of water or a railroad. Starting in 1862, Congress incentivized Americans to travel westward and populate the territories with a series of Homestead acts, which gave away public lands, called "homesteads," for free. In total, the United States gave away 270 million acres of public land to support the country's expansion.

Civil War

Congress repeatedly attempted to compromise on slavery, especially as to whether it would be expanded into new territories. The first such attempt was the Missouri Compromise of 1820, which included three parts. First, Missouri was admitted as a slave state. Second, Maine was admitted as a free state to maintain the balance between free and slave states. Third, slavery was prohibited north of the 36°30' parallel in new territories, but the Supreme Court overturned this in Dred Scott v. Sandford (1837).

The Compromise of 1850 admitted California as a free state, allowed popular sovereignty to determine if Utah and New Mexico would be slave states, banned slavery in Washington D.C., and enforced a harsh Fugitive Slave Law. The Kansas-Nebraska Act of 1854 started a mini civil war, as slave owners and abolitionists rushed into the new territories. Slavery eventually caused the collapse of the Whigs, the dominant political party of the early and middle 19th century. The Northern Whigs created the anti-slavery Republican Party.

1. Missouri Compromise of 1820 - overturned by Dred Scott case
2. Compromise of 1850
3. KS, NE Act of 1854

194

1861, Fort Sumter begins Civil War
Appomattox CH- Lee surrenders

Republican Abraham Lincoln won the election of 1860. Before his inauguration, seven Southern states seceded from the United States and established the Confederate States of America to protect slavery. On April 12, 1861, the first shots of the Civil War were fired by Confederate artillery at Fort Sumter, South Carolina. On January 1, 1863, after the particularly bloody Battle of Antietam, President Lincoln issued the Emancipation Proclamation, freeing the Confederacy's 3 million slaves; however, slavery continued in Union-controlled states and territories.

Later that year, the Battle of Gettysburg gave the Union Army a decisive victory, turning back the Confederacy's advances into the North. President Lincoln's famous Gettysburg Address called for the preservation of the Union and equality for all citizens. After a series of Union victories, Confederate General Robert E. Lee surrendered at Appomattox Court House and ended the Civil War in April 1865. Less than one week after Lee's surrender, John Wilkes Booth assassinated President Lincoln during a play at Ford's Theater.

Vice President Andrew Johnson assumed the presidency and battled the Radical Republicans in Congress over the Reconstruction Amendments. Federal troops were deployed across the South to enforce the new amendments, but Reconstruction concluded in 1877. Immediately after the troops withdrew, the Southern states enacted Jim Crow laws to rollback African Americans' right to vote and enforce segregationist policies.

Industrial Revolution

The First Industrial Revolution exploded in the United States during the War of 1812, as more American industrialists adopted British textile innovations. New manufacturing firms utilized the assembly line to increase production speed and accuracy. Each worker completed one individualized task on the assembly line, and the team of workers collectively produced the goods. New England manufacturers adopted the Waltham-Lowell labor and production system to maximize the use of new technologies such as the spinning jenny, spinning mule, and water frame. Eli Whitney's cotton gin was similarly revolutionary for the cotton industry.

The Second Industrial Revolution began after the Civil War and lasted until World War I. Technology again drove the economic changes, particularly in factory machinery and steel production. This era transformed the United States from an agricultural and textile economy into an industrial powerhouse. The invention of the telegraph and innovations in transportation like railways, canals, and steamboats further connected the economy.

Industrialization drove urbanization, as most new jobs were in booming city centers. To accommodate new arrivals from rural areas, cities had to adopt urban planning strategies to create a sewer system and facilitate the supply of gas and water. Economic opportunity also attracted waves of immigrants to American cities. Before 1880, most immigrants were English and Irish, but from 1880 to 1920, more than 20 million immigrants came from Central, Eastern, and Southern Europe. *late 19th, early 20th*

Despite the explosion in wealth creation, the Second Industrial Revolution caused crises in political corruption, working conditions, and wealth inequality. Political machines, like Tammany Hall in New York, consolidated political power in major American cities under a party boss who doled out special favors to his constituents. A lack of government regulation also created unsafe labor conditions. Most laborers worked twelve-hour shifts, with minimal breaks, six or seven days every week, and child labor was rampant. The long hours, dangerous machines, and young workers led to workplace accidents, and death rates soared. Wages were also low, and income inequality exploded, which is why the Second Industrial Revolution is often referred to as the "Gilded Age."

Gilded Age

Labor began to organize in response to dangerous working conditions and meager pay. Between 1881 and 1905, labor unions organized 37,000 strikes across every major industry. Anarchists, populists, and socialists challenged the political establishment, demanding reform for the working poor. These movements led to the rise of the Progressive Era (the 1890s to the 1920s). Progressives passed the direct election of U.S. Senators (17th Amendment), anti-corruption laws, anti-trust laws, women's suffrage, and the prohibition of alcohol.

Early American Foreign Policy

In the late 19th century, a public debate raged over the United States' international role. Part of the public wished to heed George Washington's famous farewell address in which he warned against intervening in foreign conflicts. Another faction supported military intervention to free colonies, as France had done for the United States. The final group called for following the European model of imperialism.

Issued in 1823, the Monroe Doctrine promised that the United States wouldn't meddle in existing European colonies, but it also vowed that the U.S. would consider any future European intervention to be a hostile act. President Theodore Roosevelt would later strengthen the Monroe Doctrine during his State of the Union address in 1904, explicitly threatening unilateral military intervention in Latin America whenever it suited American interests.

In 1898, the American battleship **USS Maine** exploded in Havana Harbor, and President McKinley declared war on Spain. In less than five months, the United States had defeated Spain and assumed control over her first overseas colonies—Puerto Rico, Guam, and the Philippines.

The outbreak of World War I in 1914 presented a serious challenge to the United States. President Woodrow Wilson attempted to keep the nation neutral, but his hand was forced. In 1915, German U-boats (submarines) torpedoed a British passenger ship **RMS Lusitania** carrying American passengers, and two years later, Britain intercepted the Zimmerman Telegram, which showed that Germany was attempting to conspire with Mexico to invade the United States. President Wilson had run out of options, and the United States declared war on Germany and joined the Triple Entente (Britain, France, and Russia). More than 116,000 Americans lost their lives serving in World War I, but the conflict was a turning point in American history, marking the arrival of the United States as a global power.

In the interwar period, known as the Roaring Twenties, there was rampant stock market speculation. On "Black Tuesday," October 29, 1929, the stock market crashed, sending the global economy off a cliff into the Great Depression. Immediately after winning the 1932 presidential election, Franklin D. Roosevelt launched the New Deal to increase employment, stimulate demand, and increase regulation over capital. Much of the current social welfare state—Social Security, unemployment insurance, disability, labor laws, and housing and food subsidies—date back to the New Deal. President Lyndon B. Johnson later introduced a series of legislation modeled after the New Deal collectively referred to as the War on Poverty or the Great Society. His aim was to alleviate poverty by increasing access to education, health care, and housing.

After World War II broke out in Europe, the United States again tried to remain neutral, but on December 7, 1941, Japan bombed Pearl Harbor. In response, President Roosevelt declared war on Japan. Germany preemptively declared war on the United States, who did the same in return. On June 6, 1944, referred to as "D-Day," American forces landed on the beaches of Normandy, France, and by May 1945, American and Soviet forces had conquered Germany. However, the Japanese continued to fight in the Pacific theater. To avoid what would've been a costly invasion of Japan's mainland, the United States dropped nuclear bombs on Nagasaki and Hiroshima, ending World War II.

Cold War Era

The United States and Soviet Union emerged from World War II as the world's preeminent superpowers. The Americans and Soviets considered each other to be an existential threat, but the development of nuclear weapon technology forced the two superpowers to avoid a direct conflict, which is why this period is known as the Cold War.

American Cold War era foreign policy followed the **domino theory**—the idea that if one country turned communist, so would neighboring countries. The United States also created the North Atlantic Treaty Organization (NATO) in 1949 to protect against Soviet aggression in Europe.

On June 25, 1950, North Korea invaded South Korea, and the United States entered the war to protect its ally and to prevent communism spreading across Asia. When General MacArthur disobeyed President Truman and crossed the 38th parallel, China entered the war on the side of North Korea, and the war turned into a bloody stalemate. All three combatants signed the Armistice Agreement on July 27, 1953, though the war never officially ended. The Korean War's brutality left a lasting impression on North Korea, heavily influencing the dictatorship's approach to the United States. ✕

In August 1964, Congress passed the Gulf of Tonkin Resolution. Although Congress didn't declare war, the Resolution authorized President Lyndon B. Johnson's use of military force in Vietnam. As in Korea, the United States feared that if North Vietnamese communists prevailed, communism would spread across Asia. The Vietnam War was a military success, but it was a political disaster. The draft proved to be enormously unpopular, and President Richard Nixon's decision to invade Cambodia and bomb Laos further buried public opinion. Domestic protests forced the United States to withdraw in 1973.

The United States also regularly conducted covert operations, trained rebels, and funded political opposition through the Central Intelligence Agency (CIA) to overthrow democratically elected socialist governments.

Non-exhaustive list of successful Cold War interventions
- Iran (1953)
- Guatemala (1954)
- Dominican Republic (1961)
- Brazil (1964)
- Congo (1965)
- Indonesia (1965)
- Ghana (1966)
- Guyana (1968)
- Chile (1973)

never Cuba

Socialist governments were often replaced with strongman dictators, and the transition frequently resulted in civil wars. The United States also directly armed morally dubious proxy forces. President Ronald Reagan covertly sold weapons to Nicaraguan death squads, the "Contras," funding it through weapon sales to Iran in violation of an American arms embargo. Similarly, during the Soviet-Afghan War (1979-1989), the Carter and Reagan administrations gave $3 billion of taxpayer money to the mujahedeen (Islamic extremists) who fought alongside Osama bin Laden.

Besides military conflict and interventions, the United States competed with the Soviet Union in the Space Race. In addition to national pride, both superpowers hoped to advance their spying and rocket capabilities. As such, they both invested heavily in technology, some of which was enormously beneficial for society, like increased computing power. To the great surprise of Americans, on October 4, 1957, the Soviet Union launched the world's first satellite, Sputnik 1, into orbit. Less than four years later, Soviet cosmonaut Yuri Gagarin became the first human to enter space. On July 20, 1969, the United States struck back by landing the first humans on the Moon during the Apollo 11 mission. The Soviet Union repeatedly failed to land a crew on the Moon. Besides technological and scientific advancements, the Space Race also played a role in *détente*—the easing of tensions between the Cold War rivals—after the Soviets and Americans launched the Apollo-Soyuz Project (1971), their first joint space mission.

For domestic politics, the Cold War era was tumultuous. Throughout the 1950s, U.S. Senator Joseph McCarthy led a series of increasingly conspiratorial criminal investigations. McCarthyism exploited Americans' fear of the Soviet Union, referred to as the "Red Scare."

The Watergate scandal was the most dramatic domestic political event during the Cold War era. Although Richard Nixon was a popular incumbent on track for a landslide victory over Democrat George McGovern in the 1972 presidential election, Richard Nixon ordered accomplices to burglarize and spy on the Democratic National Committee headquarters. Then Nixon attempted to use intelligence agencies to cover up his involvement. After a tape surfaced of Nixon ordering the coverup, the House of Representatives impeached Nixon, and he resigned before the Senate convicted him. On September 8, 1974, President Gerald Ford controversially pardoned Nixon. Besides Nixon, Andrew Johnson and Bill Clinton are the only presidents to be impeached, but no president has ever been convicted (removed from office) by the Senate.

Martin Luther King's civil disobedience is one of the most successful forms of nonviolent protest in world history, particularly his March on Washington in 1963, which concluded with King's famous "I Have a Dream" speech. King's leadership during the Civil Rights movement directly led to the Civil Rights Act of 1964 and Voting Rights Act of 1965. Despite these legislative victories, political assassinations, bombings, and riots were commonplace in the United States from the late 1960s to the 1970s.

Shocking the world, the Berlin Wall fell in 1989, and national revolutions swept out the Soviets' puppet government in Eastern Europe. By late 1991, the Soviet Union had collapsed. Considerable credit is attributed to President Ronald Reagan for escalating the arm's race, which the Soviets couldn't afford, while simultaneously holding talks with Soviet General Secretary Mikhail Gorbachev.

Post-Cold War Era

Following the collapse of the Soviet Union, the United States became an uncontested superpower. No country in the world could match its economic and military might until China's emergence as a world power in the 2010s.

September 11, 2001 was a traumatic day for the United States, as terrorists hijacked four commercial airliners and crashed three of them into the World Trade Center and Pentagon. Osama bin Laden, the Saudi-born leader of Al-Qaeda, plotted the attacks from his base in Afghanistan. President George W. Bush responded by launching the War on Terror. Less than one month after the attack, the United States invaded Afghanistan to dismantle Al-Qaeda's training camps, but Osama bin Laden evaded the American military for a decade. American Special Forces killed bin Laden at his Pakistani compound during the Obama administration. The War in Afghanistan is the longest war in American history.

More controversially, Bush invaded Iraq in 2003 based on his administration's claims that Iraqi dictator Saddam Hussein collaborated with Al-Qaeda and was producing "weapons of mass destruction." Shortly after toppling and executing Saddam Hussein, Iraq erupted in a bloody, sectarian civil war. One faction in the Iraqi Civil War would later form the Islamic State and carve a caliphate out of Syria and Iraq.

Opposition to the Iraq War became so fierce that it helped Barack Obama and Donald Trump—who share little else in common politically—win the presidency. President Obama withdrew from Iraq in December 2007, but an American-led coalition returned in 2014 to fight the Islamic State. President Obama expanded the War on Terror, relying on drone strikes and Special Operations forces to hunt terror cells in more than six countries.

The financial crisis of 2007-2008 was a pivotal moment in recent American history. Large investment banks created an artificial bubble in the mortgage sector, and when it burst, the American government bailed them out at taxpayers' expense to prevent the economy from collapsing. Both sides of the political spectrum erupted in anger, directly leading to the socialist Occupy Wall Street Movement and partially contributing to the growth of the libertarian Tea Party.

Geography, Anthropology, and Sociology

World and Regional Geography

The modern world is divided into seven continents and five oceans. The seven continents are Africa, Antarctica, Asia, Australia (Oceania), Europe, North America, and South America. The five oceans are the Arctic Ocean, Atlantic Ocean, Indian Ocean, Pacific Ocean, and Southern (Antarctic) Ocean. However, these are human distinctions based on geographic features. For example, some countries don't recognize the Southern Ocean as a fifth ocean.

The study of world and regional geography has five general themes. First, **location** is the absolute and relative position of an area on Earth. The absolute position consists of the exact coordinates where an area can be found on a map. Relative position refers to the area's proximity to other regions, including economic and political structures. Absolute and relative positions have tremendous impact on the other four themes.

Second, **place** consists of the physical and human characteristics that play a determinative role in how the area develops and grows. Examples include the climate, total population, population density, and availability of resources. For example, a bounty of resources like potable water and arable land facilitates population growth and thereby increases the labor pool to support economic growth.

Third, **environmental** and **human factors** change the physical landscape. Environmental factors influence societies' ability to change and adapt to the land. For example, Americans took advantage of the climate and arable land in the Midwest, turning the native tallgrass prairie biome into the Corn Belt. Consequently, less than 1 percent of the original biome remains.

Fourth, a **region** is any area with a unifying characteristic. New England is a cohesive region based on its shared history that dates to the Thirteen Colonies, the influence of English and Irish cultures, and economic connection to the Atlantic Ocean, among other factors. Regions can be divided in any number of ways if there are shared characteristics. As such, some places can be a part of several regions. For example, Ohio is considered part of the Midwest and Rust Belt.

Fifth, **migration** and **communication** drive interaction between the world's different regions, and those interactions change the regions. Migration of Europeans to North America devastated Native Americans, and every new wave of immigration has generated tension with the previous arrivals. On the other hand, migration can increase a region's labor pool, foster innovation, and enrich culture. Technological innovations from the telegraph to the Internet have increased the speed of communication around the world.

Maps are the most common tool for analyzing world and regional geography. Most maps contain essential elements, like a title, grid, compass, scale, and legend. Physical maps include the landscape's features, such as mountains, rivers, and lakes. One type of physical map, topographic maps, uses contour lines to illustrate changes in elevation. Other types of maps illustrate climate, population density, roadways, and any other feature that can be placed over a landscape.

Political maps reflect the state of political boundaries across a region or multiple regions for a designated period, whether in the present or past. Compared to physical maps, political maps are much more subjective, varying based on the mapmakers' interpretation of territorial disputes. For example, 19th century political maps differed on the boundaries between the competing European colonies, as well as what constituted Native American territory. Crimea and Taiwan are examples of subjective present-day territorial dispute.

The concept of a **nation-state** is based on the existence of distinct territorial boundaries. If territorial disputes can't be resolved through diplomacy, they always lead to war. President James K. Polk's administration engaged in both forms of conflict resolution. Polk negotiated a treaty with Great Britain to settle territorial boundaries in Oregon in order to avoid a third war, and when diplomacy failed, he invaded Mexico to push the newly acquired Texas territory's border to the Rio Grande, a more defensible position for the American military.

Interaction of Physical and Human Systems

A **physical system** refers to a region's landmass, environment, climate, and weather. **Human systems** are a group of people participating in a joint enterprise. Human systems adapt to and manipulate the physical system, and in doing so, they change the physical system. The extraction of resources is why physical systems change.

Human systems require the consumption of natural resources—air, fossil fuels, iron, land, minerals, sunlight, water, wind, wood, etc. Some resources are renewable, such as oxygen, fresh water, and solar energy, while others are finite. Nonrenewable resources, like fossil fuels, take so long to form that once they're depleted, they're gone. The variety and availability of resources plays an integral role in the human system's development, and the fight over resources also changes human systems when there's conflict.

The interaction between human and physical systems is most evident in economic development, particularly agriculture. Some regions are entirely barren, while others are rich in natural resources. Where a human system is located within that range will have an important, if not decisive, impact on its future. For example, an advanced human system has never developed in the Sahara Desert due to the lack of water and arable land. As such, the human system adapted to the harsh physical system by embracing a nomadic lifestyle. In contrast, nearly all ancient empires were located on or near a large river delta. The nutrient-rich soil enabled agriculture, and the resulting food production supported a large population. With a larger population, human systems based on agriculture could diversify their economies with the excess labor, form governments, and raise armies to conquer more land. All of this would be impossible in the Sahara without implementing some future technological innovation to moderate the physical system.

The interaction between the Native Americans and Europeans resulted in the rapid decline of the Native American system and drastic changes to the physical system. The European system's large-scale production of crops and livestock sustained permanent settlements, which facilitated the establishment of a centralized system of government. In contrast, the Native Americans were nomadic, making it easier for Europeans to drive native tribes off their land. Old World diseases also overwhelmed the Native American population, reaching some of the western tribes even before the arrival of European colonists. In addition, the Europeans were armed with superior weaponry—steel and firearms. As a result, the European system devastated the Native American system. The indigenous population in California dropped from 150,000 to 15,000 between 1848 and 1900.

The American takeover dramatically altered the physical system. Agriculture, industrialization, and urbanization have caused a sharp decline in wilderness, which now accounts for less than 5 percent of total American land. Similarly, the United States outside of Alaska has lost 60% of its natural vegetation. As wilderness and habitats decline, so does biodiversity. In the United States, 539 native species are extinct or missing, and more than one-third of all species are at risk. These trends are mirrored across the world as more countries industrialize. Only 23 percent of the world's wilderness remains, and the rate of habitat destruction has markedly increased over the last few decades. If current trends continue, two-thirds of all wild animal species will be extinct by 2020.

Uses of Geography

History is the story of interaction and conflict between interests, movements, cultures, societies, nations and empires. Geography is the key to understanding history. World leaders always include geographic considerations in their decision-making. As such, understanding geography helps explain the past, interpret the present, and plan for the future. This is especially true for any armed conflict due to the strategic importance of higher ground, supply routes, defensible borders, etc. The field of studying political power through the lens of geography is called **geopolitics**.

The three theories of geopolitical power with the most historic, contemporary, and future significance are the Heartland Theory, Rimland Theory, and Organic Theory.

Published in 1904, Halford John MacKinder's Heartland Theory emphasizes the strategic importance of Eastern Europe, Russia, and Western China. These three regions form the "Heartland," occupying a central position on the "World Island"—Africa, Asia, and Europe. MacKinder considered the rest of the world to be mere islands floating around the World Island. This reflects the Heartland Theory's Eurocentric approach. Due to their military power and geographical proximity to Eastern Europe, MacKinder correctly identified Germany and Russia as the greatest threats to global security in the early 20th century.

The Cold War also heavily featured the Heartland, as the Soviet Union controlled most of Eastern Europe and worked closely with China. As a result, American foreign policymakers' primary goal was to weaken the Soviets' dominance in the Heartland. American forces used covert operations to sow dissent and discord throughout the region. For example, the Central Intelligence Agency (CIA) covertly funded Radio Free Europe—an American government program that broadcast news across Eastern Europe. In addition, the United States courted China as an ally, which culminated in President Richard Nixon's state visit to China in February 1972. Following the Soviet Union's loss of the Heartland and subsequent dissolution, the United States encouraged Eastern Europe to join the North Atlantic Treaty Organization (NATO), an American-led military alliance.

Like the Heartland Theory, the Rimland Theory is Eurocentric, prioritizing the Eurasian continent above all other regions. However, the Rimland Theory differs in its emphasis on the "Rimland" (Eurasian coasts). Accordingly, the European coast, Middle East, and Asiatic coasts have the most geopolitical value. The Rimland Theory's author, Nicholas John Spykman, believed these regions served as a buffer between land

[handwritten margin note: "World Island" HEARTLAND.]

and sea power. The theory predates the widespread use of airplanes, which detracts from some of the coastal regions' importance. However, the United States remains a military superpower through naval superiority.

Rather than name a strategically important region, the Organic Theory argues that nation-states need to consolidate political power and acquire new geographic territory in order to sustain themselves. In this concept, the nation-state operates like a living organism, and new territory provides the resources it needs to survive. First published by German Friedrich Ratzel in 1897, the Organic Theory was often combined with Social Darwinism—the idea that Darwin's natural selection applies to humans—to justify imperialism and racism. Nazi Germany was one of the Organic Theory's most vocal advocates.

Empires and nation-states have historically pursued their self-interest by consolidating political power and acquiring foreign territory. Mercantilism, colonialism, and imperialism are all related to conquering territory, and they were common European policies for centuries. The Roman Empire is another illustrative example. Rome started as a single city-state, conquered the Italian Peninsula, and then seized most of Europe, North Africa, the Balkans, and Asia Minor. Once a territory was captured, the Romans enslaved large populations of people, collected taxes, and extracted resources from the land. Each conquest increased Rome's political power, and Rome collapsed partially due to its inability to conquer and hold new territory.

The Organic Theory also helps explain why nation-states resist fracturing into smaller, independent states. If acquiring territory is the nation-state's lifeblood, then losing territory is a direct harm. In addition to undermining the government's legitimacy, losing territory could decrease the labor pool, natural resources, and military strength. It also means sharing a new border with what could be a hostile neighbor. This was the case in the American Civil War. President Abraham Lincoln didn't initially deploy military force to free the slaves. In fact, several of the border slave states remained in the Union for the entire conflict. Instead, President Lincoln wanted to preserve the Union and prevent the loss of territory, economic power, military power, and natural resources. Lincoln's reasoning was consistent with the Organic approach to geopolitics.

The present-day United States is not a traditional empire. Past empires have conquered and directly ruled over their territories. The United States hasn't added a major piece of territory since the Spanish-American War. Nevertheless, the United States' leverage over many nation-states is impossible to overstate. The United States has acquired political power by wielding military force to coerce countries and money to make them willing partners. The United States outspends its rivals on its military by a significant margin every year, though some of the difference can be attributed to higher labor costs.

American foreign policy revolves around geopolitics. The United States maintains approximately 800 military bases in 70 different countries, and the bases surround every potential challenger to American hegemony. The U.S. Navy operates nineteen aircraft carriers, while the rest of the world has nine altogether. Consequently, the United States can exercise control over five oceans, challenge any coastal region it desires, and send military planes anywhere in the world at a moment's notice.

Other than a genuine interest in combatting terrorism, the wars in Afghanistan and Iraq served American geopolitical interests in the Middle East, a region that holds most of the world's oil reserves. Some think the Iraq War was motivated by the goal of "stealing" Iraqi oil, but that theory goes too far. The United States was more interested in exercising American power vis-a-vis Iran, Iraq's geographical neighbor. The United States is allied with all of the Sunni Muslim oil-producing countries (Saudi Arabia, Qatar, United Arab Emirates, etc.), and they are Iran's geopolitical rivals. As a result, the United States is constantly trying to prevent Iranian influence from spreading outside its territorial borders, as has happened in Lebanon and Syria.

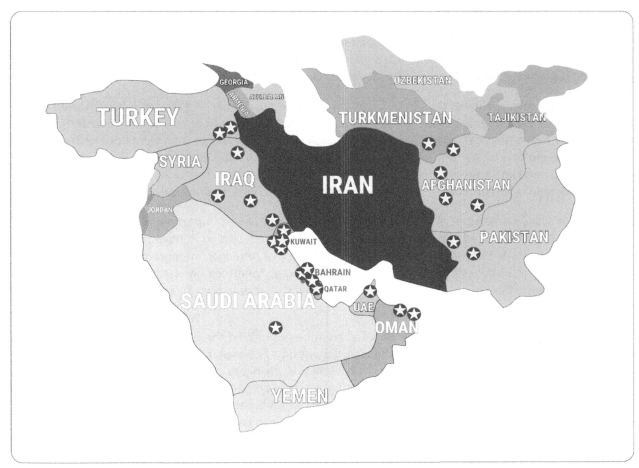

Like its impact on predicting and understanding armed conflict, geopolitics is important for understanding trade and foreign aid decisions. Human systems have almost always emphasized trading with their geographic neighbors. In addition to generating wealth, trade improves diplomatic relations and avoids conflict. Depending on the measure, the United States is either the largest or second-largest (after China) economy in the world, and the U.S. leads the global financial industry. Consequently, the United States can curry favor by promising greater economic cooperation and donates twice the amount of foreign aid as the next-largest donor.

Cultural Differences

Culture refers to a group of people's shared customs, norms, traditions, and values. Expressions of culture can be seen in art, language, literature, dance, music, religion, and technology. **Anthropology** is the study of human societies' development and culture. Similarly, **sociology** investigates the patterns, relationships, and interactions within societies and cultures.

Different cultures have different relationships with their environment, family, and communities. The difference between Native Americans and Europeans illustrates how these differences impact cultures' lived experiences and worldview. Before Europeans' arrival, Native American tribes lived in hunter-gatherer systems, consuming the physical system's resources in a sustainable manner. Native Americans consider themselves to be part of the physical system. For example, when a Native American kills a buffalo, the animal is used to provide shelter, food, weapons, spiritual artifacts, and toys. Native Americans also live in extended kinship networks where might be defined as the nuclear family, extended family, tribal members, and/or entire nation. Native American tribes include fictive (non-blood related) kin as family members. Tribes further differ as to whether they're patriarchal (male leadership) or matriarchal (female leadership). When Native Americans marry outside of the tribe, there's variation as to whether the couple moves into the husband or wife's tribe after marriage (patrilocal v. matrilocal).

In contrast, Europeans believed the physical system was merely an obstacle that could be mastered and exploited. Under their mercantilist economic system, European powers built colonies for transferring resources out of the physical system for the home country's benefit. Rather than worshipping the Earth, Europeans prayed to a higher power in the form of a divine human. The European family network is also much smaller than Native Americans'. Most Europeans only live with nuclear or extended family members, and fictive kinship is less common. Europeans are more patriarchal and patrilocal.

Nevertheless, Native Americans and European immigrants both placed importance on the community. While Native Americans lived in tribes, European immigrants often settled in neighborhoods with similar ethnic compositions. At the turn of the 19th century, the bulk of American immigrants settled in urban areas, carving ethnic enclaves in American cities, referred to as "ghettoes." Many present-day American cities still have areas known as "Little Italy" and "Chinatown" that date back to this period of self-segregating immigrant communities.

Within a single group of people, culture works as an adhesive to bind the group. A **monoculture** is a group with a single dominant culture, so there's greater unity; however, a monoculture lacks variation. If the monoculture doesn't otherwise broaden its perspective, problems might arise when the group encounters a different culture. The monoculture might not be able to recognize other group's motives, priorities, and rituals. In contrast, multicultural societies have a broader perspective, but multiculturalism requires the assimilation (integration) of different cultures, which can lead to conflict.

New cultures are primarily injected into a monoculture through immigration. If they come from a different geographic region than the resident population, the new arrivals are likely to challenge the existing culture. This can happen unintentionally. The mere presence of people speaking a different language, practicing different religions, and eating foreign food can cause controversy. Most nation-states have actively tried to integrate immigrants in order to gain the benefits of a larger labor pool without suffering internal strife.

There are two theoretical frameworks for integrating new cultures. First, the "salad bowl" approach treats different cultures like salad ingredients mixed in a bowl without changing the ingredients' individual structure. Second, the "melting pot" approach merges the different cultures forming something entirely unique. The American integration strategy is a combination of the salad bowl and melting pot. A fluid but distinct American identify is the culture's foundation, which is itself influenced by the presence of different cultures. The different cultures then provide a second layer with the individual cultures retaining more of their structural identity. Compared to the salad bowl or melting pot, the United States is more like a pizza with a lot of toppings.

The early 20th century was full of challenges to the American identity. In the early 20th century, African Americans fled the Jim Crow South en masse. During this Great Migration (1916–1970), more than 6 million African Americans left the American South and settled in the Northeast, Midwest, and West. Additionally, a series of actual and threatened revolutions disrupted Europe and led to a new wave of immigrants arriving in the United States at the turn of the 19th century.

While the colonists and first wave of immigrants were mostly from the British Isles, the new arrivals were from China, Germany, Italy, Russia, and southeastern Europe. Early on, the United States was a Protestant nation with pockets of Catholicism. English was spoken as a primary language by colonists. In contrast, the new wave of immigrants spoke dozens of different languages and practiced different religions. A major point of tension was the rapid increase in the Catholic and Jewish populations. Federal, state, and local governments responded to this cultural crisis by adopting Americanization policies. By 1910, more than 30 states had passed Americanization laws to teach immigrants English, American values, and civics. Labor unions and urban community centers, like the YMCA and YWCA, similarly focused on integrating immigrants into American society.

Although Americanization was effective, there was considerable conflict between American residents and immigrants. Demographic trends led to a hysteria driven by the fear of being replaced. For example, the Know Nothing reactionary movement supported an anti-Catholic and anti-immigrant political agenda, harassing the flood of German and Irish immigrants during the 1840s and 1850s. Chinese immigrants were also heavily discriminated against. The Chinese Exclusion Act of 1882 prohibited Chinese immigrants from coming to America.

By the end of the 19th century, the once-victimized Irish immigrants were themselves advocating for anti-immigration policies targeting southern and eastern European immigrants. Bowing to intense political pressure, Congress passed the Immigration Act of 1924. The Act applied restrictive quotas to limit immigration from southern and eastern European countries. More recently, quotas have been used to limit immigration from Mexico, Central America, and South America.

World History and Economics

Contributions of Classical Civilizations

Classical civilizations developed many innovations that contributed to our postmodern world—metal tools and weapons, written languages, calendars, representative government, professional militaries, urban planning, and large-scale farming, among others. These innovations allowed classical civilizations to conquer huge territories and establish historic empires. Examples of classical civilizations include Egypt, Greece, Persia, China, and Rome.

Egypt → Greece, Persia, Rome [handwritten]

Ancient Egypt
Ancient Egypt's first ruling dynasty was established in the 32nd century B.C., and over the next three thousand years, Egyptian innovations were adopted by many other classical civilizations. In addition, Egypt was conquered and controlled by three of those civilizations—Greece, Persia, and Rome.

Developed out of necessity to limit the Nile River's annual flooding, Egyptian irrigation techniques changed the world. Where floods once washed away crops and settlements, Egyptian irrigation left a rich delta that could grow enough food to support an empire. To govern their empire, the Egyptians independently developed a writing system (hieroglyphs) and created a professional bureaucracy of clerks and writers (scribes). Egypt also signed the earliest formal peace treaty during a war with the Hittites. Egyptian pharaohs built enormous burial structures, such as the Great Pyramid. The demand for these massive public works incentivized the invention of new quarrying, surveying, and construction techniques.

Greece
Greek city-states, such as Sparta and Athens, started to develop in the 8th century B.C. Some of the city-states united to fend off the Persian Empire, and in 4th century B.C., Alexander the Great conquered a then-unprecedented empire that included Greece, Egypt, Persia, Syria, Mesopotamia, central Asia, and

northern India. Alexander the Great's empire marks the start of the Hellenistic period, which lasted until the Roman Republic conquered the eastern Mediterranean and turned Greece into a Roman province.

Greek political systems and philosophy have had a major influence on Western civilization. The Greek city-states invented the principle of self-government and *demokratia* (direct democracy). Although Greece is considered the birthplace of democracy, the city-states were slave societies, and only the wealthy elite could participate politically. Still, Greece served as a model for Rome and early modern Europe on how to govern, collect taxes, and militarize.

The three most famous Greek scholars are Socrates, Plato, and Aristotle. All three are considered the fathers of Western philosophy, and their work continues to be studied in classrooms across the world. Plato's *Republic* and *Laws* are foundational texts in the field of political philosophy, and Aristotle's work in the physical sciences and logic were the basis for European scholarship throughout the Middle Ages. In addition to philosophy, Aristarchus was the first person to theorize that the Earth revolved around the Sun; Archimedes discovered pi (π); and Euclid's *Elements* is a collection of mathematical definitions, theorems, and proofs that went unchallenged until the 19th century.

Persia

Cyrus the Great founded the first Persian Empire, the Achaemenid Empire, in the 6th century B.C., effectively turning a group of nomadic shepherds into one of the largest empires in history. His successor, Darius I, further expanded the empire from Eastern Europe to Central and South Asia. Alexander the Great overthrew Darius III and conquered the Persian Empire in 330 B.C.

The Persian Empire was multicultural, consisting of multiple civilizations with varying religions, languages, and ethnicities. Persian rulers took a "carrot or stick" approach to diplomacy. If a civilization willingly joined the Empire and paid taxes, they would receive some degree of self-government and enjoy better economic relations. If the civilization resisted, they were invaded and enslaved.

The Persian Empire was organized under a federal system, much like the American model of government. Persian rulers functioned as the central government, and they appointed satraps (governors) and records-keepers to every region. The satraps allowed for limited local self-government, depending on the region's relationship with the Persian Empire. In exercising control over their vast empire, Persians developed innovative roadway and postal systems that the Romans later expanded upon.

China

Ancient China was ruled under successive dynasties, beginning with the Xia dynasty (21st century B.C.) and ending with the Qing dynasty (1911). The dynasties legitimized their power through the Mandate of Heaven—the belief that a higher power selected the ruler. The Mandate of Heaven contributed to the concept of legitimization in political philosophy.

The Han dynasty (206 B.C.—220 A.D.) was a golden era for Chinese trade, technological innovation, and scientific advancement. Han rulers opened the Silk Road, a series of trade routes connecting China with the rest of the Asian continent and Roman territory. The Silk Road linked the Far East and West for the first time. To facilitate this multicultural trade, Han rulers issued one of the world's first uniform currencies. Han Chinese technological innovations included papermaking, wheelbarrows, steering rudders, mapmaking (grids and raised-relief), and the seismometer (measure earthquakes). In science and math, Han scholars discovered herbal remedies, square roots, cube roots, the Pythagorean theorem, negative numbers, and advanced pi (π) calculations.

Rome

The city of Rome was founded in the 8th century B.C. and initially ruled under a monarchical government. Rome transitioned into a republic in the latter half of the 6th century B.C. In the 1st century B.C., a series of civil wars destabilized the Roman Republic, which culminated with Gaius Julius Caesar seizing absolute power. Caesar's victory caused Rome's transition from a republic to an empire. The Roman Empire would become the largest in history. Political corruption, religious conflict, economic challenges, and repeated invasions by German tribes led to the empire splitting into Western and Eastern halves in 395 A.D. The Eastern half, known as the Byzantine Empire, outlasted the Western Empire, surviving until 1453.

Rome is often referred to as the birthplace of Western civilization, and its influence on world history cannot be overstated. James Madison used the Roman Republic's separation of powers as a model for the United States Constitution. Rome spread Greek philosophy and culture across its many territories, including advancements in architecture and urban planning. Roman law influenced the development of many legal practices, like trials by juries, contracts, wills, corporations, and civil rights. All Romantic languages evolved from Latin—French, Italian, Spanish, and Portuguese. Roman numerals are still commonly used. Rome adopted and mastered Persian theories related to bureaucracy, civil engineering, "carrot and stick" diplomacy, and multiculturalism. To build their large infrastructure projects, the Romans invented a superior form of concrete. The largest religion in the world, Christianity, also started in a Roman province (Judea), spread across the empire, and eventually became Rome's state-sanctioned religion.

20th Century Developments and Transformations

The major themes of the 20th century are industrialization, imperialism, nationalism, global conflict, independence movements, technological advancement, and globalization.

The United States and Europe completed the transition from agrarian to industrial economies in the early 20th century, and by the end of the 20th century, most of the world had at least started industrializing. Industrialization created global wealth, exponentially improving the global standard of living, but it also caused explosive population growth and environmental destruction. Over the 20th century, the global population increased from 1.6 billion people to 6 billion people. This unprecedented population growth is driving rapid deforestation, as more land is cleared for agriculture and settlements. In addition, industrialization has polluted the Earth's atmosphere, land, and oceans. As a result, temperatures are increasing, sea levels are rising, and biodiversity is declining. The 21st century will face dire consequences, like mass migration and global instability, if these trends aren't reversed.

The 20th century opened with much of Asia and Africa divided into European colonies. Nationalism was on the rise and used to justify European imperialism and militarism. Nationalism, imperialism, and militarism also markedly increased in the United States and Japan. The overwhelming majority of present-day countries didn't achieve independence until after the World Wars or the Cold War.

Early 20th century nation-states were entangled in a complex web of military alliances, and when Serbian nationalists assassinated Archduke Franz Ferdinand of Austria (1914), those alliances triggered a global conflict, World War I. Russia joined the Triple Entente alliance with Great Britain and France, but in 1917, Vladimir Lenin's Bolsheviks (communists) led an armed insurrection against the Russian Tsar, Nicholas II. Following the Russian Revolution, the Bolsheviks won a victory against the European-backed counter-revolutionaries, paving the way for the creation of the Union of Soviet Socialist Republics (USSR).

The Treaty of Versailles ended World War I in June 1919, and it included several of American President Woodrow Wilson's Fourteen Points. Wilson was an advocate for countries' right to self-determination, and his Fourteen Points helped discredit colonialism and imperialism as legitimate foreign policy goals. Part I of the Treaty established Wilson's League of Nations, but Germany was prohibited from joining until 1926. The United States also refused to join, further undermining the League's legitimacy. The Treaty of Versailles also forced Germany to claim total responsibility for causing World War I and pay extensive reparations. This amounted to a national humiliation for Germany, fueling a reactionary right-wing movement that culminated in Adolf Hitler's rise to power in the 1930s.

The global women's rights movement gained support because of World War I. When the men left to fight overseas, women joined the workforce and contributed to the war effort. British Parliament granted women the right to vote in 1918, and Germany did the same in the following year. President Woodrow Wilson also reversed his previous position and declared his support for the 19th Amendment (1920), establishing women's suffrage in the United States.

The Great Depression occurred between the World Wars, lasting from 1929 until the late-1930s. A stock market crash triggered a depression in the United States that quickly spread around the world. The Great Depression put enormous stress on Western governments to alleviate poverty and lessen the appeal of communist revolution. Some governments, like the United States and Great Britain, increased their public investment to increase employments and social services. Other governments, like Germany and Italy, transitioned from militarized nationalism into outright far-right fascism.

Hitler's Nazi Party exploited global instability in his efforts to right the perceived injustices inflicted on Germany during World War I. First, Nazi Germany remilitarized the Rhineland and stopped paying reparations under the Treaty of Versailles. Second, Hitler enforced collective punishments on German Jews as retribution for their alleged disloyalty to the state, previewing what would become the Holocaust. Third, Hitler supported Italy's invasion of Ethiopia (1935), and German forces fought a proxy war to assist the fascist Francisco Franco during the Spanish Civil War (1936-1939). Fourth, Hitler annexed two territories in 1938—Austria and the Sudetenland in Czechoslovakia—under the pretext of protecting ethnic Germans. Much of Europe was horrified by these events, but the leadership mostly followed a policy of appeasement, hoping to avoid a second global conflict.

One year later, in September 1939, the Nazis invaded Poland to clear *lebensraum* (living space) for Germans. Two days later, France and Britain declared war on Germany, igniting World War II. Germany, Italy, and Japan formed the Axis alliance. Japan immediately conquered China and the Korean Peninsula, and Germany added the conquest of mainland Europe and North Africa. Germany also signed a nonaggression pact with Joseph Stalin's Soviet Union, but Hitler broke the pact and invaded the Soviet Union in June 1941. This decision was disastrous, as it forced the Nazis into an expensive and bloody war of attrition. Hitler also committed significant resources to the Holocaust—his plan to exterminate Jews, gypsies, homosexuals, Afro-Europeans, and disabled people.

The United States entered World War II in 1941, changing the tides of war. In 1942 alone, the U.S. Navy defeated Japan at the Battle of Midway; the Allies routed Italy and Germany in North Africa; and the Soviet Union decisively defeated Germany at Stalingrad. Nazi Germany agreed to an unconditional surrender on May 8, 1945, and an American nuclear attack forced Japan to surrender in September 1945.

With most of Europe and Asia lying in ruins, the United States and the Soviet Union were the only global superpowers to survive World War II. The Soviet Union's resilience was remarkable, considering the intense suffering Soviets endured, but they did benefit from consolidating power in Eastern Europe under Soviet-controlled satellite governments. The two superpowers engaged in a series of proxy wars, but the threat of nuclear war deterred a direct conflict. However, there were several close calls, any of which would have ended life on Earth.

The Cuban Missile Crisis (1962) began after the failed American Bay of Pigs invasion angered Cuba and the Soviet Union. The Soviets also objected to American ballistic missiles in Turkey, and they responded by covertly sending ballistic missiles to Cuba. American generals urged President John F. Kennedy to preemptively launch a nuclear strike against the Soviet Union, but an agreement was reached at the last minute. The Soviets dismantled their Cuban missile system, and the United States publicly promised not to invade Cuba. In addition, the United States secretly promised to dismantle her Turkish missile system.

At the end of the Cold War, the United States was the world's only remaining superpower. Without formal military opposition, the United States has increasingly used trade as a foreign policy tool. Until the Trump presidency, every American presidential administration has advocated for free-trade policies, such as the North American Free Trade Agreement (NAFTA). The United States has even helped potential rivals join the international community to prevent large-scale conflict and achieve American goals. For example, the United States integrated China into the world economy by pushing through their membership in the World Trade Organization. American economists argue that free trade benefits everyone in the increasingly globalized world. The rise and proliferation of Internet-based technologies has also contributed to the rapid development of a global marketplace.

The Digital Revolution has increased globalization through technological innovations like the internet and social media. Now, people anywhere in the world, no matter how far away, can communicate instantaneously. This has resulted in greater appreciation of people's different backgrounds and lived experiences, an economic boom in the computer-based economic sector, and lower costs for many businesses. However, the Digital Revolution has also threatened privacy, increased automation's threat on employment, and allowed nation-states to spread dissent in foreign countries. For better or worse, the internet has been the most disruptive technological innovation since Gutenberg's printing press (1439).

Cross-Cultural Comparisons in World History

Cross-cultural comparisons are inherently difficult to make due to the highly subjective nature of culture and lived experience. Cultures differ in their values, traditions, and customs, even for some ideals that appear to be universal. There are three major obstacles for effective cross-cultural comparisons.

First, the comparison is likely to involve some degree of **moral relativism**, the practice of prescribing moral judgments on foreign cultures. Some philosophers and policymakers argue it's impossible to compare different culture's values, traditions, and customs, while others believe some values are universal.

Second, cross-cultural comparisons are often used to draw **moral equivalencies**, the rejection of a proposed moral comparison between two group's actions or tactics. Cold-War-era American policymakers regularly accused their political opponents of moral equivalency to silence legitimate policy objections, especially when the objections compared American and Soviet imperialism. Those American policymakers argued that the United States is moral, while the Soviet Union is not; therefore, any attempt at moral comparison is inherently flawed.

Third, cross-cultural comparisons have historically been used to spread ideas of cultural superiority, including **scientific racism**, the use of pseudoscience to defend assertions of racial superiority or inferiority. Scientific racism was popular through World War II, and it was typically used to justify colonialism and imperialism. When comparing Western culture with African or native peoples, European colonizers assumed their culture was superior. As such, Europeans considered it their duty to spread their culture to the "noble savages." More often than not, this meant colonizing, converting, or enslaving non-Europeans.

Despite these challenges, cross-cultural comparisons can be useful analytical tools for studying world history. To avoid those three pitfalls, historical context and political ideology are especially valuable, as both influence how cultures develop.

History refers to the culture's preexisting experiences, which influence how societal institutions, communal values, and public attitudes develop. Political ideology is another useful tool for cross-cultural comparisons. Some cultures have representative government based on liberalism, like the United States and Europe. As a result, the sharing of political power amongst citizens places more cultural value on individual rights. In contrast, other cultures have more experience with top-down political ideologies, including totalitarianism. For example, Russia was a monarchy that transitioned into a communist dictatorship. Similarly, family dynasties ruled China for more than 3,000 years, and the Chinese Communist Revolution established another absolutist government. Chinese and Russian culture place more emphasis on authority and security than individual freedom.

Economics

Economists study the production, distribution, and consumption of wealth as expressed through commodities, goods, and services. **Commodities** are raw materials or agricultural products—gold, silver, gas, oil, corn, barley, etc. Goods are physical, tangible items, such as computers, bathing suits, refrigerators, televisions, etc. Services are activities based on labor and/or skills, like the work of lawyers, waiters, engineers, computer programmers, etc.

The government's role is to implement an economic system to distribute resources. In a centrally planned economic system, the government makes all decisions related to production and distribution. In addition, price controls are common, if not pervasive. Communist countries have a centrally planned economic system, and they attempt to abolish private property, transfer the means of production to the public, and distribute profits on an equitable basis.

In contrast, capitalism is a market economic system. The free market is what sets prices based on the existing supply and demand, and private firms make all decisions related to production and distribution. Market economic systems are based on merit, meaning that resources are distributed unequally. Under a pure **laissez-faire** free-market system, the government can't regulate, tax, subsidize, or otherwise interfere with the free market. The only rule in **laissez-faire** economics is **caveat emptor** (buyer beware).

Nearly all economies are mixed economic systems where the public and private sectors share the means of production and profits. As such, all governments with a mixed economic system collect taxes, set tariffs, and spend resources on public projects; however, they differ on the amount of control over the free market. For example, some governments implement price controls to regulate certain economic sectors for a designated period.

When a free market is present, the price and quantity are based on supply and demand. **Supply** is the amount of a commodity, good, or service that's available for consumption, and **demand** is the desire of buyers to acquire the commodity, good, or service. **Money** refers to the method of payment, whether it's a government currency, credit, digital currency, or precious metal.

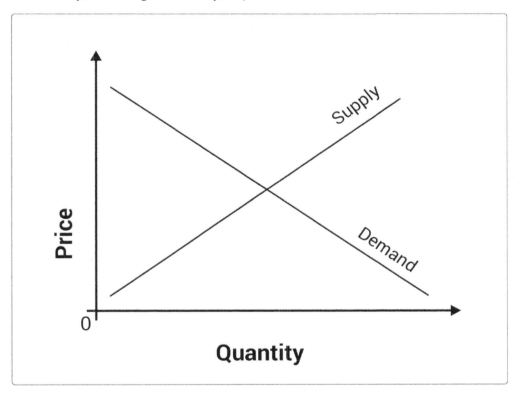

Governments can create their own currencies, and they can typically control the amount of currency in circulation, as well as the cost of short-term borrowing. Most countries designate a central bank or government agency to set and enforce monetary policies to control inflation and interest rates. **Inflation** is a period of increased prices and decreased currency values. **Interest rates** are what lenders charge borrowers to receive loans or credit. For example, governments sell bonds to borrow money for a designated period, and when the period ends, the buyer receives an interest payment plus the amount of the original debt.

In general, economics is a source of domestic and foreign conflict due to the scarcity (shortage) of resources like money, raw materials, and skills. Within a country, the needs and wants of the population are unlimited, while many resources are scarce. The same is also true in the context of international resources—the supply of resources is limited, while demand is unlimited.

Countries' domestic economic policy agendas involve raising revenue through taxes and spending money to enact and enforce policy decisions. Foreign economic policy agendas involve tariffs for imported goods. Tariffs are mostly used to protect industries with a special value to the homeland or to punish foreign countries.

Governments make production and trade policy decisions based on comparative advantage—the principle that countries produce the goods and services that have the least opportunity cost. Opportunity cost measures the loss of potential gain if the country had produced some other good or service. As such, in a free market, countries specialize at what they can do most efficiently relative to their competitors.

Most governments sign free-trade agreements with close allies and major trading partners. Free-trade agreements lower or eliminate tariffs. The agreements can be bilateral (2 countries) or multilateral (3+ countries). For example, the Gulf Cooperation Council is a multilateral free-trade agreement between Arab states in the Persian Gulf. In addition, many countries join intergovernmental organizations to borrow money, donate aid, or settle disputes. The World Trade Organization provides structural support for trade negotiations and offers dispute resolution services. The International Money Fund tries to increase global economic cooperation. The World Bank attempts to alleviate poverty by loaning money to developing countries for large projects.

Income inequality and perceptions of unfairness stir domestic unrest. In effect, worsening economic conditions cause political conflicts. The public might object to tax policies, stagnant or falling incomes, shortages of resources, underfunded social services, or any other specific policy. If the economic situation continues to deteriorate, the public might seek to overthrow the government. For example, during the French Revolution (1789-1799), King Louis XVI was executed after the monarchy amassed enormous war debts, enforced regressive taxes on their poorest citizens, and publicly flaunted their wealth in front of an increasingly poor public.

Technological innovation can both drive economic growth and send economies spiraling into a depression. Throughout history, technology has increased the efficiency of human labor. If the excess labor migrates to a different economic sector, the economy will grow. Many emerging technologies create new economic sectors, but some economic sectors are hurt by this transition. For example, the printing press expanded the markets for writers, records-keepers, and librarians. On the other hand, the printing press destroyed the market for scribes. Typically, free-market economic systems generate more technological advancements since the private firms are incentivized to pursue profits, which drives innovation. However, public spending can also lead to groundbreaking advances. For example, the Space Race revolutionized the computer-based economic sector, and the American military created ARPANET, the foundation for what would later become the Internet.

Due to comparative advantage in the free market, developing countries handle most of the world's labor-intensive work, like manufacturing. Developed countries benefit from the cheaper labor in lower costs, but there are fewer jobs for blue-collar workers. These workers often don't have the necessary skills to smoothly transition into a new field, especially as fields become increasingly specialized. Automation has a similar impact—decreased costs, increased unemployment, and a skills gap in the labor market. Consequently, governments must enact economic policies that maximize the advantages of cheaper labor and lower costs, while also protecting the economic system's legitimacy. The legitimacy of an economic system is context-specific, depending on historical and cultural forces. However, systems with higher standards of living and less income disparity enjoy more widespread legitimacy with the public.

Practice Questions

1. What type of boat offered early European explorers more maneuverability to navigate coastal waters?
   a. Caravel
   b. Steamship
   c. Astrolabe
   d. Quadrant

   parts of caravel

2. Which of the following was the first European colony established in North America?
   a. St. Augustine
   b. Roanoke
   c. Jamestown
   d. Hudson's Bay

   A

3. When did immigration to the United States shift from Great Britain to southeastern Europe?
   a. Early 18th century
   b. Early 19th century
   c. Early 20th century
   d. Early 21st century

   C

4. What was the Zimmerman Telegram?
   a. A famous telegram from Germany to the United States describing the experiences of a Jewish German family during the Holocaust
   b. An intercepted communication from Germany to Mexico stating Germany's willingness to help Mexico invade the United States
   c. A telegram that announced Germany's invasion of the Sudetenland
   d. A new type of telegraph invented during the Second Industrial Revolution

5. Which one of the following civilizations first developed advanced irrigation techniques?
   a. Greece
   b. Rome
   c. Egypt
   d. Persia

6. What event led to France and England ending their policy of appeasement toward Hitler's Germany?
   a. Germany's remilitarization of the Rhineland
   b. Germany's use of proxy forces during the Spanish Civil War
   c. Germany's invasion of Poland
   d. Germany's annexation of Austria

7. Which of the following best describes the interaction of physical systems and human systems?
   a. Physical systems and human systems exist independently of each other
   b. Physical systems and human systems influence and change each other
   c. Physical systems change human systems, but human systems can't change physical systems
   d. Human systems change physical systems, but physical systems can't change human systems

8. What was the primary role of party bosses in 19th century American government?
    a. Vote to elect U.S. senators and presidential electors
    b. Raise money for state and federal elections
    c. Ensure the integrity of local elections
    d. Consolidate power under a political machine

9. Which of the following did NOT contribute to European colonization of the Americas?
    a. Disease
    b. Sustainable land use — Native Americans
    c. Superior weaponry
    d. Permanent settlements

10. What event triggered the Occupy Wall Street movement?
    a. The War in Afghanistan
    b. The Iraq War
    c. The financial crisis of 2007–2008
    d. The Supreme Court's decision in *Citizens United v. Federal Election Commission*

11. What principle ensures that political power isn't completely centralized?
    a. Checks and balances
    b. Sovereignty
    c. Legitimacy
    d. Federalism

12. Which of the following most accurately describes manifest destiny?
    a. The belief that America is exceptional and has a duty to spread its virtues westward
    b. The belief that America is destined to be a global superpower
    c. The belief that Mexico should be invaded and enslaved
    d. The belief that the Union must be preserved at all costs

13. What power is exclusive to state governments in the United States?
    a. Establish lower federal courts
    b. Enact and enforce immigration laws
    c. Charter corporations
    d. Hold and regulate elections

14. What is a difference between present-day civil rights and civil liberties?
    a. Civil liberties are unconditional, and civil rights are conditional.
    b. The federal government guarantees civil liberties but not civil rights.
    c. Civil rights apply to a broader class of Americans.
    d. Civil rights are freedom from unequal treatment based on a characteristic, and civil liberties are universal.

15. What countries formed the Triple Entente in World War I?
    a. The United States, Britain, and Canada
    b. The United States, Britain, and France
    c. Britain, France, and Russia
    d. Austria-Hungary, Germany, and Italy

16. What did President Franklin Delano Roosevelt call his legislative agenda?
    a. The War on Poverty
    b. The New Deal
    c. The Great Society
    d. Social Security

17. When it was founded, what was the Republican Party's primary issue?
    a. States' rights
    b. Tax cuts
    c. Manifest destiny
    d. Abolition of slavery

18. What is the Organic Theory's thesis?
    a. Naval and air power is more important than territorial control.
    b. Africa, Asia, and Europe form the World Island, which is the most important landmass for geopolitics.
    c. Countries need to acquire political power and territory to survive.
    d. Communism will grow organically unless there's early military intervention.

19. Which of the following maps is the most subjective?
    a. Climate maps
    b. Political maps
    c. Population density maps
    d. Topographic maps

20. How did Jim Crow laws impact the American South?
    a. African American slaves could vote for the first time in American history.
    b. The South diversified from a one-crop economy.
    c. The South industrialized, following the Northern example.
    d. The Southern states contravened the Reconstruction Amendments.

21. What is the difference between the melting pot and salad bowl approaches to cultural integration?
    a. The melting pot approach can accommodate more cultural diversity than the salad bowl approach.
    b. The salad bowl approach can accommodate more cultural diversity than the melting pot approach.
    c. The melting pot approach preserves most of the culture's unique characteristics, while the salad bowl approach doesn't.
    d. The salad bowl approach preserves most of the culture's unique characteristics, while the melting pot approach doesn't.

22. Which of the following best describes the 10th Amendment to the U.S. Constitution?
    a. The 10th Amendment reserves all non-specified powers to the states and people.
    b. The 10th Amendment establishes the existence of rights not named in the document.
    c. The 10th Amendment protects the right to bear arms.
    d. The 10th Amendment protects a series of rights for people accused of crimes.

23. What was the primary cause of widespread urbanization in the United States?
    a. The First Industrial Revolution
    b. The Second Industrial Revolution
    c. The Great Migration
    d. Successive waves of immigration

24. What is the government's role in a centrally planned economic system?
    a. The government distributes resources based solely on merit.
    b. The government allows the private market to set all prices based on supply and demand.
    c. The government makes all decisions related to production, distribution, and price.
    d. The government balances a private and public sector to stabilize the economy.

25. What was NOT included in the Missouri Compromise of 1820?
    a. Slavery was banned in Washington, D.C. → *Connecticut Comp.*
    b. Missouri was admitted as a slave state.
    c. Slavery was prohibited in future northern territories.
    d. Maine was admitted as a free state.

26. Which of the following best describes commodities?
    a. Physical, tangible items
    b. Activities based on labor or skill
    c. Raw materials or agricultural products
    d. High-demand products

27. The American Continental Army won which of the following battles?
    a. Antietam
    b. Appomattox
    c. Quebec
    d. Saratoga

28. What is a monoculture's primary weakness?
    a. Compared to a multicultural society, a monoculture is more likely to increase domestic unrest.
    b. A monoculture is a recent development, so there's a limited historical precedent.
    c. Compared to a multicultural society, a monoculture is more likely to be warlike.
    d. A monoculture has a narrow perspective, limiting societal understanding of external forces.

29. What caused the Korean War?
    a. Soviet and North Korean forces invaded South Korea.
    b. Chinese and North Korean forces invaded South Korea.
    c. North Korean forces invaded South Korea.
    d. South Korean forces invaded North Korea.

30. What treaty ended the American Revolution?
    a. Treaty of Paris
    b. Treaty of Ghent
    c. Treaty of Alliance
    d. Treaty of Versailles

31. What is the usual effect of inflation?
    a. Increased regulation and decreased growth
    b. Decreased regulation and increased growth
    c. Increased prices and decreased currency values
    d. Decreased prices and increased currency values

32. What was included in the Connecticut Compromise?
    a. Two legislative bodies with different methods of representation
    b. Two legislative bodies with the same method of representation
    c. One legislative body with representation based on population
    d. One legislative body with one vote per state

33. What happened to the global population during the 20th century?
    a. The population declined due to repeated global conflicts.
    b. The population declined due to worsening global poverty.
    c. The population increased rapidly in the first half of the century before declining in the second half of the century.
    d. The population increased the most in world history.

34. What is the Space Race's legacy?
    a. The United States dismantled its space exploration program after beating the Soviets to the Moon.
    b. The superpowers' relations improved, and the United States withdrew from the Vietnam War.
    c. The underlying technology led to the Digital Revolution.
    d. The Soviet Union collapsed due to its repeated failure to put a man on the Moon.

35. Which of the following powers is exclusive to the federal government in the United States?
    a. Regulate immigration
    b. Regulate local government
    c. Implement welfare and benefit programs
    d. Levy taxes

36. What was the domino theory?
    a. An economic theory that caused the Great Depression
    b. An American foreign policy approach to contain communism
    c. A framework for analyzing how military alliances caused World War I
    d. A British attempt to integrate French Canada into the British Empire

37. What was a major achievement during the Han dynasty?
    a. The Han dynasty installed the world's first representative government.
    b. The Han dynasty defeated Alexander the Great's legendary military.
    c. The Han dynasty invented a new, more powerful form of concrete.
    d. The Han dynasty connected the Far East with the West for the first time.

38. How did large-scale agriculture facilitate European colonization in the Americas?
    a. Large-scale agriculture increased American exports to Europe, and the colonies received military aid in return.
    b. Large-scale agriculture led to the development of new technologies that were applied to the military.
    c. Large-scale agriculture supported the development of major cities in the American South, and Native Americans couldn't pierce the city's defenses.
    d. Large-scale agriculture produced a food surplus that supported a larger population, permanent settlements, and a centralized government.

39. Which of the following laws was NOT a major cause of the American Revolution?
    a. Indian Removal Acts
    b. Proclamation of 1763
    c. Quebec Act
    d. Townshend Acts

40. In what way did Native American and European colonists' family structures differ?
    a. Men served as the primary provider of resources.
    b. European colonists lived more sustainably.
    c. Native Americans included broader kinship networks.
    d. European colonists were more likely to honor their elders.

41. What event exposed the Articles of Confederation as a deeply flawed system of government?
    a. Publication of The Federalist Papers
    b. John Brown's raid at Harper's Ferry
    c. Whiskey Rebellion
    d. Shays' Rebellion

42. The United States has NOT successfully overthrown the government in which of the following countries?
    a. Iran (1953)
    b. Cuba (1961)
    c. Dominican Republic (1961)
    d. Chile (1973)

43. Which of the following presidential administrations conquered and annexed the most territory from a foreign power?
    a. Polk administration
    b. Madison administration
    c. Monroe administration
    d. Jackson administration

44. What is the consequence of economic comparative advantage?
    a. Countries increase tax rates to subsidize more industries.
    b. Countries enforce high tariffs on products they can't produce efficiently.
    c. Countries specialize at what they can do most efficiently relative to their competitors.
    d. Countries increase spending to stimulate economic growth.

45. What country successfully launched the first satellite into orbit?
    a. Japan
    b. Soviet Union
    c. Germany
    d. United States

46. What two American presidential campaigns most featured the candidates' opposition to the Iraq War?
    a. Barack Obama and Hillary Clinton
    b. Barack Obama and Donald Trump
    c. Hillary Clinton and John McCain
    d. Hillary Clinton and Donald Trump

47. What contributed to the First Industrial Revolution in the United States?
   a. Cotton gins
   b. Steel
   c. Electricity
   d. Railroads

48. Which of the following was achieved during the Progressive Era?
   a. Emancipation of all slaves
   b. Direct election of United States Senators
   c. Annexation of Texas
   d. Victory in the Mexican-American War

49. What intergovernmental organization primarily offers dispute resolution services?
   a. Organization for Economic Cooperation and Development
   b. The World Bank
   c. The World Trade Organization
   d. The International Monetary Fund

50. Which of the following was NOT one of the original Thirteen Colonies?
   a. Maine
   b. Maryland
   c. Massachusetts
   d. New Hampshire

51. Who was Cyrus the Great?
   a. Egyptian pharaoh who built the Great Pyramid of Giza
   b. Greek general, politician, and orator who led the Delian League
   c. Persian ruler who founded the Achaemenid Empire
   d. Roman general who crossed the Rubicon River during the Roman Civil War

52. Which of the following civilizations most influenced the drafting of the U.S. Constitution?
   a. China
   b. Egypt
   c. Greece
   d. Rome

53. What area has the most geopolitical importance under the Heartland Theory?
   a. Arab Gulf and Central Mesopotamia
   b. Eastern Europe, Russia, and Western China
   c. Eurasian coastal land
   d. North America and South America

54. President Andrew Jackson refused to enforce what Supreme Court decision?
   a. United States v. Windsor
   b. Worcester v. Georgia
   c. Dred Scott v. Sandford
   d. Plessy v. Ferguson

Answer Explanations

1. A: Choice *A* is the correct answer. The caravel is a smaller and more maneuverable ship first developed in the 15th century by the Portuguese to explore the West African coast. Astrolabes and quadrants are naval navigation tools, not types of boats. The steamship wasn't invented until the early 19th century.

2. A: Spanish explorers established St. Augustine in 1565. All other colonies were founded at least a decade later. Sir Walter Raleigh founded Roanoke in 1585, making it the first British colony, but it was abandoned in 1590. Established in 1607, Jamestown was the first successful British colony. The British explorer Henry Hudson explored Hudson's Bay in the 1610s, and the French established trading outposts in the area during the 1670s. Thus, Choice *A* is the correct answer.

3. C: Choice *C* is the correct answer. American immigrants' homeland first changed dramatically in the early 20th century. The American colonists were mostly British, and immigration until the late 19th century was mostly confined to the British Isles. In the late 19th century and early 20th century, immigrants arrived from southeastern Europe en masse. This placed considerable strain on American society, as the current residents were Protestant, and the new immigrants were Catholic and Jewish.

4. B: Choice *B* is the correct answer. The Zimmerman Telegram was a message from Germany to Mexico that stated Germany's willingness to help Mexico invade America. Great Britain intercepted the Zimmerman Telegram and delivered it to the American government, hoping it would persuade the United States to join the Triple Entente. Germany didn't invade the Sudetenland until World War II, and the Zimmerman Telegram wasn't a type of telegram or related to the Holocaust.

5. C: Founded in the 31st century B.C., Ancient Egypt is one of the oldest civilizations in world history. The Egyptians settled on the Nile River, and they developed advanced irrigation techniques to harness the Nile's rich delta for agriculture. This occurred more than 10,000 years before the ancient Greek, Persian, and Roman civilizations were established. Consequently, Choice *C* is the correct answer.

6. C: In September 1939, France and England declared war on Germany two days after the Germans invaded Poland; therefore, Choice *C* is the correct answer. Previously, France and England had followed a policy of appeasement, allowing Adolf Hitler to remilitarize the Rhineland (1936), deploy proxy forces in the Spanish Civil War (1936-1939), and annex Austria (1938).

7. B: Physical systems and human systems influence and change each other. Humans alter the physical system through the extraction of resources, like fossil fuels, iron, land, minerals, water, and wood. Likewise, the variety and availability of the physical system's resources has a strong influence on the human system's development. Thus, Choice *B* is the correct answer.

8. D: A party boss was the head of a political machine, a system of government common in 19th century American cities. The party boss consolidated political power by doling out special favors to constituents. So, Choice *D* is the correct answer. Before the passage of the Seventeenth Amendment (1913), the state legislature elected U.S. Senators, not party bosses. Some party bosses raised money for their state and/or national political party, but this was not their primary function. The party bosses didn't protect election integrity. If anything, they committed corruption and voter fraud, which the Progressive Era later sought to rectify.

9. B: The question asks what answer did NOT help the Europeans colonize the Americas. While the Native Americans lived sustainably, the Europeans exploited the land to extract the maximum possible value, so Choice *B* is the correct answer. The European colonists did establish permanent settlements, which facilitated their centralized system of government. Old World diseases did overwhelm the Native American population, decimating some of the western tribes even before the arrival of European colonists. The Europeans were also armed with superior weaponry—steel and firearms.

10. C: The Occupy Wall Street movement was a direct response to the irresponsible investment banking practices that caused the financial crisis of 2007-2008; therefore, Choice *C* is the correct answer. The War in Afghanistan has never led to large-scale protests, and while the Iraq War became incredibly unpopular, it wasn't directly related to Occupy Wall Street. *Citizens United v. Federal Election Commission* (2010) effectively legalized unlimited campaign contributions, and the Occupy Wall Street movement vehemently opposed it. However, the Occupy Wall Street movement predates the Court's decision, so it couldn't have been a triggering event.

11. D: Choice *D* is the correct answer. Federalism is the principle that divides political power between the federal, state, and local government. In the United States, federalism is rooted in the Tenth Amendment. The federal government can limit or prohibit the states from enacting certain policies, and state governments exercise exclusive control over local government. Sovereignty refers to a government's ability to exercise control over a defined territory and population. Legitimacy is the population's acceptance of the government's authority to rule. American constitutional checks and balances divide the power within the federal government, not between the federal government and local governments.

12. A: Manifest destiny is the belief that Americans hold special virtues; the United States has a duty to spread those virtues westward; and success is a certainty. Choice *A* best captures this sentiment. Manifest destiny influenced American confidence in the country's potential to be a global superpower, but it was originally applied to territorial expansion. Annexing Mexican land was a consequence of manifest destiny, not the entire idea, and the United States didn't attempt to enslave Mexicans. President Lincoln used the preservation of the Union to defend his decision to fight the Civil War, but it wasn't directly related to manifest destiny.

13. D: The power to hold and regulate elections is reserved to the states, so Choice *D* is the correct answer. The powers to enforce immigration laws and establish lower federal courts are exclusive to the federal government. The federal and state governments share the power to charter corporations.

14. D: In the present day, civil liberties are universal, and civil rights safeguard the freedom of people with certain protected characteristics, such as race and gender; therefore, Choice *D* is the correct answer. Civil liberties are conditional—under some special circumstances, like wartime, the government can restrict citizens' civil liberties. The federal government guarantees both civil liberties and civil rights. Civil rights only apply to a narrow class of Americans, those with protected characteristics.

15. C: Britain, France, and Russia formed the Triple Entente in World War I, so Choice *B* is the correct answer. Canada and the United States both joined the Triple Entente, but they were not original members. Austria-Hungary and Germany fought against the Triple Entente. Italy allied with Austria-Hungary and Germany before the war broke out, but the Italians held out and later joined the Triple Entente once it appeared they would be victorious.

16. B: Choice *B* is the correct answer. President Franklin Delano Roosevelt's legislative agenda was called the New Deal, and it created the modern-day welfare state—Social Security, unemployment insurance, disability, labor laws, and housing and food subsidies. The War on Poverty and Great Society were Lyndon B. Johnson's agenda, though they were influenced by the New Deal. Social Security was part of the New Deal, not Roosevelt's legislative agenda.

17. D: Northern Whigs and Free Soil Democrats created the Republican Party to advocate for the abolition of slavery, so Choice *D* is the correct answer. Abraham Lincoln was the first Republican to be elected president. The Republicans exposed the Southern theory of states' rights, and their pro-business agenda didn't develop until after the Civil War. Manifest destiny also wasn't the Republicans primary issue; it was slavery.

18. C: The Organic Theory argues that nation-states need to consolidate political power and acquire new geographic territory in order to sustain themselves. Under this conception, the nation-state operates like a living organism, and new territories provide the resources it needs to survive. Thus, Choice *C* is the correct answer. The Rimland Theory emphasizes the importance of naval power and coastal land, and the World Island is part of the Heartland Theory. In the Cold War era, American foreign policymakers created the domino theory to justify military intervention for limiting the spread of communism.

19. B: Choice *B* is the correct answer. Political maps are the most subjective, because territorial boundaries are frequently contested or otherwise in dispute. For example, 19th century political maps differed on the boundaries between the competing European colonies, as well as what constituted Native American territory. In the present day, there's dispute over who owns Crimea. In contrast, climate, population density, and topographic maps are all based on objective data.

20. D: Immediately after the federal government withdrew troops from the South, ending Reconstruction, the Southern states enacted Jim Crow laws. These laws contravened the Reconstruction Amendments by preventing African Americans from voting and enforcing segregationist policies. Therefore, Choice *D* is the correct answer. African Americans voted for the first time during Reconstruction, but following the passage of Jim Crow laws, they couldn't vote until the 1960s Civil Rights Movement. The South didn't diversify from a one-crop economy (cotton) or industrialize until the 20th century. In addition, it wasn't related to Jim Crow. If anything, Jim Crow contributed to the continued focus on cotton as sharecropping replaced slavery.

21. D: The salad bowl preserves more of the culture's unique characteristics than the melting pot, so Choice *D* is the correct answer. Under the salad bowl approach, the "salad" has several ingredients (cultures), and they're mixed together in a bowl without changing the ingredients' individual structure. In contrast, under a melting pot approach, the ingredients (cultures) are all poured into a pot, creating something unique. Neither approach is proven to be more effective at accommodating more cultural diversity, and in practice, most countries use a mixture of the two approaches.

22. A: The Tenth Amendment reserves all non-specified powers to the states or people, establishing the principle of federalism. So, Choice *A* is the correct answer. The Ninth Amendment establishes the existence of unnamed rights. The Second Amendment protects the right to bear arms. The Fourth, Fifth, and Sixth Amendments include procedural protections for people accused of crimes.

23. B: Choice *B* is the correct answer. The United States first industrialized during the First Industrial Revolution to replace the decline in British imports caused by the War of 1812. However, this development was limited to towns in the Northeast. Urbanization didn't occur until after the Civil War, and it was caused by the Second Industrial Revolution's technological innovations, like steel production, railways, and more sophisticated factory machinery. The Great Migration and successive waves of immigration increased the pace of urbanization, supplying labor to the urban boom. Yet, urbanization wouldn't have occurred without the Second Industrial Revolution transforming America from an agricultural to industrial economy.

24. C: The government makes all decisions related to production, distribution, and price in a centrally planned economic system; therefore, Choice *C* is the correct answer. This allows communist governments to oversee price control, and, as a result, the production and distribution of resources is less efficient but more equitable. If a government distributes resources solely based on merit and allows private markets to set prices, then the economy is operating under a free-market system. A government that balances a private and public sector is characteristic of a mixed economic system.

25. A: The question is asking what was NOT included in the Missouri Compromise of 1820. The Missouri Compromise had three parts: Maine was admitted as a free state; Missouri was admitted as a slave state; and slavery was prohibited in new territories north of the 36°30′ parallel. The only answer that doesn't name a part of the Missouri Compromise is Choice *D*, so it must be correct. The Compromise of 1850 banned slavery in Washington, D.C.

26. C: Choice *C* is the correct answer. Commodities are raw materials or agricultural products—gold, silver, gas, oil, corn, barley, etc. Physical, tangible items are goods. Activities based on labor or skills are services. High-demand products typically have a higher price in a free-market system, depending on the supply.

27. D: The American Continental Army was victorious in the Battle of Saratoga during the Revolutionary War; thus, Choice *D* is the correct answer. The Battle of Quebec was a Revolutionary War battle, but the Continental Army was defeated. Antietam was a Civil War battle, and President Lincoln issued the Emancipation Proclamation five days after it concluded. The Battle of Appomattox was one of the final battles in the Civil War, and it ended with Confederate General Robert E. Lee surrendering to Union General Ulysses S. Grant.

28. D: A monoculture is a group of people with a single culture. Compared to a multicultural society, a monoculture usually offers greater unity. However, monocultures often have a narrow worldview, limiting the society's understanding of the greater world. Thus, Choice *D* is the correct answer. Multicultural societies require assimilation, which can cause domestic unrest under the best of circumstances.

29. C: The Korean War started with North Korea invading South Korea, so Choice *C* is correct. The United States entered the war to protect its ally and prevent communism spreading across Asia. China didn't enter the conflict until General MacArthur led the American military across the 38th parallel. The Soviets provided material support to communist North Korea, but they never formally entered the war.

30. A: The Treaty of Paris concluded the American Revolution, securing American independence. Thus, Choice *A* is the correct answer. The Treaty of Ghent ended the War of 1812. The United States and France signed the Treaty of Alliance during the American Revolution, and French support turned the tides of war for the Americans. The Treaty of Versailles ended World War I, and its failure to establish a lasting peace partially caused World War II.

31. C: Inflation is a period of increased prices and decreased currency values, so Choice *C* is the correct answer. Most countries designate a central bank or government agency to set and enforce monetary policies to control inflation and interest rates. Regulation typically correlates with growth, but that relationship is not inflation.

32. A: Delegates at the American Constitutional Convention agreed on the Connecticut Compromise, establishing two legislative bodies. Representation in one house was based on population (House of Representatives), and the other granted each state two votes (Senate). As such, Choice *A* is the correct answer. The New Jersey Plan proposed a single legislative body with one vote per state, but it was rejected in favor of the Connecticut Compromise.

33. D: The global population increased in both halves of the 20th century. From 1900 to 2000, the global population increased from 1.6 billion people to 6 billion people, marking the largest increase in world history. Therefore, Choice *D* is the correct answer.

34. C: During the Space Race, the United States and Soviet Union invested in computer-based technology to advance their rocket and satellite capabilities. These advancements in computing power led to the Digital Revolution, so Choice *C* is the correct answer. The United States never dismantled its space exploration program, and the Soviet Union collapsed more than a decade after they gave up trying to put a man on the Moon. Although the Space Race improved the superpowers' relationship, this didn't influence the American withdrawal from Vietnam. Instead, mounting domestic protests caused the United States to leave Vietnam.

35. A: The power to regulate immigration is exclusive to the federal government; so, Choice *A* is the correct answer. The powers to regulate local government and implement welfare programs are reserved to the states. Both the federal and state governments enjoy the power to levy taxes.

36. B: American Cold War foreign policy followed the domino theory, the idea that if one country turned communist, so would all of the neighboring countries. Consequently, the United States regularly intervened militarily to contain communism, which happened in Korea and Vietnam. Therefore, Choice *B* is the correct answer. None of the other answer choices are related to American foreign policy in the Cold War era.

37. D: The Han dynasty created the Silk Road, a series of trade routes that linked the Far East and West for the first time in world history. Thus, Choice *D* is the correct answer. The Greeks installed the first representative government; Indian rulers defeated Alexander the Great's legendary military; and the Romans invented a superior type of concrete.

38. D: The European system's large-scale production of crops and livestock produced a food surplus that sustained permanent settlements and centralized government. So, Choice *D* is the correct answer. The European colonies didn't trade agriculture for military aid; agriculture didn't lead to military technological advancements; and the American South didn't urbanize for several centuries.

39. A: The question is asking what was NOT a major cause of the American Revolution. The Proclamation of 1763 angered colonists by prohibiting colonial expansion west of the Appalachian Mountains. Likewise, the Quebec Act and Townshend Act increased resentment. The Quebec Act granted rights to French Canadians at the same time Great Britain passed a series of laws to increase taxes in the Thirteen Colonies, like the Townshend Acts. The Indian Removal Acts weren't passed until the Andrew Jackson administration; so, Choice *A* is the correct answer.

40. C: Native Americans traditionally live in extended kinship networks. As such, Native Americans define family as the nuclear family, extended family, tribal members, and/or entire nation. Fictive (non-blood related) kin are also commonly included as family members. In contrast, European colonists' families typically only included the nuclear and extended family. Therefore, Choice *C* is the correct answer. Men served as the primary provider of resources in both family structures; the European colonists didn't live more sustainably than Native Americans; and Native Americans also honored their elders.

41. D: From 1786 to 1787, Revolutionary War veteran Daniel Shays led an armed insurrection in western Massachusetts, and the government's inability to quash the rebellion exposed the Articles of Confederation's flaws. Thus, Choice *D* is the correct answer. The *Federalist Papers* were published during the ratification process, and, at that time, the Articles of Confederation was widely considered to be untenable. The question was what form of government would replace it. John Brown's raid at Harper's Ferry increased regional tension before the Civil War, and President George Washington's suppression of the Whiskey Rebellion demonstrated the strength of the U.S. Constitution.

42. B: The question is asking which government was NOT overthrown with American assistance. President John F. Kennedy attempted to overthrow the Cuban government in 1961, but his Bay of Pigs invasion was a disastrous failure. The United States provided military support, training, and/or funding in Iran, the Dominican Republic, and Chile. All three governments were successfully replaced with pro-American dictators. Therefore, Choice *B* is the correct answer.

43. A: James K. Polk won the 1844 presidential election based on his promise to complete America's manifest destiny. Polk annexed the present-day American southwest and California from Mexico, and his administration settled border disputes with Great Britain in the Oregon territory. None of the administrations in the other answer choices annexed a comparable amount of territory; therefore, Choice *A* is the correct answer.

44. C: Comparative advantage is the principle that countries produce the goods and services that have the least opportunity cost. When a country has a comparative advantage, they'll specialize in that industry because it's more efficient. Thus, Choice *C* is the correct answer. A country might implement the other three policies, but it's less likely when the country enjoys a comparative advantage.

45. B: On October 4, 1957, the Soviet Union launched the first satellite, Sputnik 1, into orbit; therefore, Choice *B* is the correct answer. The United States was shocked by the Soviets' achievement, and they redoubled their efforts, culminating in the Apollo 11 mission's Moon landing. The Japanese and German space exploration program weren't active until 1969, and they weren't major competitors to the American and Soviet programs.

46. B: Choice *B* is the correct answer. Barack Obama used his opposition to the Iraq War to differentiate himself from his opponent, John McCain, who wanted to increase the number of American troops in Iraq. Although it's unclear whether Donald Trump opposed the Iraq War before the invasion, he was one its earliest and most vocal public critics. Like Obama, Trump raised the issue to paint his opponent, Hillary Clinton, as the candidate more likely to start another war. Clinton had voted for the Iraq War as a Senator, but she had since publicly recognized it as a mistake.

47. A: Eli Whitney invented the cotton gin in 1793, and the cotton industry exploded. Following its invention, American cotton production doubled every decade until the latter half of the 19th century. As a result, New England textile mills enjoyed access to more cotton at cheaper prices, facilitating the First Industrial Revolution in the United States. Therefore, Choice *A* is the correct answer. The other three answer choices contributed to the Second Industrial Revolution.

48. B: The Progressive Era (1890-1920) strengthened American democracy in a variety of ways. One of those legislative achievements was the 17th Amendment, which established the direct election of U.S. Senators. Previously, state legislatures elected Senators. Thus, Choice *B* is the correct answer. The 13th amendment freed slaves after the end of the Civil War; Texas was annexed in 1845; and the United States defeated Mexico in 1848.

49. C: Choice *C* is the correct answer. The World Trade Organization provides structural support for trade negotiations and offers dispute resolution services. The International Money Fund tries to increase global economic cooperation. The World Bank attempts to alleviate poverty by loaning money to developing countries for large projects. The Organization for Economic Cooperation and Development (OECD) was created to administer American aid under the Marshall Plan. Now, OECD members collaborate on free trade policies to drive global economic growth.

50. A: Maine was NOT one of the original Thirteen Colonies; therefore, Choice *A* is the correct answer. The Thirteen Colonies were Connecticut, Delaware, Georgia, Maryland, Massachusetts, New Hampshire, New Jersey, New York, North Carolina, Pennsylvania, Rhode Island, South Carolina, and Virginia. Maine was admitted in the Missouri Compromise of 1820.

51. C: Cyrus the Great founded the first Persian Empire, the Achaemenid Empire, in the 6th century B.C., effectively turning a group of nomadic shepherds into one of the largest empires in world history. Thus, Choice *C* is the correct answer. Egyptian Pharaoh Khufu built the Great Pyramid of Giza. Pericles was an Athenian general, politician, and orator who led the Delian League in the Peloponnesian Wars against Sparta. Julius Caesar was the Roman general who famously crossed the Rubicon River and won the Roman Civil War, establishing the Roman Empire.

52. D: Choice *D* is the correct answer. James Madison used the Roman Republic's separation of powers as a model for the U.S. Constitution. Greece generally influenced the U.S. Constitution in its implementation of the world's first direct democracy, but the Roman influence is more specific. China and Egypt didn't influence the Constitution's drafting.

53. B: Halford John MacKinder's Heartland Theory emphasizes the strategic importance of Eastern Europe, Russia and Western China due to their central position on the World Island. Thus, Choice *B* is the correct answer. The Eurasian coastal land is prioritized in the Rimland theory. The Arab Gulf, Mesopotamia, North America, and South America all have immense geopolitical value in America's foreign policy approach.

54. B: President Andrew Jackson refused to enforce the Supreme Court's decision in *Worcester v. Georgia* (1832), which established the concept of tribal sovereignty. Instead, Jackson encouraged the colonization of Native American land. *United States v. Windsor* (2013) established the right to same-sex marriage. *Dred Scott v. Sandford* (1857) overturned the Missouri Compromise's prohibition on slavery in northern territories. *Plessy v. Ferguson* (1896) upheld the South's "separate but equal" segregation.

Science

Earth Science

The Structure of the Earth System

The structure of the Earth has many layers. Starting with the center, or the **core,** the Earth comprises two separate sections: the inner core and the outer core. The innermost portion of the core is a solid center consisting of 760 miles of iron. The outer core is slightly less than 1400 miles in thickness and consists of a liquid nickel-iron alloy. The next section out from the core also has two layers. This section is the **mantle,** and it is split into the lower mantle and the upper mantle. Both layers of the mantle consist of magnesium and iron, and they are extremely high in temperature. This hot temperature causes the metal contained in the lower mantle to rise and then cool slightly as it reaches the upper mantle. Once the metal begins to cool, it falls back down toward the lower mantle, restarting the whole process again. The motion of rising and falling within the layers of the mantle is the cause of plate tectonics and movement of the outermost layer of the Earth. The outermost layer of the Earth is called the **crust.** Movements between the mantle and the crust create effects such as earthquakes and volcanoes.

The Earth's atmosphere is composed of five primary layers. These layers consist of gases that are held in place by the force due to the effects of Earth's gravity. The breakdown of the gases includes mostly nitrogen (78 percent), and less than one-quarter oxygen (21 percent); the rest is other gases (1 percent in total). Most of the weather and clouds exist in the closest layer to the Earth's surface, called the **troposphere**. After this first layer, the atmosphere thins out because each layer is farther away from the surface of the Earth and therefore less impacted by the effects of gravity. This thinning of layers continues until the atmosphere meets space. The layer closest to the Earth contains half of the actual atmosphere, reaches twelve miles vertically, and is heated by the surface of the Earth. As this first layer becomes farther away from the surface, it cools off and contains water vapor, which forms clouds.

The second layer of the atmosphere from the surface of the Earth, called the **stratosphere,** is very dry and contains ozone, which helps to absorb potentially harmful wavelengths from solar radiation. The second layer is also where airplanes and weather balloons fly.

The third layer from the surface of the Earth, the **mesosphere,** is the coldest. This layer is where meteors will burn up if they enter the atmosphere. The fourth layer, the **thermosphere,** has very low air density and is where the space shuttle and the International space station orbit. The fifth, and final thin layer, called the **exosphere,** consists of hydrogen and helium.

Processes of the Earth System

The Earth system is complex, made of interrelated parts; processes in one area or of a certain type can significantly impact other components. The planet can be thought of as consisting of four main parts: the hydrosphere, the atmosphere, the **geosphere** (referring to any physical matter that makes up the Earth), and the **biosphere** (referring to all living organisms across the planet).

Different chemical, physical, and energetic cycles give rise to the activities that take place across the Earth system. These include processes such as evaporation/precipitation (which drive how water is dispersed over the planet) and oceanic convection currents (which influence weather patterns and animal migration patterns, among others). Most of these cycles are initially triggered by the radiation provided by the Sun. For example, **photosynthesis** refers to the process of plants converting sunlight to chemical energy that plants can better utilize. This process is also the primary basis of converting carbon dioxide to oxygen, a critical component for the biosphere, atmosphere, and geosphere, for the reasons listed below:

- Biosphere: Animals need oxygen to survive
- Atmosphere: Imbalanced levels of carbon dioxide or oxygen can cause repercussions such as climate change
- Geosphere: Plants also need to take water and other nutrients from their surrounding soil for the full functions of photosynthesis to take place

However, other events may be triggered by processes within the Earth itself. For example, **plate tectonics** refers to how plates that make up the surface of the Earth's crust move. When plates move, they can create earthquakes, volcanic eruptions, mountain ranges, or deep trenches. These impact the physical makeup of the geosphere, as well as the existence of a number of organisms in the biosphere.

The cycle of water on the Earth is called the **hydrologic cycle.** This cycle involves the water from the surface of the Earth evaporating from the oceans, lakes, and rivers, into the air. This evaporating water cools as it rises in the air. As the cooling occurs, the water condenses into clouds contained within the atmosphere, which eventually allows the water to return to the surface of the Earth in some form of precipitation. Precipitation can occur as snow, rain, hail, or sleet. Areas experiencing drought receive little or no precipitation; therefore, little to no water is available to run off into the surrounding bodies of water. The hydrologic cycle becomes imbalanced and often dormant in affected regions.

The terms *weather* and *climate* are often mistakenly interchanged, even though they describe different phenomena on Earth. **Weather** on Earth is constantly changing, while **climate** describes a long-term state. Factors that can affect the weather include latitude, elevation, wind, proximity to a large body of water, and ocean currents. Latitude influences weather based upon distance from the equator; for instance, the sections of the Earth nearest to the equator receive more direct sunlight from the positioning of the Earth on its axis, and therefore are warmer. The higher the elevation of a location above sea level, the colder the temperature. Wind, resulting from the Earth's rotation (trade winds), can affect the temperatures of the surrounding areas. Large bodies of water can store heat, which influences the weather of surrounding areas and the effect ocean currents have on the rising and falling of warm air. This phenomenon occurs around lakes and surrounding areas; at times, for instance, areas on one side of a lake will experience heavier amounts of snowfall due to what is called "lake effect snow." This occurs when the lake is at a higher temperature than the atmosphere, and winds, picking up some of this energy, cause a larger amount of snowfall on the other side of the lake.

Earth History

Scientists have theorized that the universe was formed during the "Big Bang" ten to fifteen billion years ago. The **Big Bang** describes an initial expansion of the universe from a high-density, high-temperature state. The belief also posits that the entire universe has been expanding ever since the occurrence of the Big Bang; this expansion of gases and matter into condensed clouds formed the galaxies, and more specifically, the components of the solar system. The progression in the stages of the formation of the universe is referred to as **evolution**. The term *evolution* is also used to describe the development of organisms in a biological progress.

The Earth is proposed to be 4.5 billion years old, resulting from solar nebula remnants that dispersed after the Sun was formed. The theory is that the Earth was originally hot and gaseous with no oxygen. Most of the activity that took place on the face of this "Early Earth" would have been that of frequent volcanic eruptions. Over a period of half a billion years, it is believed that the Earth cooled to where a solid layer was able to form. It would be during this time that liquid water appeared on the surface and original life began. Once the crust solidified, the beginnings of rock and fossil records would have formed. As rocks show physical changes due to heat, chemicals, and erosion, they can provide some insight into the type of environment that existed in the past. Fossils, as organic matter, can provide a more accurate timeline of events than rock records. Additionally, the process of dating such substances involves calculating the **half-life** (all radioactive materials decay at an exponential rate referred to as its half-life) of these radioactive materials and determining when they would have come into existence. It is believed that living organisms first appeared 1 billion years ago and that these early organisms did not need much oxygen. It is believed that plants capable of photosynthesis appeared between 2.5 to 3 billion years ago; their appearance contributed more oxygen to the Earth's atmosphere.

The study of the age of the Earth and the materials on the Earth is called **paleontology,** a science often considered a bridge between biology and geology. Not only does paleontology study the existence and history of fossils and materials on Earth, it attempts to determine the causes of their existence. A process used to determine the date of an organic object is through **carbon dating**. This a process that takes a sample of the Carbon 14 isotope in question and compares it to the known values of Carbon 12, in order to determine the amount of carbon that has decayed into nitrogen. The discrepancy between the two values provides a proposed timeframe from which to trace the organic object's existence. Another element used for dating nonorganic objects is uranium. Uranium is believed to have always had a consistent and predictable decay rate to lead that can be used for comparison.

Dating Rocks

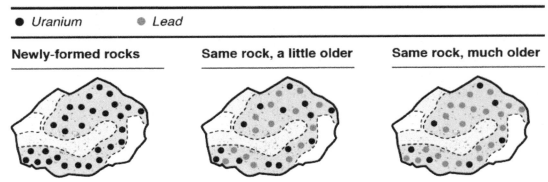

● Uranium   ● Lead

Newly-formed rocks   **Same rock, a little older**   **Same rock, much older**

Earth and the Universe

The **universe** is defined as the largest entity made by space and time, and it includes all of the smaller entities contained within it. The largest known systems within the universe are known as **galaxies**. Scientists believe there are over 100 billion galaxies within the universe. Galaxies can be made up of different gases, cosmic debris, stars, planets, moons, black holes, and other bits of matter. Billions of these entities can make up a single galaxy. They primarily appear in either spiral or elliptical shapes. Galaxies that cannot be categorized as these shapes are known as irregularly-shaped galaxies. These different shapes are made based on the masses of the various entities within the galaxy. The gravitational pull of these objects upon one another creates not only the shape of the galaxy, but also influences how other systems operate within the galaxy. Galaxies can be hundreds of thousands to millions of light years across in size.

Within galaxies, the next largest system is a **solar system**. These systems contain of one or more stars with a massive gravitational pull. Various planets, moons, and debris orbit the star or stars as a result. Stars form because of the gravitational collapse of explosive elements (primarily hydrogen and helium). The center of the star continues in a state of thermonuclear fusion that creates the star's internal gravitational pull. Over many thousands of years, the central thermonuclear activity will slowly cease until the star collapses, resulting in the absorption of orbiting bodies. The Earth is part of a solar system in the Milky Way galaxy. Its solar system consists of one sun, eight planets, their moons, and other cosmic bodies, such as meteors and asteroids (including an asteroid belt that orbits the Sun in a full ring). In order of proximity to the Sun, the planets in this solar system are Mercury, Venus, Earth, Mars, Jupiter, Saturn, Uranus, and Neptune. Beyond Neptune is a dwarf planet named Pluto, and at least four other known dwarf planets. While the Earth has only a single moon, most other planets have multiple moons (although Mercury and Venus have none). Based on their mass, moons, and position from the Sun, each planet takes a different period to orbit the Sun and rotate upon its axis. The Earth takes 24 hours to rotate on its axis and 365 days to orbit the Sun.

Solar eclipses occur on Earth when the moon's orbit appears to cross between the Earth and the Sun, while lunar eclipses occur when the Earth's orbit crosses between the Sun and the moon. Additionally, the moon's gravitational pull on the Earth impacts the water on the planet, causing high and low tides throughout the day. The difference in tidal height varies based on the location of the moon in its orbit around the Earth (as well as different features of the water body and shoreline).

The positioning of the moon between the Earth and the Sun at different positions in the Earth's orbit results in the phases of the moon. While a common misconception is that the phases are simply caused from the shadow the Earth casts on the moon, the different phases we see are actually due to the position of the moon relative to the Sun. A portion of the moon that is not visible or shadowed is turned away from the Sun. At all times, half of the moon is illuminated while half is shadowed, yet our perception of different phases is caused by the moon's position relative to us on Earth.

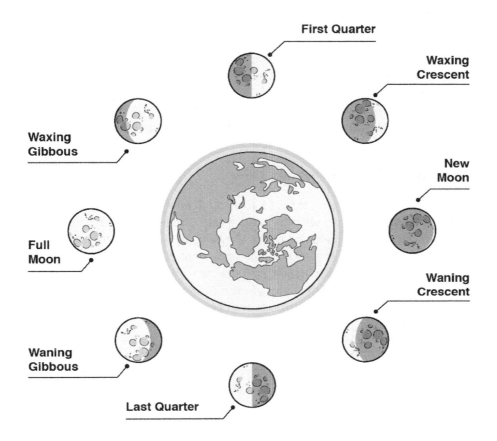

Earth Patterns, Cycles, and Change

Several patterns and cycles take place on Earth that create and influence the most unique feature of the planet: its ability to host life. One feature that influences these patterns and cycles is Earth's position relative to the Sun. The Earth is located 93 million miles from the Sun; variations in this distance would make the planet too hot or too cold to support life. As the Earth tilts closer to or further from the Sun, different parts of the planet experience different patterns of weather known as **seasons**. As the top hemisphere of the Earth tilts toward the Sun, those geographical areas experience spring and summer, while the bottom hemisphere, which has tilted away from the Sun, experiences fall and winter. As the Earth tilts the opposite way, the seasons across each northern and southern hemisphere flip. It takes one year for an area far from the **equator** (the equidistant point between the north and south poles of the Earth) to experience four seasons. Areas that are close to the equator have the same temperature year-round but may experience differences in climate, such as rainier or drier seasons. These are impacted by ocean currents that travel around the Earth and can be warm or cool based on the Earth's positioning, natural variances (such as the El Niño and La Niña phenomena), and human activities that contribute to temperature changes.

Important cycles on the Earth include the water cycle, which involves the evaporation of surface water into the atmosphere that later returns as precipitation, and the carbon cycle, a complex system that creates the atmospheric conditions on the planet. Carbon is an element found in all organic chemical compounds, and is therefore found in the air, living organisms, the ocean, rocks and other solid matter, and in the Earth's deeper layers. Carbon is exchanged across these entities through processes such as photosynthesis, volcanic eruptions, oceanic currents, and the water cycle. Without human activities that contribute to excess carbon production, the carbon present on Earth stays the same through these exchanges, except for a few distinct periods in history, such as ice ages. Human activities such as burning fossil fuels, concentrated animal feeding operations, and deforestation have contributed to a steady increase in the levels of carbon and carbon dioxide present in the atmosphere. In turn, this traps more heat near the Earth's surface and deposits more carbon into the hydrosphere through acid rain. An ocean temperature increase of just two degrees Celsius causes shifts in ocean ecosystems and convection currents that can disrupt weather and climate patterns, such as abnormally hot or cool temperatures, increased precipitation or aridity, and the timing, intensity, and location of natural disasters such as hurricanes.

Science as a Human Endeavor, a Process, and a Career

The field of science utilizes systematic processes to investigate an event and provide reasoning from a base of evidence. As a human endeavor, scientific inquiry and discovery are ways for people to observe, understand, and reason with the world around them. They also allow people to analyze and determine patterns to predict future occurrences that directly impact human life. The **scientific method** is comprised of concrete steps that encompass all these activities. It begins with making an observation, forming a question around that observation, and forming a hypothesis to answer the proposed question. Then, an experiment that produces data allows for the observer to confidently determine whether the hypothesis was correct or incorrect.

Not all ideas, methods, or results are popular or accepted by those in society. Thus, the pursuit of science is often riddled with controversy. This has been an underlying theme since the early days of astronomical discovery. Copernicus was excommunicated from his religious establishment when he announced his belief that the Sun, not the Earth, was the controlling body of the heavens known to humans at the time. Despite Copernicus having documented observations and calculations, those opposed to his theory could not be convinced; therefore, Copernicus experienced great ridicule and suffering due to his scientific research and assertions. In addition, other scientists have faced adverse scrutiny for their assertions, including Galileo, Albert Einstein, and Stephen Hawking. In each case, logical thoughts, observations, and calculations were used to demonstrate their ideas, yet opposition to their scientific beliefs still exists.

The possibilities for careers involving science range from conducting research, to the application of science and research (engineering), to academia (teaching). All of these avenues require intensive study and a thorough understanding of respective branches of science and their components. An important factor of studying and applying science is being able to concisely and accurately communicate knowledge to other people. Many times, this is done utilizing mathematics or demonstration. The necessity of communicating ideas, research, and results brings people from all nationalities together. This often lends to different cultures finding common ground for research and investigation, and it opens lines of communication and cooperation.

Science as Inquiry

Design of a Scientific Investigation

Scientific investigation is seeking an answer to a specific question using the scientific method. The scientific method is a procedure that is based on an observation. For example, if someone observes something strange, and they want to understand the process, they might ask how that process works. If we were to use the scientific method to understand the process, we would formulate a hypothesis. A hypothesis explains what you expect to happen from the experiment. Then, an experiment is conducted, data from the experiment is analyzed, and a conclusion is reached. Below are steps of the scientific method in a practical situation:

- Observation: One day, a student observes that every time he eats a big lunch, he falls asleep in the next period.

- Experimental Question: The question the student asks is, what is the relationship between eating large meals and energy levels?

- Formulate a Hypothesis: The student hypothesizes that eating a big meal will lead to lower energy due to the body using its energy to digest the food.

- Conduct an Experiment (Materials and Procedure): The student has his whole class eat two meals for lunch for a week, then he measures their energy levels in the next period. The next week, the student has them eat a small lunch, and then measures their energy levels in the next period.

- Analyze Data: The data in the student's experiment showed that in the first week, sixty percent of the students felt sleepy in the next period class and that in the second week, only twenty percent of the students felt sleepy in the next period class.

- Conclusion: The student concluded that the data supported his hypothesis: student energy levels decrease after the consumption of a large meal.

An important component of scientific research after the experiment is conducted is called **peer review**. This is when the article written about the experiment is sent to other scientists to "review." The reviewers offer feedback so that the editors can decide whether or not to publish the findings in a scholarly or scientific journal.

Critiquing a Scientific Explanation Using Logic and Evidence

According to the scientific method, one must either observe something as it is happening or as a constant state, or prove it through experimenting, to say it is a fact. Scientific experiments are found reliable when they can be replicated and produce comparable results regardless of who is conducting them or making the observations. However, historically many beliefs have been considered facts at the time, only to be disproven later when objective evidence became accessible. For example, in ancient times many people believed the Earth was flat based on limited visual evidence. Ancient Greek philosophers Pythagoras in the 6th century BCE and Aristotle in the 4th century BCE believed the earth was spherical. This was eventually borne out by observational evidence. Aristotle estimated the Earth's circumference; Eratosthenes measured it c. 240 BCE; in the 2nd century CE, Ptolemy had mapped the globe and developed the latitude, longitude, and climes system.

While many phenomena have been established by science as facts, technically many others are actually theories, though many people mistakenly consider them facts. As one example, gravity per se is a fact; however, the scientific explanation of how gravity functions is a theory. Though a theory is not the same as a fact, this does not presume theories are merely speculative ideas. A scientific theory must be tested thoroughly and then applied to established facts, hypotheses, and observations. Moreover, for a theory to be accepted or even considered scientifically, it must relate and explain a broad scope of observations which would not be related without the theory. People sometimes state opinions as if they were facts to persuade others. For example, advertising might claim a product is the best without concrete evidence. To evaluate information, one must consider both its source and any supporting evidence to ascertain its veracity.

Identifying Basic Scientific Measurement Using Laboratory Tools

A Newton meter or force meter is a standardized instrument for measuring the force exerted by different elements in the universe that cause movement when they act upon objects by pulling, pushing, rotating, deforming, or accelerating them, such as gravity, friction, or tension. Force is measured in units called Newtons (N), named after Sir Isaac Newton, who defined the laws of motion, including forces. One common example of a force meter is a bathroom scale. When someone steps on the scale, the force exerted on the platform is measured in the form of units of weight. Force meters contain springs, rubber bands, or other elastic materials that stretch in proportion to force applied. A Newton meter displays 50-Newton increments, with four 10-Newton marks in between. Thus, if a Newton meter's needle rests on the third mark between 100 and 150, this indicates 130N.

Using Resource and Research Material in Science

Part of the process of scientific inquiry is researching a problem or question. Before an experiment can be designed, proper research must be conducted into the question at hand. The initial question needs to be well formed and based on logical reasoning. A literature review should be conducted on existing material pertaining to the subject in question, and confirmation of any experimentation on the question that has been conducted previously. It is important to use high-quality resources and research materials in scientific practices. This means that materials should come from reputable sources that are free from bias, and information presented in the materials should follow stringent data collection and analysis.

Using resource and research materials in science allows the researcher to better understand an event he or she has observed. Materials may show that an evidence-based and widely-accepted scientific explanation for an event has been established, or they may identify a gap upon which the researcher can base his or her scientific inquiry. Science libraries (often found on large academic campuses), publications through reputable print and online scholarly journals, and interviews conducted with experts in the field (normally with post-graduate level education and work experience) can be valuable, high-quality sources of science information.

Some examples of reputable materials include those distributed by the public National Science Foundation and by academic institutions, such as public and private universities. Materials are often divided by the discipline they cover (i.e., chemistry versus physics). All works utilized in future scientific experiments that lead to publication or other public dissemination of findings should be comprehensively cited, with credit given to the original source of information.

It is common for different scientists in the same place, or even varying countries, to be conducting experiments to test the same hypothesis. This does not always lead to a race to see who finishes first, but it can lead to cooperative research and shared acclaim if the results prove successful. Awards for research, discoveries, and scientific application are often used by the scientific community to show appreciation for advancements in science.

The Unifying Processes of Science

While the field of science can cover a variety of disciplines, certain processes are utilized across the spectrum. For example, all scientific inquiries follow the basic systematic process outlined in the scientific method. Additionally, all scientific fields organize information, events, and entities into systems and orders based on recurrent themes.

Scientific systems focus on entities comprised of different parts that make up a whole and are often related and/or dependent on the function of one another. For example, the Earth's climate is a system dependent on factors such as temperature, barometric pressure, the carbon cycle, the water cycle, and the Earth's position in space. Other science systems include machines, ecological systems, and the human body.

Scientific order expresses how similar events typically occur within similar parameters; established aspects of scientific order (such as the order of the universe) can be utilized to predict future events, although some predictions may be less accurate due to the precision of an established order. While it can be difficult to predict all future events when all influential variables are not fully understood, even small bits of information can help extrapolate the findings of an observation or experiment into a larger hypothesis. For example, if a scientist observes that one species of birds in the northern hemisphere migrates toward the equator in the fall, he or she may predict that other species of birds do the same. However, this finding would not necessarily apply to all birds (e.g., penguins) due to variables that may not apply to migratory species.

Relationships Among Events, Objects, and Procedures
When we determine relationships among events, objects, and procedures, we are better able to understand the world around us and make predictions based on that understanding. With regards to relationships among events and procedures, we will look at cause and effect.

Cause
The cause of a particular event is the thing that brings it about. A causal relationship may be partly or wholly responsible for its effect, but sometimes it's difficult to tell whether one event is the sole cause of another event. For example, lung cancer can be caused by smoking cigarettes. However, sometimes lung cancer develops even though someone does not smoke, and that tells us that there may be other factors involved in lung cancer besides smoking. It's also easy to make mistakes when considering causation. One common mistake is mistaking correlation for causation. For example, say that in the year 2008 a volcano erupted in California, and in that same year, the number of infant deaths increased by ten percent. If we automatically assume, without looking at the data, that the erupting volcano *caused* the infant deaths, then we are mistaking correlation for causation. The two events might have happened at the same time, but that does not necessarily mean that one event caused the other. Relationships between events are never absolute; there are a myriad of factors that can be traced back to their foundations, so we must be thorough with our evidence in proving causation.

Effect
An effect is the result of something that occurs. For example, the Nelsons have a family dog. Every time the dog hears thunder, the dog whines. In this scenario, the thunder is the cause, and the dog's whining is the effect. Sometimes a cause will produce multiple effects. Let's say we are doing an experiment to see what the effects of exercise are in a group of people who are not usually active. After about four weeks,

the group experienced weight loss, rise in confidence, and higher energy. We start out with a cause: exercising more. From that cause, we have three known effects that occurred within the group: weight loss, rise in confidence, and higher energy. Cause and effect are important terms to understand when conducting scientific experiments.

Life Science

Living Characteristics and Cells

Things are characterized as "living" due to a number of widely accepted factors. First, all living things must be made up of one cell (**unicellular**) or more (**multicellular**) that can perform the basic functions needed for living. These include the utilization of a nutrient source for energy to carry out other processes, respiration, the ability to move, the ability to create and remove waste, the ability to grow larger in some capacity, the ability to reproduce, and the ability to seek out and sense factors in the environment that contribute to survival and reproduction. Organisms consist of eukaryotic or prokaryotic cells. Animals, people, plants, fungi, and insects are **eukaryotes**, while bacteria are **prokaryotic** cells. Prokaryotic cells are much simpler than eukaryotic cells; they do not have a nucleus or other membrane-bound, intracellular components.

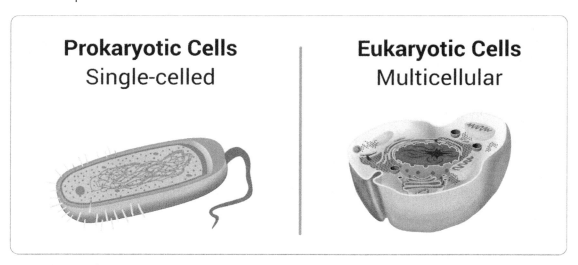

The smallest known living organism that fits these characteristics is a prokaryotic micro-bacterium; 150,000 could fit on the tip of a human hair. It was discovered in 2015 by University of California, Berkeley scientists, who reason that there are many undiscovered microbes that may be as small or smaller. The largest living thing is an intact, parasitic fungus that spans four miles of forest in Oregon.

The Cell

All living organisms are made up of cells. They are considered the basic functional unit of organisms and the smallest unit of matter that is living. Most organisms are multicellular, which means that they are made up of more than one cell and often they are made up of a variety of different types of cells. Cells contain organelles, which are the little working parts of the cell, responsible for specific functions that keep the cell and organism alive.

Plant and animal cells have many of the same organelles but also have some unique traits that set them apart from each other. Plants contain a cell wall, while animal cells are only surrounded by a phospholipid plasma membrane. The cell wall is made up strong, fibrous polysaccharides and proteins. It protects the cell from mechanical damage and maintains the cell's shape. Inside the cell wall, plant cells also have plasma membrane. The plasma membrane of both plant and animal cells is made up of two layers of phospholipids, which have a hydrophilic head and hydrophobic tails. The tails converge towards each other on the inside of the bilayer, while the heads face the interior of the cell and the exterior environment. Microvilli are protrusions of the cell membrane that are only found in animal cells. They increase the surface area and aid in absorption, secretion, and cellular adhesion. Chloroplasts are also only found in plant cells. They are responsible for photosynthesis, which is how plants convert sunlight into chemical energy.

The list below describes major organelles that are found in both plant and animal cells.

- Nucleus: The nucleus contains the DNA of the cell, which has all of the cells' hereditary information passed down from parent cells. DNA and protein are wrapped together into chromatin within the nucleus. The nucleus is surrounded by a double membrane called the nuclear envelope.

- Endoplasmic Reticulum (ER): The ER is a network of tubules and membranous sacs that are responsible for the metabolic and synthetic activities of the cell, including synthesis of membranes. Rough ER has ribosomes attached to it while smooth ER does not.

- Mitochondrion: The mitochondrion is essential for maintaining regular cell function and is known as the powerhouse of the cell. It is where cellular respiration occurs and where most of the cell's ATP is generated.

- Golgi Apparatus: The Golgi Apparatus is where cell products are synthesized, modified, sorted, and secreted out of the cell.

- Ribosomes: Ribosomes make up a complex that produces proteins within the cell. They can be free in the cytosol or bound to the ER.

Organ Systems

An **organ system** refers to a group of organs that work together to carry out biological functions. In organ systems, each organ is dependent on other organs to function properly. Animal species typically have a number of organ systems. These include the respiratory system, in which organs such as the lungs and diaphragm function to allow the organism to breathe; the digestive system, in which organs such as the stomach, intestines, and pancreas break down nutrients to deliver to the rest of the body or eliminate in the form of solid wastes; the cardiovascular system, in which organs such as the heart and blood vessels pump and carry oxygenated blood throughout the body while transporting deoxygenated blood back to the lungs; the urinary system, in which organs such as the kidneys and bladder balance the body's fluid and chemical levels and eliminate liquid waste; and the integumentary system, which consists of the skin (the body's largest organ) and other tissues.

While these are all individual systems, they also work closely together within the body as a whole, and the body cannot function well if one system is not working properly. For example, if the respiratory system is unable to bring in oxygen, the cardiovascular system will be unable to circulate oxygenated blood. If the digestive system is unable to break down foods into nutrients, then nutrients cannot be transported through the circulatory system to cells that need energy.

Vascular plants are also considered to have organ systems that protect individual and bundled cells, store transport nutrients, and conduct photosynthesis. These plants also have reproductive systems that are visible in flowers or fruits.

Growth and Development

All living things grow and develop, whether through cell division or by cell replication. When cells divide, the newly created cell may have some differences from the original copy, whereas cells that replicate are identical. Cell division is often seen in periods of overall development, such as when a fetus grows in utero or a plant shoot turns into a flower. Cell replication is typically seen when a single entity becomes larger, such as when a child's bone becomes bigger as he or she ages. Growth and development are fueled by nutrition, hydration, and respiration. Animal growth requires water, macro- and micro-nutrients (carbohydrates, proteins, fats, vitamins, and minerals), and respiration to keep the body oxygenated and remove waste. Other factors that support animal growth include adequate sleep and recovery, as well as hormonal factors. Some hormonal issues may be congenital and lead to pathologies, while others may be impacted by external stressors (such as poor nutrition or sleep).

Plant growth takes place as a seedling sprouts root into soil matter and absorbs nutrients such as water, nitrogen, potassium, and phosphorus. Plants also take carbon dioxide from the air and need sunlight exposure to carry out photosynthesis, which provides their main source of energy for growth. Different plants also have different temperature requirements that aid in growth and the development of reproductive structures, such as the pistil and stamen found within flowers.

Like animals and plants, bacteria take in nutrients for physical growth. They also typically require some level of warmth and humidity to grow and reproduce. Most bacteria are unicellular and asexual; when they can no longer grow larger and still meet the needs of the cell, they split through a process called **binary fission**. During this split, the unicellular organism divides into two duplicate cells containing the exact same DNA.

Basic Macromolecules in a Biological System

There are six major elements found in most biological molecules: carbon, hydrogen, oxygen, nitrogen, sulfur, and phosphorus. These elements link together to make up the basic macromolecules of the biological system, which are lipids, carbohydrates, nucleic acids, and proteins. Most of these molecules use carbon as their backbone because of its ability to bond four different atoms. Each type of macromolecule has a specific structure and important function for living organisms.

Lipids

Lipids are made up of hydrocarbon chains, which are large molecules with hydrogen atoms attached to a long carbon backbone. These biological molecules are characterized as hydrophobic because their structure does not allow them to form bonds with water. When mixed together, the water molecules bond to each other and exclude the lipids. There are three main types of lipids: triglycerides, phospholipids, and steroids.

Triglycerides are made up of one glycerol molecule attached to three fatty acid molecules. Glycerols are three-carbon atom chains with one hydroxyl group attached to each carbon atom. Fatty acids are hydrocarbon chains with a backbone of sixteen to eighteen carbon atoms and a double-bonded oxygen molecule. Triglycerides have three main functions for living organisms. They are a source of energy when carbohydrates are not available, they help with absorption of certain vitamins, and they help insulate the body and maintain normal core temperature.

Phospholipid molecules have two fatty acid molecules bonded to one glycerol molecule, with the glycerol molecules having a phosphate group attached to it. The phosphate group has an overall negative charge, which makes that end of the molecule hydrophilic, meaning that it can bond with water molecules. Since the fatty acid tails of phospholipids are hydrophobic, these molecules are left with the unique characteristic of having different affinities on each of their ends. When mixed with water, phospholipids create bilayers, which are double rows of molecules with the hydrophobic ends on the inside facing each other and the hydrophilic ends on the outside, shielding the hydrophobic ends from the water molecules. Cells are protected by phospholipid bilayer cell membranes. This allows them to mix with aqueous solutions while also protecting their inner contents.

Steroids have a more complex structure than the other types of lipids. They are made up of four fused carbon rings. Different types of steroids are defined by the different chemical groups that attach to the carbon rings. Steroids are often mixed into phospholipid bilayers to help maintain the structure of the cell membrane and aid in cell signaling from these positions. They are also essential for regulation of metabolism and immune responses, among other biological processes.

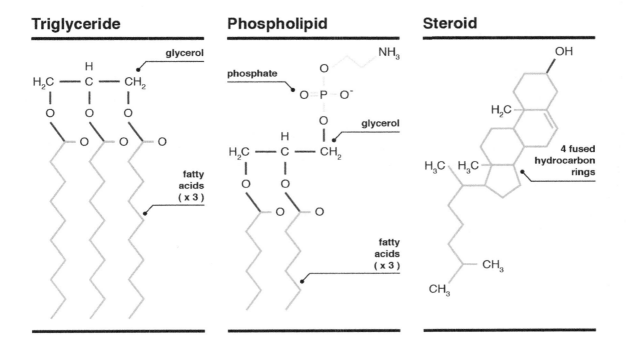

Carbohydrates

Carbohydrates are made up of sugar molecules. Monomers are small molecules, and polymers are larger molecules that consist of repeating monomers. The smallest sugar molecule, a monosaccharide, has the chemical formula of CH_2O. Monosaccharides can be made up of one of these small molecules or a multiple of this formula (such as $C_2H_4O_2$). Polysaccharides consist of repeating monosaccharides in lengths of a few hundred to a few thousand linked together. Monosaccharides are broken down by living organisms to extract energy from the sugar molecules for immediate consumption. Glucose is a common monosaccharide used by the body as a primary energy source which can be metabolized immediately. The more complex structure of polysaccharides allows them to have a more long-term use. They can be stored and broken down later for energy. Glycogen is a molecule that consists of 1700 to 600,000 glucose units linked together. It is not soluble in water and can be stored for long periods of time. If necessary, the glycogen molecule can be broken up into single glucose molecules in order to provide energy for the body. Polysaccharides also form structurally strong materials, such as chitin, which makes up the exoskeleton of many insects, and cellulose, which is the material that surrounds plant cells.

Nucleic Acids

Nucleotides are made up of a five-carbon sugar molecule with a nitrogen-containing base and one or more phosphate groups attached to it. Nucleic acids are polymers of nucleotides, or polynucleotides. There are two main types of nucleic acids: deoxyribonucleic acid (DNA) and ribonucleic acid (RNA). DNA is a double strand of nucleotides that are linked together and folded into a helical structure. Each strand is made up of four nucleotides, or bases: adenine, thymine, cytosine, and guanine. The adenine bases only pair with thymine on the opposite strand, and the cytosine bases only pair with guanine on the opposite strand. It is the links between these base pairs that create the helical structure of double-stranded DNA. DNA is in charge of long-term storage of genetic information that can be passed on to subsequent generations. It also contains instructions for constructing other components of the cell. RNA, on the other hand, is a single-stranded structure of nucleotides that is responsible for directing the construction of proteins within the cell. RNA is made up of three of the same nucleotides as DNA, but instead of thymine, adenine pairs with the base uracil.

Proteins

Proteins are made from a set of twenty amino acids that are linked together linearly, without branching. The amino acids have peptide bonds between them and form polypeptides. These polypeptide molecules coil up, either individually or as multiple molecules linked together, and form larger biological molecules, which are called **proteins**. Proteins have four distinct layers of structure. The primary structure consists of the sequence of amino acids. The secondary structure consists of the folds and coils formed by the hydrogen bonding that occurs between the atoms of the polypeptide backbone. The tertiary structure consists of the shape of the molecule, which comes from the interactions of the side chains that are linked to the polypeptide backbone. Lastly, the quaternary structure consists of the overall shape that the protein takes on when it is made up of two or more polypeptide chains. Proteins have many vital roles in living organisms. They help maintain and repair body tissue, provide a source of energy, form antibodies to aid the immune system, and are a large component in transporting molecules within the body, among many other functions.

Primary protein structure

is sequence of a chain of amino acids

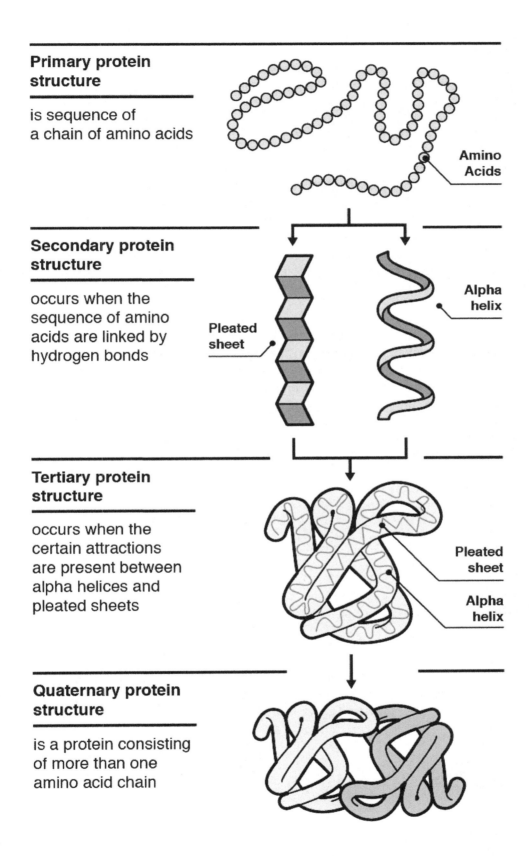

Amino Acids

Secondary protein structure

occurs when the sequence of amino acids are linked by hydrogen bonds

Pleated sheet

Alpha helix

Tertiary protein structure

occurs when the certain attractions are present between alpha helices and pleated sheets

Pleated sheet

Alpha helix

Quaternary protein structure

is a protein consisting of more than one amino acid chain

Life Processes
Cellular Respiration

Cellular respiration in multicellular organisms occurs in the mitochondria. It is a set of reactions that converts energy from nutrients to ATP and can either use oxygen in the process, which is called aerobic respiration, or not, which is called anaerobic respiration.

Aerobic respiration has two main parts, which are the citric acid cycle, also known as Krebs cycle, and oxidative phosphorylation. Glucose is a molecule that is used for energy production within the cell. Before the citric acid cycle can begin, the process of glycolysis converts glucose into two pyruvate molecules. Pyruvate enters the mitochondrion, is oxidized, and then is converted to a compound called acetyl CoA. There are eight steps in the citric acid cycle that start with acetyl CoA and convert it to oxaloacetate and NADH. The oxaloacetate continues in the citric acid cycle and the NADH molecule moves on to the oxidative phosphorylation part of cellular respiration. Oxidative phosphorylation has two main steps, which are the electron transport chain and chemiosmosis. The mitochondrial membrane has four protein complexes within it that help to transport electrons through the inner mitochondrial matrix. Electrons and protons are removed from NADH and $FADH_2$ and then transported along these and other membrane complexes.

Protons are pumped across the inner membrane, which creates a gradient to draw electrons to the intermembrane complexes. Two mobile electron carriers, ubiquinone and cytochrome C, are also located in the inner mitochondrial membrane. At the end of these electron transport chains, the electrons are accepted by O_2 molecules and water is formed with the addition of two hydrogen atoms. Chemiosmosis occurs in an ATP synthase complex that is located next to the four electron transport complexes. As the complex pumps protons from the intermembrane space to the mitochondrial matrix, ADP molecules become phosphorylated and ATP molecules are generated. Four to six ATP molecules are generated during glycolysis and the citric acid cycle and twenty-six to twenty-eight ATP molecules are generated during oxidative phosphorylation, which makes the total amount of ATP molecules generated during aerobic cellular respiration thirty to thirty-two.

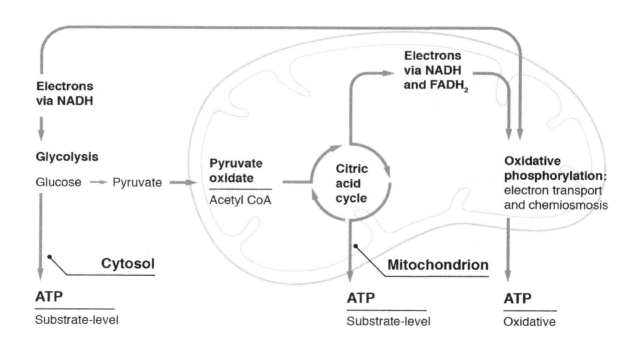

Since not all environments are oxygen-rich, some organisms must find alternate ways to extract energy from nutrients. The process of anaerobic respiration is similar to that of aerobic respiration in that protons and electrons are removed from nutrient molecules and are passed down an electron transport chain, with the end result being ATP synthesis. However, instead of the electrons being accepted by oxygen molecules at the end of the electron transport chain, they are accepted by either sulfate or nitrate molecules. Anaerobic respiration is mostly used by unicellular organisms, or prokaryotic organisms.

Photosynthesis
Photosynthesis is a set of reactions that occur to convert light energy into chemical energy. The chemical energy is then stored as sugar and other organic molecules inside the organism or plant. Within plants, the photosynthetic process takes place within chloroplasts. The two stages of photosynthesis are the light reactions and the Calvin cycle. Within chloroplasts, there are membranous sacs called thylakoids and within the thylakoids are a green pigment called chlorophyll. The light reactions take place in the chlorophyll. The Calvin cycle takes place in the stroma, or inner space, or the chloroplasts.

During the light reactions, light energy is absorbed by chlorophyll. First, a light-harvesting complex, called photosystem II (PS II), absorbs photons from light that enters the chlorophyll and then passes it onto a reaction-center complex. Once the photon enters the reaction-center complex, it causes a special pair of chlorophyll *a* molecules to release an electron. The electron is accepted by a primary electron acceptor molecule, while at the same time, a water molecule is dissociated into two hydrogen atoms, one oxygen atom, and two electrons. These electrons are transferred to the chlorophyll *a* molecules that just lost their electrons.

The electrons that were released from the chlorophyll *a* molecules move down an electron transport chain using an electron carrier, called plastoquinone, a cytochrome complex, and a protein called plastocyanin. At the end of the chain, the electrons reach another light-harvesting complex, called photosystem I (PS I). While in the cytochrome complex, the electrons cause protons to be pumped into the thylakoid space, which in turn provides energy for ATP molecules to be produced. A primary electron acceptor molecule accepts the electrons that are released from PS I and then passes them onto another electron transport chain, which includes the protein ferredoxin. At the end of the light reactions, electrons are transferred from ferredoxin to NADP+, producing NADPH. The ATP and NADPH that are produced through the light reactions are used as energy to drive the Calvin cycle forward.

The three phases of the Calvin cycle are carbon fixation, reduction, and regeneration of the CO_2 acceptor. Carbon fixation occurs when CO_2 is introduced into the cycle and attaches to a five-carbon sugar, called ribulose bisphosphate (RuBP). A six-carbon sugar is split into two three-carbon sugar molecules, known as 3-phosphoglycerate. Next, during the reduction phase, an ATP molecule loses a phosphate group and becomes ADP. The phosphate group attaches to the 3-phosphoglycerate molecule, making it 1,3-bisphosphate. Then, an NADPH molecule donates two electrons to this new molecule, causing it to lose a phosphate group and become glyceraldehyde 3-phosphate (G3P), a sugar molecule. At the end of the cycle, one G3P molecule exits the cycle and is used by the plant for energy. Five other G3P molecules continue in the cycle to regenerate RuBP molecules, which are the CO_2 acceptors of the cycle. When every photon has been used up, three RuBP molecules are formed from the rearrangement of five G3P molecules and wait for the cycle to start again. It takes three turns of the cycle and three CO_2 molecules entering the cycle to generate just one G3P molecule.

Take a look here:

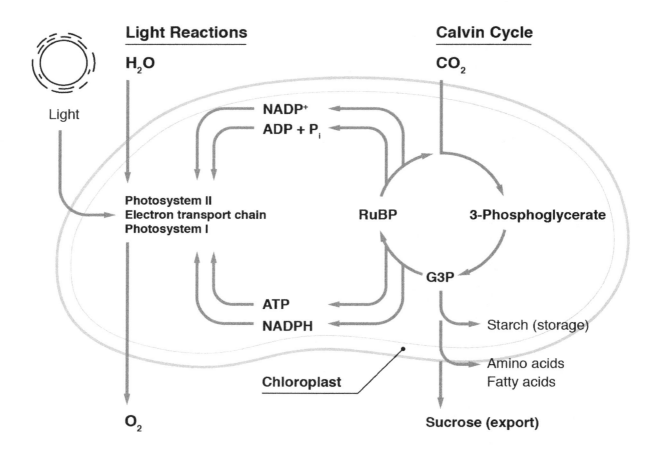

Reproduction and Heredity

Chromosomes

A **chromosome** is a molecule of DNA that contains the genetic material of an organism, located in the nucleus of the cell. It is a threadlike structure made up of genes that is coiled tightly around proteins called **histones.** The histones support the more fragile form of the chromosome. Chromosomes are too small to even be seen under a microscope when a cell is not dividing. However, when a cell is undergoing division, the DNA making up the chromosomes becomes much more tightly packed and microscopically visible. During cell division, each chromosome makes an exact copy of itself that it is attached at a constriction point called the **centromere**. The double chromosome structure, called **sister chromatids**, has an X shape, with one set of the chromosome's arms being longer than the other. In other words, the centromere is located closer to one end of the chromosome than the other. The shorter part of the chromosome sticking out from the centromere is called the **p-arm**, and the longer arm is called the **q-arm**.

For genetic information to be conserved from one generation to the next, chromosomes must be replicated and divided within the parent cell before being passed on to the daughter cell. Humans have twenty-three pairs of chromosomes. Twenty-two pairs are **autosomes**, or body chromosomes that contain most of the genetic hereditary information, and one pair is an **allosome**, or sex chromosome. Some genetic traits are sex-linked, so those genes are located on the allosome. Chromosomes are divided in humans during the process of meiosis. **Meiosis** is a special type of cell division in which a parent cell produces four daughter cells, each with half the number of chromosomes as the parent cell. As a precursor to meiosis, each chromosome replicates itself to form a sister chromatid. When a sperm cell meets an egg cell, each brings with it twenty-three sister chromatids. When meiosis starts, the homologous chromosomes pair up and undergo a crossing-over event where they can switch gene alleles. The remixed sister chromatids move toward the center of the cell along spindles and then are pulled to opposite poles and divided into two cells. These two cells divide again, breaking up the sister chromatids, and leaving each of the four cells with one set of chromosomes.

The process of meiosis

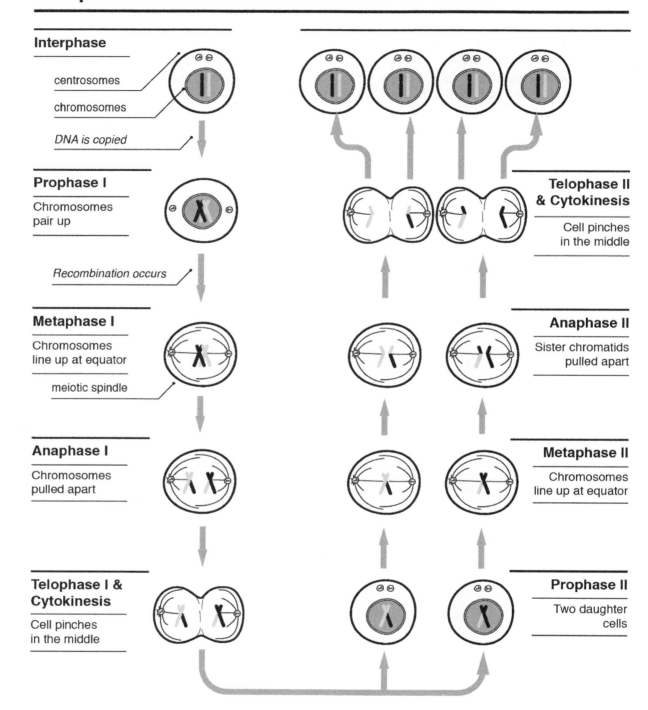

Interphase

centrosomes

chromosomes

DNA is copied

Prophase I

Chromosomes
pair up

Recombination occurs

Metaphase I

Chromosomes
line up at equator

meiotic spindle

Anaphase I

Chromosomes
pulled apart

**Telophase I &
Cytokinesis**

Cell pinches
in the middle

**Telophase II
& Cytokinesis**

Cell pinches
in the middle

Anaphase II

Sister chromatids
pulled apart

Metaphase II

Chromosomes
line up at equator

Prophase II

Two daughter
cells

Genes

Genes are made up of DNA and are the basic functional unit of heredity. They can be as short as a few hundred DNA base pairs in length to over 2 million DNA base pairs long. Humans have between 20,000 and 25,000 genes on their twenty-three pairs of chromosomes. Each chromosome contains two *alleles,* or variations, of each gene—one inherited from each parent. Genes contain information about a specific trait that was inherited from one of the individual's parents. They provide instructions for making proteins to express that specific trait. One allele of a gene has a more dominant *phenotype,* or physical characteristic, than the other. This means that when both variations are present on a gene, the dominant variation or phenotype would always be expressed over the recessive phenotype.

Since the dominant phenotype is always expressed when present, the recessive phenotype is only expressed when the gene only contains two recessive phenotype alleles. Although this is the case for almost all genes, some gene alleles have either codominance or incomplete dominance expression. With codominance, if both alleles are present, they are equally expressed in the phenotype. For example, certain cows can have red hair with two red hair alleles and white hair with two white hair alleles. However, when one of each allele is present, these cows have a mix of red and white hair on their bodies, not pink hair. Incomplete dominance occurs when two different alleles on a gene produce a third phenotype. For example, in certain types of flowers, two red alleles produce red flowers, and two white alleles produce white flowers. One of each allele produces pink flowers, a completely different color of flower.

Gene Mutations

Sometimes when genes are replicated, a permanent alteration in the DNA sequence occurs, and a gene mutation is formed. Mutations can be small and affect a single DNA base pair or be large and affect multiple genes in a chromosome. They can either be **hereditary**, which means they were present in the parent cell as well, or **acquired**, which means the mutation occurred at some point during cell replication within that individual's lifetime. Acquired mutations do not get passed on to subsequent generations. Most mutations are rare and occur in very small portions of the population. When the genetic alteration occurs in more than 1 percent of the population, it is called a **polymorphism.** Polymorphisms cause many of the variations seen in normal populations, such as hair and eye color, and do not affect a person's health. However, some polymorphisms put an individual at greater risk of developing some diseases.

DNA

DNA is the material that carries all of the hereditary information about an individual. It is present in every cell of the human body. DNA is a double-stranded molecule that coils up into a helical structure. Each strand is made from a sequence of four chemical bases, which are adenine, guanine, cytosine, and thymine. Each base pairs with only one of the four other bases when it is linked to the second strand— adenine with thymine and guanine with cytosine. The order of the base pairs and length of the strand determine what type of information is being coded. It varies for each gene that it makes up.

DNA Replication

An important characteristic of DNA is its ability to replicate itself. Each strand of the double-stranded DNA structure serves as a template for creating an exact replica of the DNA molecule. When cells divide, they require an exact copy of the DNA for the new cell. During DNA replication, the helical molecule is untwisted, and the strands are separated at one end. Specific replication proteins attach to each separated strand and begin forming new strands with matching base pairs for each of the strands. While some of the DNA molecule is untwisted, the remainder becomes increasingly twisted in response. Topoisomerase enzymes help relieve the strain of the excess twisting by breaking, untwisting, and rejoining the DNA strands. Once the replication proteins have copied the strands from one end to the other, two new DNA molecules are formed. Each DNA molecule is made from one original base pair strand and one newly synthesized base pair strand joined together.

Mendel's Laws of Heredity

Gregor Mendel was a monk who came up with one of the first models of inheritance in the 1860s. He is often referred to as the father of genetics. At the time, his theories were criticized because biologists did not believe that these ideas could be applicable and could also not apply to different species. They were later rediscovered in the early 1900s and given more credence by a group of European scientists. Mendel's original ideas have since been combined with other theories of inheritance to develop the ideas that are studied today.

Between 1856 and 1863, Gregor Mendel experimented with about five thousand pea plants that had different color flowers in his garden to test his theories of inheritance. He crossed purebred white flower and purple flower pea plants and found that the results were not a blend of the two flowers; they were instead all purple flowers. When he then fertilized this second generation of purple flowers with itself, both white flowers and purple flowers were produced, in a ratio of one to three. Although he used different terms at the time, he proposed that the color trait for the flowers was regulated by a gene, which he called a **factor**, and that there were two alleles, which he called **forms**, for each gene. For each gene, one allele was inherited from each parent. The results of these experiments allowed him to come up with his Principles of Heredity.

There are two main laws that Mendel developed after seeing the results of his experiments. The first law is the **Law of Segregation**, which states that each trait has two versions that can be inherited. In the parent cells, the allele pairs of each gene separate, or segregate, randomly during gamete production. Each gamete then carries only one allele with it for reproduction. During the process of reproduction, the gamete from each parent contributes its single allele to the daughter cell. The second law is the **Law of Independent Assortment**, which states that the alleles for different traits are not linked to one another and are inherited independently. It emphasizes that if a daughter cell selects allele A for gene 1, it does not also automatically select allele A for gene 2. The allele for gene 2 is selected in a separate, random manner.

Mendel theorized one more law, called the Law of Dominance, which has to do with the expression of a genotype but not with the inheritance of a trait. When he crossed the purple flower and white flower pea plants, he realized that the purple flowers were expressed at a greater ratio than the white flower pea plants. He hypothesized that certain gene alleles had a stronger outcome on the phenotype that was expressed. If a gene had two of the same allele, the phenotype associated with that allele was expressed. If a gene had two different alleles, the phenotype was determined by the dominant allele, and the other allele, the recessive allele, had no effect on the phenotype.

Measuring Temperature

As those familiar with word roots can determine, thermometers measure heat or temperature (*thermo-* is from Greek for heat and *meter* from Greek for measure). Some thermometers measure outdoor or indoor air temperature, and others measure body temperature in humans or animals. Meat thermometers measure temperature in the center of cooked meat to ensure sufficient cooking to kill bacteria. Refrigerator and freezer thermometers measure internal temperatures to ensure sufficient coldness. Although digital thermometers eliminate the task of reading a thermometer scale by displaying a specific numerical reading, many thermometers still use visual scales. In these, increments are typically two-tenths of a degree. However, basal thermometers, which are more sensitive and accurate, and are frequently used to track female ovulation cycles for measuring and planning fertility, display increments of one-tenth of a degree. Whole degrees are marked by their numbers; tenths of degrees are the smallest marks in between.

Cellular Reproduction

Cellular reproduction is the process that cells follow to make new cells with the same or similar contents as themselves. This process is an essential part of an organism's life. It allows for the organism to grow larger itself, and as it ages, it allows for replacement of dying and damaged cells. The process of cellular reproduction must be accurate and precise. Otherwise, the new cells that are produced will not be able to perform the same functions as the original cell. Mutations can occur in the offspring, which can cause anywhere from minor to severe problems. The two types of cellular reproduction that organisms can use are mitosis or meiosis. Mitosis produces daughter cells that are identical to the parent cell and is often referred to as asexual reproduction.

The process of mitosis

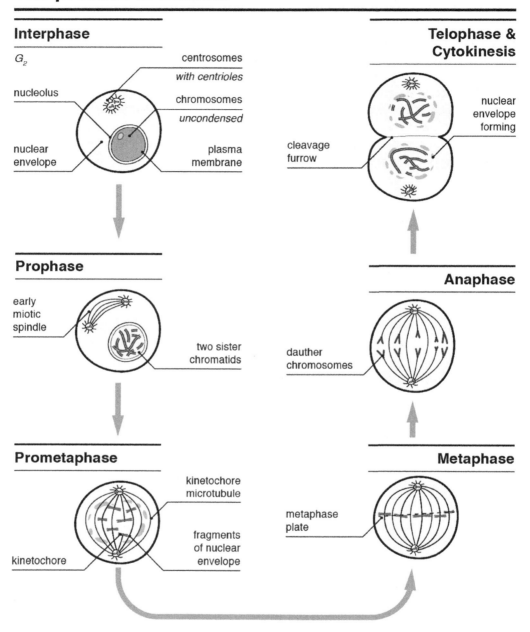

Interphase

G_2

nucleolus

nuclear envelope

centrosomes with centrioles

chromosomes uncondensed

plasma membrane

Prophase

early miotic spindle

two sister chromatids

Prometaphase

kinetochore microtubule

fragments of nuclear envelope

kinetochore

Telophase & Cytokinesis

nuclear envelope forming

cleavage furrow

Anaphase

dauther chromosomes

Metaphase

metaphase plate

Meiosis has two stages of cell division and produces daughter cells that have a combination of traits from their two parents. It is often referred to as sexual reproduction. Humans reproduce by meiosis. During this process, the sperm, the male germ cell, and the egg, the female germ cell, combine and form a parent cell that contains both sets of chromosomes. This parent cell then divides into four daughter cells, each with a unique set of traits that came from both of their parents.

In both processes, the most important part of the cell that is copied is the cell's DNA. It contains all of the genetic information for the cell, which leads to its traits and capabilities. Some parts of the cell are copied exactly during cellular reproduction, such as DNA. However, certain other cellular components are synthesized within the new cell after reproduction is complete using the new DNA. For example, the endoplasmic reticulum is broken down during the cell cycle and then newly synthesized after cell division.

Change Over Time in Living Things

All living things change over time. Individual living things change over the period of a single lifespan through growth, development, and aging; evolution proposes that entire species can change over the course of thousands of years (called species **evolution**).

Individual lifespans of organisms can last anywhere from a few hours (some species of flies) to hundreds of years (some species of ocean clams). In fact, one species of jellyfish has the ability to regenerate any injured or stressed part and could, in theory, live forever. Regardless of the lifespan, all organisms follow the basic processes of a **life cycle**, including birth, growth and development, reproduction, and death. These are typically marked by visible transitions. In humans, for example, an implanted zygote (a female egg that has been fertilized by a male sperm) transforms from a single cell into a fully formed baby over the course of nine months.

After birth, different milestones mark the baby's growth and development: height, weight, head circumference, motor abilities, communication abilities, and visible understanding of the world. Puberty in adolescents indicates that reproduction is possible; pregnancy and birth provide the next generation of the species. Signs of aging may indicate that reproduction is no longer possible (i.e., menopause) or that organ systems are not functioning as well as they used to (degeneration). Eventually, all living creatures die from natural aging, disease, or trauma. Similarly, many animals follow similar cycles, though gestation, reproductive ages, reproductive capacity, and length of lifespan vary across species.

The plant life cycle begins with a seed that has been placed in nutrient-rich soil with additional access to adequate water and sunlight. As the seed grows, indicators of development include an established root system, shoots, and leaves. A mature plant will have reproductive parts such as flowers or fruit, and eventually, these plants will be able to create and spread new seeds, which will begin the plant life cycle again.

While most plants and animals experience genetic recombination with a partner to reproduce, bacteria typically do not. Bacteria simply reproduce through **binary fission,** where one cell replicates itself. If the bacteria do not have appropriate conditions in which do this (such as a freezing environment), the life cycle may end. Some species of bacteria can spore, creating a protective environment in which the bacteria can remain dormant and protect its DNA structures until environmental conditions are better. Spores are highly resistant to external factors that the bacteria may not be able to withstand.

Mutations refer to a change in a cell's or organism's DNA. Mutations may or may not be physically visible; they may be advantageous (an **adaptation**) or detrimental. Organisms that have detrimental mutations are less likely to survive, whereas organisms with advantageous mutations are more likely to survive and pass on their genes. This phenomenon is referred to as **natural selection**. Over time, this is how a species can evolve so that the initial mutation, which might have once been a rarity in the population, becomes common in the population. This can be beneficial to the evolved species, but it may be harmful to other species. For example, a number of bacteria have evolved to become resistant to antibiotic medications. This ensures the survival of the bacteria but can cause extreme illness or death in humans who now have less recourse for treatment. Consequently, it is possible that humans could evolve to withstand bacterial infections, as weaker groups die out and stronger ones remain in the gene pool.

Regulation and Behavior

Homeostasis refers to the way living organisms regulate their internal environment to remain functional. Across most living organisms, this process focuses on controlling internal body temperature, respiration, hormone release, and the delivery of nutrients to various parts of the body. Controlling these aspects of the body allows optimal environments for the different organ systems to function in a stable way, rather than with large and unpredictable variation. However, the introduction or lack of various stimuli can cause an organism's internal environment to fall out of homeostasis. For example, if a human does not drink enough water, individual cells will have more intracellular water than that in the extracellular space. Consequently, cells will pass fluid into the bloodstream through osmosis, but may dehydrate themselves in the process. People will tend to feel thirsty at this time, but if fluids are not replaced, the body attempts to stop fluids from leaving the bloodstream, using methods such as limiting the urge to urinate or decreasing sweat output. All of these hydration processes are controlled through chemical and hormone signaling from the cells and kidneys, and hydration affects every organ system; therefore, the body strives to maintain fluid and electrolyte homeostasis.

This urge to maintain homeostasis across all internal domains strongly dictates the external behavior of the living organism. Organisms seek inputs that will support homeostasis; sense and perception play a role in this. For example, cold-blooded reptiles will seek safe but warm areas when their internal body temperature drops too low. Most species show vastly different hormonal variations between males and females. These regulate reproductive conditions as well as mating and reproductive behaviors. For example, it is believed that high levels of testosterone in males drive them to display showier and more aggressive mating behaviors in order to reproduce.

Neuromuscular System
The **neuromuscular system** is composed of all of the muscles in the human body and the nerves that control them. Every movement that the body makes is controlled by the brain. The nervous system and the muscular system work together to link thoughts and actions. Neurons from the nervous system can relay information from the brain to muscle tissue so fast that an individual does not even realize it is happening. Some body movements are voluntary, but others are involuntary, such as the heart beating and the lungs breathing.

Nervous System
The nervous system is made up of the central nervous system (CNS) and the peripheral nervous system (PNS). The CNS includes the brain and the spinal cord, while the PNS includes the rest of the neural tissue that is not included in the CNS. Neurons, or nerve cells, are the main cells responsible for transferring and processing information between the brain and other parts of the body. Neuroglia are cells that support the neurons by providing a framework around them and isolating them from the surrounding environment.

Central Nervous System
The CNS is located within the dorsal body cavity, with the brain in the cranial cavity and the spinal cord in the spinal canal. The brain is protected by the skull, and the spinal cord is protected by the vertebrae. The brain is made up of white and gray matter. The white matter contains axons and oligodendrocytes. **Axons** are the long projection ends of neurons that are responsible for transmitting signals through the nervous system, while **oligodendrocytes** act as insulators for the axons and provide support for them. The gray matter consists of neurons and fibers that are unmyelinated. **Neurons** are nerve cells that receive and transmit information through electrical and chemical signals. Glial cells and astrocytes are located in both types of tissue. Different types of glial cells have different roles in the CNS. Some are immunoprotective,

while others provide a scaffolding for other types of nerve cells. Astrocytes provide nutrients to neurons and clear out metabolites. The spinal cord has projections within it from the PNS. This allows the information that is received from the areas of the body that the PNS reaches to be transmitted to the brain. The CNS as a whole is responsible for processing and coordinating sensory data and motor commands. It receives information from all parts of the body, processes it, and then sends out action commands in response. Some of the reactions are conscious, while others are unconscious.

Infections of the CNS include **encephalitis**, which is an inflammation of the brain, and **poliomyelitis**, which is caused by a virus and causes muscle weakness. Other developmental neurological disorders include ADHD and autism. Some diseases of the CNS can occur later in life and affect the aging brain, such as Alzheimer's disease and Parkinson's disease. Cancers that occur in the CNS can be very serious and have high mortality rates.

Peripheral Nervous System
The PNS consists of the nerves and ganglia that are located within the body outside of the brain and spinal cord. It connects the rest of the body, organs, and limbs to the CNS. Unlike the CNS, the PNS does not have any bony structures protecting it. The PNS is responsible for relaying sensory information and motor commands between the CNS and peripheral tissues and systems. It has two subdivisions, known as the afferent, or sensory, and efferent, or motor, divisions. The afferent division relays sensory information to the CNS and supplies information from the skin and joints about the body's sensation and balance. It carries information away from the stimulus back to the brain.

The afferent division provides the brain with sensory information about things such as taste, smell, and vision. It also monitors organs, vessels, and glands for changes in activity and can alert the brain to send out appropriate responses for bringing the body back to homeostasis. The efferent division transmits motor commands to muscles and glands. It sends information from the CNS to the organs and muscles to provide appropriate responses to sensations. The electrical responses from the neurons are initiated in the CNS, but the axons terminate in the organs that are part of the PNS. The efferent division consists of the autonomic nervous system (ANS), which regulates activity of smooth muscle, cardiac muscle, and glands, and allows the brain to control heart rate, blood pressure, and body temperature, and the somatic nervous system (SNS), which controls skeletal muscle contractions and allows the brain to control body movement.

Diseases of the PNS can affect single nerves or the whole system. Single nerve damage, or mononeuropathy, can occur when a nerve gets compressed due to trauma or a tumor. It can also be damaged as a result of being trapped under another part of the body that is increasing in size, such as in carpal tunnel syndrome. These diseases can cause pain and numbness at the affected area.

Autonomic Nervous System
The autonomic nervous system is made up of pathways that extend from the CNS to the organs, muscles, and glands of the body. The pathway is made up of two separate neurons. The first neuron has a cell body that is located within the CNS, for example, within the spinal cord. The axon of that first neuron synapses with the cell body of the second neuron. Part of the second neuron innervates the organ, muscle, or gland that the pathway is responsible for.

The autonomic nervous system consists of the sympathetic nervous system and the parasympathetic nervous system. The sympathetic nervous system is activated when mentally stressful or physically dangerous situations are faced, also known as "fight or flight" situations. Neurotransmitters are released that increase heart rate and blood flow in critical areas, such as the muscles, and decrease activity for nonessential functions, such as digestion. This system is activated unconsciously. The parasympathetic system has some voluntary control. It releases neurotransmitters that allow the body to function in a restful state. Heart rate and other sympathetic responses are often decreased when the parasympathetic system is activated.

Somatic Nervous System and the Reflex Arc

The somatic nervous system is considered the voluntary part of the PNS. It comprises motor neurons whose axons innervate skeletal muscle. However, nerve muscles and muscle cells do not come into direct contact with each other. Instead, the neurotransmitter acetylcholine transfers the signal between the nerve cell and muscle cell. These junctions are called **neuromuscular junctions**. When the muscle cell receives the signal from the nerve cell, it causes the muscle to contract.

Although most muscle contractions are voluntary, reflexes are a type of muscle contraction that is involuntary. A **reflex** is an instantaneous movement that occurs in response to a stimulus and is controlled by a neural pathway called a **reflex arc**. The reflex arc carries the sensory information from the receptor to the spinal cord and then carries the response back to the muscles. Many sensory neurons synapse in the spinal cord so that reflex actions can occur faster, without waiting for the signal to travel to the brain and back. For somatic reflexes, stimuli activate somatic receptors in the skin, muscles, and tendons. Then, afferent nerve fibers carry signals from the receptors to the spinal cord or brain stem. The signal reaches an integrating center, which is where the neurons synapse within the spinal cord or brain stem. Efferent nerve fibers then carry motor nerve signals to the muscles, and the muscles carry out the response.

Muscular System

There are seven hundred muscles in the body. They are attached to the bones of the skeletal system and make up half of the body's weight. There are three types of muscle tissue in the body: skeletal muscle, smooth muscle, and cardiac muscle. An important characteristic of all types of muscle is that they are **excitable**, which means that they respond to electrical stimuli.

Skeletal Muscles

Skeletal muscle tissue is a voluntary striated muscle tissue, which means that the contractile fibers of the tissue are aligned parallel so that they appear to form stripes when viewed under a microscope. Most skeletal muscle are attached to bones by intermediary tendons. Tendons are bundles of collagen fibers. When nerve cells release acetylcholine at the neuromuscular junction, skeletal muscle contracts. The skeletal muscle tissue then pulls on the bones of the skeleton and causes body movement.

Smooth Muscles

Smooth muscle tissue is an involuntary nonstriated muscle tissue. It has greater elasticity than striated muscle but still maintains its contractile ability. Smooth muscle tissue can be of the single-unit variety or the multi-unit variety. Most smooth muscle tissues are single unit where the cells all act in unison and the whole muscle contracts or relaxes. Single-unit smooth muscle lines the blood vessels, urinary tract, and digestive tract. It helps to move fluids and solids along the digestive tract, allows for expansion of the urinary bladder as it fills and helps move blood through the vessels. Multi-unit smooth muscle is found in the iris of the eye, large elastic arteries, and the trachea.

Cardiac Muscles

Cardiac muscle tissue is an involuntary striated muscle that is only found in the walls of the heart. The cells that make up the tissue contract together to pump blood through the veins and arteries. This tissue has high contractility and extreme endurance, since it pumps for an individual's entire lifetime without any rest. Each cardiac muscle cell has finger-like projections, called **intercalated disks**, at each end that overlap with the same projections on neighboring cells. The intercalated disks form tight junctions between the cells so that they do not separate as the heart beats and so that electrochemical signals are passed from cell to cell quickly and efficiently.

Endocrine System

The endocrine system is made up of ductless tissues and glands and is responsible for hormone secretion into either the blood or the interstitial fluid of the human body. **Hormones** are chemical substances that change the metabolic activity of tissues and organs. **Interstitial fluid** is the solution that surrounds tissue cells within the body. This system works closely with the nervous system to regulate the physiological activities of the other systems of the body in order to maintain homeostasis. While the nervous system provides quick, short-term responses to stimuli, the endocrine system acts by releasing hormones into the bloodstream, which then are distributed to the whole body. The response is slow but long lasting, ranging from a few hours to even a few weeks. While regular metabolic reactions are controlled by enzymes, hormones can change the type, activity, or quantity of the enzymes involved in the reaction. They can regulate development and growth, digestive metabolism, mood, and body temperature, among many other things. Often very small amounts of a hormone will lead to large changes in the body.

There are eight major glands in the endocrine system, each with its own specific function. They are described below.

- Hypothalamus: This gland is a part of the brain. It connects the nervous system to the endocrine system via the pituitary gland and plays an important role in regulating endocrine organs.

- Pituitary gland: This pea-sized gland is found at the bottom of the hypothalamus. It releases hormones that regulate growth, blood pressure, certain functions of the reproductive sex organs, and pain relief, among other things. It also plays an important role in regulating the function of other endocrine glands.

- Thyroid gland: This gland releases hormones that are important for metabolism, growth and development, temperature regulation, and brain development during infancy and childhood. Thyroid hormones also monitor the amount of circulating calcium in the body.

- Parathyroid glands: These are four pea-sized glands located on the posterior surface of the thyroid. The main hormone that is secreted is called **parathyroid hormone (PTH)** and helps with the thyroid's regulation of calcium in the body.

- Thymus gland: This gland is located in the chest cavity, embedded in connective tissue. It produces several hormones that are important for development and maintenance of normal immunological defenses.

- Adrenal glands: One adrenal gland is attached to the top of each kidney. Its major function is to aid in the management of stress.

- Pancreas: This gland produces hormones that regulate blood sugar levels in the body.

- Pineal gland: The pineal gland secretes the hormone melatonin, which can slow the maturation of sperm, oocytes, and reproductive organs. Melatonin also regulates the body's **circadian rhythm**, which is the natural awake-asleep cycles.

Reproductive System

The reproductive system is responsible for producing, storing, nourishing, and transporting functional reproductive cells, or gametes, in the human body. It includes the reproductive organs, also known as **gonads,** the reproductive tract, the accessory glands and organs that secrete fluids into the reproductive tract, and the perineal structures, which are the external genitalia. The human male and female reproductive systems are very different from each other.

The male gonads are called **testes**. The testes secrete androgens and produce and store one-half billion **sperms cells**, which are the male gametes, each day. An **androgen** is a steroid hormone that controls the development and maintenance of male characteristics. Once the sperm are mature, they move through a duct system where they are mixed with additional fluids that are secreted by accessory glands, forming a mixture called **semen.** The sperm cells in semen are responsible for fertilization of the female gametes to produce offspring. The male reproductive system has a few accessory organs as well, which are located inside the body. The prostate gland and the seminal vesicles provide additional fluid that serves as nourishment to the sperm during ejaculation. The vas deferens is responsible for transportation of sperm to the urethra. The bulbourethral glands produce a lubricating fluid for the urethra that also neutralizes the residual acidity left behind by urine.

The female gonads are called **ovaries**. Ovaries produce one immature gamete, or **oocyte,** per month. The ovaries are also responsible for secreting the hormones estrogen and progesterone. When the oocyte is released from the ovary, it travels along the uterine tubes, or Fallopian tubes, and then into the uterus. The uterus opens into the vagina. When sperm cells enter the vagina, they swim through the uterus. If they fertilize the oocyte, they do so in the Fallopian tubes. The resulting zygote travels down the tube and implants into the uterine wall. The uterus protects and nourishes the developing embryo for nine months until it is ready for the outside environment. If the oocyte is not fertilized, it is released in the uterine, or menstrual, cycle. The **menstrual cycle** usually occurs monthly and involves the shedding of the functional part of the uterine lining. Mammary glands are a specialized accessory organ of the female reproductive system. The mammary glands are located in the breast tissue of females. During pregnancy, the glands begin to grow as the cells proliferate in preparation for lactation. After pregnancy, the cells begin to secrete nutrient-filled milk, which is transferred into a duct system and out through the nipple for nourishment of the baby.

Unity and Diversity of Life, Adaptation, and Classification

Living organisms vary in many ways, yet there are a number of similarities that help define a "living" creature. It is estimated that there are millions of distinct species; while 1.5 million have been categorized, some scientists believe there could anywhere from three to 100 million distinct species on Earth. Species are classified in a hierarchical system based on similarities in genetic composition, physical manifestations, behaviors, and other features that define how the organism survives. All species can be categorized into three domains: Bacteria, Archaea, and Eukaryotes. Bacteria and Archaea are single-cell and prokaryotic (having no internal structures within the cell). Archaea are considered the simplest of living organisms. Eukaryotes are far more complex; they can be single-cell or multicellular organisms. Each cell in a living organism has a variety of internal structures called organelles. **Organelles** carry out various functions that contribute to the living functions of the organism. Because different organisms evolved and adapted to external stressors in order to survive and reproduce, the need arose for a classification system to group and distinguish organisms.

After the three domains, organisms can further be classified across five kingdoms: Bacteria, Protists, Fungi, Plants, and Animals. All organisms in the Bacteria and Archaea domains fall under the Bacteria kingdom.

Protists are eukaryotic, single-celled organisms that do not qualify as bacteria or archaea. There are few commonalities among protists; these organisms simply cannot fit the classification requirements of the other five kingdoms. Fungi are eukaryotic organisms that are unique in that their cell walls are made of chitin polymers. Plants are primarily eukaryotic multicellular organisms that create energy through the process of photosynthesis. The plant kingdom is considered to be the driver for all other living organisms, as they serve as food sources, create oxygen, and balance other gases in the atmosphere. Organisms that are not classified as Bacteria, Protists, Fungi, or Plants are in the Animal kingdom. Animals are multicellular and eukaryotic organisms that are highly diverse.

After Kingdoms, organisms are categorized into a Phylum. There are numerous Phyla within each kingdom; new Phyla have been created to categorize new species that did not fit into the distinctions of previously established Phyla. After Phyla, species are categorized respectively into a Class, a Family, a Genus, and a Species. Distinct organisms may be referred to by their genus-species name; for example, when humans are referred to as "homo sapiens," this refers to their categorized genus ("homo") and their categorized species ("sapiens"). While a number of organisms can share Domain, Kingdom, Phyla, Class, Family, and Genus, Species is a distinct term.

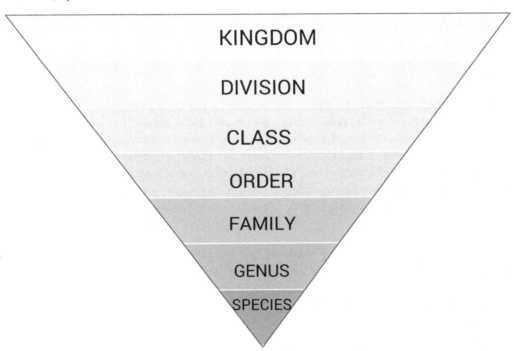

The Interdependence of Organisms

Organisms on Earth are interdependent within their species and across different species. For example, all organisms are dependent on plants for food and the balance of gases in the atmosphere (i.e., producing oxygen and using carbon dioxide). However, plants benefit from the presence of some fungi, which can support the nutrient composition uptake from the soil that the plant uses in photosynthesis. Humans benefit from the presence of a variety of bacteria in the gut that promote healthy digestion and nutrient absorption; in turn, the human gut provides a hospitable home for such bacteria. These types of supportive two-way interactions are called **symbiotic relationships**. Consequently, it is also important to note that many organisms can be detrimental to others; for example, some fungi are toxic to plants, and many bacteria cause illnesses in larger species.

An **ecosystem** refers to a specific physical area and the components—living and non-living—that make up the area. In an ecosystem, each component plays a functional role that can be positive or negative for the overall system. A stable, healthy ecosystem houses a precise balance of relationships between each component that allows the ecosystem to thrive. For example, a freshwater stream in a rainforest serves as the water source for animals and plants. The same animals graze and produce waste in the area, which fertilizes the soil for the plants. The plants contribute to the composition of the atmosphere. Additionally, a completely unique ecosystem of aquatic life exists within the water itself, which is affected by the atmosphere. For example, a more oxygen-rich atmosphere may contribute to cleaner runoff into the water when it rains; this, in turn, will affect the type of life in the water, as well as the animals and plants that use the water. Introducing new entities into a healthy ecosystem can cause harmful shifts and disruption in the area. This can occur due to natural events (such as an earthquake or hurricane) or human activity (such as waste dumping).

Populations of organisms typically form communities in which they can thrive off of mutually beneficial relationships. Populations refer to groups of one single species that live together or in close proximity and reproduce with one another; communities refer to members of a population that are working together toward a common goal or benefit for the species (such as procuring resources or protecting the community's physical space). Healthy populations and communities are able to work together to ensure future survival for the species.

Personal Health

Personal health encompasses different aspects that support a person's ability to be well and thrive. These aspects include social factors (such as relationships and friendships), emotional factors (such as the ability to cope with stressors), spiritual factors (believing in a greater purpose or meaning to one's life), environmental factors (exposure to and relationship with the physical space in which one lives), job satisfaction (including health and safety in one's place of work), and physical wellness (taking care of one's mind and body). These factors are often interdependent. For example, a person's social circle and social activities often influence the types of foods he or she eats or the recreational activities in which he or she engages.

Nutrition refers to the energy sources and nutrients that people consume in order to grow, reproduce, and function on a daily basis. The choice and availability of nutrients contribute significantly to the individual and community health status. Nutrient-poor foods may cause deficiencies or diseases, while nutrient-rich foods can prevent or correct deficiencies or diseases. Individuals may make poor nutrition choices due to lack of education, lack of access (physical access or lack of financial resources), or for psychosocial reasons.

Communicable diseases are infectious and spread easily from one person to another. They are typically triggered by a bacteria or virus. Based on the type of bacteria or virus that causes the disease, it can be spread through touch, air, or bodily fluids. If one member of a species contracts a disease, it typically means that any member of the species is susceptible to that disease; some diseases can spread across species (such as rabies), though symptoms and severity may present differently. **Immunocompromised** individuals (the very young, very old, or otherwise ill) are most susceptible to communicable diseases. Infection risk can be reduced through frequent and thorough hand-washing, access to clean food and water, utilizing proper cooking techniques, vaccinations, and utilizing protective barriers in situations where bodily fluids may be exchanged.

Substance abuse refers to using any ingestible material in a way that is physically, mentally, or emotionally harmful to oneself or others. Substance abuse can lead to serious problems beyond physical health issues, such as legal consequences, job loss, and relationship breakdowns. Common substances that are abused are alcohol, tobacco, and a number of both illegal and legal pharmaceutical drugs (such as cocaine or prescription narcotics). However, even food can be abused; people experience food addictions in which they cannot control the amount and types of food they eat, which can lead to chronic diseases. Substance abuse can result from genetic predisposition or psychosocial factors. **Cognitive therapy** can be a critical component for understanding and correcting the factors that may be contributing to a substance abuse problem.

Physical Science

The Physical and Chemical Properties and Structure of Matter

Measurable Properties of Atoms
Atoms are the smallest units of all matter and make up all chemical elements. They each have three parts: protons, neutrons, and electrons.

Although atoms are very small in size, they have many properties that can be quantitatively measured. The **atomic mass** of an atom is equal to the sum of the protons and neutrons in the atom. The **ionization energy** of an atom is the amount of energy that is needed to remove one electron from an individual atom. The greater the ionization energy, the harder it is to remove the electron, meaning the greater the bond between the electron and that atom's nucleus. Ionization energies are always positive because atoms require extra energy to let go of an atom. On the other hand, **electron affinity** is the change in energy that occurs when an electron is added to an individual atom. Electron affinity is always negative because atoms release energy when an electron is added. The **effective nuclear charge** of an atom is noted as Z_{eff} and accounts for the attraction of electrons to the nucleus of an atom as well as the repulsion of electrons to other neighboring electrons in the same atom. The **covalent radius** of an atom is the radius of an atom when it is bonded to another atom. It is equal to one-half the distance between the two atomic nuclei. The **van der Waal's radius** is the radius of an atom when it is only colliding with another atom in solution or as a gas and is not bonding to the other atom.

The Periodic Table and Periodicity
Periodic Table
The **periodic table** is a chart that describes all the known elements. Currently, there are 118 elements listed on the periodic table. Each element has its own cell on the table. Within the cell, the element's abbreviation is written in the center, with its full name written directly below. The atomic number is recorded in the top left corner, and the atomic mass is recorded at the bottom center of the cell in atomic mass units, or **amus**. The first ninety-four elements are naturally occurring, whereas the last twenty-four can only be made in laboratory environments.

The rows of the table are called **periods,** and the columns are called **groups.** Elements with similar properties are grouped together. The periodic table can be divided and described in many ways according to similarities of the grouped elements. When it is divided into blocks, each block is named in accordance with the subshell in which the final electron sits. The blocks are named alkali metals, alkaline earth metals, transition metals, basic metals, semimetals, nonmetals, halogens, noble gases, lanthanides, and actinides. If the periodic table is divided according to shared physical and chemical properties, the elements are often classified as metals, metalloids, and nonmetals.

The Periodic Table of the Elements

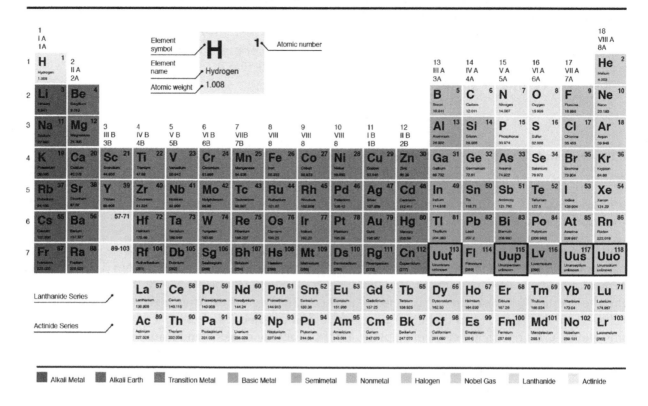

Periodicity

Periodicity refers to the trends that are seen in the periodic table among the elements. It is a fundamental aspect of how the elements are arranged within the table. These trends allow scientists to learn the properties of families of elements together instead of learning about each element only individually. They also elucidate the relationships among the elements. There are many important characteristics that can be seen by examining the periodicity of the table, such as ionization energy, electron affinity, length of atomic radius, and metallic characteristics. Moving from left to right and from bottom to top on the periodic table, elements have increasing ionization energy and electron affinity. Moving in the opposite directions, from top to bottom and from right to left, the elements have increasing length of atomic radii. Moving from the bottom left corner to the top right corner, the elements have increasing nonmetallic properties, and moving in the opposite direction from the top right corner to the bottom left corner, the elements have increasing metallic properties.

Protons

Protons are found in the nucleus of an atom and have a positive electric charge. At least one proton is found in the nucleus of all atoms. Protons have a mass of about one atomic mass unit. The number of protons in an element is referred to as the element's atomic number. Each element has a unique number of protons and therefore its own unique atomic number. Hydrogen ions are unique in that they only contain one proton and do not contain any electrons. Since they are free protons, they have a very short lifespan and immediately become attracted to any free electrons in the environment. In a solution with water, they bind to a water molecule, H_2O, and turn it into H_3O+.

Neutrons

Neutrons are also found in the nucleus of atoms. These subatomic particles have a neutral charge, meaning that they do not have a positive or negative electric charge. Their mass is slightly larger than that of a proton. Together with protons, they are referred to as the nucleons of an atom. Interestingly, although neutrons are not affected by electric fields because of their neutral charge, they are affected by magnetic fields and are said to have magnetic moments.

Electrons

Electrons have a negative charge and are the smallest of the subatomic particles. They are located outside the nucleus in orbitals, which are shells that surround the nucleus. If an atom has an overall neutral charge, it has an equal number of electrons and protons. If it has more protons than electrons or vice versa, it becomes an ion. When there are more protons than electrons, the atom is a positively charged ion, or cation. When there are more electrons than protons, the atom is a negatively charged ion, or anion.

The location of electrons within an atom is more complicated than the locations of protons and neutrons. Within the orbitals, electrons are always moving. They can spin very fast and move upward, downward, and sideways. There are many different levels of orbitals around the atomic nucleus, and each orbital has a different capacity for electrons. The electrons in the orbitals closest to the nucleus are more tightly bound to the nucleus of the atom. There are three main characteristics that describe each orbital. The first is the principle quantum number, which describes the size of the orbital. The second is the angular momentum quantum number, which describes the shape of the orbital. The third is the magnetic quantum number, which describes the orientation of the orbital in space.

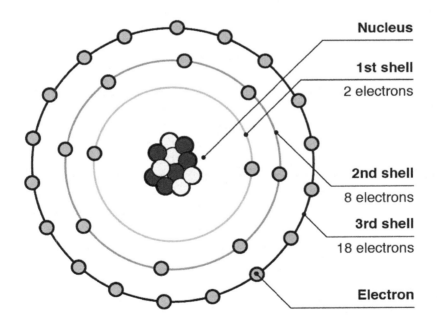

Chemical Bonds Between Atoms

Chemical bonds are formed from attractions between atoms that then create chemical compounds or molecules. The bonds can be strong or weak depending on how the bond is formed. A stable compound formed with the total energy of the molecular unit is lower than that of the atoms separately. There are many different types of chemical bonds that can form between atoms, including covalent bonds, ionic bonds, metallic bonds, and hydrogen bonds.

Covalent Bonds

An important characteristic of electrons is their ability to form covalent bonds with other atoms to form molecules. A covalent bond is a chemical bond that forms when two atoms share the same pair or pairs of electrons. There is a stable balance of attraction and repulsion between the two atoms. When these bonds are formed, energy is released because the electrons become more spatially distributed instead of being pulled toward the individual atom's nucleus. There are several different types of covalent bonds. Sigma bonds are the strongest type of covalent bond and involve the head-on overlapping of electron orbitals from two different atoms. Pi bonds are a little weaker and involve the lateral overlapping of certain orbitals. While single bonds between atoms, such as between carbon and hydrogen, are sigma bonds, double bonds, such as when carbon is double-bonded to an oxygen atom, are usually one sigma bond and one pi bond.

Covalent bonds can also be classified as nonpolar or polar. Nonpolar covalent bonds are formed when two atoms share their electrons equally, creating a very small difference of electronegativity between the atoms. Compounds that are formed with nonpolar covalent bonds do not mix well with water and other polar solvents and are much more soluble in nonpolar solvents. Polar covalent bonds are formed when electrons are not evenly shared between the atoms. Therefore, the electrons are pulled closer to one atom than the other, giving the molecule ionic properties and an imbalance of charge. The electronegative difference between the atoms is greater when polar bonds are formed compared to nonpolar bonds.

Coordinate covalent bonds, or dipolar bonds, are formed when the two shared electrons of the molecule come from the same atom. The electrons from one atom are shared with an empty orbital on the other atom, making one atom the electron pair donor and the other atom the electron pair acceptor. The electrons are shared equally when these bonds are created.

Ionic Bonds

When ionic bonds are formed, instead of sharing a pair of electrons, the electrons are transferred from one atom to another, creating two ions. One of the ions is left with a positive charge, and the other one is left with a negative charge. This results in a large difference in electronegativity between the ions. The ionic bonds result from the attraction between the oppositely charged ions. However, the same two ions are not always paired with each other. Each ion is surrounded by ions with the opposite charge but are constantly moving around. Ionic bonds form in metal salts. Metals have few electrons in their outermost orbitals, and by losing those electrons, they become more stable. By taking these electrons away from the metallic atoms, nonmetals can fill their valence shells and also become more stable. For example, when sodium atoms and chloride atoms combine to form sodium chloride, the sodium atom loses an electron and becomes positively charged with a closed shell of electrons, and the chloride atom gains an electron, leaving it with a full shell of electrons.

Metallic Bonds

Metallic bonds occur when the electrons in the outer shell of an atom become delocalized and free-moving. They become shared by many atoms as they move in all directions around the positively charged metal ions. The free-floating electrons create an environment that allows for easy conduction of heat and electricity between the atoms. They also contribute to the **luster**, or surface reflectivity, that is often characteristic of metals, as well as the high tensile strength of metallic material. Metallic bonds are often seen as a sea of electrons with positive ions floating between them.

Hydrogen Bonds
Hydrogen bonds are different from the previously mentioned bonds because they are formed between a hydrogen atom that is present in one molecule and another atom that is already part of a molecular complex. These types of bonds are intermolecular instead of intramolecular. The hydrogen atom is attracted to an atom that has a high electronegativity in the other molecule. The large difference in electronegativity between the molecules creates a strong electrostatic attraction between the molecules. If a hydrogen atom forms a polar covalent bond with another atom, such as an oxygen atom, the hydrogen end of the molecule remains slightly positively charged, and the oxygen end of the molecule remains slightly negatively charged. The hydrogen of this molecule would then be attracted to other atoms with a slightly negative charge in nearby molecules. Hydrogen bonding is also important in the formation of the DNA double helix molecule. The nitrogenous bases on each strand are situated so they can form hydrogen bonds with the bases that are directly opposite them on the other strand.

Characteristic Properties of Substances
Properties of Water
Water is a polar compound formed from one oxygen atom bonded to two hydrogen atoms. It has many unique properties, such as its ability to exist as a solid, liquid, and gas on Earth's surface. It is the only common substance that can exist in all three forms in this environment. Water is also self-ionizing, breaking itself up into H^+ and OH^- ions, which also makes it both an acid and a base.

The polarity of water and its attraction to other polar molecules is an important characteristic. **Cohesion** is the attraction of water molecules to each other. The slight negative charge of the oxygen atom in one molecule attracts the slightly positively charged hydrogen atoms of other water molecules. This attraction allows water to have surface tension. Insects, such as water striders, can actually walk across the surface of a pool of water. **Adhesion** is the attraction of water molecules to other molecules with which it can form hydrogen bonds. This attraction creates capillary action. **Capillary action** is the ability of water to "climb" up the side of a tube as it is attracted to the material of the tube. Its polarity also helps it break up ions in salts and bond to other polar substances, such as acids and alcohols. It is used to dissolve many substances and is often described as a **universal solvent** because of its polar attraction to other atoms and ions.

While most compounds become denser when they become solid, ice, the solid form of water, is actually less dense than the liquid form of water. The hydrogen bonds that form between the water molecules become ice crystals and more stable. The bonds remain spaced apart as the liquid freezes, creating a low density in the solid structure. Ice, therefore, floats to the top of a glass of liquid water.

Water is also a great moderator of temperature because of its high specific heat and high heat of vaporization. **Specific heat** is the amount of energy that is needed to change the temperature of one gram of a substance 1°C. When a substance has a high specific heat, it requires a lot of energy to change the temperature. Since water molecules form a lot of hydrogen bonds, it takes a lot of energy to break up the bonds. Since there are a lot of hydrogen bonds to absorb and release heat as they break and form, respectively, temperature changes are minimized. Similarly, **heat of vaporization** is the amount of energy needed to change 1 gram of liquid into gas. It takes a lot of energy to break the hydrogen bonds between liquid water molecules and turn them into water vapor.

Characteristic Properties of Molecules
There are two basic types of properties that can help characterize substances: physical and chemical. Physical properties can be detected without changing the substance's identity or composition. If a substance is subject to a physical change, its appearance changes, but its composition does not change at

all. Common physical properties include color, odor, density, and hardness. Physical properties can also be classified as extensive or intensive. Extensive physical properties depend on the amount of substance that is present. These include characteristics such as mass and volume. Intensive properties do not depend on how much of the substance is present and remain the same regardless of quantity. These include characteristics such as density and color.

Chemical properties are characteristics of a substance that describe how it can be changed into a different chemical substance. A substance's composition is changed when it undergoes a chemical change. Chemical properties are measured and observed only as the substance is undergoing a change to become a different substance. Some examples of chemical properties are flammability, reactivity, toxicity, and ability to oxidize. These properties are detected by making changes to the substance's external environment and seeing how it reacts to the changes. An iron shovel that is left outside can become rusty. Rusting occurs when iron changes to iron oxide. While iron is very hard and a shiny silver color, iron oxide is flaky and a reddish-brown color. Reactivity is the ability of a substance to combine chemically with another substance. While some substances are very reactive, others are not reactive at all. For example, potassium is very reactive with water, and even a small amount causes an explosive reaction. Helium, on the other hand, does not react with any other substance.

It is often important to quantify the properties that are observed in a substance. Quantitative measurements are associated with a number, and it is imperative to include a unit of measure with each of those measurements. Without the unit of measure, the number may be meaningless. If the weight of a substance is noted as 100 without a unit of measure, it is unknown whether the substance is equivalent to 100 of something very light, such as milligram measurements, or 100 of something very heavy, such as kilogram measurements. There are many other quantitative measurements of matter that can be taken, including length, time, and temperature, among many others. Contrastingly, there are many properties that are not associated with a number; these properties can be measured qualitatively. The measurements of qualitative properties use a person's senses to observe and describe the characteristics. Since the descriptions are developed by individual persons, they can be very subjective. These properties can include odor, color, and texture, among many others. They can also include comparisons between two substances without using a number; for example, one substance may have a stronger odor or be lighter in color than another substance.

Changes in States of Matter
The universe is composed completely of matter. **Matter** is any material or object that takes up space and has a mass. Although there is an endless variety of items found in the universe, there are only about one hundred elements, or individual substances, that make up all matter. These elements are different types of atoms and are the smallest units that anything can be broken down into. Different elements can link together to form compounds, or molecules. Hydrogen and oxygen are two examples of elements, and when they bond together, they form water molecules. Matter can be found in three different states: gas, liquid, or solid.

Gases
Gases have three main distinct properties. The first is that they are easy to compress. When a gas is compressed, the space between the molecules decreases, and the frequency of collisions between them increases. The second property is that they do not have a fixed volume or shape. They expand to fill large containers or compress down to fit into smaller containers. When they are in large containers, the gas molecules can float around at high speeds and collide with each other, which allows them to fill the entire container uniformly. Therefore, the volume of a gas is equal to the volume of its container. The third distinct property of a gas is that it occupies more space than the liquid or solid from which it was formed.

One gram of solid CO_2, also known as **dry ice**, has a volume of 0.641 milliliters. The same amount of CO_2 in a gaseous state has a volume of 556 milliliters. Steam engines use water in this capacity to do work. When water boils inside the steam engine, it becomes steam, or water vapor. As the steam increases in volume and escapes its container, it is used to make the engine run.

Liquids

A liquid is an intermediate state between gases and solids. It has an exact volume due to the attraction of its molecules to each other and molds to the shape of the part of the container that it is in. Although liquid molecules are closer together than gas molecules, they still move quickly within the container they are in. Liquids cannot be compressed, but their molecules slide over each other easily when poured out of a container. The attraction between liquid molecules, known as **cohesion**, also causes liquids to have surface tension. They stick together and form a thin skin of particles with an extra strong bond between them. As long as these bonds remain undisturbed, the surface becomes quite strong and can even support the weight of an insect such as a water skipper. Another property of liquids is adhesion, which is when different types of particles are attracted to each other. When liquids are in a container, they are drawn up above the surface level of the liquid around the edges. The liquid molecules that are in contact with the container are pulled up by their extra attraction to the particles of the container.

Solids

Unlike gases and liquids, solids have a definitive shape. They are similar to liquids in that they also have a definitive volume and cannot be compressed. The molecules are packed together tightly, which does not allow for movement within the substance. There are two types of solids: crystalline and amorphous. Crystalline solids have atoms or molecules arranged in a specific order or symmetrical pattern throughout the entire solid. This symmetry makes all of the bonds within the crystal of equal strength, and when they are broken apart, the pieces have straight edges. Minerals are all crystalline solids. Amorphous solids, on the other hand, do not have repeating structures or symmetry. Their components are heterogeneous, so they often melt gradually over a range of temperatures. They do not break evenly and often have curved edges. Examples of amorphous solids are glass, rubber, and most plastics.

Matter can change between a gas, liquid, and solid. When these changes occur, the change is physical and does not affect the chemical properties or makeup of the substance. Environmental changes, such as temperature or pressure changes, can cause one state of matter to convert to another state of matter. For example, in very hot temperatures, solids can melt and become a liquid, such as when ice melts into liquid water, or sublimate and become a gas, such as when dry ice becomes gaseous carbon dioxide. Liquids can evaporate and become a gas, such as when liquid water turns into water vapor. In very cold temperatures, gases can depose and become a solid, such as when water vapor becomes icy frost on a windshield, or condense and become a liquid, such as when water vapor becomes dew on grass. Liquids can freeze and become a solid, such as when liquid water freezes and becomes ice.

Here's an illustration:

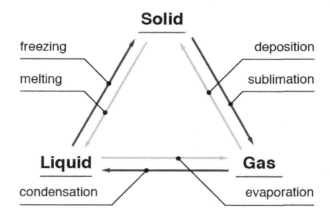

Chemical Reactions

A chemical reaction is a process that involves a change in the molecular arrangement of a substance. One set of chemical substances, called the reactants, is rearranged into a different set of chemical substances, called the products, by the breaking and re-forming of bonds between atoms. In a chemical reaction, it is important to realize that no new atoms or molecules are introduced. The products are formed solely from the atoms and molecules that are present in the reactants. These can involve a change in state of matter as well. Making glass, burning fuel, and brewing beer are all examples of chemical reactions.

Types of Chemical Reactions

Chemical reactions are thought to involve changes in positions of electrons with the breaking and re-forming of chemical bonds, without changes to the nucleus of the atoms. The three main types of chemical reactions are combination, decomposition, and combustion.

Combination

In combination reactions, two or more reactants are combined to form one more complex, larger product. The bonds of the reactants are broken, the elements rearranged, and then new bonds are formed between all of the elements to form the product. It can be written as A + B → C, where A and B are the reactants and C is the product. An example of a combination reaction is the creation of iron (II) sulfide from iron and sulfur, which is written as:

$$8Fe + S_8 \rightarrow 8FeS$$

Decomposition

Decomposition reactions are the opposite of combination reactions. They occur when one substance is broken down into two or more products. The bonds of the first substance are broken, the elements rearranged, and then the elements bonded together in new configurations to make two or more molecules. These reactions can be written as C → B + A, where C is the reactant and A and B are the products. An example of a decomposition reaction is the electrolysis of water to make oxygen and hydrogen gas, which is written as:

$$2H_2O \rightarrow 2H_2 + O_2$$

Combustion

Combustion reactions are a specific type of chemical reaction that involves oxygen gas as a reactant. This mostly involves the burning of a substance. The combustion of hexane in air is one example of a combustion reaction. The hexane gas combines with oxygen in the air to form carbon dioxide and water.

The reaction can be written as:

$$2C_6H_{14} + 17O_2 \rightarrow 12CO_2 + 14H_2O$$

Oxidation and Reduction

Oxidation/reduction (redox or half) reactions involve the oxidation of one species and the reduction of the other species in the reactants of a chemical equation. This can be seen through three main types of transfers.

The first type is through the transfer of oxygen. The reactant gaining an oxygen is the oxidizing agent, and the reactant losing an oxygen is the reduction agent.

For example, the oxidation of magnesium is as follows:

$$2Mg(s) + O_2(g) \rightarrow 2MgO(s)$$

The second type is through the transfer of hydrogen. The reactant losing the hydrogen is the oxidizing agent, and the other reactant is the reduction agent.

For example, the redox of ammonia and bromine results in nitrogen and hydrogen bromide due to bromine gaining a hydrogen as follows:

$$2 NH_3 + 3Br_2 \rightarrow N_2 + 6 HBr$$

The third type is through the loss of electrons from one species, known as the **oxidation agent**, and the gain of electrons to the other species, known as the **reduction agent**. For a reactant to become "oxidized," it must give up an electron.

For example, the redox of copper and silver is as follows:

$$Cu(s) + 2 Ag^+(aq) \rightarrow Cu^{2+}(aq) + 2 Ag(s)$$

It is also important to note that the oxidation numbers can change in a redox reaction due to the transfer of oxygen atoms. A standard set of rules for finding the oxidation numbers for a compound is listed below:

1. The oxidation number of a free element is always 0.

2. The oxidation number of a monatomic ion equals the charge of the ion.

3. The oxidation number of H is +1, but it is −1 when combined with less electronegative elements.

4. The oxidation number of O in compounds is usually −2, but it is −1 in peroxides.

5. The oxidation number of a Group 1 element in a compound is +1.

6. The oxidation number of a Group 2 element in a compound is +2.

7. The oxidation number of a Group 17 element in a binary compound is −1.

8. The sum of the oxidation numbers of all the atoms in a neutral compound is 0.

9. The sum of the oxidation numbers in a polyatomic ion is equal to the charge of the ion.

These rules can be applied to determine the oxidation number of an unknown component of a compound.

For example, what is the oxidation number of Cr in $CrCl_3$?

From rule 7, the oxidation number of Cl is given as −1. Since there are 3 chlorines in this compound, that would equal 3×-1 for a result of −3. According to rule 8, the total oxidation number of Cr must balance the total oxidation number of Cl, so Cr must have a total oxidation number equaling:

$$+3 (-3 + +3 = 0)$$

There is only 1 Cr, so the oxidation number would be multiplied by 1, or the same as the total of +3, written as follows:

$$\overset{+3 \quad -1}{\underset{+3 \quad -3}{CrCl_3}}$$

Balancing Chemical Reactions

The way the hexane combustion reaction is written above ($2C6H14 + 17O2 \rightarrow 12CO2 + 14H2O$) is an example of a chemical equation. Chemical equations describe how the molecules are changed when the chemical reaction occurs. The "+" sign on the left side of the equation indicates that those molecules are reacting with each other, and the arrow, "→," in the middle of the equation indicates that the reactants are producing something else. The coefficient before a molecule indicates the quantity of that specific molecule that is present for the reaction. The subscript next to an element indicates the quantity of that element in each molecule. In order for the chemical equation to be balanced, the quantity of each element on both sides of the equation should be equal. For example, in the hexane equation above, there are twelve carbon elements, twenty-eight hydrogen elements, and thirty-four oxygen elements on each side of the equation. Even though they are part of different molecules on each side, the overall quantity is the same. The state of matter of the reactants and products can also be included in a chemical equation and would be written in parentheses next to each element as follows: gas (g), liquid (l), solid (s), and dissolved in water, or aqueous (aq).

Catalysts

The rate of a chemical reaction can be increased by adding a catalyst to the reaction. Catalysts are substances that lower the activation energy required to go from the reactants to the products of the reaction but are not consumed in the process. The **activation energy** of a reaction is the minimum amount of energy that is required to make the reaction move forward and change the reactants into the products. When catalysts are present, less energy is required to complete the reaction. For example, hydrogen peroxide will eventually decompose into two water molecules and one oxygen molecule. If potassium permanganate is added to the reaction, the decomposition happens at a much faster rate. Similarly, increasing the temperature or pressure in the environment of the reaction can increase the rate of the reaction. Higher temperatures increase the number of high-energy collisions that lead to the products. The same happens when increasing pressure for gaseous reactants, but not with solid or liquid reactants.

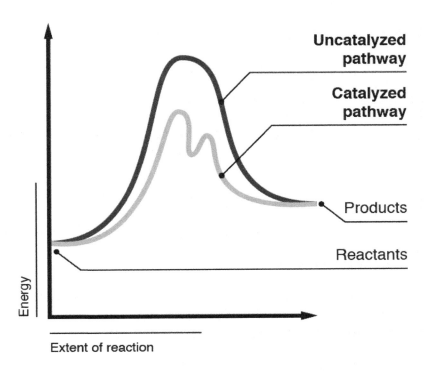

Enzymes

Enzymes are a type of biological catalyst that accelerate chemical reactions. They work like other catalysts by lowering the activation energy of the reaction to increase the reaction rate. They bind to substrates and change them into the products of the reaction without being consumed by the reaction. Enzymes differ from other catalysts by their increased specificity to their substrate. They can also be affected by other molecules. Enzyme inhibitors can decrease their activity, whereas enzyme activators increase their activity. Their activity also decreases dramatically when the environment is not in their optimal pH and temperature range.

An enzyme can encounter several different types of inhibitors. In biological systems, inhibitors are many times expressed as part of a feedback loop where the enzyme is producing too much of a substance too quickly and the reaction needs to be stopped. Competitive inhibitors and substrates cannot bind to the enzyme at the same time. These inhibitors often resemble the substrate of the enzyme. Noncompetitive inhibitors bind to the enzyme at a different location than the substrate. The substrate can still bind with the same affinity, but the efficiency of the enzyme is decreased. Uncompetitive inhibitors cannot bind to the enzyme alone and can only bind to the enzyme–substrate complex. Once an uncompetitive inhibitor binds to the complex, the complex becomes inactive. An irreversible inhibitor binds to the enzyme and permanently inactivates it. It usually does so by forming a covalent bond with the enzyme.

pH

In chemistry, **pH** stands for the potential of hydrogen. It is a numeric scale ranging from 0 to 14 that determines the acidity and basicity of an aqueous solution. Solutions with a pH of greater than 7 are considered basic, those with a pH of less than 7 are considered acidic, and solutions with a pH equal to 7 are considered neutral. Pure water is considered neutral with a pH equal to 7. It is important to remember that the pH of solutions can change at different temperatures. While the pH of pure water is 7 at 25°C, at 0°C it is 7.47, and at 100°C it is 6.14. pH is calculated as the negative of the base 10 logarithm of the activity of the hydrogen ions in the solution and can be written as $pH = -\log_{10}(a_H+) = \log_{10}(1/a_H+)$.

One of the simplest ways to measure the pH of a solution is by performing a litmus test. Litmus paper has a mixture of dyes on it that react with the solution and display whether the solution is acidic or basic depending on the resulting color. Red litmus paper turns blue when it reacts with a base. Blue litmus paper turns red when it reacts with an acid. Litmus tests can be crude measurements of pH and not very precise. A more precise way to measure the pH of a solution is to use a pH meter. These specialized meters act like voltmeters and measure the electrical potential of a solution. Acids have a lot of positively charged hydrogen ions in solutions that have greater potential than bases to produce an electric current. The voltage measurement is then compared with a solution of known pH and voltage. The difference in voltage is translated into the difference in pH.

Acids and Bases

Acids and bases are two types of substances with differing properties. In general, when acids are dissolved in water, they can conduct electricity, have a sour taste, react with metals to free hydrogen ions, and react with bases to neutralize their properties. Bases, in general, when dissolved in water, conduct electricity, have a slippery feel, and react with acids to neutralize their properties.

The Brønsted-Lowry acid–base theory is about how acid–base reactions work. **Acids** are defined as substances that dissociate in aqueous solutions and form hydrogen ions. **Bases** are defined as substances that dissociate in aqueous solutions and form hydroxide (OH^-) ions. The basic idea behind the theory is that when an acid and base react with each other, a proton is exchanged, and the acid forms its conjugate base, while the base forms its conjugate acid. The acid is the proton donor, and the base is the proton acceptor. The reaction is written as $HA + B \leftrightarrow A^- + HB^+$, where HA is the acid, B is the base, A^- is the conjugated base, and HB^+ is the conjugated acid. Since the reverse of the reaction is also possible, the reactants and products are always in equilibrium. The equilibrium of acids and bases in a chemical reaction can be determined by finding the acid dissociation constant, K_a, and the base dissociation constant, K_b. These dissociation constants determine how strong the acid or base is in the aqueous solution. Strong acids and bases dissociate quickly to create the products of the reaction.

In other cases, acids and bases can react to form a neutral salt. This happens when the hydrogen ion from the acid combines with the hydroxide ion of the base to form water, and the remaining ions combine to form a neutral salt. For example, when hydrochloric acid and sodium hydroxide combine, they form salt and water, which can be written as:

$$HCl + NaOH \rightarrow NaCl + H_2O$$

Forces and Motions

Nature of Motion

Cultures have been studying the movement of objects since ancient times. These studies have been prompted by curiosity and sometimes by necessity. On earth, items move according to guidelines and have motion that is fairly predictable. To understand why an object moves along its path, it is important to understand what role forces have on influencing its movements. The term **force** describes an outside influence on an object. Force does not have to refer to something imparted by another object. Forces can act upon objects by touching them with a push or a pull, by friction, or without touch like a magnetic force or even gravity. Forces can affect the motion of an object.

To study an object's motion, it must be located and described. When locating an object's position, it can help pinpoint its location relative to another known object. Comparing an object with respect to a known object is referred to as **establishing a frame of reference**. If the placement of one object is known, it is easier to locate another object with respect to the position of the original object.

Motion can be described by following specific guidelines called **kinematics**. Kinematics use mechanics to describe motion without regard to the forces that are causing such motions. Specific equations can be used when describing motions; these equations use time as a frame of reference. The equations are based on the change of an object's position (represented by x), over a change in time (represented by t). This describes an object's velocity, which is measured in meters/second (m/s) and is described by the following equation:

$$v = \frac{\Delta x}{\Delta t} = \frac{x_f - x_i}{\Delta t}$$

Velocity is a vector quantity, meaning it measures the magnitude of something (how much) and the direction it is moving. Both of these components are essential to understanding and predicting the motion of objects. The scientist Isaac Newton did extensive studies on the motion of objects on earth and came up with three primary laws to describe motion.

Law 1: An object in motion tends to stay in motion unless acted upon by an outside force. An object at rest tends to stay at rest unless acted upon by an outside force (also known as the law of inertia).

For example, if a book is placed on a table, it will stay there until it is moved by an outside force.

Law 2: The force acting upon an object is equal to the object's mass multiplied by its acceleration (also known as F = ma).

For example, the amount of force acting on a bug being swatted by a flyswatter can be calculated if the mass of the flyswatter and its acceleration are known. If the mass of the flyswatter is 0.3 kg and the acceleration of its swing is 2.0 m/s², find the force of its swing.

$$m = 0.3 \, kg$$
$$a = 2.0 \, m/s^2$$
$$F = m \times a$$
$$F = (0.3) \times (2.0)$$
$$F = 0.6 \, N$$

Law 3: For every action, there is an equal and opposite reaction.

For example, when a person claps their hands together, the right hand feels the same force as the left hand, as the force is equal and opposite.

Another example is if a car and a truck run head on into each other, the force experienced by the truck is equal and opposite to the force experienced by the car, regardless of their respective masses or velocities. The ability to withstand this amount of force is what varies between the vehicles and creates a difference in the amount of damage sustained.

Newton used these laws to describe motion and derive additional equations for motion that could predict the position, velocity, acceleration, or time for objects in motion in one and two dimensions. Since all of Newton's work was done on earth, he primarily used earth's gravity and the behavior of falling objects to design experiments and studies in free fall (an object subject to earth's gravity while in flight). On earth, the acceleration due to the force of gravity is measured at 9.8 meters per second^2 (m/s^2). This value is the same for anything on the earth or within the earth's atmosphere.

Acceleration
Acceleration is how much change in velocity there is over a change in time. It is given by the following equation:

$$a = \frac{\Delta v}{\Delta t} = \frac{v_f - v_i}{\Delta t}$$

Since velocity is the change in position over a change in time, it is necessary for calculating an acceleration. Both of these are vector quantities, meaning they have magnitude and direction (or some amount in some direction). Acceleration is measured in units of distance over time^2 (meters/second^2 or m/s^2 in metric units).

For example, what would be the acceleration of a vehicle that has an initial velocity of 35 m/s and a final velocity of 10 m/s over 5.0 s?

Using the givens and the equation:

$$a = \frac{\Delta v}{\Delta t} = \frac{v_f - v_i}{\Delta t}$$

V_f = 10 m/s

V_i = 35 m/s

Δt = 5.0 s

$$a = \frac{10 - 35}{5.0} = \frac{-25}{5.0} = -5.0 \, m/s^2$$

The vehicle is decelerating at −5.0 m/s^2.

If an object is moving with a constant velocity, its velocity does not change over time and therefore has no (or 0) acceleration.

It is common to misuse vector terms in spoken language. For example, if someone is pulled over by law enforcement for going above the posted speed limit while driving, they might be told they have been pulled over for "speeding." This is not a correct use of the term, as they would be speeding with direction, or traveling with too much velocity.

Another misconception is if something has a negative acceleration, it must be slowing down. If the change in position of the moving object is in a negative direction, it could have a negative velocity. If the acceleration is in the same direction as this negative velocity, it would be increasing the velocity in the negative direction, thus resulting in the object increasing in velocity.

For example, if west is designated to be a negative direction, a car increasing in speed to the west would have a negative velocity. Since it is increasing in speed, it would be accelerating in the negative direction, resulting in a negative acceleration.

Another common misconception is if a person is running around an oval track at a constant velocity, they would have no (or 0) acceleration because there is no change in the runner's velocity. This idea is incorrect because the person is changing direction the entire time they are running around the track, so there would be a change in their velocity, and therefore they would have an acceleration.

One final point regarding acceleration is that it can result from the force a rotating body exerts toward its center. For planets and other massive bodies, it is called **gravity**. This type of acceleration can also be utilized to separate substances, as in a centrifuge.

Projectile Motion
When objects are launched or thrown into the air, they exhibit what is called **projectile motion.** This motion takes a parabolic (or arced) path as the object rises and/or falls with the effect of gravity. In sports, if a ball is thrown across a field, it will follow a path of projectile motion. Whatever angle the object leaves the horizon with is the same angle with which it will return to the horizon. The height the object goes is referred to as the y component, and the distance along the horizon the object travels is referred to as the x component. To maximize the horizontal distance an object travels, it should be launched at an angle 45 degrees to the horizon. The following shows the range, or x distance, an object can travel when launched at various angles.

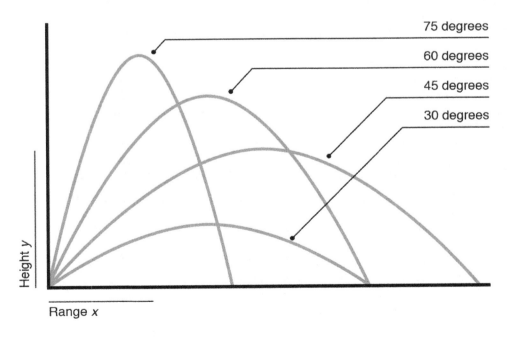

If something is traveling through the air without an internal source of power or any extra external forces acting upon it, it will follow these paths. All projectiles experience the effects of gravity while on earth;

therefore, they will experience a constant acceleration of 9.8 m/s² in a downward direction. While on its path, a projectile will have both a horizontal and vertical component to its motion and velocity. At the launch, the object has both vertical and horizontal velocity. As the object increases in height, the y component of its velocity will diminish until the very peak of the object's path. At the peak, the y component of the velocity is zero. Since the object still has a horizontal, or x component, to its velocity, it would continue its motion. There is also a constant acceleration of 9.8 m/s² acting in the downward direction on the object the entire time, so at the peak of the object's height, the velocity would then switch from zero to being pulled down with the acceleration. The entire path of the object takes a specific amount of time, based on the initial launch angle and velocity. The time and distance traveled can be calculated using the kinematic equations of motion. The time it takes the object to reach its maximum height is exactly half of the time for the object's entire flight.

Similar motion is exhibited if an object is thrown from atop a building, bridge, cliff, etc. Since it would be starting at its maximum height, the motion of the object would be comparable to the second half of the path in the above diagram.

Newton's Laws of Motion

Newton's laws of motion describe the relationship between an object and the forces acting upon that object, and its movement responding to those forces. Newton has three laws:

Law of Inertia: An object at rest stays at rest and an object in motion stays in motion unless otherwise acted upon by an outside force. For example, gravity is an outside force that will affect the speed and direction of a ball; when we throw a ball, the ball will eventually decrease in speed and fall to the ground because of the outside force of gravity. However, if the ball were kicked in space where there is no gravity, the ball would go the same speed and direction forever unless it hits another object in space or falls into another gravity field.

Newton's Second Law: This law states that the heavier an object, the more force has to be used to move it. This force has to do with acceleration. For example, if you use the same amount of force to push both a golf cart and an eighteen-wheeler, the golf cart will have more acceleration than the truck because the eighteen-wheeler weighs more than the golf cart.

Newton's Third Law: This law states that for every action, there is an opposite and equal reaction. For example, if you are jumping on a trampoline, you are experiencing Newton's third law of motion. When you jump down on the trampoline, the opposite reaction pushes you up into the air.

Friction

As previously stated with Newton's laws, forces act upon objects on the earth. If an object is resting on a surface, the effect of gravity acting upon its mass produces a force referred to as **weight.** This weight touches the surface it is resting on, and the surface produces a normal force perpendicular to this surface. If an outside force acts upon this object, its movement will be resisted by the surfaces rubbing on each other.

Friction is the term used to describe the force that opposes motion, or the force experienced when two surfaces interact with each other. Every surface has a specific amount with which it resists motion, called a **coefficient of friction**. The coefficient of friction is a proportion calculated from the force of friction divided by the normal force (force produced perpendicular to a surface).

$$\mu_s = \frac{F_s}{F_N}$$

There are different types of friction between surfaces. If something is at rest, it has a static (non-moving) friction. It would require an outside force to begin its movement. The coefficient of static friction for that material multiplied by the normal force would need to be greater than the force of static friction to get the object moving. Therefore, the force required to move an object must be greater than the force of static friction.

$$F_s \leq \mu_s \times F_N$$

Once the object is in motion, the force required to maintain this movement only needs to be equivalent to the value of the force of kinetic (moving) friction. To calculate the force of kinetic friction, simply multiply the coefficient of kinetic friction for that surface by the normal force.

$$F_k = \mu_k \times F_N$$

The force required to start an object in motion is larger than the force required to continue its motion once it has begun.

$$F_s \geq F_k$$

Friction not only occurs between solid surfaces; it also occurs in air and liquids. In air, it is called **air resistance**, or drag, and in water, it is called **viscosity**.

For example, what would the coefficient of static friction be if a 5.0 N force was applied to push a 20 kg crate, from rest, across a flat floor?

First, the normal force could be found to counter the force from the weight of the object, which would be the mass multiplied by gravity.

$$F_N = mass \times gravity$$

$$F_N = 20 \, kg \times 9.8 \, \frac{m}{s^2}$$

$$F_N = 196 \, N$$

Next, the coefficient of static friction could be found by dividing the frictional force by the normal force.

$$\mu_s = \frac{F_s}{F_N}$$

$$\mu_s = \frac{5.0 \, N}{196 \, N}$$

$$\mu_s = 0.03$$

Since it is a coefficient, the units cancel out, so the solution is unitless. The coefficient of static friction should also be less than 1.0.

Rotation

An object moving on a circular path has momentum (a measurement of an object's mass and velocity in a direction); for circular motion, it is called **angular momentum**, and this value is determined by rotational inertia, rotational velocity, and the distance of the mass from the axis of rotation, or the center of rotation.

If objects are exhibiting circular motion, they are demonstrating the conservation of angular momentum. The angular momentum of a system is always constant, regardless of the placement of the mass. As stated above, the rotational inertia of an object can be affected by how far the mass of the object is placed with respect to the center of rotation (axis of rotation). A larger distance between the mass and the center of rotation means a slower rotational velocity. Reversely, if a mass is closer to the center of rotation, the rotational velocity increases. A change in the placement of the mass affects the value of the rotational velocity, thus conserving the angular momentum. This is true as long as no external forces act upon the system.

For example, if an ice skater is spinning on one ice skate and extends their arms out (or increases the distance between the mass and the center of rotation), a slower rotational velocity is created. When the skater brings their arms in close to their body (or lessens the distance between the mass and the center of rotation), their rotational velocity increases, and they spin much faster. Some skaters extend their arms straight up above their head, which causes the axis of rotation to extend, thus removing any distance between the mass and the center of rotation and maximizing the rotational velocity.

For example, if a person is selecting a horse on a merry-go-round, the placement of their selection can affect their ride experience. All the horses are traveling with the same rotational speed, but to travel along the same plane as the merry-go-round, a horse closer to the outside will have a greater linear speed due to being farther away from the axis of rotation. Another way to think of this is that an outside horse must cover more distance than a horse near the inside to keep up with the rotational speed of the merry-go-round platform. Based on this information, thrill seekers should always select an outer horse to experience a greater linear speed.

Uniform Circular Motion

When an object exhibits circular motion, its motion is centered around an axis. An axis is an invisible line on which an object can rotate. This type of motion is most easily observed on a toy top. There is actually a point (or rod) through the center of the top on which the top can be observed to be spinning. This is called the **axis**. An axis is the location about which the mass of an object or system would rotate if free to spin.

In the instance of utilizing a lever to lift an object, it can be helpful to calculate the amount of force needed at a specific distance, applied perpendicular to the axis of motion, to calculate the torque, or circular force, necessary to move something. This is also employed when using a wrench to loosen a bolt. The equation for calculating the force in a circular direction, or perpendicular to an axis, is as follows:

$$Torque = F_\perp \times distance\ of\ lever\ arm\ from\ the\ axis\ of\ rotation$$

$$\tau = F_\perp \times d$$

For example, what torque would result from a 20 N force being applied to a lever 5 meters from its axis of rotation?

$$\tau = 20\ N \times 5\ m$$

$$\tau = 100\ N \times m$$

The amount of torque would be 100 N×m. The units would be Newton meters because it is a force applied at a distance away from the axis of rotation.

When objects move in a circle by spinning on their own axis, or because they are tethered around a central point (also considered an axis), they exhibit circular motion. Circular motion is similar in many ways to linear (straight line) motion; however, there are some additional facts to note. When an object spins or rotates on or around an axis, a force that feels like it is pushing out from the center of the circle is created. The force is actually pulling into the center of the circle. A reactionary force is what is creating the feeling of pushing out. The inward force is the real force, and this is called **centripetal force.** The outward, or reactionary, force is called **centrifugal force.** The reactionary force is not the real force; it just feels like it is there. This can also be referred to as a **fictional force.** The true force is the one pulling inward, or the centripetal force. The terms **centripetal** and **centrifugal** are often mistakenly interchanged.

For example, the method a traditional-style washing machine uses to spin a load of clothes to expunge the water from the load is to spin the machine barrel in a circle at a high rate of speed. During this spinning, the centripetal force is pulling in toward the center of the circle. At the same time, the reactionary force to the centripetal force is pressing the clothes up against the outer sides of the barrel, which expels the water out of the small holes that line the outer wall of the barrel.

Linear Momentum and Impulse
The motion of an object can be expressed as momentum. This is a calculation of an object's mass times its velocity. Momentum can be described as the amount an object will continue moving along its current course. Momentum in a straight line is called **linear momentum**. Just as energy can be transferred and conserved, so can momentum.

Momentum is denoted by the letter p and calculated by multiplying an object's mass by its velocity.

$$p = m \times v$$

For example, if a car and a truck are moving at the same velocity (25 meters per second) down a highway, they will not have the same momentum because they do not have the same mass. The mass of the truck (3500 kg) is greater than that of the car (1000 kg); therefore, the truck will have more momentum. In a head-on collision, the truck's momentum is greater than the car's, and the truck will cause more damage to the car than the car would to the truck. The equations to compare the momentum of the car and the truck are as follows:

$p_{truck} = mass_{truck} \times velocity_{truck}$ $p_{car} = mass_{car} \times velocity_{car}$

$p_{truck} = 3500 \ kg \ \times 25 \ m/s$ $p_{car} = 1000 \ kg \ \times 25 \ m/s$

$p_{truck} = 87,500 \ N$ $p_{car} = 25,000 \ N$

The momentum of the truck is greater than that of the car.

The amount of force during a length of time creates an impulse. This means if a force acts on an object during a given amount of time, it will have a determined impulse. However, if the length of time can be extended, the force will be less due to the conservation of momentum.

For a car crash, the total momentum of each car before the collision would need to equal the total momentum of the cars after the collision. There are two main types of collisions: elastic and inelastic. For the example with a car crash, in an elastic collision, the cars would be separate before the collision, and they would remain separated after the collision. In the case of an inelastic collision, the cars would be separate before the collision, but they would be stuck together after the collision. The only difference would be in the way the momentum is calculated.

For elastic collisions:

$$total\ momentum_{before} = total\ momentum_{after}$$

$$(mass_{car\ 1} \times velocity_{car\ 1}) + (mass_{car\ 2} \times velocity_{car\ 2})$$
$$= (mass_{car\ 1} + mass_{car\ 2}) \times velocity_{car\ 1\ \&\ car\ 2}$$

The damage from an impact can be lessened by extending the time of the actual impact. This is called the **measure of the impulse of a collision.** It can be calculated by multiplying the change in momentum by the amount of time involved in the impact.

$$I = change\ in\ momentum\ \times time$$

$$I = \Delta p \times time$$

If the time is extended, the force (or change in momentum) is decreased. Reversely, if the time is shortened, the force (or change in momentum) is increased. For example, when catching a fast baseball, it helps soften the blow of the ball to follow through or cradle the catch. This technique is simply extending the time of the application of the force of the ball so the impact of the ball does not hurt the hand.

For example, if a martial arts expert wants to break a board by executing a chop from their hand, they need to exert a force on a small point on the board, extremely quickly. If they slow down the time of the impact from the force of their hand, they will injure their hand and not break the board.

Often, law enforcement officials will use rubber bullets instead of regular bullets to apprehend a criminal. The benefit of the rubber bullet is that the elastic material of the bullet bounces off the target but hits the target with the same momentum as a regular bullet. Since the amount of time the rubber bullet is in contact with the target is decreased, the amount of force from the bullet is increased. This method can knock a subject off their feet by the large force and the short time of the impact without causing any lasting harm to the individual. The difference in the types of collisions is noted through the rubber bullet bouncing off the individual, so both the bullet and the subject are separate before the collision and separate after the collision. With a regular bullet, the bullet and subject are separate before the collision, but a regular bullet in many cases would not be separated by the subject after the collision.

Universal Gravitation
Every object in the universe that has mass causes an attractive force to every other object in the universe. The amount of attractive force depends on the masses of the two objects in question and the distance that separates the objects. This is called the **law of universal gravitation** and is represented by the following equation:

$$F = G\frac{m_1 m_2}{r^2}$$

In this equation, the force between two objects, m_1 and m_2, is indirectly proportional to the square of the distance separating the two objects. A general gravitational constant G ($6.67 \times 10^{-11}\ \frac{N \cdot m^2}{kg^2}$) is multiplied by the equation. This constant is quite small, but for the force between two objects to be noticeable, they must have sizable masses.

To better understand this on a large scale, a prime representation could be viewed by satellites (planets) in the solar system and the effect they have on each other. All bodies in the universe have an attractive force between them. This is closely seen by the relationship between the earth and the moon. The earth and the moon both have a gravitational attraction that affects each other. The moon is smaller in mass than the earth and therefore will not have as big of an influence as the earth does on the moon. The attractive force from the moon is observed by the systematic push and pull on the water on the face of the earth by the rotations the moon makes around the earth. The tides in oceans and lakes are caused by the moon's gravitational effect on the earth. Since the moon and the earth have an attractive force between them, the moon pulls on the side of the earth closest to the moon, causing the waters to swell (high tide) on that side and leave the ends 90 degrees away from the moon, causing a low tide there. The water on the side of the earth farthest from the moon experiences the least amount of gravitational attraction and also collects on that side in a high tide.

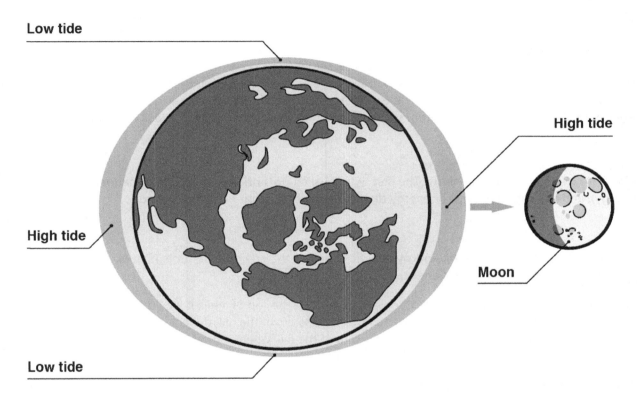

The universal law of gravitation is taken primarily from the works of Johannes Kepler and his laws of planetary motion. These include the fact that the paths of the orbits of the planets are not perfect circles, but ellipses, around the sun. The area swept out between the planet and the sun is equal at every point in the orbit due to fluctuation in speed at different distances. Finally, the period (T) of a planet's motion squared is inversely proportional to the distance (r) between that planet and the sun cubed.

$$\frac{T^2}{r^3}$$

Isaac Newton used this third law and applied it to the idea of forces and their effects on objects. The effect of the gravitational forces of the moon on the earth are noted in the tides, and the effect of the forces of the earth on the moon are noted in the fact that the moon is caught in an orbit around the earth. Since the moon is traveling at a velocity tangent to its orbit around the earth and the earth keeps attracting it in, the moon does not escape and does not crash into the earth. The moon will continue this course due to the attractive gravitational force between the earth and the moon. Albert Einstein later applied Newton's adaptation of Kepler's laws. Einstein was able to develop a more advanced theory, which could explain the motions of all the planets and even be applied beyond the solar system. These theories have also been beneficial for predicting behaviors of other objects in the earth's atmosphere, such as shuttles and astronauts.

Energy

Energy refers to definable units of power formed from mechanical, chemical, thermal, nuclear, sonic, or other resources that can be converted to create power. **Mechanical energy** refers to power that comes from movement, such as a light wave. **Chemical energy** refers to power found within chemicals, usually within bonds between the atoms that make up the chemical. Typically, bonds must be broken for a chemical reaction to occur and energy to be released, such as when wood is ignited to create a fire. Most fossil fuel consumption is an example of chemical energy. **Thermal energy** represents power that comes from heat or changes in temperature. For example, someone who warms his or her cold hands on a cup of hot tea is experiencing a thermal energy exchange; the hot cup is radiating heat, and the cold hands are absorbing the heat. **Nuclear energy** results from the fission or fusion of the nuclei in atoms. **Sonic energy** refers to power produced from sound waves, such as when sound vibrations have the ability to shatter a piece of glass.

Kinetic Energy and Potential Energy
There are two main types of energy. The first type is called **potential energy** (or gravitational potential energy), and it is stored energy, or energy due to an object's height from the ground.

The second type is called **kinetic energy**. Kinetic energy is the energy of motion. If an object is moving, it will have some amount of kinetic energy.

For example, if a roller-coaster car is sitting on the track at the top of a hill, it would have all potential energy and no kinetic energy. As the roller coaster travels down the hill, the energy converts from potential energy into kinetic energy. At the bottom of the hill, where the car is traveling the fastest, it would have all kinetic energy and no potential energy.

Another measure of energy is the **total mechanical energy** in a system. This is the sum (or total) of the potential energy plus the kinetic energy of the system. The total mechanical energy in a system is always conserved. The amounts of the potential energy and kinetic energy in a system can vary, but the total mechanical energy in a situation would remain the same.

The equation for the mechanical energy in a system is as follows:

$$ME = PE + KE$$

$$(Mechanical\ Energy\ =\ Potential\ Energy\ +\ Kinetic\ Energy)$$

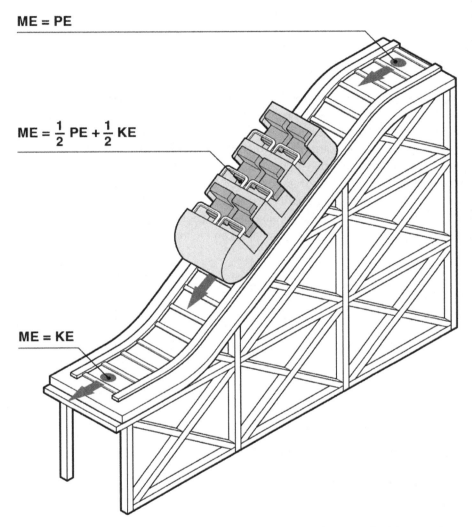

ME = PE

$$ME = \frac{1}{2}\ PE + \frac{1}{2}\ KE$$

ME = KE

Energy can transfer or change forms, but it cannot be created or destroyed. This transfer can take place through waves (including light waves and sound waves), heat, impact, etc.

There is a fundamental law of thermodynamics (the study of heat and movement) called **conservation of energy.** This law states that energy cannot be created or destroyed, but rather energy is transferred to different forms involved in a process. For example, a car pushed beginning at one end of a street will not continue down that street forever; it will gradually come to a stop some distance away from where it was originally pushed. This does not mean the energy has disappeared or has been exhausted; it means the energy has been transferred to different mediums surrounding the car. Some of the energy is dissipated by the frictional force from the road on the tires, the air resistance from the movement of the car, the sound from the tires on the road, and the force of gravity pulling on the car. Each value can be calculated in a number of ways, including measuring the sound waves from the tires, the temperature change in the tires, the distance moved by the car from start to finish, etc. It is important to understand that many processes factor into such a small situation, but all situations follow the conservation of energy.

Just like the earlier example, the roller coaster at the top of a hill has a measurable amount of potential energy; when it rolls down the hill, it converts most of that energy into kinetic energy. There are still additional factors such as friction and air resistance working on the coaster and dissipating some of the energy, but energy transfers in every situation.

Simple Machines

Simple machines refer to basic mechanisms that are able to change the direction or magnitude of an applied force, often to make a process less burdensome. There are six types of simple machines: inclined planes, pulleys, levers, wedges, wheel and axles, and screws. An **inclined plane** refers to any ramp that removes the physical work of lifting a load. A **pulley** consists of one or more wheels and a rope to which a load can be attached; the **wheel** is then spun in order to move the rope and the attached load. A **lever** moves a load around a **fulcrum**, the point upon which the lever rests and moves. A **wedge** can be made out of numerous materials, but it must be thick on one end and thin on the other. A wedge can be used between two different objects to separate them or forced between a single object to separate it. **Wheel and axle** machines are made of a wheel attached to a rotational force (axle); both rotate in order to transfer force between them to move a load. Finally, **screws** move in a circular fashion to move something from the bottom of the screw toward the top (similar to an inclined plane). They can also hold objects together.

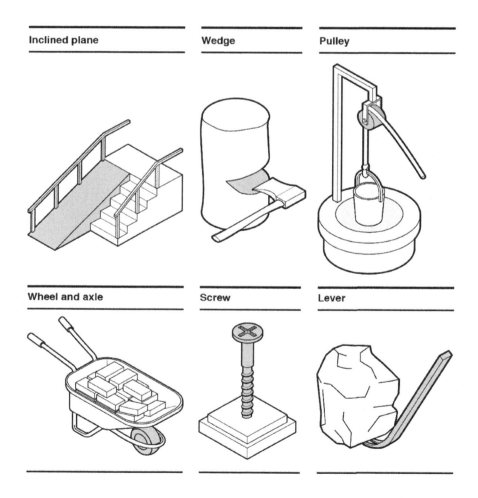

Inclined plane   Wedge   Pulley

Wheel and axle   Screw   Lever

The six simple machines utilize the transfer of energy to the advantage of the user. These machines function based on an amount of energy input from the user and accomplish a task by distributing the energy for a common purpose.

The use of simple machines can help by requiring less force to perform a task with the same result. This is referred to as a **mechanical advantage.**

For example, if a person is trying to lift a child into the air with their arms to pick an apple from a tree, it would require less force to place the child on one end of a teeter totter and push the other end of the teeter totter down to elevate the child to the same height to pick the apple. In this example, the teeter totter is a lever.

Interactions of Energy and Matter

Energy can exist in many different forms, which include heat, sound, light, and electricity. Energy can travel in different mediums in order to transfer among objects or environments, through mechanical waves. When molecules move, they can increase the temperature or pressure in an area, thus causing an increase in heat. When waves move through air and matter, they can cause vibrations that result in sound. When charge moves across a potential difference, it causes electricity. When electromagnetic waves travel, they do not need a medium and can travel in a vacuum. Light can travel as an electromagnetic wave and transfer energy. Another form of energy comes from magnets. Due to the alignment of electrons in an object (primarily metals), objects can have fields present around them. Fields around magnets can induce a current, thus causing an energy transformation.

Waves and Sound
Mechanical waves are a type of wave that pass through a medium (solid, liquid, or gas). There are two basic types of mechanical waves: longitudinal and transverse.

A **longitudinal wave** has motion that is parallel to the direction of the wave's travel. It can best be shown by compressing one side of a tethered spring and then releasing that end. The movement travels in a bunching and then unbunching motion, across the length of the spring and back until the energy is dissipated through noise and heat.

A **transverse wave** has motion that is perpendicular to the direction of the wave's travel. The particles on a transverse wave do not move across the length of the wave but oscillate up and down to create the peaks and troughs observed on this type of wave.

A wave with a mix of both longitudinal and transverse motion can be seen through the motion of a wave on the ocean, with peaks and troughs, oscillating particles up and down.

Mechanical waves can carry energy, sound, and light. Mechanical waves need a medium through which transport can take place. However, an electromagnetic wave can transmit energy without a medium, or in a vacuum.

Sound travels in waves and is the movement of vibrations through a medium. It can travel through air (gas), land, water, etc. For example, the noise a human hears in the air is the vibration of the waves as they reach the ear. The human brain translates the different frequencies (pitches) and intensities of the vibrations to determine what created the noise.

A tuning fork has a predetermined frequency because of the size (length and thickness) of its tines. When struck, it allows vibrations between the two tines to move the air at a specific rate. This creates a specific tone (or note) for that size of tuning fork. The number of vibrations over time is also steady for that tuning fork and can be matched with a frequency (the number of occurrences over time). All sounds heard by the human ear are categorized by using frequency and measured in hertz (the number of cycles per second).

The intensity (or loudness) of sound is measured on the **Bel scale**. This scale is a ratio of one sound's intensity with respect to a standard value. It is a logarithmic scale, meaning it is measured by factors of ten. But the value that is 1/10 of this value, the decibel, is the measurement used more commonly for pitches heard by the human ear.

The Doppler effect applies to situations with both light and sound waves. The premise of the Doppler effect is that, based on the relative position or movement of a source and an observer, waves can seem shorter or longer than they are. When the Doppler effect is experienced with sound, it warps the noise being heard by the observer by making the pitch or frequency seem shorter or higher as the source is approaching and then longer or lower as the source is getting farther away. The frequency and pitch of the source never actually change, but the sound in respect to the observer's position makes it seem like the sound has changed. This effect can be observed when an emergency siren passes by an observer on the road. The siren sounds much higher in pitch as it approaches the observer and then lower after it passes and is getting farther away.

The Doppler effect also applies to situations involving light waves. An observer in space would see light approaching as being shorter wavelengths than it was, causing it to seem blue. When the light wave is getting farther away, the light would seem red due to the apparent elongation of the wavelength. This is called the red-blue shift.

A recent addition to the study of waves is the gravitational wave. Its existence has been proven and verified, yet the details surrounding its capabilities are still under inquiry. Further understanding of gravitational waves could help scientists understand the beginnings of the universe and how the existence of the solar system is possible. This understanding could also include the future exploration of the universe.

Light
The movement of light is described like the movement of waves. Light travels with a wave front and has an **amplitude** (a height measured from the neutral), a cycle or wavelength, a period, and energy. Light travels at approximately 3.00×10^8 m/s and is faster than anything created by humans.

Light is referred to by its measured **wavelengths**, or the length for it to complete one cycle. Types of light with the longest wavelengths include radio, TV, micro, and infrared waves. The next set of wavelengths are detectable by the human eye and make up the visible spectrum. The visible spectrum has wavelengths of 10^{-7} m, and the colors seen are red, orange, yellow, green, blue, indigo, and violet. Beyond the visible spectrum are even shorter wavelengths (also called the **electromagnetic spectrum**) containing ultraviolet light, x-rays, and gamma rays. The wavelengths outside of the visible light range can be harmful to humans if they are directly exposed, especially for long periods of time.

When a wave crosses a boundary or travels from one medium to another, certain actions take place. If the wave travels through one medium into another, it experiences refraction. This is the bending of the wave from one medium's density to another, altering the speed of the wave.

For example, a side view of a pencil in half a glass of water appears as though it is bent at the water level. What the viewer is seeing is the **refraction** of light waves traveling from the air into the water. Since the wave speed is slowed in water, the change makes the pencil appear bent.

When a wave hits a medium that it cannot pass through, it is bounced back in an action called **reflection**. For example, when light waves hit a mirror, they are reflected, or bounced off, the back of the mirror. This can cause it to seem like there is more light in the room due to the doubling back of the initial wave. This is also how people can see their reflection in a mirror.

When a wave travels through a slit or around an obstacle, this is known as **diffraction.** A light wave will bend around an obstacle or through a slit and cause a diffraction pattern. When the waves bend around an obstacle, it causes the addition of waves and the spreading of light on the other side of the opening.

Optics
The dispersion of light describes the splitting of a single wave by refracting its components into separate parts. For example, if a wave of white light is sent through a dispersion prism, the light wave appears as its separate rainbow-colored components due to each colored wavelength being refracted in the prism.

When wavelengths of light hit boundaries, different things occur. Objects can absorb certain wavelengths of light and reflect others, depending on the boundaries. This becomes important when an object appears to be a certain color. The color of the object is not actually within the makeup of that object, but by what wavelengths are being transmitted by that object. For example, if a table appears to be red, that means the table is absorbing all wavelengths of visible light except those of the red wavelength. The table is reflecting, or transmitting, the wavelengths associated with red back to the human eye and therefore appears red.

Interference describes when an object affects the path of a wave or another wave interacts with that wave. Waves interacting with each other can result in either constructive interference or destructive interference based on their positions. For constructive interference, the waves are in sync and combine to reinforce each other. In the case of deconstructive interference, the waves are out of sync and reduce the effect of each other to some degree. In scattering, the boundary can change the direction or energy of a wave, thus altering the entire wave. Polarization changes the oscillations of a wave and can alter its appearance in light waves. For example, polarized sunglasses take away the "glare" from sunlight by altering the oscillation pattern observed by the wearer.

When a wave hits a boundary and is completely reflected back or cannot escape from one medium to another, it is called **total internal reflection**. This effect can be seen in a diamond with a brilliant cut. The angle cut on the sides of the diamond causes the light hitting the diamond to be completely reflected back inside the gem and makes it appear brighter and more colorful than a diamond with different angles cut into its surface.

When reflecting light, a mirror can be used to observe a virtual (not real) image. A plane mirror is a piece of glass with a coating in the background to create a reflective surface. An image is what the human eye sees when light is reflected off the mirror in an unmagnified manner. If a curved mirror is used for reflection, the image seen will not be a true reflection, but will either be magnified or made to appear smaller than its actual size. Curved mirrors can also make an object appear closer or farther away than its actual distance from the mirror.

Lenses can be used to refract or bend light to form images. Examples of lenses are the human eye, microscopes, and telescopes. The human eye interprets the refraction of light into images that humans understand to be actual size. When objects are too small to be observed by the unaided human eye, microscopes allow the objects to be enlarged enough to be seen. Telescopes allow objects that are too far away to be seen by the unaided eye to be viewed. Prisms are pieces of glass that can have a wavelength of light enter one side and appear to be broken down into its component wavelengths on the other side, due to the slowing of certain wavelengths within the prism, more than other wavelengths.

Atomic Structure

The Bohr model of the atom is the one most commonly used in science today. It was proposed by physicist Niels Bohr and caused some controversy with its configuration of the electrons and their location within the atom. The Bohr model of the atom consists of the nucleus, or core, which is made up of positively charged protons and neutrally charged neutrons. The neutrons are theorized to be in the nucleus with the protons. This pairing of protons and neutrons provides a "balance" at the center of the atom. The nucleus of the atom consists of more than 99 percent of the mass of an atom. Surrounding the nucleus are orbitals containing negatively charged electrons. The entire structure of an atom is too small to be seen with the unaided eye and has contributed to the differing ideas about its structure. Most research has been focused around recording the reactions of the atom or the energy emitted from the electrons to test any theories about its structure.

Bohr's Model

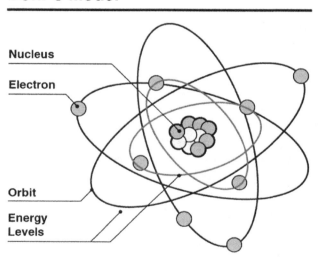

Each atom has an atomic number that is assigned by the number of protons within the atom's nucleus. If a substance is made up of atoms that all have the same atomic number, it is called an **element.** Elements are organized by their atomic number and grouped by similar properties in a chart called the **Periodic Table.**

Adding the total number of protons to the total number of neutrons in an atom provides the mass number. Most nuclei of atoms are electronically neutral, and all atoms of one type have the same atomic number. However, there are some atoms of the same type that have a different mass number. This variation is due to an imbalance of neutrons. These atoms are called **isotopes.** For isotopes, the atomic number (determined by the number of protons) is the same, but the mass number (determined by adding the protons and neutrons) is different. This is a result of there being a different number of neutrons.

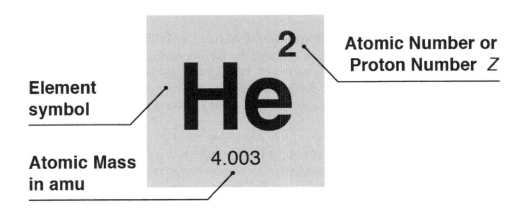

The Periodic Table arranges elements by atomic number, similar characteristics, and electron configurations in a tabular format. The vertical lines are called **columns** and are sorted by similar chemical properties/characteristics, such as appearance and reactivity. This is seen in the shiny texture of metals, the softness of post-transition metals, and the high melting points of alkali earth metals. The horizontal lines are called **rows** and are arranged by electron valance configurations. The columns are referred to as **groups**, and the rows are **periods.**

The Nature of Electricity
Electrostatics is the study of electric charges at rest. A balanced atom has a neutral charge from its number of electrons and protons. If the charge from its electrons is greater than or less than the charge of its protons, the atom has a charge. If the atom has a greater charge from the number of electrons than protons, it has a negative charge. If the atom has a lesser charge from the number of electrons than protons, it has a positive charge. Opposite charges attract each other, while like charges repel each other, so a negative attracts a positive, and a negative repels a negative. Similarly, a positive repels a positive. Just as energy cannot be created or destroyed, neither can charge; charge can only be transferred. The transfer of charge can occur through touch, or the transfer of electrons. Once electrons have transferred from one object to another, the charge has then transferred.

For example, if a person wears socks and scuffs their feet across a carpeted floor, they are transferring electrons to the carpeting through the friction from their feet. Additionally, if that person then touches a light switch, they will receive a small shock. This "shock" is the person feeling the electrons transferring from the switch to their hand. Since the person lost electrons to the carpet, giving them a positive charge, the electrons from the light switch are attracted to the person for the transfer. The shock felt is the electrons moving from the switch to the person's finger.

Another method of charging an object is through induction. **Induction** occurs when a charged object is brought near two touching stationary objects. The electrons in the objects will attract and cluster near another positively charged object and repel away from a negatively charged object held nearby. The stationary objects will redistribute their electrons to allow the charges to reposition themselves closer or farther away. This redistribution will cause one of the touching stationary objects to be negatively charged and the other to be positively charged. The overall charges contained in the stationary objects remain the same but are repositioned between the two objects.

Another way to charge an object is through polarization. Polarization can occur simply by the reconfiguration of the electrons within a single object.

For example, if a person rubs a balloon on their hair, the balloon could then cling to a wall if it were brought close enough. This would be because rubbing the balloon causes it to become negatively charged. When the balloon is held against a neutrally charged wall, the negatively charged balloon repels all the wall's electrons, causing a positively charged surface on the wall. This type of charge is temporary, due to the massive size of the wall, and the charges will quickly redistribute.

An electric current is produced when electrons carry charge across a length. To make electrons move so they can carry this charge, a change in voltage must be present. On a small scale, this is demonstrated through the electrons traveling from the light switch to a person's finger in the example where the person had run their socks on a carpet. The difference between the charge in the switch and the charge in the finger causes the electrons to move. On a larger and more sustained scale, this movement would need to be more controlled. This can be achieved through batteries/cells and generators. Batteries or cells have a chemical reaction that takes place inside, causing energy to be released and charges to move freely. Generators convert mechanical energy into electric energy for use after the reaction.

For example, if a wire runs touching the end of a battery to the end of a lightbulb, and then another wire runs touching the base of the lightbulb to the opposite end of the original battery, the lightbulb will light up. This is due to a complete circuit being formed with the battery and the electrons being carried across the voltage drop (the two ends of the battery). The appearance of the light from the bulb is the visible presence of the electrons in the filament of the bulb.

Electric energy can be derived from a number of sources, including coal, wind, sun, and nuclear reactions. Electricity has numerous applications, including being transferable into light, sound, heat, or magnetic forces.

Magnetism and Electricity

Magnetic forces occur naturally in specific types of materials and can be imparted to other types of materials. If two straight iron rods are observed, they will naturally have a negative end (pole) and a positive end (pole). These charged poles follow the rules of any charged item: opposite charges attract, and like charges repel. When set up positive to negative, they will attract each other, but if one rod is turned around, the two rods will repel each other due to the alignment of negative to negative poles and positive to positive poles. When poles are identified, magnetic fields are observed between them. If small iron filings (a material with natural magnetic properties) are sprinkled over a sheet of paper resting on top of a bar magnet, the field lines from the poles can be seen in the alignment of the iron filings, as pictured below.

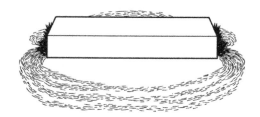

These fields naturally occur in materials with magnetic properties. There is a distinct pole at each end of such a material. If materials are not shaped with definitive ends, the fields will still be observed through the alignment of poles in the material. For example, a circular magnet does not have ends but still has a magnetic field associated with its shape, as pictured below.

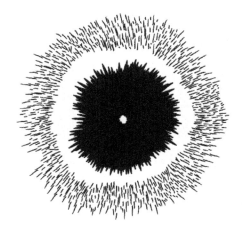

Magnetic forces can also be generated and amplified by using an electric current. For example, if an electric current is sent through a length of wire, it creates an electromagnetic field around the wire from the charge of the current. This force is from the moving of negatively charged electrons from one end of the wire to the other. This is maintained as long as the flow of electricity is sustained. The magnetic field can also be used to attract and repel other items with magnetic properties. A smaller or larger magnetic force can be generated around this wire, depending on the strength of the current in the wire. As soon as the current is stopped, the magnetic force also stops.

Magnetic energy can be harnessed, or manipulated, from natural sources or from a generated source (a wire carrying electric current). When a core with magnetic properties (such as iron) has a wire wrapped around it in circular coils, it can be used to create a strong, non-permanent electromagnet. If current is run through the wrapped wire, it generates a magnetic field by polarizing the ends of the metal core, as described above, by moving the negative charge from one end to the other. If the direction of the current is reversed, so is the direction of the magnetic field due to the poles of the core being reversed. The term **non-permanent** refers to the fact that the magnetic field is generated only when the current is present, but not when the current is stopped. The following is a picture of a small electromagnet made from an iron nail, a wire, and a battery.

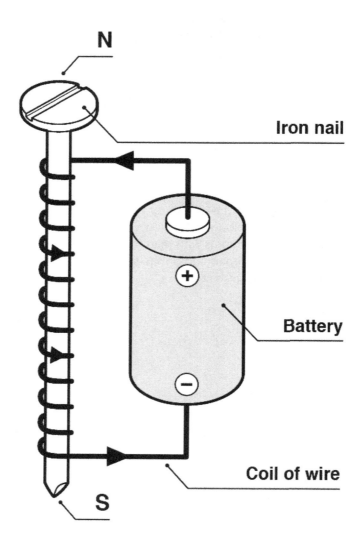

This type of electromagnetic field can be generated on a larger scale using more sizable components. This type of device is useful in the way it can be controlled. Rather than having to attempt to block a permanent magnetic field, the current to the system can simply be stopped, thus stopping the magnetic field. This provides the basis for many computer-related instruments and magnetic resonance imaging (MRI) technology. Magnetic forces are used in many modern applications, including the creation of super-speed transportation. Super magnets are used in rail systems and supply a cleaner form of energy than coal or gasoline. Another example of the use of super-magnets is seen in medical equipment, specifically MRI. These machines are highly sophisticated and useful in imaging the internal workings of the human body. For super-magnets to be useful, they often must be cooled down to extremely low temperatures to dissipate the amount of heat generated from their extended usage. This can be done by flooding the magnet with a super-cooled gas such as helium or liquid nitrogen. Much research is continuously done in this field to find new ceramic–metallic hybrid materials that have structures that can maintain their charge and temperature within specific guidelines for extended use.

Practice Questions

1. How do neuroglia support neurons?
   a. Provide nutrition to them
   b. Provide a framework around them and protect them from the surrounding environment
   c. Relay messages to them from the brain
   d. Connect them to other surrounding cells

2. Which nerve system allows the brain to regulate body functions such as heart rate and blood pressure?
   a. Central
   b. Somatic
   c. Autonomic
   d. Afferent

3. Which of the following organs is NOT considered an accessory organ of the male reproductive system?
   a. Testes
   b. Prostate
   c. Vas deferens
   d. Bulbourethral glands

4. How many gametes do the ovaries produce every month?
   a. One million
   b. One
   c. One-half billion
   d. Two

5. In what part of the female reproductive system do sperm fertilize an oocyte?
   a. Ovary
   b. Mammary gland
   c. Vagina
   d. Fallopian tubes

6. Which is a distinct characteristic of tissues and glands that are a part of the endocrine system?
   a. Lack a blood supply
   b. Act quickly in response to stimuli
   c. Secrete bile
   d. Ductless

7. Which endocrine gland is found at the bottom of the hypothalamus?
   a. Pituitary
   b. Thymus
   c. Thyroid
   d. Pancreas

8. Which endocrine gland regulates the blood sugar levels of the body?
   a. Pineal
   b. Parathyroid
   c. Pancreas
   d. Adrenal

9. Which molecule is the simplest form of sugar?
   a. Monosaccharide
   b. Fatty acid
   c. Polysaccharide
   d. Amino acid

10. Which type of macromolecule contains genetic information that can be passed to subsequent generations?
    a. Carbohydrates
    b. Lipids
    c. Proteins
    d. Nucleic acids

11. What is the primary unit of inheritance between generations of an organism?
    a. Chromosome
    b. Gene
    c. Gamete
    d. Atom

12. Which one of Mendel's laws theorizes that the alleles for different traits are NOT linked and can be inherited independently of one another?
    a. The Law of Dominance
    b. The Law of Segregation
    c. The Law of Independent Assortment
    d. None of the above

13. In which situation is an atom considered neutral?
    a. The number of protons and neutrons are equal.
    b. The number of neutrons and electrons are equal.
    c. The number of protons and electrons are equal.
    d. There are more electrons than protons.

14. Which is an example of a physical property of substances?
    a. Odor
    b. Reactivity
    c. Flammability
    d. Toxicity

15. Which type of matter has molecules that cannot move within its substance and breaks evenly across a plane caused by the symmetry of its molecular arrangement?
    a. Gas
    b. Crystalline solid
    c. Liquid
    d. Amorphous solid

16. What type of reactions involve the breaking and re-forming of bonds between atoms?
    a. Chemical
    b. Physical
    c. Isotonic
    d. Electron

17. What is the instrument used for measuring the force exerted by different elements in the universe that cause movement when they act upon objects by pulling, pushing, rotating, deforming, or accelerating them?

    a. Isaac force

    b. Newton meter

    c. Micrometer Caliper

    d. Vernier Scale

18. Which of the following describes an invention used to measure small fractions within already small divisions?

    a. A tape measure

    b. A ruler

    c. A yardstick

    d. Vernier Scale

19. When are scientific experiments found reliable?

    a. When all the materials needed for the experiment are used

    b. When the scientists conducting them are credible

    c. When they prove the hypothesis to be true

    d. When they can be replicated

20. Which of the following scenarios describes mistaking correlation for causation?

    a. In the same year, the drinking water was contaminated by a nearby chicken farm, and stomach cancer in the area increased 3 percent. The contaminated water obviously caused stomach cancer to increase.

    b. Victoria notices that every time she turns on the stove burner underneath a pot with water in it, the water boils. Victoria realizes that putting heat under water causes it to boil.

    c. We saw that the thunderstorm that day caused all the neighborhoods in the East Village to flood. We could hardly get to the movie that night because of all the rain!

    d. Hector learned in school that when tectonic plates shift, it causes earthquakes to happen. There had been many earthquakes when Hector lived in California, and now he knew that the shifting of plates is what caused them.

21. Harley's sister, Camille, is pushing her on the swing. Camille notices that every time she pushes Camille forward, the swing propels back just as far. This is an example of which of the following of laws?

    a. Law of Inertia

    b. Newton's Second Law

    c. Newton's Third Law

    d. Law of Segregation

22. In the model of the scientific method, which of the following best explains the step of formulating a hypothesis?

    a. Forming a question that relates to the observation.

    b. Writing out an expectation of what's going to happen.

    c. Gathering the materials needed for the procedure.

    d. Summarizing the results of the experiment.

23. When would a peer review be conducted in an experiment?
    a. Before the experiment.
    b. During the experiment.
    c. After the experiment is over and before it is published.
    d. After the experiment is over and published.

24. Which layer of the Earth is 760 miles wide and comprised primarily of nickel and iron?
    a. The crust
    b. The atmosphere
    c. The mantle
    d. The inner core

25. Earthquakes and the formation of mountain ranges are two natural events influenced directly by which of the following geological processes?
    a. Underground sulfur springs
    b. Lunar cycles
    c. Plate tectonics
    d. Atmospheric pressure shifts

26. The interaction between the Earth's atmosphere and the Earth's hydrosphere creates which of the following cycles?
    a. The carbon cycle
    b. The water cycle
    c. The Krebs cycle
    d. The life cycle

27. Which of the following terms refers to all living organisms on Earth, regardless of species?
    a. Biosphere
    b. Geosphere
    c. Biodome
    d. Binomial nomenclature

28. Scientists believe there may be up to how many distinct species on Earth?
    a. 100 million
    b. 500 million
    c. 1 billion
    d. 5 billion

29. Gases, cosmic debris, solar systems, and black holes can all be found in which of the following cosmic entities?
    a. Galaxies
    b. Nebulas
    c. Dark matter
    d. Constellations

30. Which two elements play a key role in the physical formation of stars?
    a. Nickel and iron
    b. Helium and hydrogen
    c. Nitrogen and carbon
    d. Copper and carbon

31. Which planets in the solar system have no moons?
    a. Pluto and Neptune
    b. Jupiter and Saturn
    c. Mercury and Venus
    d. Mercury and Mars

32. Which aspect of the Earth is scientifically proven to be strongly influenced by its moon?
    a. The high and low tides of the oceans
    b. The onset of labor in pregnant female mammals
    c. Daily predictions of personal events
    d. Seismic activity

33. Which area of the Earth experiences nearly the same temperature year-round, without the distinction of four seasons?
    a. The North pole
    b. The South pole
    c. The Equator
    d. The International Date Line

34. In recent decades, which of the following have contributed to an unprecedented increase in carbon dioxide levels in the Earth's atmosphere?
    a. Fossil fuel consumption
    b. Concentrated animal feeding operations
    c. Deforestation
    d. All of the above

35. Which event takes place when the moon's orbit causes it to cross between the Sun and the Earth?
    a. High tide
    b. Solar eclipse
    c. Lunar eclipse
    d. The end of the calendar year

36. Which of the following is NOT part of the Earth's hydrosphere?
    a. Oceans
    b. Water vapor in the atmosphere
    c. Whales
    d. The Antarctic ice sheet

37. What is the primary difference between the Earth's inner core and outer core?
    a. The inner core is made of nickel, while the outer core is made of iron
    b. The inner core is solid, while the outer core is molten
    c. The inner core is inaccessible to people, while the outer core is accessible to people
    d. The inner core is hot, while the outer core is cool

38. Which of the following simple machines utilizes a fixed fulcrum to move a load?
    a. Wheel and axle
    b. Lever
    c. Pulley
    d. Inclined plane

39. The separation of a single radioactive element to create a powerful force is known as what type of process?
    a. Nuclear fission
    b. Nuclear meltdown
    c. Thermodynamics
    d. Proton pump inhibitor

40. Combining two or more atoms of a single radioactive element to create a powerful force is known as what type of process?
    a. Nuclear fission
    b. Nuclear meltdown
    c. Nuclear fusion
    d. Nuclear dynamic

41. A dinner plate that rests inside a kitchen cabinet is an example of which type of energy?
    a. Kinetic energy
    b. Potential energy
    c. Mechanical energy
    d. Magnetic energy

42. What defines a covalent bond?
    a. The sharing of electron pairs between non-metal atoms
    b. The repelling of electron pairs between non-metal atoms
    c. The sharing of electron pairs between metal atoms
    d. The repelling of electron pairs between metal atoms

43. Which of the following events indicates that a chemical reaction has occurred?
    a. A bike shows an intact coat of paint
    b. A banana shows brown spots
    c. A book rests on a table
    d. A phone rings

44. The Industrial Revolution led to pollution which made the air, buildings, and trees grey or darker in color. It was observed that moths in the area also became darker in color. What would this an example of?
    a. Natural selection
    b. Climate change
    c. Acclimation
    d. Anomaly

45. A tiny ball rests in the absolute center of an untouched, vacuum-sealed, underground container for 40 years. During this time, nobody checks on the ball or the container. At the end of the 40 years, the container is examined and the ball is still in the exact same spot in the center of the container. This is an example of what scientific principle?
    a. Theory of Relativity
    b. First Law of Motion
    c. Gravity
    d. Space-time continuum

46. In what type of chemical reaction is heat absorbed from the surrounding environment?
   a. Exothermic
   b. Endothermic
   c. Rusting
   d. Freezing

47. Which of the following is an example of friction?
   a. A rubber band that is pulled taut then snapped
   b. Jumping on the end of a diving board
   c. Throwing a baseball at an angle
   d. Applying a car's brakes at a red light

48. Isaac is reducing strawberry jam to make a dessert sauce. He takes the jam out of the refrigerator and spoons some into a saucepan. The jam is a cold, thick glob and takes a few minutes to slowly fall off the spoon and into the pan. Isaac turns the stove top on medium heat and the jam begins to turn runny and bubble. What factor of the jam did the heat affect?
   a. Its flavor
   b. Its mass
   c. Its viscosity
   d. Its caloric energy

49. Objects in which molecules are closest together can be described as which of the following in comparison to objects in which molecules are farther apart?
   a. High vibrational
   b. Dense
   c. Forceful
   d. Pressurized

50. The process in which a gas becomes a liquid is known as which of the following?
   a. Melting
   b. Sublimation
   c. Vaporization
   d. Condensation

51. Which of the following is an example of a homogenous mixture?
   a. Distilled water
   b. Sand
   c. Shallow tidal pools
   d. Deep ocean water

52. In chemical reactions, what is the state in which reactants and products no longer change formally known as?
   a. End state
   b. Equilibrium
   c. Finality
   d. Termination

53. Tropical clownfish are often found living among sea anemone. The clownfish eat algae and dead material off the sea anemone, which keeps the anemones clean and the clownfish fed. The sea anemone also provides a protective environment for the clownfish. What is this an example of?
    a. Aquatic friendship
    b. Evolution
    c. Symbiotic relationship
    d. Conservation

54. What is one way to mitigate transmission of communicable disease?
    a. Getting vaccinations
    b. Traveling by car versus traveling by plane
    c. Avoiding people who have traveled abroad in the last 12 months
    d. Following a diet high in biotin

55. Which is the defining feature of organisms found in the Archaea and Bacteria domains?
    a. They are eukaryotes
    b. They are prokaryotes
    c. They contain the most recently evolved organisms
    d. They are all multicellular

Answer Explanations

1. B: Neurons are responsible for transferring and processing information between the brain and other parts of the body. Neuroglia are cells that protect delicate neurons by making a frame around them. They also help to maintain a homeostatic environment around the neurons.

2. C: The autonomic nerve system is part of the efferent division of the peripheral nervous system (PNS). It controls involuntary muscles, such as smooth muscle and cardiac muscle, which are responsible for regulating heart rate, blood pressure, and body temperature. The central nervous system, Choice *A*, includes only the brain and the spinal cord. The somatic nervous system, Choice *B*, is also part of the efferent division of the PNS and controls voluntary skeletal muscle contractions, allowing for body movements. The afferent division of the PNS, Choice *D*, relays sensory information within the body.

3. A: The testes are the main reproductive organ of the male reproductive system. They are the gonads; they secrete androgens and produce and store sperm cells. The prostate, vas deferens, and bulbourethral glands are all accessory organs of the male reproductive system. The prostate provides nourishment to sperm, the vas deferens transports sperm to the urethra, and the bulbourethral glands produce lubricating fluid for the urethra.

4. B: The ovaries produce only one mature gamete each month. If it is fertilized, the result is a zygote that develops into an embryo. The male reproductive system produces one-half billion sperm cells each day.

5. D: Once sperm enter the vagina, they travel through the uterus to the Fallopian tubes to fertilize a mature oocyte. The ovaries are responsible for producing the mature oocyte. The mammary glands produce nutrient-filled milk to nourish babies after birth.

6. D: The tissues and glands of the endocrine system are all ductless. They secrete hormones, not bile, into the blood or interstitial fluid of the human body. The endocrine system has a slow, long-lasting response to stimuli, unlike the nervous system, whose response is quick and short termed.

7. A: The pituitary gland is a pea-sized gland that is found at the bottom of the hypothalamus. The hormones that it releases regulate growth, blood pressure, and pain relief, among other things. The thymus, Choice *B*, is located in the chest cavity and produces hormones that are important for the development and maintenance of immune responses. The thyroid gland, Choice *C*, is found in the neck and releases hormones responsible for metabolism, growth and development, temperature regulation, and brain development during infancy and childhood. The pancreas, Choice *D*, is located in the abdomen and regulates blood sugar levels.

8. C: The pancreas is responsible for regulating blood sugar levels in the body. The pineal gland regulates melatonin levels, which affect maturation of gametes and reproductive organs, as well as the body's circadian rhythm. The parathyroid gland secretes a hormone that helps the thyroid regulate calcium levels in the body. The adrenal glands help with the body's management of stress.

9. A: Monosaccharides are the simplest sugars that make up carbohydrates. They are important for cellular respiration. Fatty acids, Choice *B*, make up lipids. Polysaccharides, Choice *C*, are larger molecules with repeating monosaccharide units. Amino acids, Choice *D*, are the building blocks of proteins.

10. D: Nucleic acids include DNA and RNA, which are strands of nucleotides that contain genetic information. Carbohydrates, Choice *A*, are made up of sugars that provide energy to the body. Lipids, Choice *B*, are hydrocarbon chains that make up fats. Proteins, Choice *C*, are made up of amino acids that help with many functions for maintaining life.

11. B: Genes are the primary unit of inheritance between generations of an organism. Humans each have twenty-three pairs of chromosomes (Choice *A*), and each chromosome contains hundreds to thousands of genes. Genes each control a specific trait of the organism. Gametes, Choice *C*, are the reproductive cells that contain all of the genetic information of an individual. Atoms, Choice *D*, are the small units that make up all substances.

12. C: The Law of Independent Assortment states that the alleles for different traits are inherited independently of one another. For example, the alleles for eye color are not linked to the alleles for hair color. So, someone could have blue eyes and brown hair or blue eyes and blond hair. The Law of Dominance, Choice *A*, states that one allele has a stronger effect on phenotype than the other allele. The Law of Segregation, Choice *B*, states that each trait has two versions that can be inherited. Each parent contributes one of its alleles, selected randomly, to the daughter offspring.

13. C: Atoms are considered neutral when the number of protons and electrons is equal. Protons carry a positive charge, and electrons carry a negative charge. When they are equal in number, their charges cancel out, and the atom is neutral. If there are more electrons than protons, or vice versa, the atom has an electric charge and is termed an ion. Neutrons do not have a charge and do not affect the electric charge of an atom.

14. A: Physical properties of substances are those that can be observed without changing the substances' chemical composition, such as odor, color, density, and hardness. Reactivity, flammability, and toxicity are all chemical properties of substances. They describe the way in which a substance may change into a different substance. They cannot be observed from the surface.

15. B: Solids have molecules that are packed together tightly and cannot move within their substance. Crystalline solids have atoms or molecules that are arranged symmetrically, making all of the bonds of even strength. When they are broken, they break along a plane of molecules, creating a straight edge. Amorphous solids do not have the symmetrical makeup of crystalline solids. They do not break evenly. Gases and liquids both have molecules that move around freely.

16. A: Chemical reactions are processes that involve the changing of one set of substances to a different set of substances. In order to accomplish this, the bonds between the atoms in the molecules of the original substances need to be broken. The atoms are rearranged, and new bonds are formed to make the new set of substances. Combination reactions involve two or more reactants becoming one product. Decomposition reactions involve one reactant becoming two or more products. Combustion reactions involve the use of oxygen as a reactant and generally include the burning of a substance. Choices *C* and *D* are not discussed as specific reaction types.

17. B: Newton meter. A Newton meter is used for such things such as gravity, friction, or tension. A bathroom scale or similar scale is a common example of a force meter. Choice *A* is not an existing term. Choices *C* and *D* are used to measure fractions of small numbers.

18. D: A Vernier Scale is used to measure small fractions within already small divisions. Choices *A*, *B*, and *C* are used for measuring short distances, yet do not go as small as the Vernier Scale.

19. D: Scientific experiments are found reliable when they can be replicated and produce comparable results regardless of who is conducting them or making the observations, making Choice *B* incorrect. Choice *A* is incorrect, although having all the materials needed is ideal for conducting an experiment. Choice *C* is incorrect; a hypothesis is never proven correct, but it can receive credibility if the data supports it in that particular experiment.

20. A: The drinking water being contaminated and the stomach cancer is not necessarily determined by cause and effect. The two events could have just happened at the same time, which is correlation, not causation. The other three examples are very clear examples of cause and effect; we know for a fact that when water becomes hot enough, it boils, or that earthquakes are caused by tectonic plates shifting.

21. C: Newton's Third Law. This law states that for every action, there is an opposite and equal reaction. When Camille pushes Harley forward on the swing, the opposite and equal reaction is the swing going backwards. Choice *A*, law of inertia, is Newton's first law, which states that an object at rest or at motion stays that way unless otherwise acted upon by an outside force, making Choice *A* incorrect. Choice *B*, Newton's second law, states that the heavier, an object, the more force has to be used to move it, making Choice *C* incorrect. Choice *D*, Law of Segregation, has to do with heredity, and states that each trait has two versions that can be inherited, making Choice *D* incorrect.

22. B: Formulating a hypothesis means writing out an expectation of what's going to happen. The hypothesis comes after the experimental question, which is forming a question that relates to the observation, making Choice *A* incorrect. Gathering the materials needed for the procedure is the step where we actually conduct the experiment, making Choice *C* incorrect. Summarizing the results of the experiment is the conclusion, making Choice *D* incorrect.

23. C: After the experiment is over and before it is published. A peer review is when other scientists review the experiment's findings in order to test its validity and methods. Peer review is an important part of scientific research and is a way for the scientific community to provide feedback for the experiment.

24. D: The inner core of the Earth is a solid sphere made of nickel and iron. Scientists believe that while the Earth initially formed as a molten, gaseous ball, it cooled down and its four main layers were created. While the outer three layers are made of a variety of elements and consist of different forms of matter, the inner core is very hot, yet solid.

25. C: Plate tectonics refers to a scientific theory that describes the Earth's crust as consisting of numerous plates that shift against one another. The tremendous friction and pressure that consequently take place result in earthquakes (as plates violently slide against or away from one another) or contribute to the formation of mountain ranges (as plates push into one another and create elevation where they meet). Underground bodies of water, lunar cycles, and atmospheric changes do not directly influence earthquakes or mountain formation.

26. B: The atmosphere and hydrosphere interact to create the water cycle, a unique cycle that allows Earth to have life. The water cycle is initiated by solar heat, which causes water sources on the ground to evaporate into the atmosphere. Cooler atmospheric temperature trigger precipitation, which returns water vapor to the ground. The carbon cycle primarily takes place between the atmosphere and the geosphere, while the Krebs cycle takes place within living cells as a means of energy production. The life cycle refers to an organism's life processes from birth to death.

27. A: Biosphere is the all-encompassing term that includes all living organisms on a planet. Geosphere refers to the physical components of a planet, while biodome is not a real term. Binomial nomenclature is a method of naming an organism by using its categorized genus and species.

28. A: Scientists estimate there may be up to 100 million distinct species of life, although only about 1.5 million have been categorized so far. As new species continue to be discovered, the number of Phyla in the taxonomic classification system has increased to accommodate organisms that did not fit into previously-established categorical groups.

29. A: Galaxies are the second-largest systems in the universe (after the universe itself) and are made up of gases, cosmic matter, solar systems (and their planets, moons, and other objects), and black holes; galaxies also include nebulas (gaseous entities that result from star matter), and dark matter (invisible matter that cannot be seen but appears to have mass). Our galaxy includes constellations (groups of stars).

30. B: Hydrogen and helium are easily explosive and create the gravitational collapse and internal gravitational pull that allows the star to form. The center of a star is constantly experiencing explosions similar to a nuclear bomb. All other elements listed are usually not present in star matter.

31. C: Mercury and Venus are the only planets in our solar system that do not have moons. The other planets listed have multiple moons. Pluto, which is not considered to be a planet, also has multiple moons.

32. A: The high and low tides of the ocean waters are directly influenced by the position of the moon in relation to the Earth. There is no scientific evidence that correlates the moon's influence on labor in pregnant females, daily predictions (or horoscopes), or seismic activity (which is primarily a geologic process driven by the internal environment of the Earth).

33. C: The equator is equidistant from both the north and the south pole. Therefore, this area stays at relatively the same point in space even as the Earth tilts on its own axis. While each hemisphere of the Earth will experience different temperatures and seasons, the climate of the equator stays relatively constant year-round. Areas close the equator (in both the north and south directions) may experience the same temperatures year-round, but may experience wet and dry seasons.

34. D: All of these activities are human activities that have increased carbon dioxide in the atmosphere. Burning fossil fuels for energy releases carbon into the air. Concentrated animal feeding operations result in excess energy and space needed to raise livestock, which leads to deforestation, air and water pollution, and excess pesticide use, which disrupts the carbon balance. Finally, deforestation from these operations and other human activities decreases the amount of plant life that can help regulate the amount of carbon dioxide that is in the atmosphere.

35. B: A solar eclipse occurs when the moon crosses in front of the Earth and partially or totally blocks the appearance of the Sun in the sky (known as a partial solar eclipse or total solar eclipse, respectively). High tides occur daily. Lunar eclipses occur when the Earth's orbit crosses between the Sun and the moon. The calendar year is not related to the moon's positioning, but rather human interpretation of the Earth orbits the Sun.

36. C: Whales live within the Earth's hydrosphere but are not considered part of it. The hydrosphere includes any part of Earth that is water (whether in solid, gas, or liquid form). Whales are considered part of the Earth's biosphere.

37. B: The inner and outer core are both made up of the same elements (iron and nickel), are extremely hot, and both are inaccessible to humans. However, the inner core is solid while the outer core is molten.

38. B: A lever moves a load around an attached point that can hinge or pivot. This point is known as the fulcrum. The fulcrum can be located in the center of the lever, or at one end. Wheel and axle machines use two separate rotational forces to transfer energy. Pulleys use a wheel and a rope to move a load. An inclined plane serves as a ramp upon which a load can be moved rather than lifted.

39. A: Nuclear fission occurs when the nucleus of a radioactive atomic element is split by force. This causes an explosive release of energy. A nuclear meltdown refers to any accident that occurs at a core reactor in a power plant; these are catastrophic to the surrounding geographic areas, as extreme amounts of radiation are released. Thermodynamics is the physical science of energetic relationships. Proton pump inhibitors are a class of drugs that limit intracellular pumping activity, typically to manage digestive issues.

40. C: Nuclear fusion occurs when lower-weight radioactive elements fuse and release energy rather than splitting, which occurs in the nuclear fission process. Nuclear meltdowns refer to catastrophic events at nuclear power plants, while nuclear dynamic is not a true physical science term.

41. B: Any object, even those at rest, that is composed of atoms has potential energy. Out of the options listed, a dinner plate at rest only has potential energy. Kinetic energy refers to an object that is moving. Mechanical energy refers to an object's total kinetic and potential energy. Magnetic energy refers to objects that have magnetic forces, such as the poles of the Earth.

42. A: Covalent bonds join non-metal atoms through each atom's outer electrons. Atoms that repel each other inherently cannot form a bond. Metal atoms that bond electrons are referred to as having metallic bonds.

43. B: A chemical reaction is noted by changes in color, temperature, or appearance; it is also indicated by the presence or release of a gas. Out of the options listed, the banana showing brown spots indicates that the cells of the banana have reacted to the air and oxidized to become riper in those areas. The other options listed describe unchanged objects or objects at rest.

44. A: In any environment, the fittest organisms will reproduce and pass on genes. The darkers moths could not be seen by predators as well, so they were more likely to survive than lighter-colored moths. Climate change refers to a shift in climate over time and does not address species' change. Acclimation refers to a temporary change in an organism, rather than a permanent change across a species. An anomaly is a single, unexplainable instance that is abnormal; however, many species of cacti and flora thrive in deserts, so this is not an example of an anomaly.

45. B: Newton's First Law of Motion states that any object that is at rest will remain at rest unless an outside force is applied. This law also states that any object in motion will remain in motion at the same rate, in the same direction, unless an outside force interferes. In this example, the ball in the vacuum-sealed, untouched container did not experience any external force whatsoever. Therefore, it is unsurprising that it remained where it was initially set.

46. B: Endothermic reactions consume heat from the surrounding environment to complete the chemical reaction and create a product. For example, holding an ice cube in one's hand and allowing it to melt into water (as a result of body heat) is an example of an endothermic reaction. Exothermic reactions release heat into the environment (i.e., igniting wood to create a fire). Rusting occurs when iron reacts to oxygen over a period of time. Freezing is a type of exothermic reaction.

47. D: Friction refers to any force that resists motion when one surface or material is in contact with another. In this example, the brakes are working in the opposite direction from the way the wheels are rolling. Pulling a rubber band, jumping, and throwing a ball are adding more force to an event, rather than working in the opposite manner.

48. C: Viscosity refers to a liquid material's friction or resistance in relation to another surface. Heating a viscous substance makes it less viscous. In this case, the jam was viscous when it was cold and in a more solid state; it resisted moving off the spoon and onto the pan. As Isaac heated the jam, it became less viscous and was able to easily move around the pan. Low temperature is unlikely to quickly change the taste, caloric content, or flavor of a food item.

49. B: An object's density refers to how physically close its molecules are to one another in space. Typically, as objects cool and solidify, density increases and volume decreases. As objects heat up and become more liquid or gaseous, volume increases and density decreases.

50. D: Condensation refers to the process of a gas becoming a liquid. For example, surface water on blades of grass evaporates when ground and surface temperatures are warmer in the daytime; as night time temperatures cool, the water vapor condenses into droplets. Melting is the process of turning a solid into a liquid. Vaporization is the process of turning a liquid into a gas. Sublimation is the process of turning a solid into a gas.

51. A: A homogenous mixture refers to any substance composed of two or more elements. These elements can be metal or non-metal in nature. Homogenous mixtures cannot be perceived by the five senses to have various components within them. Distilled water is the purest type of water, consisting of just hydrogen and oxygen atoms. Other types of water, such as tidal pool water and deep ocean water, will contain compounds such as salt or sea debris. Sand is also made up of various materials, such as rocks and shells. Mixtures that can be perceived to have multiple components are known as heterogeneous mixtures.

52. B: When chemical reactions reach a state of chemical equilibrium, the reactants (substances that cause the reaction) and the products (the end result of the reaction) remain in unchanged states and concentrations.

53. C: A symbiotic relationship between two entities occurs when the presence of one party benefits the other, and vice versa. Aquatic friendship is not a scientific term. Evolution refers to the way a specific organism changes over a long period of time. Conservation refers to the preservation of natural areas.

54. A: Vaccinations introduce and encourage immunity to specific contagious diseases. When large populations are vaccinated and develop immunity, the presence of specific communicable diseases within that population is mitigated. This protects the few who may not have been vaccinated through the practice of herd immunity (the larger vaccinated group is able to prevent introduction and spread of the specific disease for which the group has been vaccinated). Car travel and avoiding persons who travel do not necessarily limit interactions that would prevent the spread of communicable diseases. Biotin is a vitamin that promotes hair, nail, and skin strength; it is not involved in immunity or disease prevention.

55. B: All species in the Archaea and Bacteria domains are single-celled prokaryotes. The oldest and most primitive organisms are found in these domains, while multicellular, complex, and more recently-evolved species are found in the third domain, Eukaryotes.

Greetings!

First, we would like to give a huge "thank you" for choosing us and this study guide for your Praxis Elementary Education Multiple Subjects exam. We hope that it will lead you to success on this exam and for your years to come.

Our team has tried to make your preparations as thorough as possible by covering all of the topics you should be expected to know. In addition, our writers attempted to create practice questions identical to what you will see on the day of your actual test. We have also included many test-taking strategies to help you learn the material, maintain the knowledge, and take the test with confidence.

We strive for excellence in our products, and if you have any comments or concerns over the quality of something in this study guide, please send us an email so that we may improve.

As you continue forward in life, we would like to remain alongside you with other books and study guides in our library, such as:

Praxis Core: amazon.com/dp/1628455691

We are continually producing and updating study guides in several different subjects. If you are looking for something in particular, all of our products are available on Amazon. You may also send us an email!

Sincerely,
APEX Test Prep
info@apexprep.com

FREE

Free Study Tips DVD

In addition to the tips and content in this guide, we have created a FREE DVD with helpful study tips to further assist your exam preparation. **This FREE Study Tips DVD provides you with top-notch tips to conquer your exam and reach your goals.**

Our simple request in exchange for the strategy-packed DVD is that you email us your feedback about our study guide. We would love to hear what you thought about the guide, and we welcome any and all feedback—positive, negative, or neutral. It is our #1 goal to provide you with top quality products and customer service.

To receive your **FREE Study Tips DVD**, email freedvd@apexprep.com. Please put "FREE DVD" in the subject line and put the following in the email:

   a. The name of the study guide you purchased.

   b. Your rating of the study guide on a scale of 1-5, with 5 being the highest score.

   c. Any thoughts or feedback about your study guide.

   d. Your first and last name and your mailing address, so we know where to send your free DVD!

Thank you!

Made in the USA
Las Vegas, NV
04 May 2021